EARLY MORMON COUNTRY
TO 1846

0   100   200 Miles
Scale

BRITISH   NORTH   AMERICA

MAINE

VERMONT

Tunbridge
Sharon   Lebanon

NEW YORK

NEW
HAMPSHIRE

Toronto   Lake Ontario

Palmyra
Manchester
Mendon   Fayette

Whiting-
ham

Topsfield   Salem
Boston

Brantford   Buffalo

Albany

MASSACHUSSETTS

South Bainbridge

Colesville

CONNECTICUT   R.I.
Providence

Columbia   Harmony

Fairport   New York
Kirtland   City
Cleveland
Hiram

NEW
JERSEY

Amherst

PENNSYLVANIA

HIO

Philadelphia

Columbus

MARYLAND

DEL.

Washington, D.C.

VIRGINIA

ATLANTIC OCEAN

Huron

Lake Erie

NORTH CAROLINA

The HEAVENS RESOUND

The HEAVENS RESOUND

A History of
the Latter-day Saints in Ohio
1830-1838

Milton V. Backman, Jr.

Deseret Book Company
Salt Lake City, Utah

Library of Congress Cataloging in Publication Data

Backman, Milton Vaughn.
  The heavens resound.

  Bibliography: p.
  Includes index.
    1. The Church of Jesus Christ of Latter-day Saints—
Ohio—History. 2. Mormon Church—Ohio—History.
3. Ohio—Church history. I. Title.
BX8615.03B32 1983   289.3'771   83-12882
ISBN 0-87747-973-9

Contents

Maps

Illustrations

Tables

Preface

Every age has its challenges, its confrontations, its opportunities, and its significant developments. The decade of the 1830s was no exception. This formative era saw an extension of the foundations of a new religious movement that emerged from a series of sacred events beginning in the spring of 1820.

The founder of this new faith, Joseph Smith, was born in Vermont in 1805. His family settled in the Finger Lakes region of western New York in 1816. A quest to secure a remission of sins led the youth to investigate churches in the area where he lived, and after perceiving that the religious leaders were teaching conflicting doctrines, he decided that none of the faiths could be right. While engaged in this quest to determine religious truth, Joseph decided to ask God in prayer which church he should join. In the spring of 1820, at the age of fourteen, he went to a grove near his family's log cabin home at Manchester, New York, and knelt in prayer. Suddenly he beheld a vision, as two glorious personages—God the Father and His beloved Son, Jesus Christ—appeared to him. Joseph was told that the religious denominations taught incorrect doctrines and that he should not join any of them. He was also promised that at some future time, the fulness of the gospel would be revealed to him.

Other visions and revelations followed this first vision. In the fall of 1823 Joseph was directed by an angel named Moroni to go to a hill near his home. There he found, in a stone box, a set of metallic plates containing curious inscriptions. Four years later he removed the plates and commenced to translate them, through the gift and power of God. The record engraven on the plates described the religious history of early inhabitants of the American continent, including a visitation of the Resurrected Christ. In March 1830 this record was published as the Book of Mormon.

While this record—a new witness for Christ—was being translated, Joseph Smith and one of his associates, Oliver Cowdery, received from angelic messengers the priesthood, which they learned is the power and authority to act in the name of God.

On April 6, 1830, in Fayette, New York, Joseph Smith organized the restored Church of Christ, or The Church of Jesus Christ of Latter-day Saints, as it was later called. That summer and fall, missionaries were sent out to surrounding regions and states to proclaim the restored gospel. Shortly after they introduced their message in Ohio in October 1830, the migration of Latter-day Saints to that area commenced. The following summer members also began gathering in a second location, western Missouri. Thus, during the 1830s there were two gathering places for the Latter-day Saints, Ohio and Missouri. While more members of the Church gathered in Missouri than Ohio during that decade, Joseph Smith, their prophet, lived in Ohio during most of that period, and in large measure the headquarters of the Church was located where he resided.

The Heavens Resound is the story of developments in the Church in Ohio and other parts of eastern America between late 1830 and mid-1838. It is the story of a people who at the call of a prophet sold their homes and farms and migrated west, left their families to serve as itinerant preachers, participated in a strenuous march to western Missouri, sacrificed to build a house for the Lord, and then, amid apostate mobocracy, abandoned their homes in Ohio to start a new life on the western frontier.

As in many other eras, this age was one of paradoxes, of remarkable conversions and also apostasy, of the triumph of a build-

ing program and also the collapse of an economy, of the joy and
serenity associated with unparalleled spiritual manifestations and
also the anguish and trials accompanying flight from angry oppres-
sors.

The experience of the Latter-day Saints in Ohio was also a
period of change and adjustment. Approximately one-half of the
revealed sections or revelations currently included in the
Church's Doctrine and Covenants were recorded in Ohio.
Throughout the thirties, principles were revealed through Joseph
Smith that influenced not only beliefs but also patterns of daily
conduct. Many of these revelations described an expanding
Church government, and a number of converts were called soon
after baptism to serve in various positions of ecclesiastical responsibility, the first persons to hold these positions in this dispensation. As the Prophet continued to instruct the Saints, members of
the Church faced the challenge of constantly adjusting, of altering some of their opinions, and of harmonizing their actions with
the new directions and enlightenment they received from a latter-
day prophet.

This, then, is the story of that period, the story of the Latter-
day Saints in Ohio, 1830-1838.

Acknowledgments

hroughout the writing of this history, I
have been helped immeasurably by the
timely suggestions of many scholars. Many of my colleagues at
Brigham Young University read portions of the manuscript at various
stages of development, and to them I extend my appreciation.
I am especially grateful to Dr. Keith Perkins, Dr. Robert
J. Matthews, Dr. Larry C. Porter, Dr. Melvin J. Petersen, Dr. H.
Donl Peterson, Dr. Larry T. Wimmer, Dr. Ben Bennion, Lyndon
W. Cook, and my father, Milton V. Backman. I also extend
appreciation to Dr. Leonard J. Arrington for encouraging me to
continue my exploration of this formative period and for offering
valuable constructive criticism as the work was nearing completion.

A number of students enrolled at Brigham Young University
also helped in research, typing, and proofreading the manuscript,
and to these individuals I am grateful.

This volume could not have been prepared without the assistance
and cooperation of many librarians, especially those serving
in the historical and genealogical departments of The Church of
Jesus Christ of Latter-day Saints, Brigham Young University,
Archives of the Reorganized Church of Jesus Christ of Latter Day

Saints, the Lake County Historical Society (Mentor, Ohio), the Ohio Historical Society, the Western Reserve Historical Society, the Hiram College Library, the Hiram (Ohio) Township Historical Society, Archives at the Western Reserve University, the Geauga County Historical Society (Burton, Ohio), the Rutherford B. Hayes Library (Fremont, Ohio), the Cincinnati Historical Society, the American Jewish Archives (Cincinnati, Ohio), the Shaker Historical Society (Shaker Heights, Ohio), the Cleveland and Dayton public libraries, the Disciples of Christ Historical Society (Nashville, Tennessee), the Library of Congress, and the Bancroft Library (University of California at Berkeley).

I also extend appreciation to my family for their patience while I have devoted many hours in research and writing and for their help in various research endeavors. I am especially grateful to my wife, Kathleen, for her assistance in reading hundreds of Ohio newspapers, checking references, reading and rereading the manuscript, and offering many pertinent suggestions concerning content and style.

Chapter 1

The Birth of Mormonism in Ohio

In the latter part of October 1830, four Latter-day Saint missionaries arrived in Mentor, Ohio, carrying, as one contemporary reported, carpet bags filled with copies of the Book of Mormon. The missionaries were Oliver Cowdery, one of the three witnesses to the Book of Mormon; Peter Whitmer, one of the eight witnesses to the Book of Mormon; Ziba Peterson, an early convert; and Parley P. Pratt, a traveling preacher who was converted to the restored Church while preaching the need for a restoration.[1]

At the home of Sidney Rigdon, one of the most influential restorationist preachers living in northeastern Ohio, the Mormon elders introduced the restored gospel and presented to the preacher a copy of the ancient record. Parley P. Pratt, who had known the preacher for several years, later recalled that his ministerial friend "was much surprised," adding that "it was with much persuasion and argument that he was prevailed on to read" the book.[2] Mr. Rigdon's first reaction to the Book of Mormon was unfavorable; he had a Bible that he believed was a revelation from God, and he "had considerable doubt" concerning the divine events attested to by the missionaries. While the elders were attempting to explain their convictions, he interrupted, saying,

Oliver Cowdery

"No, young gentlemen, you must not argue with me on the subject; but I will read your book, and see what claims it has upon my faith, and will endeavor to ascertain whether it be a revelation from God or not."[3]

Sidney Rigdon granted the missionaries permission to preach in his church to members of his Reformed Baptist congregation. As the missionaries unfolded the message of the restoration to the large congregation, they explained why they themselves had embraced the restored gospel. Two of them, Oliver Cowdery and Peter Whitmer, Jr., were witnesses to the plates from which the

Parley P. Pratt

Book of Mormon was translated. Elder Cowdery also testified that he was present with Joseph Smith when an angel conferred upon them the lesser priesthood and again when holy angels restored to the earth the higher priesthood.

After the missionaries spoke, Sidney Rigdon stood and addressed the congregation. He said that the message they had received that evening was "of an extraordinary character, and certainly demanded their most serious consideration." He further exhorted them to "give the matter a careful investigation, and not turn against it without being fully convinced of its being an imposition, lest they should, possibly, resist the truth." Quoting the admonition of Paul, he concluded, "Prove all things, and hold fast to that which is good."[4]

Sidney Rigdon's original response to Mormonism was negative for several reasons. For years he had held the traditional Protestant view that the Bible was the sole standard of religious truth and that visions and revelations had ceased with the deaths of the early apostles. Now here were missionaries who informed him of new revelations from heaven and of a book other than the Bible that contained the words of God.[5] The first published account of his conversion was given in the Painesville, Ohio, *Telegraph*. The writer, who signed his report with the initials "M.S.C." (probably Matthew S. Clapp, a restorationist minister of the Christian [Disciple] church in Painesville), stated that the elders told Sidney Rigdon that converts whom he had earlier immersed for the remission of sin should now be baptized by individuals who possessed God's authority. "Rigdon seemed much displeased" when he learned that seventeen of his followers were baptized one night by the Mormon elders, the writer noted. When Mr. Rigdon again conversed with the missionaries, the article continued, he requested "proof of the truth of their book and mission." Oliver Cowdery, speaking for the missionaries, responded by bearing witness that in response to his own sincere, prayerful petition to his "Heavenly Father . . . in the name of Jesus Christ," he had received an answer from an angel sent by God.[6]

From Mentor, the missionaries walked a few miles south to the outskirts of Kirtland, where they contacted some Reformed Baptists who had established a communal society on Isaac Morley's farm. One of the first individuals they met was Lyman Wight, then preparing to move seven miles from Kirtland to Mayfield, where he anticipated organizing five families into a branch of this society. "When I had my goods about half loaded," he recorded in his journal,

there came along four men, namely: P. Pratt, O. Cowdery, P. Whitmer, and Ziba Peterson and brought with them the Book of Mormon, which they wished to introduce to us. I desired they would hold on till I got away, as my business was of vital importance, and I did not wish to be troubled with romances, nor idle speculations. But nothing daunted, they were not to be put off, but were as good natured as you please. Curiosity got uppermost, and I concluded to stop for a short time. We called a meeting, and one testified that he had seen angels, and another that he had seen the plates, and that the gifts were back in the church again, etc. The meeting became so interesting that I did not get away till the sun was about an hour high at night, and it was dark before I arrived at my new home.[7]

The success of the elders in Kirtland was immediate and remarkable. Soon news spread throughout the region that an unusual religious message was being expounded by missionaries from New York. On occasions, the roads were crowded with people traveling to Kirtland to hear the message of the restoration. Inquirers exhausted the elders with their constant questions. "The people thronged us night and day," Parley P. Pratt said, "insomuch that we had not time for rest or retirement." Some came "for curiosity, some to obey the gospel, and some to dispute or resist it."[8]

Since not enough copies of the Book of Mormon were available for all who desired to read it, some people loaned their copies on a short-term basis. Before Isaac Morley had finished reading the book, Mary Rollins, a twelve-year-old girl living in Kirtland with her widowed mother in a house belonging to her uncle, Algernon Sidney Gilbert, requested an opportunity to examine it. "I plead[ed] so earnestly for it," she recalled, that Isaac Morley finally said, "Child, if you will bring this book home before breakfast tomorrow morning, you may take it." Hurrying home, she showed the work to others, and they also expressed a desire to learn of its message. Consequently, throughout the night she and her aunt and uncle read intently. The next morning, her narrative continues, she returned the book to Isaac Morley. Amazed that she had read and learned so much, he said, "Child, take this book home and finish it. I can wait."[9]

John Murdock, a follower of Sidney Rigdon, first learned of the restoration on October 31, 1830, while he was traveling to a nearby community to deliver a Sabbath sermon. He had been associated with the Reformed Baptists for about three years and was concerned that many restorationist theologians of the day had rejected latter-day miracles, thereby denying the gift and power of the Holy Ghost.[10] Shortly before the appearance of the Latter-day Saint elders in Ohio, an inquirer asked him, "Where is the man to commence the work of baptizing? or where shall he get his authority?" John Murdock replied that no one had the authority. "If they are out of the way as we believe," he said, "they have lost all authority. There is only one way in which the priesthood of God can be restored," he added. "The Lord must either send an angel to baptize the first man, or he must give a special command to some one man to baptize another."[11]

Four days after he heard that the missionaries were in his area, John Murdock rode twenty miles to Kirtland to meet them. On two occasions during this journey he conversed with friends who tried to persuade him to return home. Undaunted by their skepticism, he continued on. He was introduced to the missionaries, who gave him a copy of the Book of Mormon and told him that it had come forth by the power of God. That night he attended a confirmation meeting at Isaac Morley's home—the first such meeting, he later said, to be conducted in Ohio. Staying overnight in the Morley home, he commenced reading the book, which was heralded as a new witness for Christ. He also conversed with Sidney Rigdon, who was still investigating the new faith. The next day he listened thoughtfully as the missionaries, led by Oliver Cowdery, responded to his questions. After being convinced that these men held the authority he had been seeking, he requested baptism. On Friday, November 5, just five days after he learned of the missionaries' presence in the area, John Murdock was baptized in the Chagrin River by Parley P. Pratt. Two days later he was confirmed by Oliver Cowdery and then ordained an elder.[12]

By the middle of November 1830, Sidney Rigdon had resolved his problems concerning the Book of Mormon, latter-day revelation, and the elders' claim of authority. As he read the Book of Mormon, he became "fully convinced of the truth of the work, by a revelation from Jesus Christ."[13] He also decided, according to

Sidney Rigdon

a non-Mormon contemporary, that Oliver Cowdery had not been deceived by an angel of the devil but had truly been visited by an angel from God.[14] Moreover, Sidney concurred that he had not previously been "legally baptized and ordained" and that he had "no authority to minister in the ordinances of God."[15]

On Sunday, November 14, 1830, Sidney Rigdon gathered his neighbors and other friends and spoke to a large congregation in the Methodist meetinghouse in Kirtland. The *Painesville Tele-*

graph reported that when he addressed this group, he was "apparently much affected and deeply impressed," seemed "exceedingly humble," and "confessed the sins of his former life." Apparently describing the same sermon, Parley P. Pratt recalled that the new convert spoke for about two hours, "during most of which time both himself and nearly all the congregation were melted into tears."[16] He was subsequently baptized, probably the following day. The *Telegraph* specified that on that occasion "he professed to be exceedingly joyful, and said he would not be where he was three days ago for the universe." Parley P. Pratt reported that after Sidney and his wife were baptized by Oliver Cowdery, they emerged from the water overwhelmed in tears. "It was," he observed, "a solemn scene."[17]

By the middle of November 1830, many of Sidney Rigdon's followers in Kirtland were convinced that the gospel of Christ had been restored to the earth, and all of the approximately fifty members of the communal society, including Isaac Morley, Titus Billings, Lyman Wight, their wives, and many of their children, had been baptized. Within a few weeks Newel K. Whitney and Frederick G. Williams also joined the Church.[18]

Many of the earliest converts in and around Kirtland in 1830 were restorationist followers of Sidney Rigdon, or Reformed Baptists. One who was not was Philo Dibble. Recently married, this twenty-four-year-old farmer had settled about five miles east of Kirtland. One morning he listened with unusual interest as two men told him about the arrival in Kirtland of four missionaries from New York. With derision, the informers explained that these peculiar preachers were carrying a "golden Bible" and that one claimed to have "seen an angel." Philo informed his bride of this report, and they drove to Kirtland. There they learned that the missionaries were in Mayfield but were expected to return the next day. The following day, Philo again hitched up his carriage and, accompanied by his wife and another family, rode to Kirtland. That evening, he attended a meeting at Isaac Morley's home. Oliver Cowdery bore witness concerning the "administration of an angel" and discussed the doctrines of repentance, baptism, and the bestowal of the Holy Ghost, promising a testimony to everyone who would embrace these principles with an honest heart. When the elder invited all who desired baptism to arise, Philo, along with William Cahoon, and three others, stood. His wife thought he was acting hastily and that further investigation was needed. "I paid no heed to her," he later recalled, "but went forth and was baptized by Parley P. Pratt. . . . When I came out of the water, I knew that I had been born of water and of the spirit, for my mind was illuminated with the Holy Ghost."[19]

Some of the followers of Sidney Rigdon were at first vehemently opposed to Mormonism and refused to accept the Book of Mormon as scripture; but they eventually were converted to the belief that his work was indeed a new witness for Christ. One of them was Orson Hyde, who was born in Connecticut in 1805, the same year that Joseph Smith was born in Vermont. After the death of his parents, this fourteen-year-old farm boy moved to Kirtland with his guardian. Four years later he set out to carve out his "fortune and destiny." He secured employment at Grandison Newell's iron foundry and later became a clerk in the Gilbert and Whitney store. While living in Kirtland, he joined the Methodist church. He was subsequently converted to the teachings of Sidney Rigdon and moved to Mentor, where he lived temporarily with this restorationist preacher, studying English and grammar under his tutelage.

In about 1829, Orson Hyde accompanied Rigdon on an itinerant crusade that included visits to the cities of Elyria and Florence. The preacher's successes in these two communities led to the creation of several new congregations, and in 1830, while teaching school in Florence, Orson Hyde served as pastor of these reformers. Shortly after he learned of the publication of the Book of Mormon, he declared it to be a hoax. A year later, while still publicly denouncing the publication, he confessed in private that his conscience told him such repudiation was wrong. A reevaluation of the work led to a powerful conversion. On October 31, 1831, Orson Hyde was baptized into the new church by his former minister, Sidney Rigdon, and on the same day he was confirmed and ordained an elder by Joseph Smith.[20]

Approximately one month after they arrived in northeastern

LDS

Frederick G. Williams

Ohio, the four Mormon missionaries, accompanied by Frederick G. Williams, resumed their journey west, heading toward Missouri. During a period of about four weeks, they had preached frequently in Kirtland, Mentor, and Mayfield and had introduced the restored gospel in Euclid, Warrensville, North Union (now Cleveland's Shaker Heights), and Painesville.[21] They had bap-

LDS

Orson Hyde

tized about 130 persons; had confirmed and ordained a number of converts, conveying to them the right to preach and baptize; and had inspired the new members to testify to friends, relatives, and strangers of the reality of the restoration. The four elders had also organized a branch of the Church in Kirtland in November, leaving Isaac Morley in charge of the congregation.[22]

A Distinct Quest for a Restoration

One reason for the remarkable growth of the Church in Ohio's Western Reserve in the fall of 1830 is that many persons living there were seeking a return to New Testament Christianity and held a number of beliefs that harmonized with doctrines taught by the Latter-day Saint missionaries. United under the leadership of Sidney Rigdon, they variously referred to themselves as Reformers, Reformed Baptists, and Reforming Baptists, but some of their critics called them Campbellites, because they endorsed sentiments popularized by a restorationist theologian named Alexander Campbell.[23]

During the 1820s, Sidney Rigdon and Alexander Campbell had shared many views concerning the need for a restoration of the pure gospel of Christ, and Rigdon was undoubtedly influenced by Campbell during that period. Born in western Pennsylvania in 1793, Sidney Rigdon had been trained by a Baptist minister and was set apart and ordained in 1819 by members of the Beaver Baptist Association (an alliance of Calvinist Baptists). After his ordination he moved to Warren, Ohio, where he met and married Phebe Brook and helped baptize about fifty converts. He next served in Pittsburgh for almost two years.[24] Meanwhile, through personal conversations with Alexander Campbell and through reading the *Christian Baptist,* a periodical published by Campbell in Bethany, West Virginia, he became acquainted with Campbell's views concerning the impropriety of creeds and the need to restore New Testament Christianity. These restorationist views conflicted with his orthodox Baptist beliefs, so he resigned from his ministerial position in the summer of 1823 and labored as a tanner for two years.[25]

In 1826 Sidney Rigdon accepted a call to become minister of a Baptist congregation in Bainbridge, Geauga County, Ohio, about fifteen miles south of Kirtland. Though the congregation had adopted a Calvinistic creed that to him was unacceptable, he was nevertheless invited to serve them without being required to endorse their local articles of faith.

Within a year of his move to Bainbridge, Sidney was invited

to serve members of another Calvinist Baptist congregation in Mentor, a few miles northeast of Kirtland Flats.[26] The Baptists of Mentor were affiliated with the Grand River Association, and he was accepted as a representative at the annual deliberations of this convention. His popularity as a preacher and his recognized leadership abilities are evidenced in part by his being invited to preach in 1826 and 1827 to delegates of an alliance of Baptist societies, the Mahoning Baptist Association.[27]

While serving as minister of the Regular Baptists in Mentor, Sidney Rigdon formally departed from the orthodox Baptist fold. Possibly his denunciation of the creeds of Christendom and his rejection of the five points of Calvinism would have been sufficient cause for members of the Grand River Association to expel him from their alliance. But his departure from traditional Baptist orthodoxy certainly advanced during the winter of 1827-28 when he began preaching that remission of sins and reception of the Holy Ghost would follow the immersion of a repentant believer. Most Baptists asserted that baptism, a symbol of acceptance of Christ, did not remit sins: such a remission was connected to faith alone. And Baptists, with few exceptions, contended that reception of the Holy Ghost did not come by repentance and baptism.

The person generally credited with being the first to popularize widely in eastern Ohio the concept that a remission of sins and the Holy Ghost follow baptism was Walter Scott, whom Sidney Rigdon had known earlier in Pittsburgh. In September 1827, Scott was called by the Mahoning Association to be a preacher, but he was not bound to creed or congregation. Shortly after this appointment, he began proclaiming six basic principles: faith, repentance, believer's baptism, remission of sins, reception of the Holy Ghost, and eternal life.[28]

Prior to the summer of 1828, Sidney Rigdon was also effectively proclaiming this same message from Mentor in the north to Mantua in the south. According to Amos Hayden, another restorationist preacher, Rigdon and Scott discussed these principles in Warren in March 1828, after which Rigdon, accompanied by Adamson Bentley, rode to Mentor to proclaim this doctrine.

After converting more than fifty persons and baptizing more than twenty into the "scriptural order of the gospel," they rode to Kirtland and converted fifty more people.[29] That summer, Alexander Campbell announced in the *Christian Baptist* that "Bishops Scott, Rigdon, and Bentley, in Ohio, within the last six months, have immersed about eight hundred persons."[30]

Members of the Grand River Association, recognizing that Sidney Rigdon and most members of his congregation had departed from the Baptist tradition, voted in September 1828 "to withdraw fellowship from the Painesville and Mentor Church." Representatives from the seventeen congregations forming this alliance further resolved that since the "sentiments and practices propagated by the leading men in the Mahoning Association were derogatory to the doctrine of Christ," fellowship with that body was terminated. In 1829 two other churches southeast of Kirtland (one in Chardon, eight miles away, and the other in Huntsburg, nineteen miles distant) were also dismissed because they had "departed from the faith of the gospel, by embracing the novel notions of A. Campbell."[31]

The Mahoning Association was dissolved in 1830 when delegates at the association's annual meeting agreed to sever all connections with the Baptist faith, to discontinue their yearly gatherings as an association, and to return to the primitive purity of the New Testament Christianity.[32] Many historians date the rise of the new denomination, the Disciples of Christ, to this move.

Early in 1830 Alexander Campbell proclaimed in the *Christian Baptist* that groups had already commenced to restore the ancient gospel. He predicted that this blissful revolution would produce many more fruits of righteousness and more peace and joy than any previous religious revolt "since the great apostasy from Christian institutions." Campbell commenced publication of another periodical, the *Millennial Harbinger*, in January 1830. The first issue was headed by a quotation from his version of Revelation 14:6: "I saw another messenger flying through the midst of heaven, having everlasting good news to proclaim to the inhabitants of the earth." This scripture was printed on the covers of subsequent issues of the magazine, which soon replaced the *Christian Baptist.*[33]

With the establishment of numerous independent congregations based on their versions of the New Testament church, Amos Hayden reported, many restorationist theologians in 1830 were proclaiming that "the millennium had now dawned, and that the long expected day of gospel glory would very soon be ushered in." This return to conditions existing in the primitive church was viewed as an initiatory movement preceding the gathering of the Jews to Jerusalem and the Second Coming of the Savior.[34]

The Break with Alexander Campbell

As Reformed Baptists of the Western Reserve compared their interpretations of the New Testament with views espoused by Alexander Campbell and other restorationist preachers, some concluded that those restorationists were teaching incorrect doctrines. In an attempt to restore New Testament Christianity more fully, Isaac Morley persuaded some of Sidney Rigdon's followers to create a communitarian system, with all things held in common. Thus, about five families, including those of Lyman Wight and Titus Billings, pooled their property and established an order called the "Family" or the "Big Family." A few families living in Mayfield organized a similar society. While Sidney Rigdon apparently approved this action, Alexander Campbell denounced the system.[35]

This was not the only issue keeping some of the followers of Sidney Rigdon from endorsing Campbell's efforts to restore New Testament Christianity. Significant disagreements also arose concerning gifts of the Holy Spirit and authority to perform ordinances. Alexander Campbell held that after individuals became the sons of God through faith and baptism, they would receive the spirit of Christ, which was the Holy Ghost. Such recipients, he taught, would be filled with peace and joy and become habitations of God.[36] He insisted, however, that those who received the gift of the Holy Ghost would not receive some of the spiritual gifts manifested in the early church; rather, they would be blessed with the fruits of the spirit. Explaining this concept, he stated that miracles similar to those wrought by the Holy Spirit during the generation of the apostles (such as healing and speaking in tongues) would not reappear in the latter days. Miracles performed by the apostles, he contended, were to confirm the new religion and prove its divine origin. Such manifestations were for a limited time, and "this limited time" had "expired."[37]

In contrast, some Reformed Baptists, especially those influenced by Sidney Rigdon, sought the same power described in the Holy Scriptures. Edward Partridge, a successful Painesville hatter, had concluded prior to the arrival of the Mormon missionaries that it was "absolutely necessary" for God to "again reveal himself to man and confer authority upon some one, or more, before his church could be built up in the last days, or any time after the apostasy." He further stated that he did not consider the subject of restoration of the priesthood until after he was convinced that God's true church was not upon the earth. Then he concluded that all men with whom he was acquainted "were without authority from God."[38]

Newell Kimball Whitney also rejected Campbell's view concerning the permanent cessation of miracles. Shortly before the introduction of Mormonism into the Western Reserve, he and his wife prayed earnestly to the Lord, requesting to know how they might be endowed with the Holy Ghost.[39]

Another settler of the Western Reserve who had been influenced by Sidney Rigdon and was seeking a restoration of the ancient gospel was Parley P. Pratt. After his marriage in New York to Thankful Halsey in September 1827, this twenty-one-year-old adventurer, accompanied by his bride, returned to a log cabin that he had built the previous winter in the wilderness of Lorain County, Ohio, about thirty miles west of Cleveland. There he erected another home, planted grain, and nurtured his young orchard of apple and peach trees.[40]

Approximately eighteen months after his marriage, Parley heard Sidney Rigdon preach his restorationist views to the settlers

Newel K. Whitney

in Lorain County. As a result of previous study of the New Testament, Parley had decided that faith, repentance, baptism by immersion for the remission of sins, and a promise of the gift of the Holy Ghost were basic principles of the gospel of Jesus Christ, and he therefore responded enthusiastically to the preacher's message. However, he also believed that one vital link was missing, a link essential to a restoration of primitive Christianity: "the authority to minister in holy things—the apostleship, the power which should accompany the form."[41] He recognized that Alexander Campbell, Sidney Rigdon, Walter Scott, and other restorationsist theologians who were then preaching in that section of America made no claims to a new commission from the Lord through a heavenly vision. Despite this deficiency, he joined the society that had been organized under Sidney Rigdon's direction in the community where he lived.[42]

In the summer of 1830, Parley P. Pratt announced that he had been called by the Holy Ghost to leave his home and preach the gospel of Christ. Since he believed that the fulness of the gospel was not upon the earth at that time, he intended to proclaim the need for a restoration of the ancient Christian order. After disposing of his property, he began to journey with his wife to their native home in Canaan, New York, near the Massachusetts border. As they traveled east along the Erie Canal near Rochester, New York, Parley felt impressed to commence preaching in that area. A few miles beyond the canal town of Palmyra, he disembarked at Newark, leaving his wife to continue the remainder of the journey alone. He walked about ten miles into a rural farming community, where he announced his intention to preach. While making the necessary arrangements, he met a Baptist deacon who informed him that a strange book had recently been published in Palmyra. He expressed a keen desire to examine the work and was told that if he returned the next day, he could secure a copy. Accordingly, the next morning he returned to the deacon's home and obtained a copy of the Book of Mormon. "I opened it with eagerness," Parley wrote in his autobiography,

and read its title page. I then read the testimony of several witnesses in relation to the manner of its being found and translated. After this I commenced its contents by course. I read all day; eating was a burden, I had no desire for food; sleep was a burden when the night came, for I preferred reading to sleep.

As I read, the spirit of the Lord was upon me, and I knew and comprehended that the book was true, as plainly and manifestly as a man comprehends and knows that he exists.[43]

After reading the Book of Mormon, Parley walked to Palmyra in search of its translator and was informed that the Smith family lived several miles outside Manchester Township. Proceeding south, Parley learned that Joseph Smith himself was then living in Pennsylvania, but that his brother Hyrum, one of the eight witnesses of the Book of Mormon plates, still lived in Manchester. He visited Hyrum Smith and listened as he explained many details concerning the coming forth of the Book of Mormon and the organization of the new church. A few days later, accompanied by Hyrum Smith, Parley walked to the Peter Whitmer farm in Fayette, New York, and, about September 1, 1830, was baptized in Seneca Lake by Oliver Cowdery. On the day of his baptism, he was also ordained to the office of elder in the Melchizedek Priesthood, receiving, as he explained, "the authority to preach, baptize, administer the sacrament, administer the Holy Spirit by laying on of hands" and preside at "meetings of worship."[44] After hastening to Canaan and telling his wife, parents, and friends of his recent spiritual experiences, he resumed his itinerant preaching. During the autumn of 1830, Parley P. Pratt not only introduced the restored gospel to a number of the inhabitants of New York, but he also baptized his brother Orson. He then returned to the area of Fayette.[45]

In October 1830, Parley P. Pratt was called by revelation to accompany Oliver Cowdery, Peter Whitmer, and Ziba Peterson on a mission to Indians living on America's frontier. After arranging for his wife to live with the Peter Whitmer family in Fayette, he proceeded west with his companions. The four elders preached to the Indians of the Catteraugus tribe near Buffalo, New York, then traveled on to Ohio.[46]

Since his conversion to the restored Church of Christ, Parley P. Pratt had not seen Sidney Rigdon. However, he sincerely believed that many in the Western Reserve would respond favorably to the message of the restoration. He knew that many of Sidney's followers had rejected the standard creeds of Christendom and sought a restoration of God's power and authority. Believing that the field was white already to harvest, Parley P. Pratt, with the assistance of three missionaries, thrust in his sickle with all his might—and reaped a fruitful harvest.

Chapter 2

Ohio in
the 1830s

In order to understand better the Ohio experience of the Latter-day Saints in the 1830s, one needs to examine social conditions and the setting of both the United States and the Western Reserve in that period. The rapid growth of the Church and the gathering of Latter-day Saints in northeastern Ohio during the 1830s, and the joys, struggles, and accomplishments they experienced there, coincided with a remarkable transformation in the young American republic. This was an era of significant increase, expansion, and concentration of the population. Modern political parties were taking shape. The Second Great Awakening, a powerful series of revivals in New England and frontier communities in Kentucky and Tennessee, was reaching a climax, and the religious vibrations of this revival combined with other forces to advance programs of humanitarian and moral reform. Meanwhile, a revolution in transportation was changing patterns of travel and communication, aiding the Latter-day Saint immigrants and missionaries.

An Era of Unusual Growth

During the threescore years preceding the American Civil War, the population of the United States almost doubled every twenty years. The five million in 1800 grew to more than nine million in 1820 and seventeen million in 1840. Although the number of immigrants arriving in the United States increased during the 1820s and 1830s, population growth during the first thirty years of the nineteenth century was due primarily to natural increase. Large families were common, and census reports of that period indicate that on the average, every household of free inhabitants had slightly more than five individuals.[1]

While the growth along the eastern seaboard remained almost stationary, there was a remarkable increase in the land west of the Appalachians. During the first decade of the century the population of New York State had almost doubled, increasing from about one-half to one million inhabitants, with the most significant growth occurring in New York City and the western part of New York State. An almost identical increase occurred during the 1820s in Ohio, and between 1820 and 1830 there was almost a fourfold increase in Wisconsin, a threefold increase in Michigan, and a doubling of the population in Missouri, Indiana, Illinois, Alabama, Mississippi, and Arkansas.

One of the remarkable changes was the rapid transformation of Ohio from a land of forests, dotted with Indian villages, to a region of mushrooming settlements. In 1800, three years before the territory became the sixteenth state, the population was approximately 72,000.[2] By 1826 it had grown to 800,000, an increase that observers noted was "perhaps without a parallel in the history of this or any other country."[3]

During the 1830s, the period of Mormon migration to Ohio, the state's population increased 581,564. Ohio had advanced from the thirteenth most populous state in 1810 to fifth in 1820, fourth in 1830. In 1840, only New York and Pennsylvania had more inhabitants than Ohio, and there were now as many people in Ohio as in the other states of the old Northwest (Indiana, Illinois, Michigan, and Wisconsin) combined.[4]

Most of the pioneers who settled in Ohio emigrated from the eastern United States. Northeastern Ohio, the area where most Latter-day Saints settled, was colonized primarily by New Englanders, while large numbers from Virginia and Kentucky

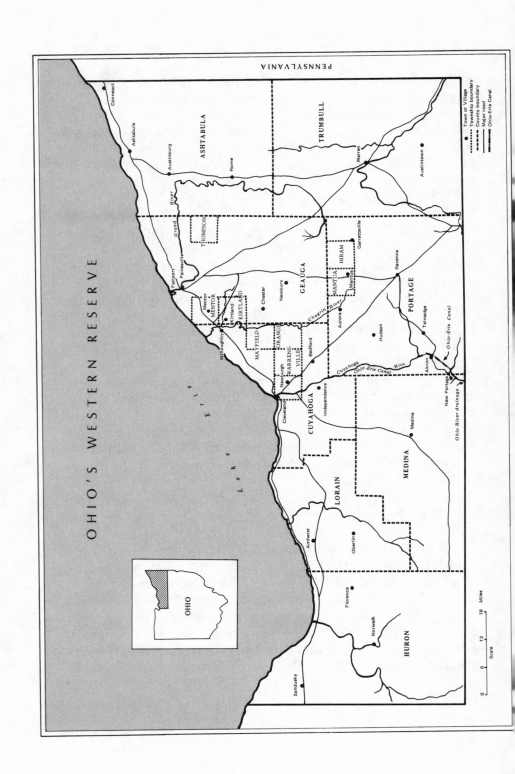

OHIO'S WESTERN RESERVE

PENNSYLVANIA

OHIO

Legend:
- Town or Village
- Township boundary
- County boundary
- Major road
- Ohio-Erie Canal

Counties: ASHTABULA, TRUMBULL, GEAUGA, PORTAGE, CUYAHOGA, MEDINA, LORAIN, HURON

Townships: THOMPSON, MENTOR, KIRTLAND, MAYFIELD, ORANGE, WARRENS-VILLE, HIRAM, MANTUA

Towns/Villages: Conneaut, Ashtabula, Austinburg, Rome, Warren, Austintown, Fairport, Painesville, Chester, Newbury, Garrettville, Ravenna, Willoughby, Kirtland, Mentor, Bedford, Aurora, Hudson, Talmadge, Akron, Newburgh, Cleveland, Independence, Medina, New Portage, Amherst, Oberlin, Florence, Norwalk, Sandusky, Mantua

Water features: Lake Erie, Grand River, Chagrin River, Cuyahoga River, Ohio-Erie Canal, Ohio River drainage

Scale: 0 6 12 18 Miles

immigrated into southern Ohio, especially the area between the Scioto and Little Miami rivers. Pennsylvanians of Scotch-Irish and German ancestry were also attracted to this region, and during the 1830s many immigrants arrived from Ireland and Germany. The Irish tended to settle in the cities, while the Germans settled not only in Cincinnati, Cleveland, Columbus, and Toledo, but also in the rural sections of the vanishing frontier.[5]

The Ohio wilderness was rapidly penetrated by the perennial march of pioneers. Throughout the first half of the nineteenth century the state remained predominantly agricultural. Extensive woodlands stretched across most of the state, these forests only slowly succumbing to the rising villages, towns, and cities.

The northeastern portion of Ohio had been known as Connecticut's Western Reserve. This area of four million acres extended north from the forty-first parallel (which included Akron) to the graceful curve of the Lake Erie shore, and stretched west 125 miles from the Pennsylvania border to about halfway across the state. Early in the colonial period the English king had given this land to Connecticut in a grant that extended from sea to sea. During and following the American Revolution, eastern states claiming western lands gradually relinquished their titles to the federal government; and by way of compromise, Connecticut retained the right to sell the northeastern section of this territory.

One group of land speculators who secured and then resold land in the Western Reserve formed the Connecticut Land Company. In 1796 directors of this joint stock company commissioned Moses Cleaveland, one of the original investors, to head an expedition and survey the land into five-mile townships. Two years later, Judge Turhand Kirtland, one of the land agents of the company, surveyed Poland and Burton townships in Geauga County, preliminary to the rapid sale of "New Connecticut." By 1800, settlements appeared along the Lake Erie shore near Cleveland—Mentor, Willoughby (known as Chagrin before 1834), and Painesville. Most of the early farms located near the lake were nestled a few miles inland in forests that gave protection from the biting winds blowing across Lake Erie.[6] New England culture spread into the region; Congregational meetinghouses were erected throughout northeastern Ohio, and schools patterned after New England educational institutions appeared in Hudson and Oberlin.

The Era of the Common Man

A new interest in politics and an extension of political democracy in the early nineteenth century coincided with the shifts in the population of the United States. Political rights of the common man were expanded as property qualifications were abandoned and opportunities to serve in government increased. Pure democracy, however, was still not a reality. Women and blacks were denied the franchise, and men watching the polls could sometimes determine how people voted.

Two parties, the Democrats and the Whigs, dominated the American political scene during the 1830s. After his triumph in 1828, Democrat Andrew Jackson served as president for two terms. He was followed by another Democrat, Martin Van Buren. Meanwhile, the Whigs (who by 1834 had changed their name from National Republicans as a symbol against executive tyranny) tried to create an anti-Jacksonian party by uniting disgruntled Democrats, dissatisfied southerners, and anti-Masons. Political confrontations led to bitter mud-slinging campaigns and even violence.

During the 1830s, Jacksonian forces succeeded in gaining political control of Ohio. Robert Lucas became the first Jacksonian Democratic governor of Ohio in 1832, and in that year Democrats gained control of both houses of the state legislature. Although most Latter-day Saints were Democrats and supported Jackson, they lived in a county that supported Henry Clay, the National Republican candidate. All counties surrounding Geauga also favored Clay.[7]

Man's Quest for Religious Truth

During the early nineteenth century, many Americans were searching for religious truth. The Second Great Awakening, a series of revivals that erupted in the late 1790s, reached its climax during the 1830s and 1840s. Methodist circuit riders, Baptist farm preachers, and traveling Presbyterian ministers were the most active and successful revivalists. Camp meetings, protracted meetings, and other unusual services were frequently held. During many of these gatherings, participants who were carried away by the intensity of their emotions exhibited their fervor through physical demonstrations, such as falling, fainting, barking, dancing, running, shouting, crying, singing, and laughing.

While the revivalist spirit was sweeping across the nation, church membership increased at a phenomenal pace. In 1800, organized religion was at a low ebb, with the ratio of ministers and church buildings to the American population standing lower than at any time since the initial English colonization of North America. But the powerful spiritual awakenings that erupted at the turn of the century prompted many persons to ask which church they should join. In 1800, only about 7 percent of the adult population in the country actively supported organized religion. The percentage of church membership increased to 13 percent by 1830, 14 percent in 1840, 17 percent in 1850, and 23 percent in 1860. As a consequence of this tremendous growth in church membership, organized religion was probably stronger, numerically speaking, in 1860 than it had been since the early days of the English colonization of America.[8]

Churches with missionary programs grew rapidly during the Jacksonian era, while faiths that failed to reach out to the great numbers of families living on isolated farms did not keep pace with the evangelistic denominations. When the new nation was born in the 1770s, the Congregational Church ranked first in membership; the Church of England, reorganized shortly thereafter as the Protestant Episcopal Church in the United States, also stood high in membership. The religious complexion in 1830 was very different, however. The Methodist and Baptist churches had become the dominant religions. According to a report in the *Cleveland Herald*, there were about twelve thousand meetinghouses in the United States in 1830, with more than one-third belonging to the combined Methodist and Baptist societies. Presbyterian congregations had 1,472 meetinghouses, followed by the Congregationalists with 1,381; Episcopalians, 922; Roman Catholics, 784; Dutch Reformed, 602; Friends, 462; Universalists, 293; Lutherans, 240; and Unitarians, 127. There were also 96 Jewish synagogues.[9]

An Age of Reform

With unprecedented numbers of Americans affiliated with various religious communities in the 1830s, a powerful spirit of reform gripped the young nation. Alexis de Tocqueville observed in the early thirties that "in no country in the world has the principle of association been more successfully used, or applied to a greater multitude of objects, than in America."[10] Ralph Waldo Emerson, the celebrated American author, remarked in 1841, "In the history of the world, the Doctrine of the Reform" had never had such "scope as at the present hour."[11]

Through the 1830s, reformers attacked the sins, evils, and burdens afflicting mankind. Abolitionists made their views heard; temperance leaders waged war against drunkenness, the saloons, the breweries, and the drinking of all intoxicating beverages; and some extended their concern to include a major reform of the popular drinking, eating, and living habits of Americans. Other reformers led crusades to improve conditions in prisons, to help the mentally incompetent, to correct abuses of the Sabbath day, to provide Americans with Bibles and religious tracts, and to establish Sunday schools in every community.

During this period, a host of voluntary associations were formed, many of which were interdenominational, drawing their support from members of various churches rather than from any single denomination. Meetings were often held in churches or public buildings and were sometimes led by ministers who either resigned from parish responsibilities to assume leadership of the organization or devoted part of the week to concentrating on reforming society.

One of the most industrious and influential educators of the age was Josiah Holbrook (1788-1854), a New England farmer. Having developed a keen interest in natural science while attending Yale, he established a mutual improvement association in Millbury, Massachusetts, in 1826. This adult-education program, which consisted in part of self-improvement courses, proved so successful that he went on to establish similar lyceums over the entire state and then to many other sections of the new nation. Holbrook eventually devoted full time toward organizing the groups. One striking evidence of his influence was the creation of the National American Lyceum in New York City in 1831, a body that represented a thousand town lyceums. By the mid-1830s more than three thousand lyceums had been formed in at least fifteen states, including Ohio.[12]

The most successful reform movement of the 1830s was the temperance crusade. Many newspapers, including some in the Western Reserve, labeled intemperance a national, social, and individual evil that corrupted the moral fiber of the country, impaired the intellect of the people, sapped the foundations of the moral and religious institutions, promoted disease and crime, and reduced the rich to poverty and the poor to wretchedness. Frequently citing observations of medical doctors, the press asserted that alcohol had an injurious effect on the brain, liver, and stomach and aggravated or produced almost every "morbid affliction to which the human body" was liable.[13]

To coordinate the activities of the emerging temperance societies, a national organization, the American Temperance Union, was constituted in 1826. By 1830 more than one thousand societies with over 100,000 members had endorsed the basic resolutions of this body. Nearly all of these organizations were formed on the principle of total abstinence from alcoholic beverages except for medicinal purposes.[14] Thirty temperance societies in Ohio were affiliated with the national union in 1830, and in January of that year, the Ohio State Temperance Society was formed in Columbus.[15] Over the next two years temperance groups were formed in nine townships in Geauga County, and these were linked together in a county society. At the annual meeting of the Geauga County Temperance Society in the summer of 1832, membership of the town associations was estimated at more than seven hundred, with the largest society, located at Kirtland, numbering 160 members. The temperance movement was supported in Kirtland by all of the Protestant churches, including Methodists, Congregationalists, Presbyterians (who worshipped with the Congregationalists), and Baptists.[16]

American newspapers and periodicals not only played a significant role in advancing the temperance crusade but also laid the foundation for a diet-reform movement that changed the eating, drinking, and chewing habits of many Americans. In 1830 the *Journal of Health* published a series of articles describing the injurious consequences of smoking and chewing tobacco and drinking tea and coffee.[17] Similar accounts, based primarily on talks delivered by reformers, were republished during the 1830s in Alexander Campbell's *Millennial Harbinger,* in the *Catholic Telegraph* (published in Cincinnati), and in a number of Ohio newspapers.[18]

One of the most controversial reform movements was the crusade for abolition of slavery. During or shortly following the American Revolution, all of the northern states acted to eradicate slavery either by immediate or by gradual emancipation. When southerners failed to take similar action, slavery became a deep wedge dividing the nation. A new antislavery movement emerged in the North about 1830, and during the thirties, the denunciation of slavery became more pronounced.[19]

The Transportation Revolution

As Ohio passed through the final stages of a pioneer period, it participated in a transportation revolution and became one of the important crossroads of the nation. New advances in the speed of travel and reduced costs of transporting goods helped facilitate the western expansion. This movement would prove beneficial to Latter-day Saints who were gathering to Ohio and Missouri and to Mormon missionaries traveling to new fields of labor.

An energetic program of road construction, especially during the years following the War of 1812, resulted in new roads across New England, New York, New Jersey, Pennsylvania, Ohio, and other sections of the country, thereby facilitating travel, especially by wagons, carriages, and stage coaches. Between 1811 and 1818 the Cumberland Road was built between Cumberland, Maryland, and Wheeling, West Virginia (then Virginia). The route then proceeded to Zanesville, Ohio, and on to Columbus in 1833; by 1840 it reached Indiana. By the standards of the day, this national highway was well built. A stone foundation was covered with gravel, and portions of the road crossing Ohio were covered with macadam seven to ten inches thick and thirty feet in width. Sturdy stone bridges with protective guard rails were erected across the rivers. To pay for the upkeep of this national pike, tolls were assessed at toll gates for nearly every object that moved on the pike, including horses, riders, coaches, cows, and hogs. Exemptions were made for preachers, soldiers, mailcoaches, and people traveling to church or school.[20]

Coinciding with the flurry of road building in America was the golden age of river steamboats. Although Robert R. Livingston and Robert Fulton had conducted a successful experiment on the Hudson River with their steamer *Clermont* in 1807, steam navigation was not inaugurated on most major American rivers and the Great Lakes until after the War of 1812. By 1830, river steamboats were carrying passengers and goods along the Ohio, the Mississippi, the Missouri, and many other major waterways.[21]

Because of the comfort and speed of steamboats, most travelers preferred them over other means of transportation. Brigham Young recalled one of his experiences while traveling by land in the spring of 1837. "We traveled by stagecoach through Ohio and Pennsylvania to Buffalo, New York, riding day and night over very rough roads." As a consequence of the swaying and jerking, he continued, "we became very weary and tarried a short time to rest ourselves."[22] Those traveling by land stopped often to recuperate in camps or wayside inns. Although some travelers on water routes suffered from seasickness, most people who journeyed by river steamer enjoyed relaxing in their berths or comfortable staterooms. If the riverboat was large, passengers could eat in spacious dining halls and even preach on open decks.

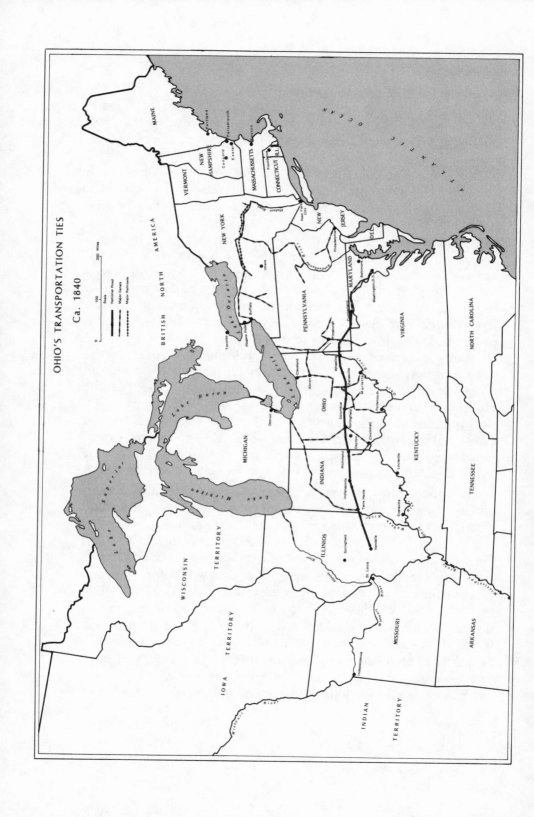

OHIO'S TRANSPORTATION TIES
Ca. 1840

Scale
0   100   200 Miles

National Road
Major Canals
Major Railroads

The advantages of water transportation during the 1830s are further evident when one considers the average speed or distance covered by different means of travel. A person walking through snow or mud a foot deep might average only a few miles a day; under more favorable conditions, they might average two to three miles an hour, depending on their determination. Teams pulling loaded wagons averaged about two miles an hour, stagecoaches about six to eight miles an hour on good roads, and western steamers almost ten miles an hour. Some of the fastest boats cut through the water at better than twenty miles an hour—and these speeds on the water continued not only during the day but also throughout the night while passengers slept. Consequently, during a twenty-four-hour period a loaded wagon might travel twenty to thirty miles, a stagecoach eighty to one hundred miles, and a steamboat almost five hundred miles. [23]

With the transportation revolution came a boom in canal building unparalleled in American history. There were only about 100 miles of canals in the nation in 1816. By 1830 there were 1,277 miles of canals, and by 1840 more than 3,326 miles had been dug—greater than the distance between New York City and Seattle. [24]

In February 1825, Ohio launched a canal building program that eventually united the waters of Lake Erie and the Ohio River, thereby connecting the Hudson River (by means of the Erie and Ohio canals) with the Mississippi and creating America's greatest system of internal waterways.

The wooden freight vessels that plied the Ohio Canal during the 1830s were usually about seventy-five feet long and fourteen feet wide. Towed by horses or mules in teams of two or more, these ungainly barges traveled three miles per hour. Since most cargo was packed in small containers, such as baskets, sacks, barrels, or boxes, travelers were often delayed as the containers were slowly unloaded. Nevertheless, most tourists preferred canal travel to its alternative, a swaying stagecoach on rutted or muddy roads. [25]

Since Kirtland was about twenty miles east of the Ohio Canal, it was generally more convenient for residents there to travel or to transport their crops and other goods northeast from Kirtland to Fairport Harbor, about ten miles distant; from Fairport, the goods could then be shipped along Lake Erie east to the Erie Canal or west to the Ohio Canal. Most of the Latter-day Saints who immigrated to Kirtland from New York in 1831 traveled west along the Erie Canal, and throughout the 1830s other Saints reported arriving at Fairport Harbor en route to the Church's headquarters in Ohio.

Before the canal boom reached its zenith, the railroad became a serious challenge to water transportation. Although the first American-built locomotive began regular service in the United States in 1830, the growth of railroads was slow in that decade. Most of the 3,328 miles of track that had been laid by 1840 were in unconnected segments east of the Appalachians. As train speeds increased and costs of transporting freight and passengers decreased, people came to recognize the advantages of the railroads over canals. The cost of constructing and maintaining railroads was less than that of canals, and trains could be operated throughout the year without being affected by most weather conditions.

One of the early leaders of the restored Church, Oliver Cowdery, reported his experience of riding on the initial run of a passenger car traveling between Utica and Schenectady, New York, in 1836. Delayed by ceremonies and confusion, he reported that the train traveled only eighty miles in six hours. Shortly after it arrived in Schenectady, he heard someone yell, "Albany baggage—the car starts in five minutes." He then witnessed a "scene of confusion, bustle and crowding." While he detected no crushed skulls or broken arms or legs, he observed a "good deal of complaining and many wry faces." Finally the trunks and people were ready for the departure, and the train proceeded slowly toward Albany. About one mile from the New York State capital, the engine was detached and pulled within one block of the statehouse by horses. After this experience, Oliver Cowdery recognized that there was a need for significant improvement in this new system of transportation.[26]

Chapter 3

The Gathering to Ohio

W hile the young nation and the maturing state of Ohio changed rapidly, the lives of one group of Americans were transformed by the light of a new religion. Responding to the message of the restoration as unfolded by a latter-day prophet, Joseph Smith, these seekers after truth embraced a new guide to direct their lives. This influence was revelation; and at the beginning of the 1830s, this religious impact was most evident in Ohio and New York. Between the end of October 1830 and early June 1831, a period of less than eight months, this new religious movement was introduced into the Western Reserve; hundreds were converted to the faith; Kirtland, Ohio, became the headquarters of a church that was less than one year old; and, at the call of the prophet, several hundred settlers from New York gathered to Geauga County (which included the area now called Lake County) to help establish a new religious center in the United States.

The Transformation of a Community

The community where members of the newly restored Church settled, Kirtland, Ohio, had changed dramatically during the two decades preceding the introduction of the Church there. In 1820, nine years after the first permanent settlers constructed their log cabins in Kirtland, the population was enumerated at 481; during

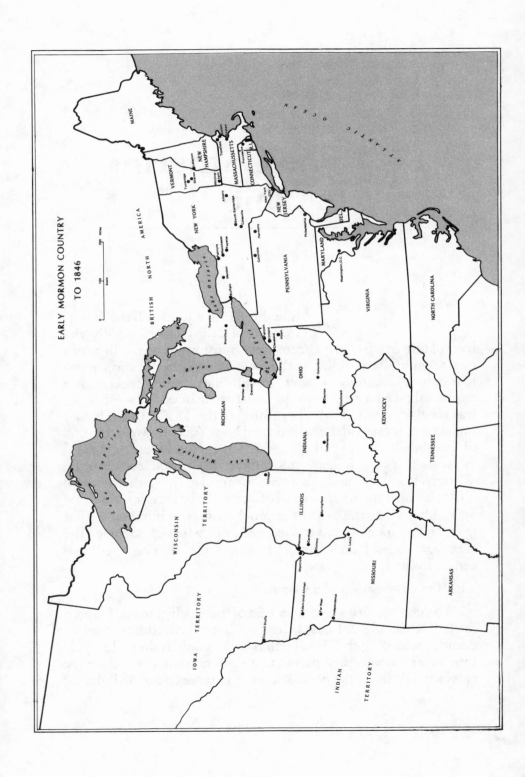

EARLY MORMON COUNTRY
TO 1846

the next decade this number doubled to 1,018, consisting of 162 families, or an average of 6.3 individuals per family.[1] Statistics, however, do not reflect the struggles and the satisfactions experienced by the pioneers as they built that community. Since much of the United States in the early nineteenth century was a vast untamed forest, many Americans gained practical experience and genuine dignity through hours of hard work, producing much of what they consumed. At least nine of the families who would join the Church in 1830 or early 1831 were among the pioneers who helped develop a civilization out of the Kirtland wilderness.[2] The lessons that young and old alike learned while building homes, manufacturing household goods, planting and harvesting crops, and establishing local political institutions proved invaluable after these pioneers joined the Church and created new communities in Missouri, Illinois, and the Great Basin of western America.

A vivid description of the Kirtland wilderness was written by one of the first settlers of that region, Christopher Gore Crary, who arrived in Kirtland from Massachusetts in May 1811. "The forest-trees," he recalled, "were of endless variety and of the tallest kinds." Beneath the trees was a "thick growth of underbrush" interspersed with "flowers of rare beauty. . . . Birds of varied plumage filled the air with their music, and the air itself was fragrant and invigorating." For centuries, he added, this region had been the home of the Indians, "and surely their most vivid imagination could have portrayed nothing more desirable or delightful" than this "celestial" abode.[3]

The Crary family guided their oxen along the narrow, winding forest paths to the homesite they had selected. While they rested during their first night in their crude home, a log cabin which they had built earlier (while staying in Mentor), they kept a bright fire burning to protect themselves from the bears and wolves. Their "beds consisted of hemlock boughs, which were," according to Crary, "perhaps better appreciated than beds of down might have been under other circumstances."[4]

One year after the Crary family began farming in Kirtland, Isaac Morley settled there. Shortly after erecting a small cabin in

Kirtland, he returned to his former home in Montague, Franklin County, Massachusetts, and married his childhood sweetheart, Lucy Gunn. Then the newlyweds traveled six hundred miles by team and wagon back to Kirtland. Shortly after they began developing the virgin land, Isaac left his wife to serve in the War of 1812. According to family histories, Lucy remained alone in the forest, seldom seeing another human, and lived in constant fear of attack by wild beasts or roaming Indians. No other settlers lived near the Morley cabin, and there were no stores, post offices, church buildings, or mills nearby.[5]

After serving for forty-one days in this second war for independence, Isaac Morley returned home, ill with chills and fever. He soon recovered, and the young couple resumed their labors. As the years passed, they cultivated a large farm and built a more commodious frame home. They planted an orchard and a grove of maple trees, later called Morley's Grove, from which they tapped maple syrup. They harvested crops of wheat and rye, made their own molasses and vinegar, and extracted honey from their beehives. Isaac also made and sold barrels, produced a peppermint oil, and made lye from ashes, while Lucy spun and wove linen cloth from flax raised on their farm and made clothes for her family from cotton yarn purchased from others and from woolen cloth made from their own sheep's wool (the wool was processed in a local mill). During their first seventeen years of married life in Kirtland, Lucy Morley gave birth to nine children. Of the seven who grew to maturity, the first six were girls and the last was a boy named after his father.[6]

Twelve years before the arrival of the first Latter-day Saint missionaries, a local government was constituted in Kirtland. In 1818, the electors of Kirtland selected their first township officials, including three trustees (one of whom was Isaac Morley), several overseers of the poor, appraisers of property, supervisors of highways, a constable, and a treasurer. The next year a justice of the peace was also elected.[7]

One of the first leaders to serve as overseer of the poor was Peter French, whose responsibility was to prevent families from remaining in the community who might become wards of the town. Such individuals were reported to the constable, who sometimes forced them to leave. Not all persons who were unable to meet their financial obligations were expelled from Kirtland and other early American communities. A few received aid from the local government; the overseers of the poor had the responsibility to provide food and clothing and sometimes to pay the medical bills of those who needed temporary economic assistance.[8]

Although Kirtland was primarily an agricultural community, stores, mills, and factories were erected in the town between 1819 and 1830. The center of the industrial and merchandising life of the township was in the eastern section, in an area known as Kirtland Flats, adjacent to the East Branch of Chagrin River. This meandering stream with its small tributaries provided the power necessary to operate the mills and factories. A sawmill was constructed near the river in 1819, and one year later a gristmill was built downstream. Shortly thereafter, a carding machine was located near the mills where settlers could take their wool for dressing. During the 1820s, Grandison Newell built a furnace in the township and added a lathe to his shop so that he could manufacture chairs, stands, beds, candle boxes, and other such wooden products. Also during these early years an ashery was constructed for turning ashes into black salts used in making soap.[9]

The first store in Kirtland was built below the hill where the Latter-day Saints would later erect a temple. Newel K. Whitney, who had initially utilized his log cabin home as a store, erected a store on the flats in 1823. There he continued to sell and trade until he and his family moved from Kirtland in the late 1830s. The Whitney store was also used as a post office, and for many years Newel K. Whitney was the commissioned postmaster of Kirtland, or Kirtland Mills, as it then was called.

Shortly before the arrival of the Latter-day Saints, Peter French built the first brick building in Kirtland, a hotel across the street from the Whitney store.[10]

Though the early settlers of Kirtland worked long hours to produce their goods, they were not too busy to construct schools and hire teachers to instruct their youth. As early as 1814, a small log-cabin school was erected; five years later the first frame school

Newel K. Whitney's store in Hiram, Ohio

was built on the flats. By 1830, Kirtland was divided into a number of school districts so that children living in different parts of the town could participate in an elementary educational program.[11]

Early Churches of Kirtland

When the first Latter-day Saint missionaries arrived in the Western Reserve, four Protestant groups were worshipping in Kirtland. Two of them (the Congregationalists and Methodists) were holding services in meetinghouses, and the other two (the Baptists and Reformed Baptists) were meeting in the homes of settlers.

Since many of the original inhabitants of Kirtland were immigrants from New England, it is not surprising that the first body of Christians to unite in worship there were Congregationalists. In September 1819, ten settlers who endorsed the basic teachings of the reformer John Calvin gathered and endorsed an article of faith prepared by the Presbytery of Grand River for the regulation of churches under their care. This creed, patterned after the

Westminster Confession of Faith, included the five points of Calvinism: total depravity of man, unconditional election or predestination, limited atonement, irresistibility of grace (man cannot reject the call), and perseverance of the saints (saved man cannot fall). Since the Presbyterians and Congregationalists agreed by the Plan of Union of 1801 to cooperate rather than compete in new settlements of America, members of both faiths worshipped together in this congregation and voted to unite under the supervision of the Presbytery of Grand River.

After meeting for three years in homes, members of the church constructed a log meetinghouse in 1822 on the site of the present old South Congregational Church, in the southern part of the town. A few years later, after the original church was destroyed by fire, the Calvinists constructed a larger frame building across the road, and there they worshipped throughout the 1830s. Although they were originally served by different ministers, the Reverend Truman Coe began a pastorate in 1833 that continued until his retirement in 1848.[12]

Shortly after the Congregationalists of Kirtland united, Methodists commenced services in the community. About 1820 they erected a small church on the corner of the cemetery lot across the street from the future Kirtland Temple site. This Methodist congregation was originally included in the Grand Circuit, consisting of forty-four preaching stations in Ashtabula, Geauga, and Trumbull counties. Every four weeks, a Methodist circuit-rider preacher traveled about two hundred miles in this vast circuit to visit classes and congregations.[13]

A Baptist society was also meeting in Kirtland in 1830. This congregation had been admitted into the 1828 alliance of closed-communion Calvinist Baptist churches called the Grand River Association; and since there was no settled minister to serve the needs of these twenty-two Protestants, they were, for almost five years, irregularly visited by elders assigned by that alliance.[14]

The Quest for Additional Knowledge

Shortly after the four missionaries who had introduced the restored gospel in Ohio had left Geauga and Cuyahoga counties for western Missouri, two of the men who had been influenced by them traveled east to continue their investigation of the restored gospel. Though Sidney Rigdon had been baptized and ordained an elder, his traveling companion, Edward Partridge, had not yet joined the Church. Lydia Partridge recalled that when her husband commenced the journey, he was not fully convinced of the truth of the gospel taught by the elders. Philo Dibble noted that Edward Partridge not only undertook this investigation for himself, but, in a sense, traveled east as a representative for the other inquirers. Since he was known as a man of integrity, Dibble suggested, there were those who felt they could rely on his observations and who therefore awaited his investigation of Joseph Smith's integrity.[15]

When they arrived in Manchester, New York, Sidney Rigdon and Edward Partridge learned that Joseph Smith was visiting his parents, who had moved to a small community located near Waterloo. They therefore continued their journey east. According to Lucy Mack Smith, the Prophet's mother, when the two men entered her home (which was probably located a few miles east of Waterloo at a place named Kingdon[16]), a meeting was being conducted by her son Joseph. During this meeting, Edward Partridge heard Joseph himself testify concerning the restoration of the everlasting gospel. As the latter-day prophet spoke, Edward was convinced that he should join the Church immediately, but because of his apparent weariness due to the long journey, Joseph recommended that baptism be delayed until the next day. On December 11, 1830, Edward Partridge was baptized by Joseph Smith, Jr., in the Seneca River. Four days later, he was ordained to the office of elder by his former minister, Sidney Rigdon.[17]

Shortly after Sidney Rigdon and Edward Partridge met Joseph Smith, the Prophet recorded a revelation addressed to Sidney and another counseling Edward. Sidney learned that he had been sent forth like John the Baptist to prepare the way for the coming of Christ. Before embracing the restored gospel, he had been preaching baptism for the remission of sins; now he was told he had been endowed with the power of God, which included the authority to heal, cast out devils, and bestow upon others the gift of

Joseph Smith

the Holy Ghost.[18] Edward Partridge learned that he too had been specially blessed by God. The revelation stated that his sins had been forgiven him, and that he should now preach the everlasting gospel to others, crying repentance to his generation.[19]

After learning of the remarkable conversions in northeastern Ohio, Joseph Smith sent John Whitmer, one of the eight witnesses of the Book of Mormon, to Kirtland to preside over the branch that had been recently organized there. Carrying handwritten copies of many revelations received by the Prophet that were to guide and strengthen the Ohio converts, Elder Whitmer arrived in the Western Reserve in mid-January, 1831.[20] There he assumed leadership of an estimated three hundred Latter-day Saints, more than twice the number reported only two months earlier.[21]

After the four missionaries had left Ohio for Missouri in November 1830, proselyting activities had been continued by the Ohio converts. One of the most successful missionaries was the former restorationist preacher, John Murdock. Between November 1830 and March 1831, this young farmer baptized more than fifty-five settlers living primarily in Cuyahoga County (in the area of Orange and Warrensville, now included in the eastern section of Cleveland).[22]

As the membership of the Church increased, the converts were organized into branches, and leaders were appointed to direct their religious life. By early 1831, there were probably four branches of the Church in Ohio—two in Geauga County and two in Cuyahoga County. John Whitmer presided over the Kirtland branch, while Sidney Rigdon led the branch in Mentor. In Cuyahoga County, John Murdock presided over the Warrensville branch; records do not reveal the name of the leader of the Mayfield branch.[23]

The Call to Gather

During a period when the Church was growing more rapidly in Ohio than anywhere else, Joseph Smith received two revelations directing that he and other members of the Church should gather to that state. The first of these revelations was recorded in the latter part of December 1830; the second, amplifying the first, was received January 2, 1831, during a conference held in Fayette, New York. "And that ye might escape the power of the enemy," this second commandment explained, "and be gathered unto me a righteous people, without spot and blameless—wherefore, for this cause I gave unto you the commandment that ye should go to the Ohio; and there I will give unto you my law; and there you shall be endowed with power from on high."[24]

There were many advantages in gathering to Ohio. With

members scattered in several states, it was impossible for the Prophet to give instructions to all, and the new converts were constantly asking questions concerning Church procedures and doctrines. Individuals who migrated to the headquarters of the Church were in a position to receive regular instructions from the man they respected as a special servant of the Lord. Consequently, this gathering helped establish and maintain doctrinal and organizational uniformity.

In many respects, the state of Ohio was a favorable location for the establishment of an ecclesiastical headquarters. As the year 1831 began, more members were in Ohio than in any other state, and Church membership was growing more rapidly in the Western Reserve than in any other area. Moreover, Ohio was centrally located. Missionaries could leave Kirtland and be in Pennsylvania or New York within a few days, and they could travel along the Erie Canal to eastern New York and from there penetrate New England. From the Western Reserve, missionaries could also skirt Lake Erie and within a few days be in eastern Canada; or they could follow the roads or canals south to the Ohio River, which bordered Kentucky and was a gateway to the South and West.

To move from New York to Ohio was also a step toward Zion. From the Book of Mormon, Latter-day Saints learned that a New Jerusalem would be built on the American continent, and that those who sought to bring forth Zion would be blessed with the gift and power of the Holy Ghost.[25] When Oliver Cowdery was called in September 1830 to serve as a missionary among the Indians, the general location of this New Jerusalem was revealed: it was to be situated "on the borders by the Lamanites."[26] This designation was a term commonly used to identify the edge of the white settlements in the United States, a frontier then located west of the Mississippi River. One of the communities on that frontier in 1830 was Independence, Missouri. After they left Ohio, the four missionaries who had introduced the gospel in the Western Reserve established a temporary residence in Independence and gathered information concerning conditions in that section of the West.

Another reason for the migration to Ohio was to "escape the power of the enemy," as expressed in the revelation. The emigration from New York was carried out in the midst of growing opposition in the form of harassment, social ostracism, threats of attack on persons and property, arrests of Joseph Smith, and a constant flood of libelous charges aimed at disrupting the missionary activities of the Prophet in the area of Colesville, New York.[27]

Although most members of the Church who attended the January conference in Fayette, New York, accepted the instructions to move to Ohio as the word of God, a few grumbled and complained, asserting that the proposed migration was formulated by Joseph Smith for his own personal well-being. In the view of John Whitmer, such thinking was evidence that the hearts of some of the converts were not in tune with the Spirit of the Lord. With very few exceptions, however, nearly every member of the Church in New York heeded the commandment and commenced preparations for the first exodus west.[28]

Between the end of January and the last part of April, most of the New York Saints sold their homes, barns, lands, cattle, and many other possessions; packed their most precious material goods; and migrated to Geauga County, Ohio. Probably about two hundred immigrants participated in this move. A few of the men preceded their families, including Joseph Smith, Sr., Hyrum Smith, Samuel Smith, and Newell Knight; most, however, traveled with their wives and children. Some walked; others traveled by sleigh or stagecoach. A few loaded their clothes and furniture in wagons and drove their teams to Kirtland. The majority of the Saints, however, traveled most of the way on canal barges and on the steamboats or sailing vessels that plied the shores of Lake Erie.[29]

The migration to Ohio was led by Joseph Smith, accompanied by his wife, Emma; Edward Partridge; and, during part of the journey, by Sidney Rigdon and possibly Joseph Knight. Leaving the Finger Lakes country, the twenty-five-year-old Prophet traveled overland by sleigh, arriving in Kirtland on or about February 1, 1831. According to an account preserved by the Newel K. Whitney family, Joseph sprang from the sleigh and entered the Gilbert

Whitney store. Extending his hand to the junior partner as though he were a familiar acquaintance, Joseph said, "Newel K. Whitney! Thou art the man!"

Newel was astonished, for he could not recall having seen this person before. "Stranger," he replied, "you have the advantage of me. I could not call you by name, as you have me."

"I am Joseph the Prophet," the stranger declared. "You've prayed me here. Now what do you want of me?"[30]

Some time after Joseph Smith had learned about the remarkable conversions in the Western Reserve, he had seen in vision Newel K. Whitney praying for him to come to Kirtland. Consequently, the family records state that Joseph Smith recognized Newel when the two men met in the store; and, as Elizabeth Whitney recalled, the Prophet's arrival in Ohio was indeed an answer to her and her husband's prayers.[31]

This encounter with Joseph Smith was not the first occasion when the Whitneys had experienced the efficacy of prayer. Before Newel K. Whitney and his wife had joined the Church of Christ, they had prayed that they might receive knowledge concerning the authority necessary to obtain the gift of the Holy Ghost. In response to this petition, Elizabeth testified, she and her husband were enwrapped in what seemed to be a cloud and felt the Spirit of the Lord. Then they heard a voice that said, "Prepare to receive the word of the Lord, for it is coming." Shortly thereafter, this couple met Latter-day Saint missionaries, and within a few weeks they joined the Church.[32]

Joseph Smith and his wife were received with kindness by the Whitneys and were invited to live temporarily with them. Joseph wrote that he and Emma lived with the Whitney family for several weeks and "received every kindness and attention which could be expected, and especially from Sister Whitney."[33]

Although Joseph Smith and a few other Saints settled in Kirtland in February, most of the members from New York were not prepared to migrate until the canal system was opened in the spring. The majority of these members immigrated to Ohio in one of two main bodies.[34] In April 1831, approximately sixty members of the Colesville branch, representing about fifteen families,

LDS

Emma Smith   *Edward Partridge*

traveled by wagon to Ithaca, New York, on the southern shore of
the Cayuga Lake. One observer said that as some of the group
passed by her father's farm with their ox-driven covered wagons,
she was reminded of a western immigrant train.[35] Another contemporary, a teamster who had been hired by these immigrants,
recalled that in the train he accompanied to Ithaca were three
baggage and eleven passenger wagons.[36] After congregating near
the lake, the Colesville Saints traveled via the Cayuga and
Seneca canals to the Erie Canal, then along this major canal to
Buffalo. Because bitter winds off Lake Erie had prevented the
winter ice in Buffalo's harbor from thawing, most of the Colesville
Saints were delayed for several weeks. Though a few proceeded
overland to Dunkirk and then took a steamer to Fairport, Ohio,
most waited until a schooner was able to leave the harbor. These
Saints then proceeded southwest to Fairport, arriving May 14.
When they reached Kirtland, they were instructed to settle in

Thompson, about sixteen miles northeast of Kirtland, on land owned by Leman Copley, a recent convert.[37]

While the Colesville Saints were migrating from eastern New York to the Western Reserve, other members residing in the area of Fayette gathered at Kingdon, near the Seneca River, at the home where Lucy Mack Smith was living. This group then boarded two canal boats, with Lucy Smith directing the activities of about fifty individuals (twenty adults and thirty children, according to her account) on the first boat, and Thomas B. Marsh leading about thirty others on the second barge. After traversing the Cayuga and Seneca canals, these Saints continued along the Erie Canal toward Lake Erie. When they arrived in Buffalo, they met the Colesville Saints, who had been there about a week.[38] Sister Smith's group boarded a different ship from that chartered by the Colesville members. While waiting for the ice to thaw, she asked the Saints to exercise their faith, that they might continue their journey. After the group petitioned God to break the twenty-foot clogs of ice that were jamming the harbor, she testified, "a noise was heard, like bursting thunder. The captain cried, 'Every man to his post.' The ice parted, leaving barely a passage for the boat, and so narrow that as the boat passed through the buckets of the waterwheel were born off with a crash. . . . We had barely passed through the avenue when the ice closed again, and the Colesville brethren were left in Buffalo, unable to follow us."[39]

One contemporary who described the movement of Saints into Geauga County in 1831 wrote that it seemed that the "whole world" was centering in Kirtland. "They came," he continued, "men, women, and children, in every conceivable manner, some with horses, oxen, and vehicles rough and rude, while others had walked all or part of the distance. The future 'City of the Saints' appeared like one besieged. Every available house, shop, hut, or barn was filled to its utmost capacity. Even boxes were roughly extemporized and used for shelter until something more permanent could be secured."[40]

Both companies of New York Saints arrived in the Western Reserve during the middle of May, completing the first phase of

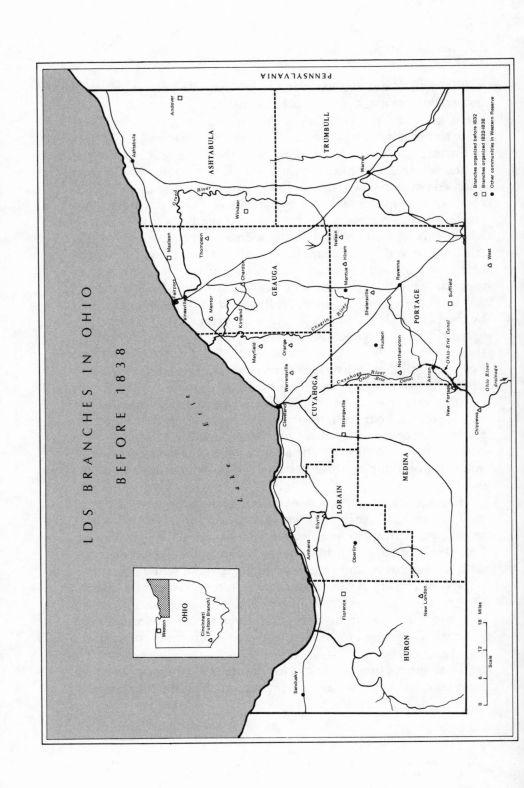

LDS BRANCHES IN OHIO

BEFORE 1838

△ Branches organized before 1832
□ Branches organized 1832-1838
● Other communities in Western Reserve

PENNSYLVANIA

Andover □

Ashtabula

ASHTABULA

TRUMBULL

Grand River

Windsor □

Warren

Madison □

Thompson △

Nelson △

Chardon

Mantua △ Hiram △

GEAUGA

Ravenna

West △

Fairport

Painesville ■

Mentor △

Kirtland △

Chagrin River

Shalersville △

PORTAGE

Suffield □

Mayfield △

Orange △

Hudson ●

Northampton △

Ohio-Erie Canal

Warrensville △

CUYAHOGA

Cuyahoga River

Ohio -Erie Canal

Akron

New Portage

Lake Erie

Cleveland

Strongsville □

Ohio River drainage

Chippewa □

MEDINA

LORAIN

Elyria

Amherst

Oberlin ●

Florence □

New London △

OHIO

Weston □

Cincinnati (Fulton Branch) △

Sandusky ●

HURON

Scale

0   6   12   18 Miles

the westward movement of Latter-day Saints. Most Americans who pushed westward in the nineteenth century were searching for free or inexpensive land, seeking adventure, or escaping creditors, or were involved in a variety of economic pursuits. But this particular migration was an unusual one in that it took place in response to what the participants believed to be a commandment from God. Commenting on this relocation of people at the call of a prophet, the *Painesville Telegraph* reported on May 17, 1831, that during the preceding week, some two hundred men, women, and children from New York had settled in Geauga County. This paper noted that these immigrants had submitted to the "spiritual and temporal" instructions of Joseph Smith, and regarded Geauga County as their "promised land."[41] Unless others arrived at the same time as the two companies, this estimate of two hundred was probably high, but it is a fairly accurate count of the total number of Latter-day Saints who emigrated from New York to Ohio between the middle of January and early June of 1831.

Although most of the New York Saints had reached Ohio by mid-May, Martin Harris, one of the three witnesses to the Book of Mormon plates, did not leave Palmyra until the end of May. Shortly after Joseph Smith had arrived in Kirtland, he wrote to Martin Harris personally, instructing him to move the Saints of Palmyra, to bring with him copies of the Book of Mormon, and to use his influence to encourage others to migrate to the new headquarters of the Church.[42] Reporting on the departure of Martin Harris from Palmyra, the *Wayne Sentinel* specified that he had been among the early settlers of that town and had "ever borne the character of an honorable and upright man." He was further regarded as a "benevolent neighbor" who had a "respectable fortune." While expressing regret that Martin Harris had united with an unpopular religious community, the paper noted that he was leaving "a large circle of acquaintances and friends" to settle in a "promised land."[43] He probably arrived in Kirtland in June, accompanied by several families.

Since there are no Church membership records dating back to the 1830s, historians of today can only estimate the number of people who, in 1830 and 1831, were influenced directly by the

LDS

*Four converts of the 1830s who later became President of the Church:
Brigham Young, top left; John Taylor; Wilford Woodruff,
bottom left; Lorenzo Snow*

message of the restoration. In the spring of 1831, one year after the Church of Christ had been organized, more than six hundred individuals had embraced the gospel, and many of these converts were then living in the Western Reserve.[44] While the actual membership in 1831 is unknown, the diaries, autobiographies, and letters of those who joined the Church during the first year of its history clearly indicate that major changes occurred in the lives of those who embraced the restored gospel. As people were caught in the gospel net, their beliefs, attitudes, goals, and aspirations changed. Many of their most important decisions were now governed by a new force: divine messages unfolded by a latter-day prophet.[45]

Table 1
Birthplaces of Kirtland Saints

State or Area	Total	Male	Female	Percentage of Total
New York	264	156	108	32
Massachusetts	126	82	44	15
Vermont	102	64	38	12
New Hampshire	66	37	29	8
Connecticut	66	37	29	8
Maine	24	13	11	3
New York and New England Combined	648	389	259	78
Canada	42	23	19	5
Ohio	33	18	15	4
Pennsylvania	33	15	18	4
England	19	6	13	2
Total other states	55	36	19	7

Source: Records of 830 husbands and wives who were members of the Kirtland Branch during the 1830s, using primarily family group sheets located in the Church Genealogical Department.

Chapter 4
The Critics
Respond

As Joseph Smith and his followers arrived in the Western Reserve and started to establish the Church's headquarters there, many non-Mormons began to respond negatively and even aggressively to the growth of this new faith. Newspaper articles generally misrepresented the history, beliefs, ambitions, and goals of the Saints, as reporters often confused improper beliefs and conduct with orthodox doctrines and behavior.

Alarmed by the spirited anti-Mormon campaign, Joseph Smith recorded in his history that in the spring of 1831, "many false reports, lies, and foolish stories, were published in the newspapers, and circulated in every direction, to prevent people from investigating the work, or embracing the faith."[1]

Reports on the Church printed in the Ohio papers before the first missionaries arrived in the Western Reserve were more favorable and unbiased than those published during the 1830s, the period of the gathering in the state. Initially the religion was more a topic of curiosity than of scorn. But after the missionaries baptized some 130 converts in Kirtland and vicinity, the number of articles relating to the Church multiplied rapidly (in fact, more articles appeared in Ohio papers between November 1830 and December 1831 than during any other period), and most of them contained derogatory statements about the Latter-day Saints, setting the tone for a propaganda offensive that continued for a number of years.

The editor who, more than any other, planted the seeds for Mormon persecution in Geauga County was Eber D. Howe, who was born in Saratoga County, New York, in 1798. Following the War of 1812, Howe was apprenticed to the publisher of the *Buffalo Gazette*. He later moved to Cleveland, Ohio, and helped establish the *Cleveland Herald* in 1818. In 1822 he moved to Painesville, where he founded the *Painesville Telegraph*. He was editor of that paper (sometimes working alone, sometimes with the help of a partner) until January 1835.[2]

During the years that E. D. Howe was editor of the *Telegraph*, more disparaging articles on Mormonism appeared in that publication than in any other Ohio newspaper. He personally wrote only a few of the articles, but he also accepted for publication many critical accounts (with truth and error garbled together) about the restored Church. Some of the articles were reproduced in other Ohio publications.[3]

Latter-day Saints were not the only targets of Howe's denunciations. He also brought his profusely slanderous language to bear against the Masons and members of various dissident or unorthodox religious societies. He opposed all secret societies in which men "swear to extricate each other . . . whether right or wrong."[4] He characterized members of one group as "deluded fanatics," "monsters," "demons," "serpents," "horned beasts," "kidnappers," "arsonists" and "murderers."[5]

Adopting the same approach, Howe and many other journalists of Ohio used discrediting terms to describe the rise of Mormonism. They referred to members of the restored Church as "fanatics," "a gang of deluded mortals," "deluded beings," the "dregs of this community," "profound believers in witchcraft, ghosts, goblins," and "inferior satellites."[6] Seldom was Joseph Smith called by his full name or even referred to as Joseph; instead, he was disparagingly called "Jo," "Joe," or "Joey."[7] The papers of Ohio branded the Book of Mormon as the "golden bible"; Joseph Smith's family as a "gang of money diggers";[8] witnesses to the Book of Mormon as "pious reprobates";[9] and the revelations recorded by Joseph Smith as "volumes of . . . trash."[10]

While engaged in this relentless attack on the Latter-day Saints, critics not only concocted the term "Mormonites," but they also formulated a derogatory definition of the word "Mormon." Quoting from a letter of "Obadiah Dogberry" (an alias of Abner Cole) in the *Palmyra Reflector*, the *Painesville Telegraph* repeated Dogberry's alleged discovery that the word "Mormon" came from the Greek word "mormoo." According to *Bailey's Dictionary*, "mormoo" meant "bugbear, hobgoblin, raw head, and bloody bones." Commenting on this definition, Howe announced that the Book of Mormon was "a fiction of hobgoblins and bugbears."[11] To correct this absurd definition of "Mormon," Joseph Smith announced that the word had not been derived from the Greek word "mormoo," but was a word that meant, literally, "more good."[12]

Speculations on the Origin of Mormonism

Numerous accounts of the rise of Mormonism appeared in the 1830s in Ohio newspapers. After publication of the Book of Mormon, several editors published descriptions of it, often accompanied by various conflicting accounts of the rise of the Church.

The author of an article entitled "The Golden Bible" in the November 25, 1830, issue of the *Cleveland Herald* (subsequently reprinted in the *Ashtabula Journal* and in the *Western Reserve Chronicle*) admitted that he had not read the book but had "perused it sufficiently to be convinced" that it was "one of the veriest impositions" of that age. The purpose of the publication, this writer concluded, was financial gain. Joseph Smith had sent forth his "twelve Apostles" to sell the book. All this was "new proof that all fools are not dead, and knavery in any garb may yet find votaries [adherents]."[13]

In another article circulated in the Western Reserve in the spring of 1831, Alexander Campbell stated that the Book of Mormon was a composite of "every error and almost every truth discussed in New York for the last ten years. He [Joseph Smith] decides all the great controversies: infant baptism, ordination, the trinity, regeneration, repentance, justification, the fall of man, the atonement, transubstantiation, fasting, penance, church government, religious experience, the call of the ministry, the general resurrection, eternal punishment, who may baptize, and even the question of free masonry, republican government, and the rights of men. All these topics are repeatedly alluded to."[14]

Many non-Mormon historians even in the twentieth century continue to publish this excerpt from Campbell's analysis. They have evidently failed to make a serious study of the Book of Mormon or even of religious history in general. They seem not to recognize that during the apostolic era, the Middle Ages, the era of the Reformation, and the seventeenth and eighteenth centuries, men debated most of the subjects enumerated by Campbell. Consequently, it is not surprising that these topics were also discussed in New York and other parts of America at the time of the publication of the Book of Mormon. In other words, even if Joseph Smith had written the kind of book that Campbell described, it would have been no indication that the book was a product of the controversial subjects "discussed in New York for the past ten years" (1820-1830). Moreover, those who have studied the book recognize that it does not contain precise answers to many of the topics mentioned by Campbell, such as the pattern of church government, free masonry, republican government, and how one receives authority (including the call to the ministry).

One of the first descriptions of the origins of the Church appeared in the *Painesville Telegraph* on September 22, 1829. This article, which had been originally printed in the *Palmyra Freeman*, alleged that Joseph Smith was visited by "the spirit of the Almighty," who informed him that an ancient record lay buried in a hill located in the town where he lived. The record had been secured and translated and was being published in Palmyra.[15] The *Ohio Star* in Ravenna, Ohio, reported on December 9, 1830, that Joseph Smith claimed to have been visited three times in a dream by the "spirit of the Almighty," which eventually led to the coming forth of the "Golden Bible."[16]

Another account of the origin of Mormonism that was originally published in the *Palmyra Reflector* and was republished in Ohio in the spring of 1831 connected the birth of the restored Church with a man named Walters. According to this story, Walters was a convicted criminal and "vagabond fortuneteller" who became a close associate of Joseph Smith. Walters, the report continued, was the instrument who persuaded the Smith family to pretend visitations and to bring forth a new book. The tale reached a crescendo with a description of the religious exercises initiated by Walters and observed by his followers, which included the Smith family. After gathering his disciples, the story read, Walters and his "money-digging impostors" carried out a ritual sacrifice of a rooster to a "foul spirit" who was supposedly the "guardian of hidden wealth."[17]

Not only did Ohio journalists of the early 1830s publish diverse and false accounts of the origin of Mormonism; they also ascribed to Mormonism various instances of unusual behavior that transpired in different parts of the world. The *Painesville Telegraph*, for example, published in 1831 a report that had appeared in the *New York Journal of Commerce*. It had no connection with the restored Church, yet was entitled "Mormonism in China." This account, which elicited complaints from Joseph Smith,[18] asserted that "a sort of revelation from the gods" had been published in China, disclosing that during the year a great pestilence would erupt. The virtuous, this bulletin added, would be spared, but the wicked would not escape; and the ground would be covered with the bodies of those stricken by the epidemic.[19]

Mormon Doctrines Denounced

Writers of the 1830s were quick to criticize the doctrines of the Latter-day Saints, especially those that differed most markedly from popular beliefs espoused by the major Protestant faiths. Most Protestants of that period believed that the Bible was the sole guide of faith; that visions, revelations, and gifts of the spirit, such as prophecy, speaking in tongues, and interpretation of tongues, had ceased with the death of the apostles; that all believers were priesthood bearers; and that anyone who received an internal call and was called by a congregation had the authority to preach and to administer the sacraments. Many further believed that since men were saved by the grace of God and the church was a congregation of believers, it was improper to say that any one particular faith was the only way leading to eternal life with God. According to the needs of the major Protestant denominations, all believers who were either elected by God or who did not fall would enter heaven, while the unregenerates, or those who fell, would suffer everlasting damnation.

It is not surprising, therefore, that the doctrines most frequently denounced by the critics related to the Church's beliefs concerning the Book of Mormon, the visions and revelations of Joseph Smith, the restoration of the priesthood, gifts of the spirit, and the reestablishment of the one and only true church of Christ on the earth. These teachings were perceived as a threat to all other religious institutions. Even though Protestants quarreled among themselves concerning some interpretations of the Bible, many united in opposition to this new faith, which, in their minds, was an unacceptable form of religious exclusiveness.

An example of the critics' response to Mormon belief was the sharp and constant criticism of the doctrine of continual revelation. When John Whitmer arrived in Kirtland in January 1831, the *Painesville Telegraph* announced that he was carrying a "new batch of revelations from God" that he pretended had "just been communicated to Joseph Smith."[20] In subsequent issues, E. D. Howe maintained that the Saints were not permitted to question "the infallibility" of Joseph Smith or of anything he might declare to be a commandment of God. All members who dared question or express doubts concerning these messages, Howe claimed, were "immediately expelled as heretics." Moreover, he insisted, many of the revelations were kept secret, not being shown to the "weaker" members.[21] After Joseph Smith moved to Hiram in September 1831, the *Telegraph* continued its barrage. It announced that he had moved to Portage County so he could manufacture additional "revelations" and could remodel the New Testament by pretending to translate it through inspiration from heaven.[22] Such comments inflamed the minds of many readers—preventing them, as Joseph Smith wrote, from gaining a correct understanding of the restoration.[23]

Journalists not only criticized the doctrinal contents of the revelations, but also ridiculed individuals whose names appeared in them, especially condemning those who complied with the commandments. Such ridicule of Church leaders was initiated during the winter of 1831-32 by the *Ohio Star* and the *Painesville Telegraph*. In March 1832, shortly after the denunciations were printed, Joseph Smith began to identify certain persons in the revelations by code names, such as "Enoch" for Joseph Smith, "Ahashdah" for Newel K. Whitney, and "Pelegoram" for Sidney Rigdon. The code names were probably used so members of the Church might avoid public ridicule.[24]

Another example of critics' responses to Latter-day Saint beliefs was their treatment of the concept of gifts of the spirit. Members of the restored Church frequently recorded in their diaries and journals experiences with such spiritual blessings as speaking in tongues, the gift of prophecy, and miraculous healings through the power of God. Editors seldom reported the miracles experienced by the Latter-day Saints, but they were quite ready to cite instances in which persons were not immediately healed following an administration by one of the elders of the Church.

Some of the misunderstandings were due to poor communication by the Saints or extravagant claims by individual Mormons. Since the Church did not operate a press in Kirtland prior to 1834, most nonmembers derived their views of the Church from members, from rumor, or from reports in local newspapers. Failings of individual Saints were sometimes cited as evidence that Mormonism was a "deluded" sect. Realizing that some members were, in fact, teaching incorrect principles and were engaged in misguided enthusiasm detrimental to the growth of the Church, Joseph Smith warned the Saints to discontinue such action. "We have reason to fear," he wrote, that many "having a zeal not according to knowledge," and "not understanding the pure principle of the doctrines of the Church, have no doubt, in the heat of enthusiasm, taught and said many things which are derogatory to the genuine character and principles of the church, and for these things we are heartily sorry, and would apologize if an apology would do any good."[25]

Yet another area of misunderstanding developed in relation to Latter-day Saint teachings concerning the Second Coming of Christ and the Millennium. Before the restored Church was introduced in the Western Reserve, Joseph Smith had taught the reality of the Second Coming of the Savior and His millennial reign. These concepts were not peculiar to the Latter-day Saints. The approach of the millennial era was a frequent topic in Alexander Campbell's *Millennial Harbinger*. Many pamphleteers in New England also discussed this subject throughout the 1830s. These facts did not, however, temper the critics' denunciations of members of the restored Church who predicted that Christ would return within a few decades or during their mortal life on earth. Shortly after the first missionaries arrived in Ohio, the *Painesville Telegraph* stated that Oliver Cowdery had predicted that the world would be destroyed "within a few years," while the *Ohio Star* reported that some Mormon elders were teaching that the world would end in fifteen years.[26]

Although newspaper reporters asserted that Latter-day Saints were predicting the destruction of the world within four to fifteen years, Joseph Smith never predicted a date for the advent of the Millennium. Nevertheless, some overly enthusiastic members evidently did express opinions contrary to the official doctrines of the Church. John Whitmer, for example, taught that "there was a tradition among some of the disciples, that those who obeyed the covenant in the last days, would never die."[27]

Spurious revelations and visions claimed by early converts of the Church provided critics with further fuel for inflammatory articles designed to cast doubt on the unusual beliefs of the Latter-day Saints. According to Joseph Smith, shortly after the first missionaries left Ohio for Missouri, "many false spirits were introduced" and "many strange visions were seen" by some of the early converts.[28] Levi Hancock recalled that one of the early converts, Heman Basset, claimed to have received a revelation in Kirtland from an angel. After reading this revelation to others, Basset would show them a picture of what he claimed to be a group of angels.[29]

George A. Smith, an early Latter-day Saint historian, reported that some of the Saints living on the Morley farm did not understand correctly the doctrine of revelation. "A false spirit," he asserted, engulfed the Saints and led to "extravagant and wild ideas." One person known as Black Pete claimed to have received messages from heaven in the form of letters floating across the sky. While seeking to obtain a closer look at one of the traveling messages, he "ran off a steep wash bank twenty-five feet high, passed through a tree top" growing parallel with the water below, and fell into the Chagrin River. George A. Smith said in conclusion that Black Pete emerged from the stream with only a few scratches, but "his ardor" was "somewhat cooled."[30]

Other persons claimed revelations that were not considered in harmony with the doctrines of the Church. John Whitmer recorded in his history that one of the early converts, "a woman by the name of Hubble," professed to be a "prophetess of the Lord" and to have received many revelations. She further insisted that she be called to serve as a "teacher in the Church of Christ."[31]

After he arrived in Kirtland and learned of these unusual claims, Joseph Smith took steps to extinguish such dangerous errors of the Saints and to teach them the correct principle of revelation. In February 1831, he received a revelation that warned the elders against the counterfeit claims and false teachings of others. This revelation emphasized that the Lord had appointed only one person, Joseph Smith, to receive revelations and commandments for the Church. Other members might receive revelation for their own needs, stewardships, and specific callings, but they did not have authority to receive revelation for the Church.[32]

Many misconceptions entertained by some of the early Latter-day Saints provided enemies with information used to malign the Church. One was the belief that physical demonstrations were proper reflections of the gifts of the spirit. In many sections of the country, settlers exhibited their religious feelings through various physical gyrations, especially at camp meetings and other revivals conducted by ministers of the Second Great Awakening. Some of the early converts to the restored Church expressed their convictions by engaging in spiritual exercises and were reported to have been seen falling to the ground and sliding around "like serpents." Others, it was reported, would jump, leap, and wave their arms as though they were engaged in a scalping exercise, run into the fields, climb on tree stumps, and commence preaching as though they were surrounded by a large congregation, seemingly oblivious to reality.[33]

Spiritual abnormalities were evident not only when Joseph Smith arrived in Kirtland, but continued in sections of Ohio into the spring of 1831. When Parley P. Pratt returned from his mission in Missouri, he observed the strange operations manifest in a number of the branches of the Church in Ohio. "Some persons," he lamented, "would seem to swoon away, and make unseemly gestures, and be drawn or disfigured in their countenances. Others would fall into ecstacies, and be drawn into contortions, which were not edifying, and which were not congenial to the doctrine and spirit of the gospel."[34]

Concerned by such spiritual excesses, Parley P. Pratt, John Murdock, and other elders in May 1831 asked Joseph Smith to seek an answer from God concerning the propriety of such behavior.[35] The Prophet responded by dictating a revelation in their presence. "There are many spirits which are false spirits," this revelation read. And "Satan hath sought to deceive you, that he might overthrow you." The means by which false spirits could be detected was then disclosed:

> That which doth not edify is not of God, and is darkness. That which is of God is light; and he that receiveth light, and continueth in God, receiveth more light; and that light groweth brighter and brighter until the perfect day. . . . If you behold a spirit manifested that you cannot understand, and you receive not that spirit, ye shall ask of the Father in the name of Jesus; and if he give not unto you that spirit, then you may know that it is not of God.[36]

Although the Prophet declared that the strange extravagances brought disgrace to the Church and caused the Spirit of the Lord to withdraw from individuals, some persons insisted that the ecstasies in which they were engaged were edifying. During the summer of 1831, missionaries Jared Carter and Sylvester Smith encountered members in Amherst, Ohio, who were participating in exercises that they called "visions." At a meeting in Amherst, Elder Carter observed a woman fall to the ground. Believing that such behavior was contrary to the counsel given in the May 1831 revelation, he suggested to Sylvester Smith that they inquire of the Lord concerning the propriety of her actions. After praying, both elders concluded that the members should desist from their spiritual excesses, but some in this congregation were still unconvinced that these instructions were correct.[37]

The process of correcting the improper behavior of the early converts was difficult. On February 17, 1834, the Kirtland high council was permanently organized, and two days later, this body tried and rebuked Elder Curtis Hodge, Sr., for engaging in a "spasm" that included shouting and screaming. Commenting on the problem, the Prophet wrote that members who refused to comply with the instructions of the authorities regarding visions and "wild, enthusiastic notions" and actions would be "tried for their fellowship," and those who did not repent and forsake their errors would be "cut off" from the Church.[38]

Despite the unseemly behavior of some members and the deliberate distortions of hostile "outsiders," however, the Church continued to grow and prosper. "The glory of God is intelligence, light, and truth," said Joseph Smith, and this influence tended to prevail.[39]

Chapter 5

The Law of Consecration

W hile the Ohio press was engaged in an aggressive campaign aimed at thwarting the growth of the restored Church, some Ohio editors and other critics were also denouncing the economic policies unfolded by Joseph Smith. Some of the opposition emerged because of misunderstanding of the economic reform program that the Prophet revealed; critics associated it with communistic systems established by various other religious communities in early America.

Prior to his arrival in Kirtland, the Prophet had informed members of the Church that a new economic system would be instituted. The revelation given in New York on January 2, 1831, instructing the Saints to gather in Ohio, also indicated that after the members settled in that state, they would receive the law of the Lord and would be endowed with power from on high. The law they would receive would include provisions related to the temporal affairs of the Church. "Let every man esteem his brother as himself," the revelation specified. A parable was related that indicated that members of Christ's Church should "be one," which apparently referred, in part, to the responsibility of members to care for the temporal needs of one another. The revelation further directed that men would be "appointed by the voice of the church" to care for the poor and needy and to "govern the affairs of the property" of the Church.[1]

After arriving in Kirtland, Joseph Smith learned that an economic program established by the "Family," the followers of Sidney Rigdon who had created a communal order on Isaac Morley's farm in the northeastern section of Kirtland township, involved both petty controversies and major conflicts. According to John Whitmer, some members of this society had decided that what belonged to one brother belonged to all; therefore they would take each other's clothes and other property and use them without permission. Such action, he observed, was leading to their temporal destruction.[2] Recognizing that problems were afflicting these members, Joseph Smith instructed them to abandon their "common stock" program for a more nearly perfect law of the Lord.[3]

Not only was there a need to provide members of the communal order in Kirtland with a better economic system, but finances were also required to support various Church programs. For example, money, goods, and property were needed immediately to help the poor and to assist immigrants who had sacrificed much to gather in Ohio. Some of the Church leaders also needed financial help. Joseph Smith lacked a home for his family; and Sidney Rigdon, after uniting with the Latter-day Saints, lost his pastoral home and the economic support he had previously received from his congregation. After Edward Partridge was called in February 1831 to devote all of his time to the Church, he was not in a position to support his family through his mercantile enterprises. Moreover, as the years passed, funds were necessary to support Church publications, educational programs, and the construction of buildings, especially the Kirtland Temple.[4]

Living in an age of social ferment, the Prophet was undoubtedly aware of some of the idealistic financial systems then being used. Prior to 1830, Shakers, Harmonites, Owenite Socialists, and Separatists of Zoar, Ohio, had initiated unusual economic systems. Some of the most successful orders had been instituted by members of the United Society of Believers in Christ's Second Appearing, commonly known as Believers or Shakers. By 1830 this faith had established twenty communistic-type communities between Maine and Kentucky; three were located in Ohio, including one a few miles west of Kirtland. Individuals who joined this order gave to the society their personal belongings and lived under a system of common ownership and use of property. Men and women slept in different dormitories, ate in a common dining room, worked on assigned tasks, and embraced the principle of celibacy.[5]

The Saints did not have to wait long for details concerning the new economic order they were to follow. On February 4, 1831, a few days after his arrival in Kirtland, the Prophet received a revelation calling Edward Partridge as the first bishop of the Church and instructing him to devote all of his time to this service.[6] Five days later, in the presence of twelve elders, Joseph Smith received another revelation that not only provided Bishop Partridge with a brief guide concerning some of his responsibilities, but also outlined the basic structure of the new system.

The economic order revealed on February 9 has been called the law of consecration and stewardship, the First United Order, the Order of Enoch, and the Order of Stewardships. An underlying basis of this new system was the concept that the earth, as well as everything on it, belongs to the Lord, and individuals, as stewards of the Lord, have a responsibility to care for the poor. Members of the Church were therefore told by revelation to consecrate their property to the Lord through the bishop and his counselors appointed for that purpose, "with a covenant and deed which cannot be broken." After receiving the property, the bishop was instructed to appoint every man "a steward over his own property," or that which he (the member) had received from the bishop, "sufficient for himself and family." The surplus was to be kept in the Lord's storehouse "to administer to the poor and needy," as determined by the bishop and the elders of the Church, for the purchase of land and for the building up of a New Jerusalem.[7]

The revelation provided a general outline of the law of consecration and stewardship; but many people, members and nonmembers alike, did not at that time understand the precise meaning of such terms as "consecration," "steward," "stewardship," and "storehouse." Consequently, as the Latter-day Saints began to live this law, additional information was revealed through the

Prophet; and as the months and years passed, Joseph Smith and other Church leaders continued to instruct the Saints in the law of consecration and stewardship.

The Saints gained a better understanding of the meaning of stewardships when, in May 1831, Joseph Smith received a revelation regarding the temporal affairs of the Saints who had recently arrived in the Western Reserve from the area of Colesville, New York. He informed these immigrants that they should settle in Thompson, Ohio, a few miles east of Kirtland, on property owned by a new convert to the Church, a former Shaker named Leman Copley. According to the revelation, the Saints in Thompson were to consecrate their property to the Lord through Edward Partridge, after which he was to "appoint" or distribute a portion to every family according to their "circumstances and . . . wants and needs."[8]

Although Bishop Partridge attempted to inaugurate the law of consecration in Thompson, conflicts developed that prevented its full implementation. While the precise reasons for the conflict are not known, selfishness and greed no doubt played a part. After Leman Copley broke a contract agreeing to let Latter-day Saints occupy his farmland and ordered them off his property, Newel Knight hastened to Kirtland to inform Joseph Smith of the difficulties.[9] Subsequently, the Prophet received a revelation in June 1831 instructing Newel Knight and others living on the Copley farm to "repent of all their sins" and "to journey into the regions westward, unto the land of Missouri, unto the borders of the Lamanites."[10] Shortly thereafter, at least fourteen families (twenty-three adults and thirty-eight children) who had emigrated from eastern New York to Ohio commenced their journey to the Missouri frontier.[11]

Another attempt to set in motion the law of consecration and stewardship was undertaken by Church leaders after members began gathering in western Missouri in the summer of 1831. Some of these immigrants had been called by revelation to colonize that region, while others immigrated there with a direct calling, that they might participate in the building of a Zion, a city of refuge and peace, in "western America." On June 4, 1831, the day following a special conference held in Kirtland, Joseph Smith received a commandment instructing twenty-eight elders to journey to Missouri.[12] Shortly after this revelation was received, Algernon Sidney Gilbert, William W. Phelps, and Joseph Coe were also called to journey west.[13]

The elders who had been called to Missouri began leaving Kirtland in pairs or small groups in the middle of June. Joseph Smith, accompanied by seven others, started west on the nineteenth and went as far as Cincinnati by wagon, canal boat, and stagecoach. From Cincinnati, they proceeded by riverboat to St. Louis; and from there, five of them—Joseph Smith, Martin Harris, William W. Phelps, Edward Partridge, and Joseph Coe—walked 240 miles across the state to Jackson County.[14] There they met Oliver Cowdery, Ziba Peterson, and Peter Whitmer, three of the missionaries who had introduced the gospel to Sidney Rigdon's followers in the Western Reserve, along with Frederick G. Williams, who had joined the missionaries in Kirtland. Parley P. Pratt had earlier left the group in Missouri to travel east to appraise conditions of the Church in Ohio and inform the Prophet of the accomplishments of the missionaries. The four missionaries were now joined by the elders from Ohio, the Saints from the Colesville branch, and a few other persons who had immigrated west.[15]

While Joseph Smith was in Jackson County during the latter part of July and in early August, he received four revelations containing information on various subjects, including the law of consecration. The revelations indicated that Missouri was "the land of promise, and the place for the city of Zion," that the inhabitants of Zion were to cleanse themselves from all unrighteousness (for Zion meant pure in heart), that they were to love and serve God and love their neighbors as themselves, and that they were to live in accordance with other laws of God. It was also revealed that the village of Independence was the "center place" of Zion and that a temple was to be built there on land west of the courthouse. William W. Phelps was called to serve as a printer for the Church, and Oliver Cowdery was to assist him in this duty.[16]

Most of the new information relating to the law of consecra-

Martin Harris

tion pertained more to assignments than to further disclosures concerning the nature of the law. Bishop Edward Partridge was given the responsibility of dividing the land among the Saints so that all who gathered could receive an inheritance. Sidney Gilbert was called to serve as a land agent for the Saints; he was to establish a merchandising store in that community and use the profits from this business to purchase land upon which the Saints could settle. Martin Harris was commanded by revelation to set a good example for other members by "laying his moneys before the bishop." He was then to receive an inheritance according to his own desires.[17]

In addition to laying a foundation for a new economic order, Joseph Smith and other Church leaders were involved in many other activities in Missouri. On August 2, 1831, the Prophet assisted the Colesville Saints in laying the first log for a house of worship in Kaw Township, twelve miles west of Independence. The log was carried by twelve men, in honor of the twelve tribes of Israel. That same day, Sidney Rigdon was in Independence consecrating and dedicating that area for the gathering of the Saints. On August 3, in the company of eight other men, Joseph Smith stood on a ten-acre plot where a temple was to be erected and dedicated the land for the building of a house of the Lord.[18]

Six days after the temple site was dedicated, the Prophet and ten others, including Oliver Cowdery and Sidney Rigdon, launched their canoes on the Missouri River and commenced the journey back to Ohio. On the third day of this trip they encountered treacherous waters. While the group was camping on the riverbank, Joseph Smith reported that William W. Phelps saw in vision "the destroyer in his most horrible power, ride upon the face of the waters." The next morning, August 12, the Prophet announced that he had received a revelation that referred to this vision and that instructed Sidney Gilbert and W. W. Phelps to continue the journey in haste by land or water, and instructed others to avoid the water route "save it be upon the canal, while journeying to their homes."[19] In accordance with this revelation, Joseph and some of the other elders continued their journey to St. Louis by land, then traveled east by stage, arriving in Kirtland on August 29, eighteen days after leaving Independence.[20]

After returning to Kirtland, Joseph Smith received several additional revelations instructing members, some named specifically, concerning their responsibilities under the law of consecration. Titus Billings and Isaac Morley were told to sell their farms in Ohio and migrate to Missouri.[21] Others, including Newel K. Whitney and Frederick G. Williams, were commanded not to sell their property but to remain in Kirtland.[22] Members of the Church in Ohio were admonished to contribute toward the purchase of land in Missouri, in order to assist in the building of Zion in Jackson County. Meanwhile, Oliver Cowdery and Newel K. Whitney were called on a mission among members of the Church to raise funds for building the New Jerusalem in western America.[23]

A major problem preventing success under the law of consecration in Kirtland in 1831 was the fact that few members of the Church there owned land or other forms of property that could be used for redistribution. Since most converts were unable to contribute significant amounts of property to the order, land was not available to be distributed in the form of inheritances. The only large acreage owned by members was the Isaac Morley farm on which the "Family" had been living. Although he sold to a nonmember approximately fifty acres of land in 1831, he retained about eighty acres; and after he had immigrated to Missouri, many members of the Church settled on this farm. In fact, this land was the principal gathering place for the Saints in Kirtland prior to 1832. Newel K. Whitney owned a store on the flats that provided his family with a source of income. A few other members (while paying taxes on horses and cattle) lived in homes on land on which they had not commenced paying taxes, indicating that, in some instances, they did not possess title to the land.[24]

Even though Latter-day Saints lacked sufficient land in Kirtland for the granting of inheritances to all, Joseph Smith continued to receive revelations during the fall of 1831 concerning the temporal responsibilities of Latter-day Saints. At a conference held in Hiram, Ohio, members agreed that some of the revelations received by the Prophet should be printed and circulated; six men—Joseph Smith, Martin Harris, Oliver Cowdery, John Whitmer, Sidney Rigdon, and William W. Phelps—were entrusted with this assignment. They organized a "literary firm" in November 1831 as a joint stewardship to publish and sell books, periodicals, and newspapers for the Church. Although none of the men owned property in Kirtland, they were commanded to be equal in "temporal things." They were to be provided with the necessities of life, but any surplus they earned was to be given into the Lord's storehouse.[25] In December, Newel K. Whitney was called to serve as bishop in Kirtland and the eastern branches of the Church. While presiding over the temporal affairs of Latter-day Saints living in Kirtland, he maintained the Lord's storehouse, kept an account of property consecrated for use by the membership of the Church, and in other respects assisted the poor in securing the necessities of life.[26]

Another attempt to implement the law of consecration and stewardship occurred in April 1832. In compliance with a revelation Joseph Smith had received in Missouri during his second trip to that state, a central council, referred to as the order, the United Order, and the United Firm, was created to manage the temporal affairs of the Church. This included the general supervision of the poor, a responsibility that was continued on a local level by the bishops of Zion (Missouri) and Kirtland. In the spring of 1832, nine leaders assembled to direct the activities of the United Firm. Five were then living in Missouri (Oliver Cowdery, Edward Partridge, Sidney Gilbert, John Whitmer, and William W. Phelps) and four were residents of Ohio (Joseph Smith, Newel K. Whitney, Sidney Rigdon, and Jesse Gause). After one of the leaders, Jesse Gause, apostatized, Frederick G. Williams became a member of the firm, as did John Johnson. After Oliver Cowdery and Martin Harris returned to Ohio, they united with the other leaders in Kirtland in directing the economic affairs of the Church in that part of the country.[27] These men functioned as a controlling body (like a board of directors that manages a corporation) and used the financial means at their disposal to finance various Church programs. While sharing the responsibilities of holding properties in trust, directors of the United Firm cared for the poor, supervised the bishop's storehouses, purchased land for those who gathered in Kirtland and Missouri, and assisted in the construction of the Kirtland Temple.[28]

Between 1832 and 1834 there was a significant increase in the amount of property owned and managed by Church leaders in Kirtland. In April 1832, shortly before the United Firm was organized, Frederick G. Williams purchased approximately 144 acres in Kirtland for two thousand dollars. This land, known as the Frederick G. Williams farm, was located on a plateau south of

NORTHERN PORTION OF KIRTLAND TOWNSHIP

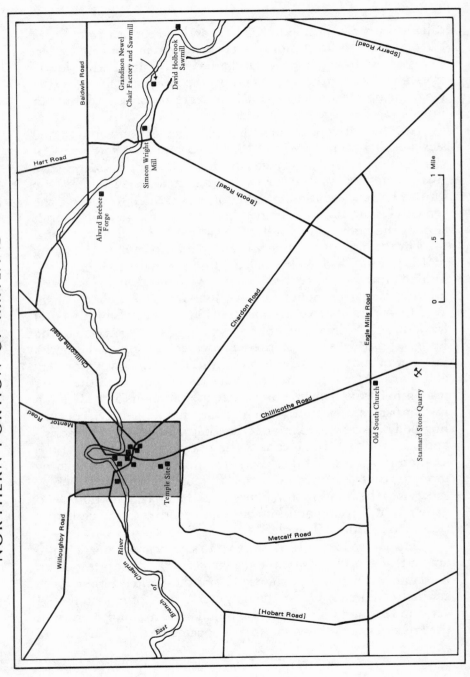

Baldwin Road

Grandison Newel
Chair Factory and Sawmill

David Holbrook
Sawmill

[Sperry Road]

Hart Road

Simeon Wright
Mill

[Booth Road]

Alvard Beebe
Forge

Chillicothe Road

Chardon Road

Mentor Road

Chillicothe Road

Eagle Mills Road

Old South Church

Stannard Stone Quarry

Temple Site

Willoughby Road

River

East Branch of Chagrin

Metcalf Road

[Hobart Road]

0   .5   1 Mile

Research by Keith Perkins

Kirtland Flats. On May 3, 1834, this property was conveyed (without monetary remuneration) to Joseph Smith, who acted as agent for the Church.[29] In April 1833, Joseph Coe and Ezra Thayer, who had been called to serve as land agents, purchased for the Church 103 acres from Peter French. The French property, which cost the Saints five thousand dollars, stretched from the Williams farm to the brow of the hill (which included the property on which the temple was built) and then down the steep slope to the east branch of the Chagrin River.[30]

Leaders of the Church not only managed the Williams, French, and Isaac Morley farmlands, but also under the steward-ship system they operated the Newel K. Whitney store, a tannery, a printing shop, and an ashery. They later also operated a steam sawmill. While some converts who gathered to Kirtland had sufficient funds to purchase land from nonmembers, others settled on Church property. Those who occupied the Church land con-tributed what they could toward Church programs, in a sense renting the land or making payments in anticipation of future ownership. Meanwhile, property taxes were paid by various Church leaders.[31]

Another significant change in the application of the law of consecration and stewardship occurred in 1834. On April 23 of that year, Joseph Smith received a revelation that separated the United Order in Kirtland from the order in Zion and, because of internal conflicts, persecution, and expulsion of the Saints from Jackson County, dissolved the organizational structure in Mis-souri.[32] This revelation also instructed the members of the United Order in Kirtland to divide among themselves some of the Church property. Instead of managing most of the Church prop-erties as a group, those in Kirtland were given specific responsibili-ties, and select property was to be their stewardship. Sidney Rig-don received the home and lot on which he was living, including a tannery. He was to direct the tannery and draw his financial sup-port from it.[33] Oliver Cowdery and Frederick G. Williams were called to direct the operation of a printing office. Elder Williams was also given stewardship over the home in which he resided, and Elder Cowdery was given the lot adjacent to the printing office.[34] John Johnson was given the home where he was living, Joseph Smith was given land near the lot where the Kirtland Temple was being built, and Martin Harris was also made steward over a plot of land.[35] Meanwhile, Newel K. Whitney not only continued to operate the general store, but he was also given the lot on which the ashery was located.[36] Although the revelation assigned many specific stewardships to certain members mentioned by name, it also made clear that every member of the Church was a steward "over earthly blessings" and was responsible to the Lord for his stewardship. The Prophet taught that it was within the stewardship of all members to "be anxiously engaged in a good cause, and do many things of their own free will, and bring to pass much righteousness," for "the power [of the Spirit of God] is in them."[37]

In 1833, while a few leaders in Kirtland were pooling their economic resources in an attempt to secure funds to support Church programs, Bishop Edward Partridge was directing in Missouri a different type of economic order. There, members voluntarily conveyed their property to the bishop and, in return, received inheritances. Instead of conveying deeds to members, Bishop Partridge, in the fall of 1832, leased land to the Saints. Under the provision of the contracts, stewards were not permitted to transfer their inheritances to their wives, children, or heirs, or to sell their property. The contracts further stipulated that if an individual left the Church, he had no legal claim to his inheritance.[38]

On several occasions, Joseph Smith wrote to Church leaders in Missouri informing them that their application of the law of consecration and stewardship was not correct. In a letter to William W. Phelps, dated November 27, 1832, the Prophet indicated that he was displeased because the Saints who had gathered in Zion had not received "their inheritance by consecrations, by order of deed from the Bishop."[39]

About five months later, the Prophet informed Bishop Partridge, in a letter dated May 2, 1833, that although stewards had no claim over their initial consecration, their inheritances belonged to them; it was their property. "Concerning inheritances," he explained, "you are bound by the law of the Lord to give a deed, securing to him who receives inheritances, his inheritance for an everlasting inheritance, or in other words, to be his individual property, his private stewardship."[40] He further taught that if an individual transgressed and left the Church, the inheritance still belonged to him. This concept became a binding principle when it was included in a revelation that was initially published in the first edition of the Doctrine and Covenants (1835). The Prophet recorded in that work a statement that removed any confusion concerning the ownership of inheritances: "And if he shall transgress and is not accounted worthy to belong to the church, he shall not have power to claim that portion which he has consecrated unto the bishop for the poor and needy of my church; therefore, he shall not retain the gift, but shall only have claim on that portion that is deeded unto him."[41]

As one studies the various revelations and instructions given through Joseph Smith on the subject of consecration and stewardship, it becomes possible to summarize and better understand this economic program. In harmony with an economic phase of the law, members were asked to deed all their property to the bishop of the Church. They then received title to a stewardship—a means of production or support for the family. This inheritance was based on the wants (inasmuch as the wants were just), needs, circumstances (including the size of the family), and abilities of the stewards. At appointed times, surplus production and increase beyond the needs of the family were to be given into the bishop's storehouse for Church projects, including the care of the poor. Should anyone leave the order, he was to receive his inheritance but not the surplus he had given to the Church. Families were to live separately, and business relations were to be conducted under a system in which stewards owned or held title to their property.

Saints who entered this order were placed on essentially the same economic level. This basic equality was to be retained by their giving periodically their surplus to the Church. This surplus was actually to be derived from two main sources: consecrations that exceeded the amount given as inheritances and contribu-

MAJOR AREA OF LDS ACTIVITY IN KIRTLAND

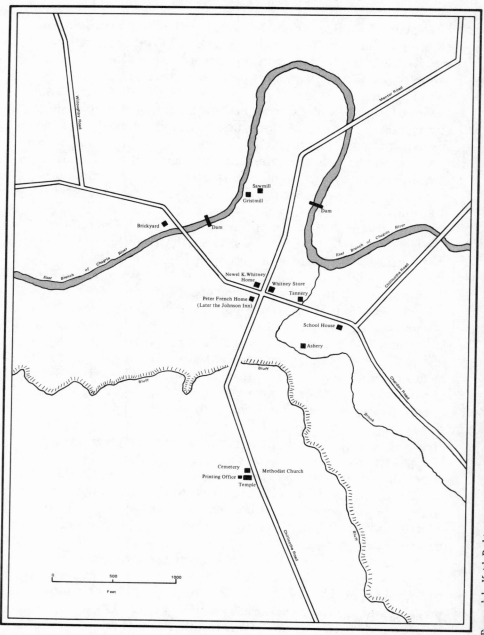

tions from the stewards. This surplus (or residue, as it is called in section 42 of the Doctrine and Covenants) was, of course, a vital part of the economic system. It was needed to support various Church programs, such as helping immigrants secure land and aiding stewards who experienced economic reversals resulting from misfortunes or disasters.

This system not only preserved the essential values of the capitalistic system, such as personal initiative, private ownership, and reward for effort, but it was also designed to eliminate some of the negative aspects of that economic system, including poverty amid plenty, inequalities of wealth, and wasteful competition. The law of consecration promoted economic equality without compromising free agency or excellence. The redistribution of wealth placed all families on essentially the same economic plane and eliminated the need for certain kinds of welfare programs by giving to everyone, including the poor, sufficient property to care for their needs. It was not aimed at establishing complete equality, for members received different kinds and types of inheritances, but it was designed to implement a principle given in a revelation recorded in Kirtland in March 1831: "It is not given that one man should possess that which is above another, wherefore the world lieth in sin."[42]

Though Joseph Smith taught the basic principles of the law of consecration and stewardship in the 1830s, only certain parts of the law were lived at that time. In some respects, the closest application of the law in Kirtland was made by the members of the United Order or United Firm. Many others, however, were living in harmony with a basic principle of the law of consecration— that of sacrificing one's time and material possessions for the building of the kingdom of God. In the mid-1830s, many Kirtland Saints sacrificed a substantial part of their material wealth to advance programs of the Church, including building the Kirtland Temple. A high percentage of the Saints were not asked to consecrate their property, and many converts who gathered in Kirtland did not purchase land in that township. Instead of owning their own farms, they lived on Church property near the temple site, where they built small frame homes and for several years de-

MAJOR CHURCH FARMS AND BUSINESSES
KIRTLAND TOWNSHIP EARLY 1830s

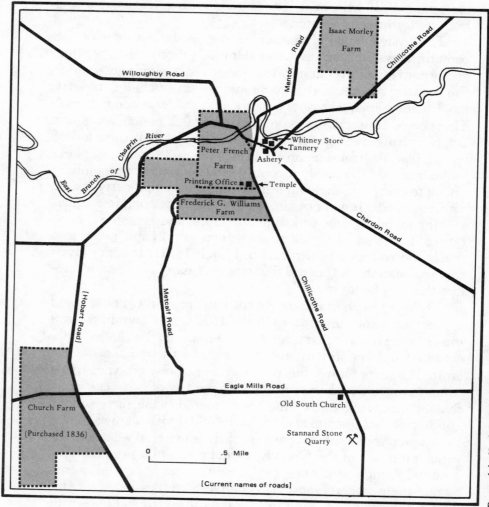

Research by Keith Perkins

voted most of their energies and economic resources to the build-ing of the temple. This application of the law of consecration in Kirtland is evident in the Geauga County tax records for the de-cade of the thirties. In March 1835, Joseph Smith identified 121 men who had assisted in building the temple, which was still under construction, and they were to receive at that time a special blessing. This list included most but not all of the men who had worked on the temple. Of these 121, some 52 percent owned land in Kirtland during the 1830s (based on tax records of land and re-corded deeds), and 13 who did not own land (11 percent) paid a personal property tax. During the years the temple was under con-struction (1833-36), only 30 percent of the temple builders pur-chased land in Kirtland. Though a few of the men lived across the township line and would have owned property in another commu-nity, many of them lived on Church property (with various Church leaders paying the assessed tax), and instead of buying land, they used their resources for the building of a house for the Lord.[43]

Although most members of the Church in Kirtland gave generously of their time, energies, and material means to build up the kingdom of God, a few converts were chastized for failing to contribute, commensurate with their means, to the poor and to the Church. In an important case tried before the Kirtland high council in June 1836, two members, an elder and a seventy, were accused of coveting their money and lacking the benevolence that should accompany one's conversion to the gospel of Christ. During one of these trials, Frederick G. Williams, a member of the First Presidency, acknowledged that the Church was poor, financially speaking, and admitted that the Church was plagued with debts that caused embarrassment to the leaders. Additional contributions, he said, were needed to alleviate this distress. Fol-lowing these remarks, another member of the First Presidency, Sidney Rigdon, discussed the relationship between property and the laws of God. "It is the duty of the Saints," he suggested, to sac-rifice their "all" for the building of the kingdom of God and to care for the poor. Christ, he reasoned, sacrificed everything so that we might be saved; thus we must follow the Savior's example and be made perfect through our suffering. One of the members was criticized for failing to help a neighbor who had fallen from a roof, injured himself, and was unable to work temporarily. The neighbor's family was experiencing economic hardships, and the accused had said that he was planning to help them, but this promise had not been realized. In one of these cases, the court ruled that the member should change his attitude toward giving, or the hand of fellowship would be withdrawn from him. In the other case, the member confessed that he did not realize his selfishness, promised to correct his failing, and asked forgiveness of God and the Church.[44]

While a few Church leaders pooled their economic resources and other members sacrificed their material wealth to advance the restoration movement in Kirtland, a more specific application of the law of consecration and stewardship was attempted in Missouri. However, problems developed there over its application, and before the full program was implemented, many Latter-day Saints were driven from their homes in Jackson County. Therefore, at no time during the 1830s did many members of the Church live the law as specifically outlined in the revelations announced in the 1830s. However, many nonmembers were convinced that the law of consecration and stewardship was controlling the economic activities of members of the Church. Such persons were not only in error regarding the Church's compliance with that law, but, largely due to newspaper misrepresentation, they misunderstood the law itself and condemned the Saints for advocating such a program.

When the initial revelation on the law of consecration and stewardship was recorded, the Church did not own a printing press. The revelation, however, was copied by some members, and one of these transcripts was obtained by a non-Mormon editor in Ravenna, Ohio. Subsequently, this revelation was published in Ravenna in the fall of 1831 and then reprinted in other papers of the Western Reserve. Critics of the Church contended that Latter-day Saint preachers had been commanded not to tell members of the economic program until they had become "strong in the faith." The revelation was published by non-Mormons under the heading "Secret Bye Laws of the Mormonites," with a caption explaining that Mormons were compelled to embrace the economic regulations. [45]

Though the critics were wrong when they stated that Latter-day Saints were compelled to live in harmony with the law of consecration and stewardship, they did not misrepresent the facts when they asserted that the Latter-day Saints were called upon to make economic sacrifices. Amid poverty, privations, and other forms of economic distress, the Kirtland Saints continued to sacrifice by gathering in Ohio and Missouri, by supporting the Church's missionary program, by building a temple for the Lord, and by helping the Saints in Missouri. [46] The restored gospel thus prepared men for a new pattern of living. While non-Mormon critics scoffed at the Saints for relinquishing some of their worldly wealth, they failed to comprehend that the converts of the Church were endowed with new incentives and were motivated by a law revealed through revelation that encouraged them to devote their time, talents, and material wealth to the building of Christ's kingdom on the earth.

Chapter 6

Revelations and Confrontations

For six and a half months—between mid-September 1831 and the end of March 1832—Hiram, Portage County, Ohio, approximately thirty miles south of Kirtland, served as a temporary headquarters of the Church. During this period, Joseph Smith and his family lived in the large frame home of John Johnson, an early convert who was one of the prosperous farmers of that community. Many Latter-day Saints traveled there to meet him, to seek his counsel, and to attend meetings held in the Johnson home. There the Prophet worked on a translation of the Bible and received some of his most profound visions and revelations. However, he also encountered serious opposition, as apostates joined forces with other settlers in an attempt to interrupt the growth of the Church in Portage County. The organized resistance led to the mobbing of Joseph Smith and Sidney Rigdon, and they fled from Hiram. Upon their return to Geauga County, many of the central developments in the history of the Church again focused on Kirtland. Although the Prophet's stay in Hiram was brief, this six-month period was one of the significant eras in the early history of the restored Church.

Joseph Smith had become acquainted with John and Elsa Johnson early in 1831 when they had gone to Kirtland to investigate reports circulating in their community concerning a restora-

tion of the everlasting gospel. [1] Others from that region, including
Ezra Booth, a Methodist minister from Mantua, accompanied the
Johnsons to Kirtland. Prior to this trip, Elsa Johnson had been afflicted with what was believed to be chronic rheumatism. For several years she had been unable to lift her hand to her head, a handi-
cap that interfered with many of her activities. As the party from
Portage County discussed the restoration with Joseph Smith in
the Newel K. Whitney home, including the manifestations of
supernatural gifts during the apostolic era, one of the inquirers
said, "Here is Mrs. Johnson with a lame arm. Has God given any
power to man now on the earth to cure her?" Before the question
was answered, the conversation shifted to another theme. Then
Joseph Smith rose, walked across the room, grasped the hand of
Elsa Johnson, and, in a "solemn and impressive manner," said,
"Woman, in the name of the Lord Jesus Christ I command thee to
be whole." Immediately thereafter, he went from the room, leaving the group stunned. Then, according to several contemporary
accounts, Elsa Johnson lifted her arm in the air. When she returned home the next day, she was able to wash her clothes without difficulty or pain. [2]

Joseph Smith's "Translation" of the Bible

On September 12, 1831, shortly after returning from his first
trip to Missouri, Joseph Smith moved with his family from Kirtland to Hiram, establishing his new residence in the John
Johnson home. There he concentrated on making corrections in
the King James Version of the Bible. Sidney Rigdon, who served
at this time as his principal scribe, also moved to Hiram and probably lived in a log cabin located near the Johnson home. [3]

Producing a new version of the Bible was not a unique idea
among religious leaders and scholars of early America. Between
1777 and 1833, more than five hundred separate editions of the
Bible or the New Testament were published in the United States.
Many of these were revisions of the King James Version, containing "'modernizations' of the language, paraphrases, and alternate
readings based on comparisons with Greek and Hebrew manuscripts." While many of the translators attempted to "clarify obso-

The John Johnson home in Hiram, Ohio

lete words and correct vague renderings," they generally did not delete portions or supply new doctrinal or historical material.[4]

Although Joseph Smith was not the only American of the early republic who worked on a translation of the Bible, he was the only editor or "translator" of that era to maintain that he had been called by God to engage in that work and to insist that he had received divine revelation during the process.[5] The content of his work was also unique. In addition to correcting biblical language, he clarified doctrines that were not clearly enunciated in the King James Version of the Bible, and he added historical material. He remarked, "It was apparent that many important points touching the salvation of men, had been taken from the Bible, or lost before it was compiled."[6] Therefore, he sought through divine revelation to recover lost historical and doctrinal truths.

Although Joseph Smith referred to this work as a translation, he did not claim knowledge of Greek or Hebrew in the early 1830s. He studied these languages later in the decade, but that study did not aid him in this particular project, for he did not have access to ancient Greek or Hebrew texts. When he used the term "translation" in connection with this activity he undoubtedly meant explanation, a rephrasing, or an expression in different words, all possible definitions of the term. However, since he himself used the word "translation," his work has been referred to as the "New Translation" and the "Inspired Translation" as well as the "Inspired Version" and the "Inspired Revision."[7]

The King James Version of the Bible used in this project was purchased by Joseph Smith and Oliver Cowdery on October 8, 1829 from E. B. Grandin, the Palmyra printer of the Book of Mormon. Day after day, the Prophet dictated changes to one of his assistants, and these scribes (including Oliver Cowdery, John Whitmer, Sidney Rigdon, and Frederick G. Williams) recorded the information. He did not write revisions in the margins or between the lines of the Bible he was using, but made marks in it to indicate where changes should be made. He also crossed out some words that were to be omitted. Meanwhile, his scribes kept a separate record on sheets of paper, recording the words of the new translation as they were dictated.[8]

During this project, Joseph Smith studied the same portions of the Bible on different occasions. Though he had earlier revised a given chapter or passage, he often made further revisions. For example, there are two successive manuscripts for parts of Genesis and two for parts of Matthew. It is apparent that the translation was a gradual process. As he studied the text, he received revelation and subsequently obtained additional knowledge of a particular subject.[9] Revelations that he received often came in response to questions he submitted to the Lord, and this project was a great stimulator of questions.[10] Many of the doctrines of the Church, including many of the revelations recorded in the Doctrine and Covenants, were disclosed while Joseph Smith was translating the Bible.[11]

The precise date on which the Prophet began his translation of the Bible is not known. His writings reveal that as early as the summer of 1830, he was involved in revising the Bible. Amid the trials and tribulations occurring in Colesville, New York, in June 1830, he recorded the visions of Moses, and he continued working on this project during the remainder of the year.[12] After immigrating to Kirtland in 1831, he resumed work on the translation. In early March he recorded a revelation that instructed him to begin a translation of the New Testament.[13] There are no records indicating that prior to this date he had worked on any section of the Bible other than Genesis. On March 8, 1831, Sidney Rigdon began copying revisions of Matthew as they were dictated by Joseph Smith.[14] There was another pause in this work while the Prophet traveled to Missouri during the summer of 1831. Then in September he moved to Hiram to again work on "the translation of the Bible."[15]

During the six months Joseph Smith resided in Hiram, he concentrated on reviewing the New Testament.[16] While engaged in this revision, he received three revelations containing some of the most important doctrines ever disclosed by the latter-day prophet. On February 16, 1832, in the home of John Johnson, Joseph Smith and Sidney Rigdon reflected on the meaning of the twenty-ninth verse of the fifth chapter of John, which states that those who have done good shall come forth in the resurrection of the just, while those who have done evil shall come forth in the resurrection of the unjust. The Prophet wrote in his history that it seemed evident that "if God rewarded every one according to the deeds done in the body the term 'Heaven,' as intended for the Saints' eternal home must include more kingdoms than one."[17] While pondering the nature of the mansions in heaven, Joseph and Sidney testified that they saw a vision and, by the power of the Spirit, beheld an impressive panorama of the past and a glimpse into the future. "We beheld the glory of the Son, on the right hand of the Father," they wrote, adding, "After the many testimonies which have been given of him, this is the testimony, last of all, which we give of him: That he lives! For we saw him, even on the right hand of God; and we heard the voice bearing record that he is the Only Begotten of the Father—that by him, and through him, and of him, the worlds are and were created, and the inhabitants thereof are begotten sons and daughters of God." They further stated that they saw "holy angels" and others who were "sanctified before his throne, worshiping God, and the Lamb."[18]

Two additional revelations recorded in Hiram seem to be directly connected with the work of translating the Bible and provide keys that unlock some perplexing concepts found in Corinthians and the book of Revelation. In response to questions arising from statements by Paul in Corinthians, Joseph Smith learned that "little children are holy, being sanctified through the atonement of Jesus Christ."[19] Later Joseph sought and received information concerning the meaning of certain terms found in Revelation, such as the sea of glass, the four beasts, the four angels, the seals, the two witnesses, and the 144,000, thereby clarifying some of the mysteries of the Bible and adding to the Latter-day Saints' understanding of the last days, the Second Coming, and the millennial reign of Christ.[20]

In addition to gaining a witness of the Father and the Son and learning about the creation of worlds whose inhabitants are "begotten sons and daughters of God," Joseph Smith and Sidney Rigdon witnessed other events of the past and saw the realities of the future. They beheld the rebellion of Lucifer, his expulsion from heaven, and his constant warfare against the saints of God. Then they beheld a scene of life beyond the grave, which shattered the usual Christian beliefs concerning the after-life. Prior to this vision, members of the Church, like other Christians, thought in terms of a heaven and a hell, a paradise and a spirit prison, a state of glory and a place of punishment. Now Joseph and Sidney learned that there are more than two places where individuals dwell in the future life, and that there is a significant difference between salvation and exaltation. They beheld that all except the sons of perdition (those who deny the Holy Spirit after having received it and whose eternal fate was not disclosed) will enter one of three degrees of glory. Following the resurrection, the most faithful children of God will enter the celestial kingdom, receive of God's fulness and glory, and dwell in the presence of God, the Eternal Father, and His Son, Jesus Christ. Honorable individuals who have neglected to embrace the fulness of the gospel of Jesus

Christ or who have not been valiant in the testimony of Christ but who have not denied the Savior are to enter the terrestrial world to receive of God's glory, but not its fulness. Those brought forth in the resurrection of the unjust (those who have not denied the Holy Spirit) will enter the lowest of the three kingdoms, the telestial glory. Whereas all mankind is assured salvation or a resurrection of the body, only the faithful and obedient will enjoy exaltation or a life with the Father and the Son. Thus a new vista concerning man's eternal home, one of eternal progression and of degrees of opportunities based upon man's works and faithfulness, unfolded. Through this revelation, Latter-day Saints received a knowledge about the hierarchy of heaven that could assist them in their quest to return to God's presence.[21]

While still in the spirit, Joseph Smith and Sidney Rigdon were commanded to write a description of this vision.[22] They then sent the recorded revelation to Independence, Missouri, for publication, and in July 1832 the vision of the degrees of glory was printed in The Evening and the Morning Star.

Philo Dibble reported that about a dozen men were in the room in the Johnson home when the vision of the glories occurred. Joseph Smith, he added, would periodically say, "What do I see?" and would then answer his own question, describing what he perceived. It seemed as though the Prophet were looking out of a window and describing to those inside things they could not behold. Meanwhile, Sidney Rigdon would confirm that he witnessed what Joseph Smith beheld. He also periodically asked, "What do I see?" Then he would describe what he experienced, after which Joseph Smith would reply, "I see the same." Others who were present remained quiet; although some felt on that occasion an unusual power, they did not see the glorious vision beheld by Joseph and Sidney.[23]

Revision of the Bible was not completed during Joseph Smith's residence in Hiram. After he and Sidney Rigdon were forced by mobs to flee from that community, they returned to Kirtland and resumed work on the project. Following the Prophet's second trip to Missouri in 1832, he continued translating.[24] By February 2, 1833, he had "completed the translation and review of the New Testament," and in a letter dated July 2, 1833, he wrote that he had "finished the translation of the Scriptures."[25] The manuscript, however, was not ready for publication. During the remaining eleven years of his life, the Prophet attempted on a number of occasions to prepare it for publication, and in doing so, he made further revisions and alterations of the text.[26] Although the translation contained about 3400 verses that are different from those appearing in the King James Version, the Prophet did not record in his manuscript all the changes in the Bible that later became known to him. He completed one phase of the project and gave some attention to every book in the Bible except the Song of Solomon which he said was not an inspired book (though in a few of the other books he made no changes). Lacking the time required to polish the work and also the necessary finances, the Prophet never published his New Translation, though he did print excerpts from this work in early Church newspapers.[27]

The Book of Commandments

While Joseph Smith was living in Hiram, a number of special meetings, called conferences, were held in the Johnson home. During one of these gatherings, held on November 1 and 2, 1831, members agreed to publish the revelations recorded by Joseph Smith.[28] Prior to this conference, Joseph had recognized the importance of preserving his revelatory experiences, and in July 1830, assisted by John Whitmer, he "began to arrange and copy the revelations."[29] There was also a need to circulate these writings to the membership of the Church. Small branches were being organized in different parts of the country, and many persons were immigrating to the newly designated Zion in Missouri. In order for the members to understand the doctrines, they needed to have access to the revelations in some authoritative form. Although some of the revelations had been copied by members who in turn referred to them in discussions with others or in sermons at public gatherings, prior to this conference they had not been compiled into a printed work.[30]

The nature of the revelations, as well as the method of their recording, varied. Some were addressed to individuals, some to groups, some to the Church, and some to the world. Some contained direct messages from heavenly beings; some were reports of visions; others were given with the aid of the Urim and Thummim; and some were spiritual confirmations that followed serious study. Some of the revelations were recorded while Joseph Smith was alone, and others were dictated to scribes in the presence of inquirers after the Prophet had been asked questions by individuals seeking religious truth. One of the methods he employed in recording revelations was described by Parley P. Pratt, who was with him when he dictated several "communications": "Each sentence was uttered slowly and very distinctly, and with a pause between each, sufficiently long for it to be recorded, by an ordinary writer, in long hand. . . . There was never any hesitation, reviewing, or reading back, in order to keep the run of the subject."[31]

On November 1, 1831, the first day of the two-day conference held in the Johnson home, elders of the Church agreed that the revelations recorded by Joseph Smith should be compiled and ten thousand copies published under the title Book of Commandments. Later the number of copies to be printed was reduced to three thousand. According to the minutes of this meeting, during the afternoon session Joseph Smith "received by inspiration" a preface to this work, now section 1 of the Doctrine and Covenants.[32] In this revelation, which contains the Lord's endorsement of the work, people were told to "search these commandments, for they are true." "Knowing the calamity which should come upon the inhabitants of the earth," the revelation reads, "I the Lord . . . called upon my servant Joseph Smith, Jun., and spake unto him from heaven, and gave him commandments." These instructions were "given unto my servants in their weakness, after the manner of their language, that they might come to understanding," that their faith might increase, and that the fulness of the gospel might be proclaimed throughout the world.[33]

During the second day of this conference, Oliver Cowdery read the preface, which Joseph Smith had received the preceding day, after which the elders who were present "bore witness to the truth of the Book of Commandments."[34]

Although the elders who attended this conference testified that the revelations were true, some of them recommended that the language of certain revelations be improved prior to their publication. After considerable discussion and prayer regarding this subject, Joseph Smith received a revelation in which the Lord challenged the wisest in the group to select the revelation considered "the least that is among them" and "make one like unto it."[35] William E. McLellin, who apparently thought himself wisest, attempted to duplicate what the Prophet had produced. It was, Joseph Smith observed, "an awful responsibility to write in the name of the Lord," and McLellin was unable to "imitate the language of Jesus Christ." This failure renewed the faith of those present and strengthened their conviction in the truthfulness of the revelations given to the Church through Joseph.[36]

The elders who attended this conference decided that Oliver Cowdery should carry the revelations to Missouri, where, under his direction, they would be printed.[37] Since the 800-mile journey was considered dangerous and Oliver Cowdery would be carrying both valuable manuscripts and contributions of the Saints for the building of Zion, John Whitmer was called to travel with him.[38]

The day following this conference, November 3, Joseph Smith received a revelation in answer to questions raised by elders regarding the gathering of the Jews in Palestine, the return of the lost tribes of Israel, and other concepts pertaining to the last days. Since this revelation was recorded after the elders had approved the publication of the Book of Commandments, it was included as an appendix in a later publication of the revelations, and in subsequent additions it was included at or near the end of the work.[39] Continuing a theme found in the preface, the revelation encouraged mankind to prepare for the coming of the Christ. The elders were commanded to preach throughout the world, taking the gospel first to the gentiles and then to the Jews. There were to be two gathering places for God's children: one (Zion) in America and the other in Jerusalem. A body of the tribes of Israel would come down from the land of the North, the wicked would be destroyed, the righteous would be spared, and the Savior would return to reign over all flesh.[40]

During the first two weeks of November, Joseph Smith attended four special conferences, recorded at least six revelations, and reviewed the commandments for publication.[41] As editor of the Book of Commandments, he chose the sixty-five revelations that were printed in the work. This did not include all the revelations he had received; some of the omitted revelations were included in later editions. In compliance with a decision of a November 8 conference, he reviewed the revelations in order to correct any errors made by scribes when they recorded the information or copied the manuscripts.[42] Before Oliver Cowdery and John Whitmer left Hiram for Independence, the Prophet was also appointed to supervise publication of the Book of Commandments, and by revelation he was told that the project was to be conducted in harmony with the law of consecration.[43]

Although Elders Cowdery and Whitmer left for Missouri in the middle of November 1831, the project was still in its initial phase when the Prophet arrived there in April 1832. By February 1832, a Church press had been established in Independence, and William W. Phelps had issued a prospectus for a forthcoming paper, *The Evening and the Morning Star*. While traveling to Missouri in April, the Prophet had stopped in Wheeling, Virginia (now West Virginia), to purchase paper for the press in Zion.[44] Some of the revelations that were to be included in the Book of Commandments were printed in the *Star*. Meanwhile, the setting of the type and preparing of the proof sheets for the collection of commandments progressed slowly.[45]

The publication of the Book of Commandments was interrupted July 20, 1833, when Missourians demanded that the Latter-day Saints immediately discontinue all publications. When Church leaders refused to comply with these and other demands, the mob destroyed the printing establishment and the living quarters of William W. Phelps. At that time "five large galley-proof sheets, each containing thirty-two pages (sixteen printed on either side of each sheet) or a total of 160 pages" had been printed.[46] The press, galley sheets, and type were thrown into the streets, but members grabbed some of the unbound copies of the Book of Commandments and hid them from the enemy.[47]

Although the destruction of the printing establishment in Missouri interrupted the publication of the Book of Commandments, copies of the galley sheets that had been preserved were later cut, bound, and distributed. When Joseph Smith secured and read a copy, he noted a few printing errors. By that time, he had also received many new revelations. Therefore, instead of recommending to the Church that the Book of Commandments be reprinted, he began in 1834 to prepare a more complete collection of the revelations; this book was printed in 1835 under the title Doctrine and Covenants.[48]

Apostasy and Mobocracy

Despite a temporary tranquillity that prevailed while Joseph Smith was studying, praying, and recording revelations, intense opposition to the Church erupted in Ohio. Criticizing the beliefs of the Latter-day Saints regarding visions, revelations, and other manifestations of God's power, critics denounced the zeal of the converts, exposed the failures of members, and complained that the Church created divisions in families. Not understanding the law of consecration and stewardship, some believed that Joseph Smith was attempting to establish a communistic society in Portage County. They argued that if the Church continued to grow there, some of the settlers might be deceived into surrendering all their property to the leaders of this new religious movement.[49]

Some of the most vocal opponents of the restoration were early converts who, after leaving the Church, persuaded others to oppose Mormonism. Two of these early dissidents were Ezra Booth and Symonds Ryder. Booth joined the Church in May 1831 and subsequently served a short-term mission in Portage County; while preaching in Hiram, he convinced Ryder that he should investigate the new religion. Impressed by Booth's testimony, Ryder traveled to Kirtland, where he heard a convert predict a destructive earthquake in China. Six weeks later, after reading about a calamity in China, he decided that a miraculous prophecy had been fulfilled, and so he joined the Church.[50]

Shortly after Ezra Booth and Symonds Ryder united with the Latter-day Saints, Joseph Smith received a revelation that referred to both of these men. Booth was commanded in June 1831 to travel to Missouri with Isaac Morley and twenty-six other missionaries,[51] and Ryder was informed that because of the transgression of Heman Basset, he was to receive the blessing previously bestowed upon Basset.[52] On June 6, 1831, Ryder was ordained an elder by Joseph Smith. After reading the revelation that pertained to him and receiving the commission as an elder in the Church, he was perplexed: his name had been spelled "Rider" instead of "Ryder." Apparently unaware that Joseph Smith often dictated revelations to scribes or recorded in his own language and spelling information he received from God, Ryder was bewildered. How could his own name be misspelled in a communication that was dictated by the Holy Spirit?[53]

When Booth returned from his mission in Missouri, he discussed with Ryder his own disenchantment with Mormonism. About the time that Joseph Smith moved to Hiram, the two dissidents decided to leave the Church. In an attempt to persuade others that Mormonism was false, Ezra Booth wrote a series of anti-Mormon articles for the *Ohio Star* in Ravenna; these were reprinted in other Ohio papers and reproduced in E. D. Howe's *Mormonism Unvailed.* In these articles, the first produced by an apostate, Ezra Booth vividly described his "justification" for leaving the Church.[54]

His complaints stemmed initially from what he regarded as a false prophecy by Joseph Smith. Prior to his leaving for Missouri, he stated, the Prophet claimed to have learned through a vision that Oliver Cowdery had established a large church in Missouri. Upon arriving in that western wilderness, Booth counted only three or four converts, all females. He further insisted that Edward Partridge was also concerned because of the size of the congregation in Missouri. When the bishop complained, the Prophet supposedly reprimanded him and said, "I see it, and it will be so."[55] From that time on, Booth said, he examined other events in the history of the Church that seemed to indicate inconsistencies. He argued, for example, that while Church leaders instructed others not to contract debts, they themselves attempted to purchase land on credit. Another of his arguments was that it seemed inconsistent for the Lord to instruct members to travel home from Missouri by water and then at McIllwaine's Bend inform them that they should proceed by land.[56]

Joseph Smith insisted that Booth had misinterpreted his teachings and church procedures. The Prophet was not disturbed when he received revelations that changed man's course of action. On a number of occasions, as in the case of Heman Basset, the blessings bestowed on one member were given to another because of transgression. When Ezra Thayer failed to accept a call to serve as a missionary in Missouri, the Prophet received a revelation commissioning Thomas B. Marsh to fulfill this responsibility. This latter alteration of an original commandment of the Lord was followed by an important revelatory statement: "Wherefore I, the Lord, command and revoke, as it seemeth me good; and all this to be answered upon the heads of the rebellious."[57]

Ezra Booth complained not only because of what he regarded as inconsistencies in the revelations and in the instructions and actions of Church leaders, but also because of the authoritarian nature of the Church polity, especially Joseph Smith's insistence that he had the sole right to receive revelation for the entire Church. Booth objected to the principle that members should pattern their conduct after the revelations that one man received. Such a tendency, he maintained, would eventually lead men into "a state of servitude," a "despotism" that would result in "unqualified vassalage."[58]

A third source of discontent stemmed from what Booth regarded as imperfections in the conduct of the latter-day prophet. He maintained that there were occasions when Joseph Smith behaved inappropriately, such as when he joked with others. This spirit of levity, Booth contended, indicated a lack of "sobriety, prudence, and stability"—qualities that should always characterize the action of God's anointed prophets.[59]

Finally, Booth was disturbed because of conflicts that divided members of the Church. During his journey to Missouri, he claimed, he had witnessed among the elders fear, selfishness, and discontent.[60]

Whereas Ezra Booth claimed that inconsistencies, authoritarianism, and the imperfections of the Prophet and other members precipitated his defection from the Church, Joseph Smith concluded that these were merely excuses that masked the real reasons for his apostasy. According to the Prophet, Booth failed to realize that "faith, humility, patience, and tribulation" precede the blessings of God and that "God brings low before He exalts." Quoting a statement from the Gospel of John (John 6:26), the Prophet remarked that men should not seek the Lord because they saw miracles, but because they partook of the gospel and were filled. Miracles were not to become the foundation for faith; rather, they were to confirm that faith that had been built upon the word of God. It was Booth's "own evil heart," Joseph concluded, that led to his apostasy; and his attempt to "overthrow the work of the Lord" exposed his "weakness, wickedness and folly" to all the world.[61]

Ezra Booth's letters indicate that his enthusiasm for the gospel dissipated as he experienced the rigors and disappointments of missionary work. As a settled Methodist preacher, he had not encountered such challenges. Not accustomed to walking long distances, he admitted that he hesitated to accept the call to travel to the promised land but went because he thought it was the will of God. After returning to Ohio, he complained that while a few leaders of the Church traveled by stage and river vessels, he had to accompany those who walked "with packs on their backs" and "subsisted by begging" until they arrived in Missouri. His problems were compounded because, as he admitted, he did not feel the Spirit of the Lord and failed to receive the gifts of the spirit that he anticipated would be manifest during his mission.[62]

In an attempt to answer the charges leveled against the Church by Ezra Booth, Church leaders called a number of missionaries to preach in Ohio and explain to others the position of the Church on various misunderstood principles. Joseph Smith, Sidney Rigdon, Reynolds Cahoon, David Whitmer, and Thomas B. Marsh were among those who campaigned against the issues introduced by this critic.[63] Sidney Rigdon challenged Ezra Booth to meet him in a debate to be held in Ravenna on Sunday, December 25, 1831. When Booth failed to appear, Elder Rigdon preached to those who gathered, assailing what he sometimes referred to as the "bundle of falsehoods." Although this public encounter did not materialize, the two continued to publicize their positions in newspaper articles and polemic sermons.[64]

Meanwhile, from early December until the second week of January 1832, Joseph Smith himself preached in Shalersville, Ravenna, and other communities of northeastern Ohio. Summarizing the purpose of this mission, he wrote that while he was "setting forth the truth," he sought to allay "the excited feelings which were growing out of the scandalous letters then being published in the *Ohio Star*." He concluded that "prejudice, blindness and darkness filled the minds of many and caused them to persecute the true Church, and reject the true light."[65]

The apostasy of Ezra Booth and Symonds Ryder helped arouse organized opposition against the Saints in Hiram. The prejudices, the misunderstandings, and the fears that were fanned concerning the possible creation of an autocratic and communistic society in that section of Ohio combined to create an ugly force. When emotions had reached a high pitch, some settlers planned a violent attack on leaders of the Church. By removing the heart of the organization, they probably thought that they could crush the expansion of Mormonism in Portage County.[66]

On March 24, 1832, an angry crowd of about fifty men attacked Joseph Smith and Sidney Rigdon.[67] Describing the turbulence of that black night, the Prophet recalled that the mob broke first into the residence of Elder Rigdon, carried him from his home, and dragged him by his heels so that his head was pulled along the rough, frozen ground. Then they covered his body with tar. One man seized a feather pillow from the Rigdon home, and the crowd tore the pillow, removed the feathers, and sprinkled them over the Church leader's tarred body.[68] The Prophet also described his own ordeal: "As I was forced out, . . . I made a desperate struggle . . . to extricate myself, but only cleared one leg," and kicked one of the men. After this man fell on the door step, the angry crowd swore that "they would kill me if I did not" remain still.[69]

Joseph was then carried into the stark darkness of a lonely

Mobbing of Joseph Smith, 1832 (painting by C.C.A. Christensen)

meadow, where he was beaten by the aroused men. As he was being carried around the corner of the Johnson home, he recounted, the man whom he had kicked caught up with the group and thrust his blood-covered hand into Joseph's face and swore, "I'll fix ye." While being carried into the field, the Prophet was choked until he became unconscious. When he awoke, he saw the tarred and bloody body of Sidney Rigdon stretched on the ground and assumed that Elder Rigdon was dead. The Prophet pleaded for mercy, after which one man cursed and said, "Call on yer God for help, we'll show ye no mercy."[70] Joseph was then carried another thirty rods or so from the Johnson home, where someone cried, "Simonds, Simonds," calling, as Joseph Smith assumed, Symonds Ryder. The Prophet said that the man replied, "Don't allow him to touch the ground, lest he should escape."[71]

Meanwhile, some members of the mob held a council. Joseph Smith thought they were trying to decide whether or not to kill him. The group decided against such action, but determined to beat him instead. They tore off all of his clothes, leaving only a shirt collar around his neck. One man fell on him like a "mad cat" and, while scratching his body with sharp nails, muttered, "That's the way the Holy Ghost falls on folks!" The mob also attempted to force into his mouth a vial of what the Prophet thought was poison, but he broke the vial with his teeth, and it fell to the ground, leaving him with a chipped tooth.[72] After being scratched and beaten, Joseph Smith was covered with a coat of tar and feathers. Some of the men tried to close his lips with the tar, and others sought to force the tar-paddle into his mouth.[73]

Eventually the mob disappeared, leaving Joseph Smith in the meadow. When he attempted to rise, he fell, but after removing some of the tar from his lips, he breathed more easily. After a while he saw two lights in the distance. He arose and made his way toward one of the lights, which was coming from the Johnson home. At the door, his wife saw his body darkened with tar, which she thought was blood, and, thinking that he had been severely crushed, she fainted. A blanket was thrown around the Prophet, and a number of friends who had gathered in the Johnson home spent the night removing the tar and washing his body.[74]

During this mobbing, two of the Saints, thinking they had encountered the enemy, fought with each other. One of them, John Poorman, ran into a cornfield to investigate a noise. At the same time, John Johnson, who had earlier been locked into his home by the mob, managed to free himself. Carrying a heavy club, he ran into the same cornfield, and when the two men met, they each supposed the other to be the foe. Poorman struck Johnson on the shoulder; then, frightened because he thought he had killed someone, he fled to the Johnson home. "Father Johnson," as he was called, recovered and struggled back to his home. Later the two men reported the incident and learned of their mistake.[75]

The next day was a Sunday, and the Latter-day Saints gathered to worship at the usual hour. During the night Joseph

Smith had been cleansed, and he was prepared to preach. "With my flesh all scarified and defaced," he wrote, he preached to the congregation as usual and noted that some of the men who had participated in the mobbing of the previous night were in attendance. During the afternoon he baptized three converts.[76]

Although Joseph Smith recovered quickly from this ordeal, others were not so fortunate. For several days Sidney Rigdon was delirious, but he eventually recovered. During the mobbing, one of the Smith twins, Joseph Smith Murdock, contracted a severe cold, and on March 29, 1832, he died. He was the first person to die as a consequence of persecution aimed at Latter-day Saints.[77]

Because of continued threats on their lives, Joseph Smith, Sidney Rigdon, and their families left Hiram in the spring of 1832. On March 31, Sidney returned to Kirtland, and on April 1, Joseph left for a mission to Missouri. Since another mob had been organized in Kirtland and "the spirit of mobocracy was very prevalent through that whole region of country," the Prophet avoided returning to Kirtland prior to this mission. He instructed his wife, for her safety, to leave Hiram, return to the Whitney home, and await his return.[78] Following his departure from Hiram, Joseph was not reunited with his family until June 1832.

Chapter 7

The Call
to Preach

During the 1830s Latter-day Saints commenced missionary work in various
parts of the world. After declaring the restored gospel to the inhabitants of New York, missionaries began preaching in Ohio and
Missouri; and while elders were serving in these three states,
others began preaching in New England, the mid-Atlantic states,
and the South. During the early 1830s, missionaries carried the
message of the restoration not only into every state of the young
nation, but into eastern Canada as well. Before the decade had
passed, missionaries from Kirtland and other parts of North
America had carried the gospel across the Atlantic to responsive
communities in England.

During most of the thirties, Kirtland was the major center for
Latter-day Saint missionary activity. Many elders received calls to
preach and, endowed with deep convictions, went forth to serve.
Sometimes, however, converts were ordained prematurely. Some
who accepted calls to preach possessed more enthusiasm than
genuine knowledge or ability. Recognizing the need to regulate
ordinations and supervise the activities of missionaries, Church
leaders residing in Kirtland provided members with instructions
and educational experiences designed to enhance their understanding of the gospel and their ability to communicate with
others.[1]

Kirtland was a favorable location for organizing and directing the missionary program. A few miles north of the community was the "Old Girdled Road," one of the main highways of the Western Reserve, which connected Cleveland with settlements in western Pennsylvania and New York. Fairport harbor was also nearby; there members could board sailing vessels that would carry them along the shores of Lake Erie. After proceeding east to Buffalo, New York, missionaries could skirt Lake Erie and Lake Ontario and penetrate upper Canada, or they could travel along the Erie Canal to the Hudson River. From the Albany region, elders could move south toward New York City or continue east into New England. While many elders went east from Kirtland, others went south and west. Like the spokes of a wheel, roads radiated from Kirtland to many sections of the Western Reserve. Kirtland was also near the Ohio Canal, which ran through the Western Reserve to the Ohio River. From this juncture individuals could continue directly overland to the southern states or proceed along the Ohio to the Mississippi, which in turn was the main western highway transporting people north and south, from Missouri and Illinois to Mississippi and Louisiana.[2]

An Internal Call to Preach

Some of the first elders who served as missionaries began preaching without having received an official call from Church leaders. They were acting in harmony with a revelation received by the Prophet, which stated: "If ye have desires to serve God ye are called to the work; for behold the field is white already to harvest."[3]

In November 1830, Frederick G. Williams joined the four elders who had introduced the gospel in Geauga County and journeyed with them to Missouri. Another Ohioan, John Murdock, met the traveling elders, was baptized, confirmed, and ordained an elder, and began preaching in the Western Reserve—all within one week's time! He had previously been engaged in an itinerant crusade, declaring the need for the recovery of New Testament Christianity; but after his conversion he began preaching the reality of the restoration. Concentrating his efforts in the eastern communities of Cuyahoga County, he baptized about seventy Ohioans within four months. He temporarily discontinued all economic pursuits, and while his family was being cared for by another member, he devoted himself to the ministry full time.[4]

Meanwhile, Levi Hancock heard that a work had been translated that contained a description of Christ's visit to his "other sheep" on the American continent. He investigated the report. After listening to the leaders of the restored Church in Mayfield, he followed them to Kirtland, where he was baptized by Parley P. Pratt. A few days later, after he was ordained an elder, he rode back to his home in Rome, Ashtabula County, and began to hold meetings. During that month, November 1830, Levi Hancock noted that he "preached from place to place where the folks were well acquainted" with him.[5]

Some of the early missionaries testified that after receiving an internal call from God to preach, they sought a confirmation from Church leaders and then went forth as the Spirit directed. Such was the case with Jared Carter. In early 1831 he left home on a business venture. He had traveled about twelve miles when he was given a copy of the Book of Mormon by a man who did not believe its contents. As he read the book, Jared prayed that the Lord might reveal the truth to him. After earnest study and prayer, Carter wrote, he was convinced by "manifestations of the Spirit of God" that the gospel of Jesus Christ had indeed been restored. Shortly thereafter he met Hyrum Smith, and in February 1831, he was baptized for the remission of sins, after which, he said, he was enwrapped by the Spirit of God. That spring he immigrated to Ohio and settled in Thompson, where his wife was baptized. They subsequently moved to Amherst, Ohio, and Jared Carter started preaching. Shortly after securing from Joseph Smith an affirmation of his duty to preach, he traveled to Vermont to proclaim the gospel to his relatives. For five months, from September 1831 to February 1832, he traveled as the Spirit guided him. Upon returning home, he learned that his three brothers, Simeon, Gideon, and John, who had been living in different parts of the nation, had all joined the Church and were actively teaching others about the new faith.[6]

This practice of serving missions without a specific call from an ecclesiastical leader continued for a number of years. Another example of an elder who went forth in the early 1830s to serve as the Spirit directed him was Zera Pulsipher, who met Jared Carter during the latter's mission in Vermont. This investigator was already interested in the message of restoration; he had secured a copy of the Book of Mormon, read it, and become convinced that it was a new witness for Christ. However, he was not certain that the Church had been reestablished on the earth, so when he met Elder Carter, he asked him if the power of the ancient church had been restored, including the gifts of the Spirit. Elder Carter responded with a firm "Yes!" Then Zera Pulsipher asked him if the sick had recovered after he had lain his hands upon them. The missionary replied that on many occasions he had witnessed the healing of the sick through the power of God, which had been restored to the earth.[7]

Zera Pulsipher was convinced that Elder Carter spoke the truth, and after asking God if the everlasting gospel was again on the earth, he received a witness of the reality of the restoration. In January 1832, he was baptized by Jared Carter.

Shortly after joining the Church, Zera Pulsipher commenced missionary work. According to a family record, while working on his farm he felt impressed to leave home and begin preaching. The impulse was so strong that shortly before noon he unyoked his oxen and turned them into the pasture, then walked to the house and asked his wife for a clean shirt and a pair of socks.

"Where on earth are you going?" she asked.

"I don't know, only that I am going to preach the gospel. The Lord will show me where to go. I am going where He guides me."

"How long will you be gone?" she inquired.

"I don't know. Just long enough to do the work the Lord has for me to do."[8]

Immediately after lunch, the new missionary traveled in the direction the Spirit indicated. He soon joined forces with another itinerant missionary, Elijah Cheney. The two elders located a school in Richland, New York, where they were allowed to preach in the evenings. One of the first converts baptized by Elder

Pulsipher in Richland was a young farmer named Wilford Woodruff, who became one of the most successful missionaries in the
history of the restoration. Within one month, the two elders had
baptized a number of individuals and organized a branch of the
Church in Richland.[9]

Another member who went forth to preach shortly after his
conversion without, apparently, receiving a direct call from
Church leaders was Brigham Young. In December 1832, eight
months after his baptism, he left his home in Mendon, New York,
together with his brother Joseph, to preach in Canada. Within
one month these two elders baptized approximately forty-five persons in the area of Kingston and organized several branches of the
Church in that region. Returning to New York, Brigham Young
continued to preach and baptize in Mendon and vicinity. Before
migrating to Kirtland in the fall of 1833, he completed a second
mission to Canada, where he strengthened the branches he had
earlier helped organize.[10]

Called by Church Leaders

Immediately after he settled in Kirtland, the Prophet Joseph
Smith commenced directing the missionary program of the
Church, calling many members by name to preach the gospel. In
addition, a number of the revelations recorded in Kirtland
included injunctions to members to preach the gospel to the
world. In the same revelation that disclosed the Law of the Lord
(including the rudiments of the law of consecration and stewardship), men of the priesthood were instructed to "go forth" to declare the gospel "to the east and to the west, to the north and to
the south," traveling two by two in the name of the Lord and with
the power of Christ.[11]

In the latter part of February 1831, the Prophet received a revelation instructing the elders to gather in Kirtland in June for a
special conference. One of the purposes of this missionary gathering was also revealed by revelation: All elders who were worthy
and able were to "go forth into the regions round about, and
preach repentance unto the people."[12] In a subsequent revelation,
they were told that when the inhabitants of the land had re-

pented, the elders were to organize churches in the name of Christ and according to the laws of the land.[13] The following year Joseph Smith received another revelation that emphasized the responsibilities of members to be involved in missionary work: "It becometh every man who hath been warned to warn his neighbor," the Lord said.[14]

In March 1831, specific instructions were given by revelation to three elders. Sidney Rigdon, Parley P. Pratt, and Leman Copley were commanded to introduce the gospel to members of the United Society of Believers in Christ's Second Appearing, known as the Shakers.[15] One of the Shaker communal societies was located a few miles west of Kirtland. In harmony with this revelation, the three men went forth and introduced the restored gospel to these Protestants.[16]

At a conference in Kirtland in June, twenty-eight men, including the Prophet, received specific missionary callings. By revelation, these elders were called and instructed to travel to Missouri, two by two, taking different routes and "preaching the word by the way."[17] Joseph Wakefield and Solomon Humphrey were called to labor in the east.[18] After the twenty-eight elders arrived in Missouri, those about to return to Ohio were instructed to preach in Cincinnati and other communities they visited on their journey home.[19]

In October 1831, William E. McLellin and Samuel Smith were called to preach in the eastern states in regions where the gospel had not yet been proclaimed.[20] After Elder McLellin failed to magnify this calling, he was called during a conference held on January 25, 1832, at Amherst, Ohio, to preach in the Southern states along with Luke Johnson, Major N. Ashley, and Burr Riggs.[21] During this conference, Orson Hyde, Samuel H. Smith, Lyman Johnson, and Orson Pratt were called by revelation to preach in the eastern states, and Asa Dodds and Calves Wilson were commanded to serve in the western states.[22] Others were called to travel two by two and preach, though they were not assigned to labor in a particular geographical area. Seven pairs of elders were called to the ministry and commanded to preach from house to house, from village to village, and from city to city.[23]

Following the Amherst conference, a few other members received missionary calls in revelations later published in the Doctrine and Covenants. In March 1832 Jared Carter was called to preach in the eastern states, in the area where he had served his first mission.[24] Instructions revealed that month to Stephen Burnett and Eden Smith specified that although it "mattereth not" in what part of the world they preached, they were to proclaim the gospel to everyone within range of their voices.[25] In August 1833, John Murdock was called to preach in the eastern states;[26] and in July 1837, Thomas B. Marsh was called to preach throughout the world.[27]

A few members were also called by revelation to serve as missionaries while they were enlisting soldiers in Zion's Camp, an army that was to travel to Missouri to aid the Saints who had been driven from their homes. Four pairs of elders, including Joseph Smith and Parley P. Pratt, Lyman Wight and Sidney Rigdon, Hyrum Smith and Frederick G. Williams, and Orson Hyde and Orson Pratt were called to serve in this dual capacity.[28]

While some elders were receiving assignments directly from Joseph Smith, others received missionary calls from lesser Church leaders. In April 1832, for example, while the Prophet was en route to Missouri, Jared Carter journeyed from Amherst to Kirtland to receive his missionary assignment. He was informed by an elders' conference that he should return to the eastern states with Calvin Stoddard, who was to serve as his companion.[29]

Sometimes missionaries were given their choice between remaining in Kirtland and attending school or leaving immediately for the mission field. When Heber C. Kimball sought counsel on this matter in May 1836, the Prophet told him that he should make this decision himself. Elder Kimball chose to return to the mission field and immediately left for New York and Vermont.[30]

A missionary assigned to a particular geographical area was sometimes allowed to trade assignments with another elder. During a missionary conference held in Kirtland in September 1837, 109 elders were called to preach the gospel. These men were divided into eight groups, and each group was assigned to a specific region. The elders in each division were instructed to hold their own meetings in preparation for their missions, and were told that those who desired to travel in a different district from the one to which they had been appointed could change with those of another region.[31]

On February 17, 1834, the Kirtland high council, a body of twelve men, was organized.[32] This body assisted the Prophet and his counselors in directing missionary activities of the Church. After receiving letters from the Saints in Canada requesting additional missionaries, the high council invited men to volunteer for this service. On February 20, the high council announced that Lyman E. Johnson, Milton Holmes, Zebedee Coltrin, Henry Harriman, Jared Carter, and Phineas Young should journey to Canada on condition that they settle their affairs at home.[33]

A major reorganization of the missionary program occurred in 1835 with the calling of men to serve in the first Quorum of Seventy and the Quorum of the Twelve Apostles. Although the precise responsibilities of members of these two quorums were not originally disclosed, individuals called to this service received general instructions to go forth and preach the gospel "in all the world."[34] On March 12, 1835, the apostles were given specific instructions by the Prophet to commence missionary work on May 4 of that year in the eastern states. The Twelve decided that during their missionary travels, they would also conduct a series of conferences. Between May 9 and October 2, they conducted four conferences in New York, two in Maine, and one each in Canada, Vermont, Massachusetts, and New Hampshire.[35]

Joseph Smith again called the seventies and apostles to serve as missionaries in 1836. In March, following the dedication of the Kirtland Temple, the seventies, the Twelve, and other bearers of the priesthood were instructed by the Prophet "to go forth and build up the Kingdom of God." That summer, nine of the apostles fulfilled missions, and during the ensuing winter, ten apostles served as missionaries.[36]

In the midst of economic troubles that struck Kirtland in 1837 and an internal crisis that caused serious divisions among members of the Church, the Prophet called Heber C. Kimball and Orson Hyde, both members of the Quorum of Twelve Apostles, to introduce the gospel in England. Elder Kimball recalled that one day, while they were in the Kirtland Temple, the Prophet approached him and said softly, "Brother Heber, the Spirit of the Lord has whispered to me, 'Let my servant Heber go to England and proclaim my Gospel and open the door of salvation to that nation.'" Elder Kimball was overwhelmed with this assignment. In his journal, he relates that he went into an upper room in the temple almost daily and poured out his soul to his Heavenly Father, asking for protection and power to fulfill an honorable mission. Although his family was almost destitute at the time, he determined that he should accept the mission call. "The cause of truth," he said, and "the Gospel of Christ, outweighed every other consideration."[37]

Accompanied by two recent converts, Willard Richards and Joseph Fielding, Elders Kimball and Hyde left for England on June 13, 1837, traveling without purse or scrip. In New York City, they were joined by three recent converts from Canada: John Goodson, Isaac Russell, and John Snyder. On July 1, the missionaries set sail for England; they arrived in Liverpool twenty days later. When Elders Kimball, Hyde, and Russell boarded a homebound ship in that same harbor exactly nine months later, they left in England more than fifteen hundred members organized into many branches of the Church.[38]

Missionary Licenses

Church authorities in Kirtland regulated missionary activities not only by issuing specific calls to preach the gospel, but also through instructions concerning ordination to the ministry and the licensing of missionaries. Some men had apparently been ordained before they were prepared to magnify their callings. In December 1833, elders were instructed not to ordain any candidate for the ministry until he had demonstrated faith, had been called and chosen by God, and could teach effectively the pure gospel of Christ.[39] On February 12, 1836, Church leaders declared that no one was to be ordained to an office in the Church in Kirtland "without the unanimous voice" of the members of a particular quorum organized in that community. Individuals who lived in other areas were not to be ordained until they had been recommended by the voice of the branch of the Church in which they resided. This recommendation was to be submitted to the ecclesiastical body that supervised activities of local branches, and the men who were appointed by Church leaders to preside over the branches were to supervise the ordinations in their respective regions.[40]

This coordination and regulation of the missionary program was designed to assure that only worthy members would serve as ambassadors of the Lord. The license that William Smith, brother of the Prophet, received included the following information: "This certifies that William Smith, a member of the Church of Christ, organized on the 6th of April, 1830, has been ordained a Priest of said Church, by authority of a conference held in Orange, Cuyahoga Co., Ohio, on the 25th day of October, A.D., 1831. This is therefore to give him authority to act in the office of his calling, according to the articles and covenants of said Church." This certificate, William commented, helped him better understand the importance of his mission to warn all men of the coming of Christ. "I accordingly made several circuits into the country round about," he wrote, "in order to declare unto them [people he met] the truths of the gospel."[41]

In March 1836 the Church's First Presidency announced that a new system was to be instituted for recording "ordinations and licenses." The license identified the office of the priesthood held by the member and stated that he was authorized to preach the gospel. Clerks were to be appointed in all the conferences to record ordinations and issue a certificate to each person who had been ordained, specifying the date of the ordination and the office to which the individual had been ordained. This information was also to be sent to Kirtland, where a record of all such transactions would be kept. Church clerks were further instructed to announce quarterly, in a Church publication, the names of all who had received licenses during the preceding three months. In addition to these procedures, the presidency decreed that all bearers of the priesthood who had previously received licenses to preach were to send their certificates to Kirtland with a letter verifying their worthiness and signed by a branch clerk, after which the faithful bearers of the priesthood would receive new licenses from the conference in which they resided.[42]

In compliance with these instructions, between March and early June 1836, 263 members received certificates from Kirtland, consisting of 244 licenses for elders, 11 for priests, 3 for teachers, and 5 for deacons. By the end of that year, 285 men had received certificates in Kirtland affirming that they were worthy to preach the everlasting gospel.[43]

Church Schools

Recognizing that an educated lay ministry has an advantage over an uneducated group, several educational institutions were organized in Kirtland, designed to train men to be effective missionaries and administrators of Church affairs. Though the schools were called by different names, such as the School of the Prophets and the School of the Elders, the general objectives of the institutions remained the same: to teach men the doctrines of the kingdom and to prepare elders to go forth to serve with increased power and effectiveness. Between 1833 and 1838, Joseph Smith, Sidney Rigdon, and other Latter-day Saint leaders taught in these schools many subjects, including English grammar, history, and theology.[44]

In a letter published in the *Evening and the Morning Star* in Kirtland in December 1833, leaders informed the elders that they should be "exceedingly careful about unnecessarily disturbing and harrowing up the feelings of the people." "Your business," the letter continued, "is to preach the Gospel in all humility and meekness, and warn sinners to repent and come to Christ." Missionaries were further told they should avoid contention and disputes with critics who did not desire to know the truth. If individuals rejected their testimony in one area, they were to travel to another community and resume preaching.[45]

After the Kirtland Temple became a seminary of learning for Latter-day Saints, the Prophet taught the elders various principles designed to aid them in their missionary labors. They were told "not to contend with others on account of their faith, or systems of religion." Rather, they were to "go in all meekness, in sobriety, and preach Jesus Christ and Him crucified."[46]

Other Characteristics of the Early Missionary Program

Church leaders directing the missionary program from Kirtland not only prescribed the communities where many missionaries would labor, but sometimes also identified the duration of their calls. Sometimes elders were called to preach for a few weeks, at other times for a much longer period. Generally, however, the early missionaries traveled as the Spirit directed and terminated their missions according to their own judgment. The completion of a mission did not necessarily mean the elder's missionary service had ended. One call followed another, so that some persons were constantly preaching. They departed in the midst of harvests and during the dead of winter, during periods of personal prosperity, and at times of economic depression. Reporting on missionary activity in June 1836, William W. Phelps wrote from Kirtland to his wife in Missouri: "The Elders are constantly coming and going. Last week Bros. Simeon Carter and Solomon Hancock started for the east. Bishop Partridge and Counselor Isaac Morley will start soon," he continued. "Last week elders Amasa M. Lyman, Peter Dustin and James Emmett returned from their missions, and Elder Oziel Stemps arrived in Kirtland this week."[47]

As missionaries went forth to proclaim the gospel, they frequently used the popular proselyting techniques of that age. They sometimes went from house to house, teaching all who would listen. In order to reach larger groups, they often made arrangements to preach in schoolhouses, courtrooms, and other public and private buildings. They often received permission to preach in Protestant meetinghouses, especially Methodist churches. They also preached in barns, in open fields, and on city sidewalks, at times engaging in public debate with members of other faiths.[48]

Between 1831 and 1837, more missionaries served in Ohio than in any other state. This was due to the fact that more elders commenced missionary work from Kirtland than any other community, and they would preach in Ohio while traveling to other parts of North America. Moreover, many missionaries served for only a few weeks or months and of necessity concentrated their efforts in communities near their homes. Consequently, Ohio was saturated with missionaries crossing and crisscrossing its plains and valleys. In December 1831, for example, Hyrum Smith and Reynolds Cahoon preached in several communities west and south of Kirtland, including Leroy, Thompson, Rome, Bloomfield, Hiram, and Wethersfield. After returning briefly to Kirtland, Hyrum was again on the move, and on January 14, 1832, he commenced another mission to communities west of Kirtland—Cleveland, Florence, and Amherst.[49]

Another active missionary in the 1830s was Lorenzo Barnes. He had been living in Norton, Medina (now Summit) County, Ohio, since 1816 and joined the Church on June 16, 1833. Less than one month after his baptism, he was ordained an elder and called on a mission by a council of high priests in Kirtland. He preached in various communities in Ohio in August and September, then returned to Kirtland to work on the temple for three or four weeks. That winter he taught school, but in the spring, he accepted the call to serve in Zion's Camp. Upon returning from Missouri in October, he began another mission that continued for more than six months. In the spring of 1835, having remained home for less than a month, Elder Barnes again returned to the mission field, preaching in Ohio and then in Pennsylvania for almost six months.[50]

Even Joseph Smith served as a traveling missionary, preaching the gospel in Ohio, Canada, and the states stretching from Massachusetts to Missouri. He was the only president of the Latter-day Saints to labor as a full-time missionary while presiding over the Church. Every year the Prophet lived in Ohio, he preached outside that state and visited members in various parts of North America. In 1831, 1832, 1834, and 1837, he traveled to western Missouri to instruct the Saints who had gathered there, finally making his home in that state in 1838.[51] Following his second trip to Missouri in 1832, he went with Newel K. Whitney to Albany, New York City, and Boston.[52] In 1833 he served a one-month mission in upper Canada.[53] In 1834 he spent nearly one

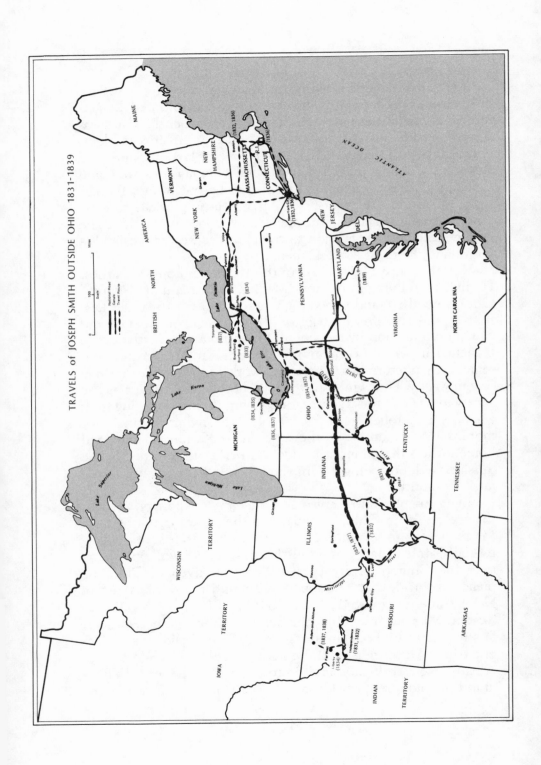

TRAVELS of JOSEPH SMITH OUTSIDE OHIO 1831-1839

month preaching in New York State, after which he proceeded to Missouri and, before the year's end, to Pontiac, Michigan.[54] The next year he returned to Michigan.[55] In 1836 he went to New York City, Boston, and Salem, Massachusetts, and made a third trip to Michigan.[56] In 1837 he traveled for the fourth time to Michigan and Missouri and made a second visit to Canada.[57]

During these fourteen known journeys outside the state of Ohio between June 19, 1831 and March 15, 1838, the Prophet traveled about 15,000 miles, averaging some 2,000 miles each year. His trips to Missouri and to the East Coast generally kept him away from home for about two and a half months at a time, and during the years of his journeys both east and west (in 1834 and 1837), he was traveling almost five months of the year. These trips were made by nearly every conceivable mode of transportation: horseback, wagon, carriage, stagecoach, canal barge, steamboat, sailing vessel, canoe, railroad car, and on foot.

On all of these trips outside of Ohio, Joseph Smith was accompanied by other members of the Church. Sidney Rigdon was his most frequent companion, traveling with the Prophet on seven of the fourteen journeys. Newel K. Whitney journeyed with the Prophet on his two long trips in 1834, his excursions to Missouri and the East Coast. Oliver Cowdery accompanied him during two of his trips to Michigan and on his journey to Salem. Frederick G. Williams accompanied him on a march to Missouri and two trips to Michigan. Parley P. Pratt served as his missionary companion when the Prophet preached in New York in 1834 and sought recruits for Zion's Camp. In addition to the several hundred men who participated in Zion's Camp, many other Latter-day Saints traveled with the Prophet, including Edward Partridge, Joseph Coe, A. S. Gilbert, Peter Whitmer, Jesse Gause, Thomas B. Marsh, and Vinson Knight.[58]

Preaching the gospel and visiting the Saints was not Joseph Smith's only concern during these journeys outside Ohio. During his four trips to Missouri, he improved the organization of the Church in that area, held conferences, transported supplies to oppressed members, and assisted Saints in establishing a new gathering place in Far West. In 1834 he traveled to New York State, accompanied by other missionaries, to recruit men for Zion's Camp and to raise money to help the Saints in Missouri and Ohio. During his missions to the East Coast in 1832 and 1836, he sought funds to finance Church programs in Ohio. He traveled to Michigan in 1837 on banking business and went to Canada that same year partly to secure help in redeeming the paper currency issued by the Kirtland Safety Society.[59]

Joseph Smith's mission to Salem in 1836 was one journey that possibly began as an attempt to secure funds for the Church but became a proselyting mission. According to Ebenezer Robinson, who worked in the printing office in Kirtland, Joseph Smith, Hyrum Smith, Oliver Cowdery, and Sidney Rigdon traveled to Salem, Massachusetts, in the summer of 1836 after hearing a report that there was a hidden treasure there.[60] Following their arrival in Salem, the Prophet received a revelation, dated August 6, that said, "I, the Lord your God, am not displeased with your coming [on] this journey, notwithstanding your follies." The Prophet was told that he should not be concerned about his debts, but he was to remain in the area and become acquainted with the men there. "And the place where it is my will that you should tarry, for the main," the revelation continued, "shall be signalized unto you by the peace and power of my Spirit, that shall flow unto you."[61] In consequence of this revelation, the Prophet and his companions remained in eastern Massachusetts for about one month, traveling from house to house, teaching people and preaching publicly when the opportunity arose.[62]

One of the most complete descriptions of a preaching mission undertaken by the Prophet Joseph Smith was his own account of his first mission to Canada in 1833. The missionary journal that he kept at that time contains an almost daily account of his activities, with about half the entries in his own handwriting and the other half in the handwriting of scribes. He had decided to travel to Canada when Freeman Nickerson, a convert from New York, and others asked him to preach to their relatives in Canada. Accompanied by Sidney Rigdon and Freeman Nickerson, the Prophet left Kirtland on Saturday, October 5, in a wagon driven by a team of horses provided by Nickerson. The following day, a

Sunday, Elder Rigdon preached to a congregation in Springfield, Ohio, and that evening the missionaries attended another meeting held in the home of one of the Saints who lived in that community.[63]

During the first week of the mission, the men traveled along the shores of Lake Erie and entered New York State, visiting members and preaching at meetings along the way. After they arrived at Freeman Nickerson's farm in Perrysburg, Cattaraugus County, western New York, on October 12, the Prophet recorded in his journal, "I feel very well in my mind. The Lord is with us, but have much anxiety about my family."[64] Soon thereafter, he received a revelation in which the Lord assured him and Sidney Rigdon that their families were well. The Prophet was also told on this occasion that he and Sidney were to declare in that region the thoughts the Lord would instill in their hearts. While Joseph was to be given power to expound the scriptures, the revelation continued, Sidney was to be a spokesman for him and would have power to bear a strong testimony to the world. "Continue your journey," the revelation admonished, "and let your hearts rejoice; for behold, and lo, I am with you even unto the end."[65]

On Sunday, October 13, Joseph and Sidney preached to a "large congregation" in western New York. The next day they continued their journey, arriving three days later at Mount Pleasant, upper Canada, at the home of Eleazer Nickerson, the second son of Freeman Nickerson.[66] During the remainder of the week, with the land covered with a fresh mantle of snow, the two missionaries sought to spread the warmth of the gospel, teaching and preaching in Mount Pleasant, Brantford, Colburn, and Weathersford.[67]

One of the highlights of this missionary experience occurred on Sunday, October 27, after Joseph and Sidney had preached to a group gathered in the Nickerson home. Twelve converts were baptized, including Freeman Nickerson's two adult sons, Moses and Eleazer, and Lydia Bailey, who later married Newel Knight in Kirtland. That evening, the Prophet conducted a confirmation meeting. After partaking of the sacrament, the missionaries laid their hands on the heads of the converts and bestowed the gift of the Holy Ghost.[68] The success of the missionaries' labors continued the following day when they baptized two additional converts and confirmed them near the water's edge. That night they held their last meeting in the area, during which they ordained Eleazer Nickerson an elder and witnessed one of the sisters speaking in tongues.[69]

The journey home required five days of traveling. When they arrived in Kirtland, one month after beginning this mission, the Prophet recorded in his journal his genuine love for his family and his deep gratitude to the Lord. "Found my family all well according to the promise of the Lord," he wrote, "for which blessing I feel to thank his holy name."[70]

Missionary work in upper Canada continued after Joseph Smith and Sidney Rigdon left that region. Writing to Sidney Rigdon on December 20, 1833, Moses Nickerson observed: "Your labors while in Canada have been the beginning of a good work: there are 34 members attached to the Church at Mt. Pleasant, all of whom appear to live up to their profession, five of whom have spoken in tongues and three sing in tongues: and we live at the top of the mountain. For my part, I feel that I cannot be thankful enough for that which I have received: the scriptures have been opened to my view beyond account."[71]

Moses Nickerson requested that other missionaries be sent to that area, and John P. Greene was called to serve there. Writing to the editor of the *Messenger and Advocate*, he reported that he had been received by the Saints with expressions of joy, and many were desirous to be instructed more perfectly in the word of the Lord. "I labored in this region about two months with a good degree of satisfaction," he stated, "and preached the gospel to many hundreds of souls."[72]

Sacrifices of the Saints

This early missionary program could not have continued without great sacrifices by the Latter-day Saints. Periodically, women surrendered their husbands so that the men of the priesthood could carry the message of the restoration to others. While enduring great loneliness, these women managed the farms and households, taught the children, and prayed for the safe return of their husbands.

Most elders left for their missions with meager funds and relied on others to provide them with the necessities of life. Like Protestant itinerant preachers of the early nineteenth century, Latter-day Saint elders walked from house to house not only preaching, but also seeking shelter and food from generous hosts. Many of them encountered trials and hardships as they traveled without adequate food, rest, or protection from the elements. During the first mission of the Twelve, Heber C. Kimball reported he suffered from fatigue and hunger, experienced a throbbing pain from his blistered feet, and sometimes found it difficult to locate a room where he could spend the night.[73]

Traveling without money was considered a severe trial by Lorenzo Snow, who joined the Church in Kirtland and later became president of the Church. The principle, he said, was contrary to his natural feeling of independence and self-respect. From the time he was old enough to work he had paid his own way, and, he asserted, nothing but a positive knowledge that God required such sacrifices would have induced him to become dependent on others for the common necessities of life.[74]

A number of the early elders were almost destitute when they entered the mission field. When George A. Smith, cousin of the Prophet, received his call to the eastern United States, he was so poor that he did not own or have the means to purchase the clothes and books he'd need. Consequently, Joseph and Hyrum Smith gave him some gray cloth, and Eliza Brown made him a coat, vest, and trousers. Brigham Young gave him a pair of shoes, while his father gave him a pocket Bible and the Prophet gave him a copy of the Book of Mormon.[75]

Erastus Snow and John E. Page were also poor when they returned to the mission field in the spring of 1836. Describing his status at the time of his departure for a mission in western Pennsylvania, Elder Snow wrote, "I left Kirtland on foot and alone with a small valise containing a few Church works and a pair of socks, with five cents in my pocket, being all my worldly wealth." Meanwhile, Elder Page informed the Prophet that he could not accept a call to preach because he was destitute of cloth-ing. "I don't even have a coat to wear," he exclaimed. The Prophet removed his own coat, gave it to Elder Page, and de-clared, "Take this and the Lord will bless you abundantly."[76]

Orson Hyde was another early convert who devoted much of his time and energy to missionary service. Every year between his baptism in 1831 and his move to Far West, Missouri, in 1838, he labored as a full-time missionary. A few days following his baptism and ordination, he was called to serve as a missionary with Hyrum Smith in northern Ohio. The following year, he received a sec-ond call to preach, this time to the eastern states with Samuel H. Smith. During this eleven-month mission (between January and December 1832), Elder Hyde traveled approximately two thousand miles, mostly by foot, in New York, Massachusetts, Pennsylvania, Maine, Connecticut, New Hampshire, and Rhode Island. In 1833, he fulfilled a mission in Pennsylvania and New York with Orson Pratt. His marriage in 1834 to Nancy Marinda Johnson, daughter of John and Elsa Johnson, did not interrupt his missionary service. In 1835, following his call to serve as one of the original members of the Quorum of the Twelve, the thirty-year-old apostle fulfilled a mission in Vermont and New Hamp-shire. In 1836, he served as a missionary in Portage County, Ohio, western New York, and eastern Canada. And in June 1837, Elder Hyde left Kirtland with Heber C. Kimball and other missionaries to introduce the gospel in England, not returning home until May 21, 1838.[77]

Some unmarried priesthood holders practically lived in the mission field during the 1830s. Such was the case of Erastus Snow. Converted in 1832 and baptized in February 1833, he was or-dained a priest in November 1834, after which he commenced preaching in his home state of Vermont. In 1835, he served as a missionary in Vermont and New Hampshire. Three months after his ordination to the office of elder in August 1836, at the age of seventeen, Elder Snow traveled seven hundred miles to Kirtland, where he attended the Elder's school, was ordained a seventy, and received a special endowment. Following his anointing in the Kirtland Temple, he returned to the mission field. Between April

and December 1836, he served a mission in Pennsylvania. Summarizing this experience, Elder Snow recorded in his journal,
"Absent 8 months and 14 days and traveled in all 1600 miles and
preached 220 times." He further noted that he baptized during
this mission about fifty individuals and obtained twenty subscriptions to the *Messenger and Advocate*.[78]

Between January 1837 and June 1838, Erastus Snow continued to devote nearly all his time to missionary work. In January
1837 he preached in Ohio. Following a brief interval during
which he attended school in Kirtland, he again headed west; and
between May and December 1837 he served as a missionary in
Ohio, Pennsylvania, and Maryland, returning to Kirtland at the
end of the year. In January 1838 he began another mission, serving primarily in Maryland. He was back in Kirtland on June 3, and
twenty-two days later, he emigrated west, thereby changing his
base of operations.[79]

From Kindness to Cruelty

The response to the message proclaimed by the early missionaries varied from community to community and from year to
year. Levi Jackman recorded in his journal that while he was
preaching in Columbus, Ohio, in 1832, people were courteous
and treated him with respect.[80] One year later Evan M. Greene
wrote that during his missionary experience in Pierpont, Ohio, a
large congregation gathered, and though the crowd did not embrace the gospel, many seemed keenly interested in his message.[81]
That same year, Orson Pratt preached in southern Ohio in the vicinity of Cincinnati and declared that a few believed and obeyed
and many were astonished by the doctrines he disclosed.[82]

While some Americans expressed an interest in the message
of the restoration, others seemed apathetic, and a few launched
aggressive campaigns against the Saints. The opposition took different forms. Sometimes critics attacked elders of the Church
after members of their congregations united with the Saints,
while some hostile individuals denounced the Mormons before elders had baptized even a single convert in their areas. Some missionaries complained that antagonists interrupted their preaching

and accused them of being deceivers and false prophets. George A. Smith wrote that once he was heckled by a minister who commenced howling, and others joined him by gnashing their teeth, as if they were going to tear him and his companion apart.[83] Missionaries also reported that vicious lies circulating about their beliefs and practices hindered people from considering the message of the restoration.[84] At times elders were denied the use of halls or meetinghouses that were generally available to traveling preachers. Though elders George A. Smith and Marcellus F. Cowdery were once denied the use of a Methodist meetinghouse, a large crowd gathered, so large that they could not all have been accommodated in the church. Consequently, the missionaries preached in a nearby field.[85]

Sometimes opponents of the Church took overt action. Mobs armed with guns and clubs threatened to beat elders and often demanded that the missionaries leave the area. Elders were also seized by angry mobs and taken before local judges, where they were accused on various false charges.[86] Some were pelted with eggs and other objects. A few fled when mobs threatened to tar and feather them.[87]

Parley P. Pratt recorded in vivid detail the circumstances of his first imprisonment. While traveling west from Kirtland in November 1831 during his mission to western Missouri, he stopped in the neighborhood where he had lived prior to his conversion. Some in that area desired to learn about the restoration, while others, he said, "were filled with envy, rage and lying." While staying at the home of Simeon Carter, he was arrested on "a very frivolous charge." Late one evening, he was taken by a magistrate before a judge who boasted that he would imprison the missionary in order to test his powers of apostleship. Various witnesses testified against Elder Pratt, and he was locked in a public house for the night.

In the morning the officer appeared and took me to breakfast; this over, we sat waiting in the inn for all things to be ready to conduct me to prison. In the meantime my fellow travelers came past on their journey, and called to see me. I told them in an undertone to pursue their journey and leave me to manage my own affairs, promising to overtake them soon. They did so.

After sitting awhile by the fire in charge of the officer, I requested to step out. I walked out into the public square accompanied by him. Said I, "Mr. Peabody, are you good at a race?" "No," said he, "but my big bull dog is, and he has been trained to assist me in my office these several years; he will take any man down at my bidding." "Well, Mr. Peabody, you compelled me to go a mile, I have gone with you two miles. You have given me an opportunity to preach, sing, and have also entertained me with lodging and breakfast. I must now go on my journey; if you are good at a race you can accompany me. I thank you for all your kindness—good day, sir."

I then started on my journey, while he stood amazed and not able to step one foot before the other. Seeing this, I halted, turned to him and again invited him to a race. He still stood amazed. I then renewed my exertions, and soon increased my speed to something like that of a deer. He did not awake from his astonishment sufficiently to start in pursuit till I had gained, perhaps, two hundred yards. I had already leaped a fence, and was making my way through a field to the forest on the right of the road. He now came hallooing after me, and shouting to his dog to seize me. The dog, being one of the largest I ever saw, came close on my footsteps with all his fury; the officer behind still in pursuit, clapping his hands and hallooing, "Stu-boy, stu-boy, take him—watch—lay hold of him, I say—down with him," and pointing his finger in the direction I was running. The dog was fast overtaking me, and in the act of leaping upon me, when, quick as lightning, the thought struck me, to assist the officer, in sending the dog with all fury to the forest a little distance before me. I pointed my finger in that direction, clapped my hands, and shouted in imitation of the officer. The dog hastened past me with redoubled speed towards the forest; being urged by the officer and myself, and both of us running in the same direction.

Gaining the forest, I soon lost sight of the officer and the dog, and have not seen them since. I took a back course, crossed the road, took round into the wilderness, on the left, and made the road again in time to cross a bridge over Vermilion River, where I was hailed by half a dozen men, who had been anxiously waiting our arrival to that part of the country, and who urged me very earnestly to stop and preach. I told them that I could not then do it, for an officer was on my track. I passed on six miles further, through mud and rain, and overtook the brethren, and preached the same evening to a crowded audience, among whom we were well entertained.

The Book of Mormon, which I dropped at the house of Simeon Carter, when taken by the officer, was by these circumstances left with him. He read it with attention. It wrought deeply upon his mind, and he went fifty miles to the church we had left in Kirtland, and was there baptized and ordained an Elder. He then returned to his home and commenced to preach and baptize. A church of about sixty members was soon organized in the place where I had played such a trick of deception on the dog.[88]

Not all local officials and juries ruled against the early missionaries; some groups protected their rights. While Parley P. Pratt was preaching in Mentor, Ohio, in 1835, a band of about fifty men interrupted his preaching by playing instruments so loud that others could not hear his sermon. Then these rowdies pelted him with eggs until his body was smeared. After Elder Pratt sued the captain of this crowd, Grandison Newell, a jury ruled that Newell should pay damages amounting to forty-seven dollars. [89]

The emphasis on missionary service continued without interruption throughout the 1830s. During a general meeting of the priesthood held in Kirtland on May 2, 1835, members agreed that when circumstances permitted, all elders should travel in the world and preach the gospel with all their might, mind, and strength. [90] A year later, during a meeting held in the Kirtland Temple, Joseph Smith told some three hundred bearers of the priesthood that they should be actively involved in missionary work. It was not necessary, he advised, for them to go forth two by two as in former times, but they should serve "in all meekness, in sobriety, and preach Jesus Christ and Him crucified." [91]

The challenge to carry the gospel to others did not change during the economic distress of the Church in 1837. Writing from Kirtland in the fall of that year, Marcellus Cowdery informed a friend in Virginia that "Brother Joseph and Sidney say that the elders must be out all winter this year. No compulsion, you know, but this is the word to the elders, and there are great promises to those who go and are faithful. From what I learn it seems to me that the cause is a greater one and of more intense interest to the children of men than I have ever before fully realized." [92]

After most of the Saints emigrated from Kirtland in 1838, the headquarters of the missionary program of the Church shifted west. The geographical change, however, had little effect on the missionary policies, procedures, and techniques that had been launched in Kirtland. And the dedication and determination of the missionaries who departed from Kirtland during the 1830s remained characteristic of the restoration movement.

Chapter 8

Growth of the Church in Kirtland

Although about nine families living in Kirtland in 1830 joined the Church shortly after the introduction of the gospel in the Western Reserve, some of these members migrated to Missouri, and only a few other settlers living in Kirtland joined the Church. Most Latter-day Saints who resided there during the thirties were converts who had emigrated from other parts of North America, especially New England, Pennsylvania, and New York. In obedience to instructions from Church leaders and missionaries, between 1831 and 1838 hundreds of Latter-day Saints settled in Kirtland to live near the Prophet and among other Latter-day Saints. During this decade, all of the men who would preside over the Church during the nineteenth century, following the martyrdom of the Prophet, were converted and traveled to Kirtland, where they became acquainted with Joseph Smith. Brigham Young, John Taylor, and Lorenzo Snow settled in Kirtland, and Wilford Woodruff used Kirtland as a base for his missionary activities.

As a consequence of the constant influx of converts into Kirtland, Latter-day Saint membership in that township continued to increase. In the years 1836 to 1838, probably half or more of all residents in Kirtland were members of the Church.[1]

The message proclaimed by the earliest missionaries and embraced by the converts of the 1830s was that the gospel of Jesus Christ had been restored to the earth through a latter-day prophet. In discussing the reality of the restoration, the missionaries informed their listeners of the disruption of the primitive church, including the alteration of beliefs and the loss of God's authority. Then they bore witness that the heavens had opened, that latter-day visions were occurring, and that the priesthood, the power and authority to act in the name of God, had been reestablished by angelic messengers. Many testified that they had experienced the power of God and knew that the gifts of the spirit evident among the early Christians were again being manifested. They also told of the coming forth of the Book of Mormon and testified that this work was a new witness for Christ.[2]

The missionaries generally concentrated on the first principles of the gospel. "Repent and embrace the gospel," they preached. When they discussed repentance, they often coupled this principle with the doctrines of faith in Christ, baptism by immersion by those in authority for the remission of sins, and the laying on of hands for the gift of the Holy Ghost.

The early missionaries also warned people to prepare for the Second Coming of the Lord Jesus Christ. Sensing an urgency to his mission, Joseph Smith frequently told of the imminence of the Second Coming and of the calamities that would occur prior to the millennial reign of Christ. In a letter intended for publication, written in January 1833 to N. E. Seaton, an editor of the *American Revivalist and Rochester Observer* in New York, the Prophet warned: "Not many years shall pass away before the United States shall present such a scene of *bloodshed* as has not a parallel in the history of our nation; pestilence, hail, famine, and earthquake will sweep the wicked of this generation from off the face of the land, to open and prepare the way for the return of the lost tribes of Israel from the north country."[3]

Three years later, at a meeting in Norton, Medina (now Summit) County, Ohio, the Prophet discussed the prophecy of Joel concerning the destructions in the latter days and predicted that after the Saints had been gathered from among the gentiles (nonmembers), desolation and destruction would plague mankind, and none would escape except the pure in heart.[4]

Missionaries carried this warning from Kirtland to many other communities. On October 1, 1831, a group of nine elders meeting in Kirtland agreed that "the duty of the elders was to go forth and warn the inhabitants of the earth of the things known in the Church of Christ in these last days."[5] Orson Hyde echoed this theme in an article printed in the *Messenger and Advocate* in 1836. "God will soon begin to manifest his sore displeasure to this generation . . . by vexation and desolating wars. . . . The war cloud will arise from an unexpected quarter," he predicted. Although he suggested that righteousness could avert this destruction, he observed that "men seemed determined to pursue their own course."[6]

The simplicity of the message declared by the missionaries is evident from notations many of them entered in their diaries. Elias Smith wrote that he preached on the "first principles," on the Second Coming, on the necessity of prophets, on the Book of Mormon fulfilling biblical prophecy (especially Isaiah, chapter 29), and on the fruits of Mormonism.[7] Orson Pratt recorded in his missionary journal some of the themes of his sermons, noting that he frequently spoke on the restoration, miracles, the first principles of the gospel, and sometimes the gathering of the Saints and the Millennium, "the thousand years of peace."[8] Joseph Fielding reported that he listened intently to Parley P. Pratt as he preached about the apostasy and the restoration of the everlasting gospel.[9] Lorenzo Barnes aptly summarized the message he and many other missionaries were proclaiming to the world when he wrote:

Our manner of teaching the people generally was—in the first place to lay before them the first principles of the gospel: faith, repentance, baptism for the remission of sins, & the laying on of the hands for the gift of the Holy Ghost. These we proved from the New Testament to the people were preached and practiced by the apostles and obeyed by the people in ancient days and Paul says if we or an angel from heaven preach any other let him be accursed & then by comparing the ancient order of things with the teachings of the present generation and [we] left the people to judge who were preaching the gospel that Paul did and who were preaching a different one.

Secondly showed what the power of Godliness was and who were denying it. Proved the necessity of more revelations wherever the Church of Christ is on the earth and then that according to the prophecies there will be more revelations given in the last days to bring about the great work that is to be accomplished. And then the prophecies concerning the restoration of the House of Israel and the means that God will make use of to bring about the great work. The covenants made to the Fathers, the coming of Christ, his kingdom and reign on earth &c. &c.[10]

Early Conversions

Many of the converts who settled in Kirtland had not been fully satisfied with the religions they had previously examined and were seeking a return to New Testament Christianity. Before he met the Latter-day Saint missionaries, Zebedee Coltrin said that he longed to see the day when apostles and prophets served the people, as described in the ancient scriptures. Meanwhile, Jonathan Crosby was concerned about the numerous divisions in the Protestant faiths and their lack of spiritual power. "Where," he asked, "is the faith and gifts of the gospel enjoyed by the ancient Saints?"[11] Nancy Alexander was also involved in a religious quest when she met the Latter-day Saint elders. Her mother was a Baptist, her aunt and uncle Presbyterians, and she was raised a Methodist by her grandmother. After studying the Bible, she became dissatisfied with the Protestant groups with which she was familiar, for none of them, she wrote, were led by apostles and prophets, and none claimed the same spiritual gifts manifest among the early Christians.[12]

For three years prior to meeting Latter-day Saint missionaries, Wilford Woodruff had been searching earnestly for the truth. He stated that the Lord had whispered to him that His Church would be established in the last days. He had also been taught this concept by an elderly friend, Robert Mason, who lived in Connecticut and who claimed to have learned from God that since the authority possessed by the apostles of old had been lost, no one had the authority to administer the ordinances of the gospel. Believing that the doctrines and practices of the religious communities he investigated did not agree with the gospel of Jesus Christ as described in the New Testament, Wilford Woodruff refused to join any church. [13]

When Wilford returned to his home following his daytime labors and learned that two missionaries were preaching in the schoolhouse, he hastened there immediately, praying that the Lord might reveal his will to him. Arriving at the school, he saw his brother Azmon, who had also come to hear the elders, and then located a chair near the front of the crowded classroom. Following a prayer and some congregational singing, Zera Pulsipher spoke for about an hour and a half on the restoration of the gospel. Wilford testified that during this sermon the Spirit of God rested upon him and bore witness of the divine authenticity of the Book of Mormon and of the mission of the Prophet Joseph Smith. Immediately following the service, he began to read the Book of Mormon. While studying this volume of scripture, he declared, he received a witness that it was the word of God. On December 31, 1833, two days after he met the elders, both Wilford and Azmon Woodruff were baptized. "The snow was three feet deep," Wilford recorded in his journal, "the day was cold, and the water was mixed with ice and snow, yet I did not feel the cold." That night he was confirmed a member of the Church, and a few days later he was ordained a teacher in the newly organized branch in Richland. A few months later, after learning from Parley P. Pratt about the request for volunteers to help the Saints in Missouri, he traveled to Kirtland. There he met Joseph Smith, and he then accompanied the Prophet as he led Zion's Camp from eastern Ohio to western Missouri. [14]

Although John Taylor was serving as a lay preacher in the Methodist church, when he heard the message of the restoration, he was not satisfied with his membership in that church. He had emigrated from England to Canada and had united with other Methodists in the Toronto area who gathered regularly to study the scriptures. During this investigation, many in this group concluded that there was a difference in the teachings of the New Testament and statements found in the popular creeds of Christendom. John Taylor and others also concluded that the churches they investigated did not possess the authority to preach the gospel and administer sacred ordinances. Shortly after listening to the "voice of warning" as declared by Parley P. Pratt, John and his wife began studying the Book of Mormon. On May 9, 1836, both joined the Church. After being ordained an elder, John went forth to preach the gospel, and in the summer of 1836 he traveled to Kirtland to meet Joseph Smith. There he received instructions to return to Canada and preside over branches of the Church that had recently been organized in that land.[15]

Also dissatisfied with the churches of his time was Lorenzo Snow. While attending school, he concluded that "if there is nothing better than is to be found here in Oberlin College, goodbye to all religions." At the close of the school term he traveled to Kirtland, not to investigate Mormonism, but to study Hebrew and visit his sister, Eliza R. Snow. While in Kirtland, he became acquainted with Joseph Smith, studied the teachings of the Church, and decided that New Testament Christianity had returned to the earth. In June 1836, Lorenzo Snow was baptized by John Boynton, a member of the Quorum of Twelve Apostles.[16]

Not all the early converts who gathered in Kirtland joined the Church quite this readily. Brigham Young investigated for two years before consenting to be baptized. In 1830 he had secured a copy of the Book of Mormon that had been given to his brother Phineas by Samuel Smith, but he had failed to receive a witness of its authenticity in just one reading. Nevertheless, he continued to study and pray. In January 1832, he traveled to Columbia, Pennsylvania, with Phineas Young and Heber C. Kimball, a neighbor, to learn more about the restoration from members of a small branch of the Church there. Immediately after returning to his home in Mendon, New York, Brigham hitched up his horse and traveled by sleigh to Kingston, Canada, to inform his brother Joseph that he had learned that the purity of the gospel had been revealed to man. On April 14, 1832, Brigham Young was baptized and confirmed a member.[17]

Eliza R. Snow also investigated the Church for a number of years before being baptized. During the 1820s she became acquainted with Sidney Rigdon, Alexander Campbell, and Walter Scott, and learned their views concerning the need to return to the ancient Christian order. When she initially heard that "the Lord was speaking from the heavens" to Joseph Smith, she thought this was "too good to be true." She met Joseph Smith during the winter of 1830-31, when the Prophet was visiting her family, and attempted to determine whether or not he was honest by watching his facial expressions. Believing in the admonition "Prove all things and hold fast to that which is good," she determined, following this visit, to investigate the Church. Four years later, on April 5, 1835, Eliza was baptized. She later testified that during the evening following this ordinance, she had "realized the baptism of the Spirit as sensibly as . . . that of the water in the stream."[18]

The Gathering

Many of the converts who gathered to Kirtland made great sacrifices after joining the Church. Some were disowned by their families; others lost the companionship of former friends. Heeding the counsel of the missionaries, many left their homes and loved ones to begin a new life among the Latter-day Saints. One such convert was Phebe W. Carter, who married Wilford Woodruff in 1837. She said that she could not have left her home in Maine had she not been sustained by her faith and trust in Israel's God. "My friends marveled at my course, as did I, but something within impelled me on," she remembered. "My mother's grief at my leaving home was almost more than I could bear. . . . My mother told me that she would rather see me buried than to cast my lot among the Mormons."

"Phebe," her mother asked, "will you come back to me if you find Mormonism false?"

"Yes, mother, I will," Phebe promised.

Because she could not endure the trial of facing her parents as she left home, Phebe wrote farewells to members of her family the night before her departure. Leaving the notes of love on a table, she ran downstairs, climbed into a carriage, and began the thousand-mile journey to Kirtland. Remembering her promise,

Phebe never returned to the parents whom she respected and loved dearly.[19]

In addition to surrendering the companionship of former friends and relatives, most Saints made financial sacrifices to gather to Kirtland. Joseph Holbrook of Weatherfield, New York, for example, attempted to sell his farm after joining the Church; however, partly because other Latter-day Saints in his community had recently sold their property and immigrated to Kirtland, he was unable to find a buyer. After Orson Hyde and Orson Pratt visited that community in March 1834 and instructed the Saints to help the oppressed members in Missouri, he decided to sacrifice his farm. He sold it for a span of mares, a wagon, some harnesses, and $150 in cash, which was in his estimate one-third the actual value of the farm. He spent part of his money traveling to Kirtland and gave half his cash to Solomon Angel to help him and his family migrate to the Mormon community in western Missouri.[20]

Another Kirtland Saint who emigrated from New York after selling his property at a financial loss was William Huntington. Following his baptism in 1835, his home in Watertown became a base of operations for many missionaries and remained so until he was instructed by Joseph Smith's father to gather with other members as soon as possible. He subsequently sold the farm for much less than anticipated and, accompanied by his family, moved to Kirtland.[21]

The immigrants who arrived in Kirtland were of varied social, religious, and economic backgrounds and came from many different sections of the nation, especially New York and New England. Husbands and wives, bachelors and widows, the young and the aged all participated in this movement. While most were farmers, some were skilled in other occupations—teachers, ministers, blacksmiths, painters, glaziers, coopers, and carpenters. After Brigham Young preached in Vermont in 1836, Mary Ann Stearns Winters recalled, "the spirit of gathering rested upon the converts" and, agreeable to the counsel given, "all who could, migrated to Kirtland." Mary Ann accompanied her widowed mother and joined the same company in which Phebe Carter was traveling. This company was led by John Carter, who was returning from a mission in New England. [22]

The immigrants made their way to Kirtland by many different routes and forms of transportation. Some walked hundreds of miles to reach their destination; others rode in wagons, carriages, and stagecoaches, or on horseback. Some traveled on canal barges and sailed on lake vessels. Some migrated alone or with members of their family, while others united in larger groups and formed covered-wagon trains. During this journey some spent nights in taverns, some rested in tents in the backs of wagons, and others slept on the ground in the open air. They proceeded along frozen paths, pushed their way through piles of drifting snow, forded turbulent streams, and wandered along dust-choked trails. They were sometimes plagued by pesky insects and frightened by poisonous serpents. They suffered hunger, thirst, and fatigue and endured monotonous meals. They migrated during winter storms, proceeded through spring rains, and sweated through summer droughts. Some were accustomed to hard work and the rigors of conquering a wilderness. For others, the journey was a severe trial. For all it was an exciting adventure leading to a new religious experience as well as a new life. [23]

A few of the immigrants were fairly prosperous when they joined the Church and could afford the most comfortable means of transportation possible. John Tanner was one of the wealthiest of these immigrants. Before his conversion to the Church in 1831, he had accumulated about twenty-two hundred acres of land west of Lake George in New York. He also owned a sawmill, a gristmill, a dairy, and a large herd of cattle. He had contracted a disease that afflicted his leg, and for five months he hobbled about on crutches. Then he met two missionaries, Jared and Simeon Carter, who informed him of the restoration of God's church. After reading the Book of Mormon, John Tanner was converted, and he was immediately healed following a prayer by one of the missionaries. As he walked without crutches, he wept and praised the Lord for sending him the gospel with its accompanying blessings. [24] He commenced selling his property, secured wagons for the journey west, and, on December 25, 1834, departed for Kirtland with three other families, making a party of forty-five. Because of his wealth, he was able to help these families and others whom they met on the journey to Kirtland.[25]

Since there were two gathering places for the Saints in the 1830s, some who arrived in Kirtland remained only briefly before continuing on to Missouri, while others settled in the Kirtland area. A few immigrants who could not decide where they should gather sought counsel from Church leaders. Some were instructed to proceed to Missouri, and others, such as John Tanner, William Huntington, and James Lake, were directed to remain in Kirtland.[26]

Although some Latter-day Saints purchased land in Kirtland, the majority of the members there lived on farms purchased by the leaders of the Church. By the end of 1836, most of the Church property had been settled, and there was relatively little room for additional families who could not afford to purchase farms of their own. Consequently, Church leaders began asking members who could not support themselves not to emigrate, and encouraged the branches to assume responsibility for providing the necessities of life for the needy.[27]

Meeting the Prophet

Many persons traveled hundreds of miles to Kirtland simply to meet Joseph Smith. Most of these visitors had been baptized by Latter-day Saint missionaries, but some delayed this ordinance until after they had conversed with the Prophet; then, following additional investigation, they were baptized in the east branch of the Chagrin River. A number of visitors returned home, sold their farms, and then began the hegira that led them back to Kirtland or to the other gathering place of the Saints in western Missouri.[28]

Most of these travelers had never before seen a man who claimed to be a prophet of God, and they approached Kirtland with various attitudes concerning the proper appearance and conduct of such a man. In Kirtland, the Prophet was likely to be found working in the fields, attending school or church meetings, or relaxing with his family. Early in November 1832, shortly after the death of his first wife, Miriam Works Young, Brigham Young, accompanied by Joseph Young and Heber C. Kimball, left his home in Mendon, New York, and traveled 325 miles in Kimball's wagon to meet Joseph Smith. When they arrived in Kirtland, they learned that the Prophet was chopping wood in a field behind the Whitney store. Guided by the sounds of the striking ax, the men hastened toward the east branch of the Chagrin River, where they found the Prophet working with his brothers.[29] There stood Joseph Smith, dressed like any common working man of his generation. He was larger, however, than most of his contemporaries, standing six feet tall and weighing about two hundred pounds. Well-built, he was closely shaven and appeared strong, active, and handsome. His complexion was light, his eyes blue, and his hair light brown. The visitors were not disappointed in the appearance or comportment of the man they had come to see.[30]

When Wilford Woodruff met Joseph Smith for the first time, in April 1834, he also found the leader engaged in physical activities. "My first introduction was not of a kind to satisfy the preconceived notions of the sectarian mind as to what a prophet ought to be, and how he should appear," Wilford commented.

It might have shocked the faith of some men. I found him and his brother Hyrum out shooting at a mark with a brace of pistols. When they stopped shooting, I was introduced to Brother Joseph, and he shook hands with me most heartily. He invited me to make his habitation my home while I tarried in Kirtland. This invitation I most eagerly accepted, and was greatly edified and blest during my stay with him. He asked me to help him tan a wolfskin which he said he wished to use upon the seat of his wagon on the way to Missouri. I pulled off my coat, stretched the skin across the back of a chair, and soon had it tanned—although I had to smile at my first experience with the Prophet.[31]

Joseph Bates Noble remembered working with the Prophet when he first became acquainted with him. Arriving in Kirtland in the summer of 1833, less than a year after his conversion, he went to Joseph Smith and informed him that he was planning on staying there for a few days. The Prophet invited Noble to join him as he headed for the hay fields. For six of the nine days that Joseph Noble remained in Kirtland, he worked with the Prophet and listened to his testimony concerning the reality of the restora-tion. The powerful conviction Noble gained helped sustain him as he moved from New York to Ohio and then joined other Latter-Saints in their march to Missouri, their flight to Illinois, their trek across the Plains, and their colonization of the Great Basin.[32]

Almost two years after his conversion, Jonathan Crosby rode to Kirtland to meet the Prophet and to find a place where he and his wife could settle. Immediately after making arrangements to stay in the Johnson Tavern, he expressed his innermost desire: "I must go and see the Prophet of God first of all." Learning where the Prophet lived, Jonathan hastened to the home and was wel-comed by Joseph Smith. They had a cordial conversation, the Prophet asking Jonathan to relate to him the incidents leading to his conversion. Some time after this conversation, Jonathan re-called his impressions of the Prophet: "He didn't appear exactly as I expected to see a Prophet of God. However, . . . I found him to be friendly, cheerful, pleasant, [and] agreeable. I could not help liking him."[33]

Joseph Smith was not always busy when immigrants and visi-tors arrived in Kirtland. Louisa Y. Littlefield recalled that he sometimes awaited the arrival of travelers who were coming to the community. As visitors arrived, she related, "Joseph would make his way to as many of the wagons as he . . . could and cordially shake the hand of each person." He was especially interested in children, she observed. He would seek out the children and babies, blessing the infants and taking the young children by the hand and speaking especially to them.[34]

Some of the converts testified that when they first met Joseph Smith, they received a powerful witness that he was a man of God. Brigham Young declared that when he first shook hands with the Prophet his joy was full, for he received a testimony, by the spirit of prophecy, that this was a prophet of God.[35] Nancy Alexander, who was converted in 1834 and who immigrated to Kirtland in the spring of 1835, testified that when she and other members of her family first met Joseph Smith, they were con-vinced that "he was inspired of God."[36]

Not all the members who eventually gathered to Kirtland had their first meeting with Joseph Smith in that community. Mary Beman, a young schoolteacher living in Avon, Livingston County, New York, who married Joseph Bates Noble, recalled that in the spring of 1834, before she joined the Church, she beheld for the first time "a Prophet of the Lord." At that time Joseph Smith was engaged in missionary work and occasionally stayed in the Beman home. "I can truly say," she wrote, "at the first sight [of Joseph Smith] . . . I had a testimony within my bosom that he was a man chosen of God to bring forth a great work in the last days." She also remembered the Prophet's persuasive testimony concerning the truth of the Book of Mormon, a witness that left a lasting impression on her mind. She further related that she appreciated cooking for and serving food to the missionaries and enjoyed many interesting conversations with the Prophet and the other traveling elders.[37]

Some of the visitors who traveled to Kirtland during the 1830s to meet the celebrated Mormon prophet were not members of the Church. He spent many hours discussing the distinguishing aspects of the restored gospel with ministers, teachers, adventurers, and curiosity seekers.[38] He frequently succored and entertained in his home both members and nonmembers. "He was a . . . friend to the poor and needy," one nonmember wrote, "and many a weary-foot-sore traveler has been the recipient of his bounty."[39]

Impact of the Gathering

As a result of the flow of immigrants into Kirtland, there was a constant need for places to house them. Many resided with other Saints until they could secure homes of their own. The first major gathering place of the Saints in Kirtland was the Isaac Morley farm; although Morley moved to Missouri in 1831 and sold a portion of his land in Geauga County, he retained a tract of approximately eighty acres, which was farmed for a brief period by other members. Some members lived on the flats near the Newel K. Whitney store. Following Joseph Smith's residency in Hiram and his second trip to Missouri in the summer of 1832, the Saints provided him and his family with an apartment in the Newel K.

Whitney store. The Smiths occupied part of the first floor and the all of second floor of the building. [40]

After the Church secured the Frederick G. Williams and the Peter French farms on the plateau south of the meandering branch of the Chagrin River and decided to build a temple there, the main gathering place for the Saints in Kirtland shifted from the Morley farm and flats to the fertile land near the temple site. Not all Latter-day Saints, however, settled near the temple. Many continued to live near the Chagrin River or in other parts of the township. Heber C. Kimball settled near a creek southwest of the Morley farm, while John Tanner, Artemus Millet, and Eliza R. Snow secured land south of the Williams farm. In October 1836 another large farm became available when the Church purchased from Peter French approximately 240 acres in the southwestern section of Kirtland Township. [41]

By the summer of 1836, the land stretching approximately one-quarter of a mile from the East Branch of the Chagrin River to the temple on the hill was dotted by small wooden homes, "generally small and inelegant," and occupied primarily by Latter-day Saints. This pattern of dwellings continued for about two miles south of the temple. A village was laid out on the plateau where the temple was built, with streets crossing each other at right angles. Most of the lots contained half an acre, and in 1836 a lot sold for fifty-five to two hundred dollars. [42]

Because of the lack of economic opportunities in Kirtland, some of the early converts who immigrated to Geauga County chose to settle in nearby towns rather than the community where the Church leaders resided. The Prophet advised the Saints not to seek employment elsewhere, but to remain in Kirtland. George A. Smith recalled that some members did not follow his counsel, preferring to settle in Chagrin, Painesville, Cleveland, and other nearby communities to gain some temporary economic advantages. Many of these settlers, he concluded, eventually drifted away from the Church. [43]

Although the Latter-day Saint population grew slowly in Kirtland during the years 1831 and 1832, the town experienced a rapid increase of Saints beginning in 1833. Most of the New York

Saints who had immigrated to Geauga County in the spring of 1831 and some of the old Kirtland residents who joined the Church immigrated to Jackson County, Missouri, that summer. Jackson County continued to be the main gathering place for the Saints until the fall of 1833; and within two years—between the summer of 1831 and the summer of 1833—more than eight hundred Saints settled in western Missouri, while only a few convert families established their homes in Kirtland. In 1832 approximately one hundred members resided in that community, compared to some twelve hundred nonmembers.

Several forces combined, however, to stimulate a remarkable growth of Church members in Kirtland beginning in 1833. After construction began on the temple in the summer of 1833, there was a need for laborers and craftsmen to assist in building a "house for the Lord." In November of that year Latter-day Saints were driven by incensed mobs from Jackson County, temporarily interrupting the flow of Saints to that region. Meanwhile, missionaries continued to encourage new members to gather in Ohio or Missouri. Consequently, in the mid-1830s Kirtland was a major gathering place for Latter-day Saints. In 1835 about 900 members were living in Kirtland with another 200 or more living near that township.[44] Three years later, more than 2,000 members were living in Kirtland and vicinity. While the non-Mormon population of that township probably remained between 1,100 and 1,300 from January 1833 to January 1838, the Latter-day Saint population increased between 200 and 500 annually, with the greatest growth occurring in 1835, 1836, and 1837.[45] During a five-year period (1833 to 1838) approximately 70 Latter-day Saint families arrived in Kirtland every year and in some years 100 families settled there or near the temple. This substantial immigration significantly changed the religious complexity and settlement pattern of a town that reported 1,000 inhabitants in 1830 and approximately 3,000 in 1837.[46] By 1837 there were about 300 homes in Kirtland, 3 churches, and 1 tavern or hotel. Kirtland was larger than Chardon, Painesville, Akron, Canton, Warren, and Youngstown and was not much smaller than Cleveland or Dayton.[47]

Table 2
Comparative Estimate of LDS and Non-LDS
in Kirtland Township, 1830-1846

Year	Total Population	Non-LDS	LDS in Kirtland
1830	1,018 (Census)	963	55[1]
1831	1,120	1,050	70
1832	1,170	1,070	100
1833	1,350	1,200	150
1834	1,540	1,140	400
1835	2,040	1,140	900
1836	2,550	1,250	1,300
1837	3,030	1,230	1,800
1838	3,230	1,230	2,000
1839	1,600	1,500	100
1840	1,778 (Census)	1,653	125
1841			350
1842			500
1843			500
1844			50
1845			20
1846			10

[1]Identifies individuals who joined the Church in the latter part of that year.

Accompanying the remarkable growth of population in Kirtland during the 1830s was an increase in the number of businesses, especially those owned and operated by Latter-day Saints. In October 1835 one group of Latter-day Saints advertised their businesses in the *Northern Times,* a newspaper published every Friday evening by Frederick G. Williams. Sarah S. Johnson announced that she had recently opened a new millinery and dress shop a few rods west of the printing office, featuring dresses, bonnets, and other items in harmony with the latest eastern ladies' fashions. Frederick G. Williams, a botanic physician, advertised a list of medicines he had for sale. Others advertised that they had facilities to tan hides and produce leather or to make furniture, and some enumerated goods available in their mercantile stores, from axes and bricks to barrels and tubs.[48] Latter-day Saints also owned a brickyard, a printing office, an ashery, a tannery, a shoe shop, a forge, a pottery firm, a carriage shop, and a steam sawmill. Meanwhile, non-Mormons owned several mercantile firms, a sawmill, a gristmill, a carding mill, and a clothing and shoe factory.[49]

Chapter 9
A Temple on a Hill

O ne of the most imposing early nineteenth century structures in Ohio is a
stately temple located on a plateau overlooking a meandering
branch of the Chagrin River. This building, erected by Saints at
the direction of the Prophet, is a remarkable symbol of faith, determination, and sacrifice. Though few in number and lacking
the wealth of the opulent merchants of the East and the aristo-
cratic planters of the South, the Saints pooled their energies and
resources and within three years, despite harassment from
threatening crowds, built a sacred house of the Lord where they
could study, worship, and obtain a special gift from God.

Less than two years after his arrival in Kirtland, Joseph Smith
received a revelation that commanded the Saints to build a sacred
temple in that community. The revelation, given in December
1832, directed that members of the Church were to organize and
"establish a house, even a house of prayer, a house of fasting, a
house of faith, a house of learning, a house of glory, a house of
order, a house of God."[1] During the ensuing summer, they further
learned that they would receive in the Lord's house an "endowment," an unusual gift or blessing from God. Undoubtedly, some
of them recalled that as early as January 1831, when the Saints
were commanded to gather in Ohio, they were told that there
they would receive an endowment from on high.[2]

The revelation instructing the Saints to build the Kirtland Temple presented major challenges. In addition to the need for architectural plans and materials for the construction of the building, they had to obtain land near the construction site where the laborers could live. Moreover, there was a need for money to purchase land and materials, food, clothing, and shelter.

The problems seem overwhelming when one considers the relative wealth of the membership in Kirtland in the early 1830s as reflected by land and tax records. In the spring of 1833, shortly after the revelation to build the temple, only ten Latter-day Saints were known to have been assessed a property (land) tax or a personal property tax (a tax on cattle, horses, and merchandise). Four of these men were assessed a tax on land (one of them, Isaac Morley, lived in Missouri), and six were assessed a tax on cattle and horses. This taxed property amounted to approximately 189 acres, representing only 1.2 percent of the assessed land in the township. Nearly 184 acres of this land consisted of two Church farms, the Isaac Morley and the former Peter French farms. Four additional acres belonged to Newel K. Whitney and one to Selah Griffin.

Church leaders did not begin paying taxes on the 143-acre Frederick G. Williams farm until 1834. Apparently some of the Saints residing in Kirtland lived on Church farms, and most of them did not own cattle. Except for Newel K. Whitney's assessment on his merchandise, not one of the Saints who were assessed a personal property tax in that year paid a tax on land, and not one of the members who paid a tax on land paid a personal property tax, indicating that the animals belonged to members who did not pay land taxes.[3]

The Latter-day Saints were so poor and so few in number early in 1833 that, according to Benjamin F. Johnson, when construction on the temple began, "there was not a scraper and hardly a plow that could be found among the Saints" to dig the foundation.[4] "Notwithstanding the Church was poor," Joseph Smith observed, "yet our unity, harmony and charity abounded to strengthen us to do the commandments of God."[5]

Securing Land for the Temple

In the spring of 1833, the Saints concentrated on purchasing land where a temple could be built and where workers could erect homes. On March 23, 1833, a committee comprising Joseph Coe, Moses Dailey, and Ezra Thayer was appointed to secure land for the building of a stake of Zion in Kirtland. Thayer reported shortly thereafter that the Peter French farm could be purchased for five thousand dollars. Following the report, Sidney Rigdon ordained Ezra Thayer and Joseph Coe as general agents of the Church to buy this property.[6]

The Peter French farm was situated immediately north of the Frederick G. Williams property and included land in lot 30, a small piece of lot 31, and most of the land in lot 17 with the exception of business property located at the crossroads and the industrial land situated near the river. The farm property was being used for farming and provided excellent lots for homes on the crest of the plateau, below the hill, and near the main businesses and mills of Kirtland. Church leaders were especially interested in the clay deposits located there. A brick kiln had already been built on this property, and it had furnished the bricks for the spacious French home, located south and across the street from the Newel K. Whitney home.[7] Although some Latter-day Saints thought the temple would be built on a lot within the Frederick G. Williams farm, after the area was surveyed members learned that the temple site would actually be located on the western edge of the French farm.[8]

Prior to the purchase of the French farm, Joseph Smith, Newel K. Whitney, Sidney Rigdon, Martin Harris, and Oliver Cowdery (the latter two being in Missouri) had already combined their economic interests and had equal claim to the properties they possessed.[9] On March 15, 1833, Frederick G. Williams was admitted into this united order and was assigned to supervise the manufacture of bricks to be used in building the temple. After John Johnson joined the order, he helped pay the mortgage on this land, and therefore the property belonged to the United Firm.[10] For several months workers tried to make bricks, but Ben-

Utah State Historical Society

The temple as viewed from Kirtland Flats

jamin F. Johnson recalled that the plan to build the temple with brick was abandoned because not far from the temple site was a stone quarry where large rocks were conveniently available.[11]

Although the Saints were faced with the problem of transporting building materials from the flats up a steep hill that became muddy during wet weather, the temple was erected in a choice location on a wooded plateau immediately south of Kirtland Flats. Following its construction, the building looked like a tower overlooking the beautiful Chagrin Valley. Viewed from the flats, it appeared to be perched on top of a hill. From other parts of the community, however, the view toward the temple was downward, for some of the hills, especially to the north and east, were higher than the temple. Whether the temple was viewed from the flats or from the hills, it appeared as a majestic structure.

In the spring of 1833, the Saints investigated purchasing additional land on the flats, but transactions were not completed, probably owing to exorbitant prices. Other landowners were willing to sell on terms acceptable to the Church. Sixteen acres of woodland west of the Elijah Smith land was secured by Newel K. Whitney from Gideon Riggs for $550. From this and other forests, trees were cut, dragged to the river, and then floated to the mill for processing. Eventually a lumber kiln was built to properly dry the wood used in building the temple.

The Church rounded out its holdings at that time by purchasing a local tannery. Sidney Rigdon was given the responsibility of directing this shop, and when the United Firm was dissolved, title to it was conveyed to him. [12]

The Saints Rebuked

Within six months after the Saints had been commanded to erect a house of the Lord, they had purchased the land but had not yet started construction. On June 1, 1833, they were chastized by revelation for not proceeding satisfactorily with the project. "Ye have sinned against me a very grievous sin," the revelation stated, "in that ye have not considered the great commandment in all things, that I have given unto you concerning the building of mine house." They were further told that if they kept the commandments of God, they would have the power necessary to construct this temple. "Let the house be built," the revelation continued, "not after the manner of the world," but "after the manner which I shall show unto three of you, whom ye shall appoint and ordain unto this power." The revelation then gave a general description of the temple. The "inner court" was to be fifty-five feet wide and sixty-five feet long. There were to be two "courts," or assembly halls. The lower court was to be dedicated as a house of worship, and the upper court was to be used as a school for the apostles. [13]

On May 4, 1833, Hyrum Smith, Reynolds Cahoon, and Jared Carter were appointed as a committee to obtain donations for the construction of a school for the elders. Shortly thereafter their responsibilities were increased, for not only was a schoolhouse to be included in the building that housed the printing office, but another school was to be included in the spacious temple. In June the three men were called to direct construction of the temple; on June 6, a conference of high priests voted they were to proceed immediately with this project and to obtain materials, including stone, brick, and lumber.[14]

Construction of the temple began in early June. Joseph Smith, Hyrum Smith, Brigham Young and his brother Lorenzo D. Young, and Reynolds Cahoon rode south in search of a quarry where stone suitable for the temple walls might be secured. They located one about two miles from the temple site and filled Lorenzo Young's wagon with stones to transport back to the temple lot. Fifteen-year-old George A. Smith also helped haul that first load of rocks from the Stannard quarry to the temple site, after which Hyrum Smith and Reynolds Cahoon began digging with their own hands a trench where the foundation was to be laid.[15]

When construction began on the temple, detailed architectural plans were not available, but the Saints had been assured by revelation that God would endow the faithful with the power to accomplish the task. On June 3, a conference of high priests called upon members of the First Presidency, Joseph Smith, Sidney Rigdon, and Frederick G. Williams, to prepare the plans.[16]

Lucy Mack Smith said that her son Joseph asked the brethren to present their views concerning a meetinghouse to accommodate the growing congregation. Some favored constructing a frame building and others suggested a log house. The Prophet reminded the men that they were not building a house for themselves but for God. "Shall we brethren build a house for our God, of logs?" he asked. "No," he replied, "I have a better plan than that. I have a plan of the house of the Lord, given by himself; and you will soon see by this, the difference between our calculations and his idea."[17]

According to Truman O. Angell, one of the supervisors in the building of the temple, the Prophet informed his counselors in the First Presidency, Sidney Rigdon and Frederick G. Williams, that the Lord would show them "the plan or model of the House to be built." The three men knelt in prayer, and the building appeared

Lucy Mack Smith, Joseph Smith's mother

before them in vision. Elder Angell reported that Frederick G. Williams later described this vision in the completed temple and said that the hall where they were then standing coincided precisely with the room he had beheld in the vision. Elder Angell further stated that when someone recommended to Joseph Smith that the seats in the building be rearranged, the Prophet said that the seats were located where he had seen them in vision.[18]

Others verified that the temple was built in harmony with a vision beheld by the Prophet. Heber C. Kimball declared that the "pattern" of the temple "was given in a revelation to Joseph Smith, Jr., Sidney Rigdon, and Frederick G. Williams."[19] George Washington Johnson, an early convert whose mother joined the Church but whose father remained a nonmember after settling in Geauga County, declared that Joseph Smith was shown in vision various details concerning the construction of the temple.[20] Truman Coe, a Presbyterian minister in Kirtland and a critic of the Church, wrote in 1836, "The completion of the temple, according to the pattern shown to Joseph in vision, is a monument of unconquerable zeal."[21] Another who confirmed the vision of the Prophet regarding the building of the Kirtland Temple was Orson Pratt. "The Lord," he said, "gave [the Latter-day Saints] the pattern by vision from heaven, and commanded them to build that house according to that pattern and order; to have the architecture, not in accordance with architecture devised by men, but to have everything constructed in that house according to the heavenly pattern that he by his voice had inspired to his servants."[22]

On July 23, 1833, six weeks after workers started digging the foundation, twenty-four men of the priesthood met on the temple site to lay the cornerstone. In order that there might be twenty-four priesthood holders participating, several men, including Joseph C. Kingsbury and Don Carlos Smith, were ordained shortly before the service. The First Presidency and three other elders commenced the ceremony by laying a stone on the southeast corner. The remaining elders were formed into three groups of six elders each, and each group laid one of the remaining cornerstones.[23]

Throughout the summer and fall of 1833, nearly every able-bodied Latter-day Saint in Kirtland worked on the temple. Only those engaged in missionary service were excused, and many of these elders assisted in this project when they were not preaching in the mission field. Joseph Smith acted as foreman in the stone quarry and frequently worked on the construction project. "Come, brethren, let us go into the stone-quarry and work for the

Front hall of the temple, showing first and second floors

Lord," he would say. After the stone had been cut, it was placed on wagons and hauled to the temple site. "Every Saturday," Heber C. Kimball observed, "we brought out every team to draw stone to the Temple." Hour after hour the men worked in cutting and hauling the stone. Usually in one day they could transport to the temple site sufficient rocks to keep the masons busy for a full week.[24]

The women also assisted in building the Lord's house. Emma Smith was in charge of sewing and cooking for the workers. The sisters, Heber C. Kimball recalled, made stockings, pantaloons, and jackets. "Our wives were continually knitting, spinning and sewing, and in fact, I may say doing all kinds of work! They were just as busy as any of us," he added.[25]

While plans were being prepared for the building of the temple, Church leaders sought individuals who could assist in supervising the work. Lorenzo Young informed the Prophet that he knew a skilled mason in Canada, a recent convert to the Church, who was qualified to assist in building the house of the Lord.

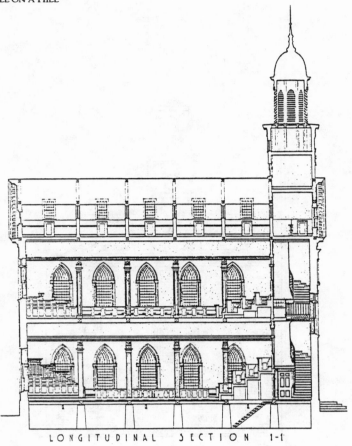

Modern architectural drawing of the Kirtland Temple (1)

Hyrum Smith subsequently wrote to the man, Artemus Millet, requesting that he move to Kirtland and help in the construction project. At that time Millet was employing thirty-six Scotch masons in his own business, but he turned the business over to his family, traveled to Kirtland, and immediately began working on the temple. Later he returned to Canada, settled his business affairs, and assisted his family in emigrating to Kirtland.[26]

Throughout the period of the building of the temple, the Church was in great financial distress. The Saints who gathered in

· F R O N T · E A S T · E L E V A T I O N ·

Modern architectural drawing of the Kirtland Temple (2)

Kirtland were unable to pay for the land they purchased in 1833, and since nearly everyone was working on the temple, funds were needed to sustain the workers. Latter-day Saints living in various parts of North America were asked to contribute to the building fund, and converts who gathered in Kirtland were requested to donate their material wealth. One of the first to contribute to this project was Vienna Jaques. After giving much of her material wealth to the Church in March 1833, she was informed by revelation that others would assist her in her journey to Missouri, and that upon her arrival in Zion, Bishop Partridge would give her "an inheritance."[27]

John Tanner also gave generously to help the Church during this period of financial distress. After migrating to Kirtland, he loaned Joseph Smith money to help pay the debt to Peter French for the temple site. He also contributed about three thousand dollars for supplies for the bishop's storehouse. To make these contributions, it was necessary for this wealthy farmer to sell his property in Bolton, New York, including about twenty-two hundred acres of land, a sawmill, and a gristmill. Throughout his residence in Kirtland, he continued to give until he had sacrificed nearly everything he owned.[28]

The three-member building committee was to supervise the collection of contributions for the temple construction. On June 1, 1833, they issued a circular to the various branches of the Church, requesting that Church officers appoint in every locality someone responsible for securing pledges of contributions, then sending the donations to Kirtland.[29]

When leaders of the Church conducted conferences in various parts of the nation, they asked the Saints to assist in building the Lord's house through their contributions. On February 9, 1834, members of New Portage, Medina County, Ohio, were asked to build a temporary meetinghouse in their community and to send contributions to Kirtland to help build a stake of Zion there.[30] Members of the Quorum of the Twelve were called to missionary service in 1835, and were asked to instruct members at conferences they conducted to send as much money as possible to Kirtland to help build the temple and assist the Saints.[31]

Meanwhile, a number of individuals were also called on missions to help raise money. In 1834, Jared Carter was sent east primarily to secure subscriptions for the house of the Lord, and others were asked to assist him in raising funds for this project.[32] One year later, Phineas Young was called on a mission to Michigan to "collect money for the relief of the building committee in Kirtland."[33] While Joseph Smith was in New York in 1834 enlisting recruits for Zion's Camp, he requested that the Saints not only

The Kirtland Temple

assist their brethren in Missouri, but also lend a helping hand to the Saints in Kirtland. Since the Saints still owed Peter French $2,000, Orson Hyde was to remain in New York until he obtained the money needed "for the relief of the brethren in Kirtland."[34]

Although members in Kirtland possessed little money, they contributed what they could for the building of the temple. One evening while Joseph Smith and Oliver Cowdery were contemplating their financial problems, Joseph prophesied that "in a short time the Lord would arrange His providences in a merciful manner" and send them assistance so that they might be delivered from debt. The two leaders covenanted that if the Lord would prosper them in their business and help them pay their debts, they would give one tenth of their increase to the poor of the Church.[35]

Responding to the plea for additional contributions, on June 18, 1835, the Saints in Kirtland subscribed $950 for the temple project. On June 25, $6,232.50 was added within one hour to the temple subscription. Additional funds were secured on September 23, 1835, when Noah Packard loaned the Church $1,000. Thirteen days later Elder Stevens loaned $600 to Frederick G. Williams and his committee, which action, according to the Prophet, "greatly relieved us of our present difficulties."[36]

Those who labored on the temple were given some economic assistance by the Church. Bishop Whitney, for example, who was in charge of the committee's storehouse, used some of the money contributed to the Church to secure goods that could be given to the workers.[37]

During the fall and winter of 1833-34, mobs threatened to tear down the walls of the temple, and men were posted to protect the walls laid during the day. "Our enemies were raging and threatening destruction upon us," Heber C. Kimball declared. He added that for weeks some men did not remove their working clothes and slept with their rifles in their arms.[38]

That fall and winter, construction of the temple was delayed not only by threats of violence but also by a lack of materials and by the immediate need for a building to house a press and a school. Work began on a structure just west of the temple, with the main floor to serve as an Elders' School or School of the Prophets, and the second floor to house the printing establishment. Though the Saints concentrated for a while on building the printing office in the fall of 1833, some continued working on the temple. Between

March 1833 and February 1834, Orson Pratt was in Kirtland only about two months (and boarded in the Prophet's home), but during that brief time between missionary journeys he managed to work on both Church buildings for about thirty days in November 1833.[39]

On October 1, 1833, Oliver Cowdery left for New York with $800 to purchase a press. He was accompanied by Bishop Newel K. Whitney, who was to secure supplies for the bishop's storehouse.[40] Two months later, on December 18, bearers of the priesthood assembled in the printing office, which was still under construction, to dedicate the newly secured press. Publication of *The Evening and the Morning Star* continued under the editorship of Oliver Cowdery. Among the first publications printed were reprints of the fourteen issues of the paper that had been printed in Missouri between June 1832 and July 1833.[41]

During the summer of 1834, when the weather provided the best conditions for working on the temple, construction practically stopped as Kirtland members prepared to assist the beleaguered Saints in Missouri. They not only devoted their energies to organizing an army, but also collected money, funds that under different circumstances could have been used for building the temple. Moreover, most able-bodied men in Kirtland participated in the long march west, so that between May and September 1834, few laborers were available to work on the Lord's house.[43]

That fall work on the temple progressed rapidly without any further interruptions. According to a notation in Joseph Smith's diary in October 1834, "Great exertions were made to expedite the work of the Lord's House."[44] William Burgess recalled that at that time the walls of the temple stood about four feet above the ground. During the winter of 1834-35, almost every able-bodied member of the Church again united to assist, and the walls rose rapidly.[45]

Since the temple walls were two feet thick and more than sixty feet high, an enormous amount of stone was needed. Most of the sandstone used in the walls was probably secured from the

Stannard quarry (located two miles south of the temple in what is today the Chapin Forest near Highway 306). Some of the larger blocks were carefully tooled, and those placed above the doorways were cut in lengths of up to eight feet.

One of the major challenges facing the builders was the raising of the huge frame, which consisted of "oak beams mortised and tenoned together and secured by wooden pins." The timbers measured ten by fourteen inches in diameter and at least fifty-five feet in length. Eight timbers, which aided in supporting the roof, were placed on stone piers in the basement and were raised so that they stood vertically seventy feet in the eaves.[46]

While some workers were hauling stone to the temple site, others were busy cutting trees in the nearby forests, taking the timber to the mills, and transporting the lumber to the temple site. The roof was made of handsplit cedar shakes. The floors were built with 1⅛-inch walnut boards cut at random widths and lengths. The gables, dormers, window frames, belfry, seats, and pulpits were also constructed of wood.[47]

In harmony with directions provided by leaders of the Church, two large auditoriums were built one above the other, while the third or attic floor was divided into five rooms. A small hall was constructed across the front of the temple, with steep winding stairs, flanked by artistically curved handrails, on the north and south sides of the vestibule. On the front of the temple was the inscription "House of the Lord. Built by the Church of Christ in 1834."

Artemus Millet and Lorenzo Young were given a contract in the amount of one thousand dollars to supervise the plastering of the temple exterior. This work was accomplished between November 2, 1835, and January 8, 1836. The stucco used on the outside walls was composed of crushed limestone mixed with clay and bluish river sand. Dishes and glassware were pulverized and mixed with the stucco so that the bluish-tinted walls glistened in the light of the sun.[48]

While the outside walls were being completed, Jacob Bump, who had received a contract for $1,500, was directing the plaster-

Upper auditorium of the temple

ing of the interior. Although most plasterers did not work during winter, Bump would build fires on the earthen floor of the basement to heat the building so that workers could work during the coldest months of the year.[49] Workers plastered all the sidewalks and ceilings, including the ceiling on the attic floor. "A barrel vault ceiling, presumably the work of Jacob Bump, showed a foundation which was constructed not of lath, but of boards an inch or so thick set on edge in the form of the vault."[50]

Under the direction of Brigham Young, a skilled painter, workers began putting the finishing touches on the building in February 1836, using primarily a pristine white paint. On February 22 he stopped attending the Hebrew class in order to devote all his energies to painting and finishing the temple's interior. He continued working full-time on the temple until March 27, when the building was sufficiently finished to be dedicated.[51]

Early in 1836, female members of the Church, under the direction of the Prophet's father, Joseph Smith, Sr., made carpets and curtains for the temple.[52] The curtains were placed on rollers so that they could be lowered from the ceiling by ropes. When lowered, they divided the main hall into either two or four rooms (depending on the number of curtains lowered), thereby enabling members to hold separate meetings simultaneously in this one spacious hall. Curtains were also placed near the ceilings above the pulpits so that they could be lowered adjacent to the pulpits and create an atmosphere of privacy at either end of the hall.[53]

In many respects, the Kirtland Temple resembled other buildings of that period, particularly some of the Congregational churches erected in New England and the Western Reserve. The rectangular building had a gabled roof, dominated by a bell tower that rose to a height of 120 feet. The outside stucco walls were painted with lines, giving the appearance of bricks. Two massive front doors, weighing about three hundred pounds each, were nine feet six inches high, five feet two inches wide, and two inches thick. Five steps led up to the doors, which opened into a ten-foot wide foyer. On the main floor, four candelabra hung by chains from the ceiling, with twelve candlestick holders in each light fixture.

Although it was similar in appearance to many other houses of worship built in the early republic, the Kirtland Temple was a unique structure.[54] Like the temple of King Solomon, it was built in compliance with the dimensions given by revelation: "Verily I say unto you, that it shall be built fifty-five by sixty-five feet in the width thereof and in length thereof, in the inner court. And there shall be a lower court and a higher court, according to the pattern which shall be given unto you hereafter."[55]

The building also blended various forms of architectural styles into one harmonious pattern. Colonial-styled windows behind the pulpits in the east and west ends of the two main halls blended with the general features of the building, while the five Gothic windows built on the two sides of the building, as well as the two erected at the west end of the temple, complemented the unusual columns erected in the lower hall. The lower auditorium was decorated with unusual carved columns and arches. Ionic fluted col-

*Lower auditorium of the temple. Beginning at top of west tier, letters
engraved on pulpits and explanations generally given of their meanings are:
M. P. C.—Melchizedek Presiding Council (presidency of the Church, which
served as presidency of the Kirtland stake); P. M. H.—Presiding
Melchizedek High Priesthood (Quorum of the Twelve or stake high
council); M. H. P.—Melchizedek High Priesthood (representing the high
priests quorum); P. E. M.—Presiding Elder Melchizedek (representing the
elders quorum). Beginning at top of east tier: B. P. A.—Bishop Presiding
[over] Aaronic [Priesthood]; P. A. P.—Presiding Aaronic Priest;
P. T. A.—Presiding Teacher Aaronic; P. D. A.—Presiding
Deacon Aaronic.* (Source: Clarence L. Fields, "History of the
Kirtland Temple," p. 28; *Times and Seasons* 6 (June 1833): 786-87;
Henry Howe, *Historical Collections of Ohio*, p. 282.)

umns pointed to delicately carved arches that contained various
patterns, including a Grecian egg-and-dart design cut into the
wooden arch above the west window. Blossoms and a trailing vine
also enriched the arches, and a design of leaves and bars decorated
the capitals of the columns that rose through the main floor of the
temple and stretched to the eaves of the building.[56]

Four tiers of pulpits, arranged like a flight of stairs, were built on the east and the west ends of the two main halls of the temple. A table leaf in the shape of a yoke was attached to the pulpits on the lower tiers and could be raised for the convenience of administering the sacrament. The other three tiers of pulpits at each end of the temple were elevated one above another. Within each tier were three pulpits, each with a seat behind it—one for the presiding officer and the other two for his counselors. The two sets of pulpits represented the two priesthoods of the Church, the Aaronic and Melchizedek, and the initials of various officers were embossed in gold letters on each pulpit. The first or highest tier of pulpits on the west side of the building was occupied by the First Presidency, the next by the president of the high priests and his two counselors, the third by the high priests, and the fourth by the president of the elders and his two counselors. The highest tier of pulpits on the east end of the temple was occupied by the bishop of the Church and his two counselors, the next by the president of the priests and his counselors, the third by the president of the teachers and his counselors, and the fourth by the president of the deacons and his two counselors.[57] Moveable benches enabled the congregation to face either end of the building.

The second story was designed for instruction and was thus constructed differently in a few respects from the first floor. Tables were available for use by students, and the pulpits on this floor were less decorative than those on the first floor.

One of the most beautiful features in the temple was found behind the pulpits at the east end of the hall on the second floor. A fan-shaped window was built above three rectangular windows, with a carving of an Egyptian water vine inserted above the window. The anthemion, a Greek flower, is the keystone design of the carving. The combined effect of the windows and carving has led to its being identified as "The Window Beautiful."

Less than three years after construction of the Kirtland Temple began, the Saints prepared to dedicate their temple as a House of the Lord. By sacrificing their time, talents, and material wealth, they had built, at a cost of from $40,000 to $60,000, the first temple in the dispensation of the fulness of times.[58]

Chapter 10

The Crisis
in Missouri

In the middle of August, 1833, Oliver Cowdery arrived in Kirtland from western Missouri with news of shocking events there. In July, settlers in the Independence area had banded together and demanded that the Latter-day Saints leave Jackson County. This body was not like the ordinary lawless band that ruthlessly raided frontier settlements, for it included prominent citizens, such as a county clerk, an Indian agent, a postmaster, a lawyer, a constable and deputy constable, two justices of the peace, and two merchants.[1]

To justify their unusual demands, non-Mormons in Jackson County prepared a long list of grievances. Evidence that there was a cultural clash between the Mormons, who had come to Jackson County primarily from northern states, and other Missourians, who had come primarily from southern states, was expressed in the sentiment that the Mormons were easterners, meaning Yankees. Although many Missourians were indifferent toward organized religion, the beliefs of the Saints also fell under attack. They were denounced for believing in visions, revelations, and modern-day miracles similar to those performed by apostles and prophets of old. They were condemned not only for teaching the reality of the restoration, but also because religion was such an all-pervasive force in their lives. Moreover, they were accused of being lazy, vicious, and poor, and of tampering with the slaves of the Missourians. Non-Mormons further complained that the Latter-day Saints believed and taught that Jackson County had been given to them by the Lord.[2]

The concept that Zion would be built by the pure in heart prior to the Second Coming of Christ was incorrectly amplified to the view that Mormons were planning on taking control of all the land and businesses in Jackson County. Were they not growing at an alarming rate? Had they not increased to about one thousand members in just two years in a county that reported three thousand citizens in 1830? And were they not pooling their property, buying goods from a Mormon store, and using the profits from their economic enterprise to purchase additional lands for the constant influx of new immigrants? Were they not thus becoming an economic and political threat? These observations, combined with vicious rumors, persuaded some of the Missourians that Mormons were ultimately planning to expel from Jackson County all who did not embrace their faith.[3]

After listing their grievances, the settlers enunciated their demands. In a written manifesto they specified that no more Mormons were to settle in Jackson County. They further demanded that Latter-day Saints living in Jackson County pledge to sell their property and leave the county immediately. The editor of the *Evening and the Morning Star* must close his office and discontinue printing works related to the Church, and stores and shops owned by Church members must close immediately.[4]

On July 20, a committee of twelve, representing hundreds of Jackson County citizens, delivered the manifesto to six Latter-day Saint leaders in Missouri. The Saints requested three months to consider the orders, since their prophet resided in Ohio, and any decisions should come from him. Their request for sufficient time to consider the demands was denied. They then asked for ten days to evaluate the decree. Again their request was denied. The Missourians granted the Saints only a few minutes to consider and accept their terms.[5]

When the Missourians failed to persuade the Saints to accept the terms outlined in the manifesto, they returned to the courthouse, where a crowd of about five hundred awaited the response.

Angered by the Saints' refusal to accept their demands, the crowd stormed to the Church-owned printing office at the home of William W. Phelps. There they grabbed his furniture and tossed it into the yard, seized the press and threw it out the window, destroyed the type, burned papers and documents, and finally destroyed the brick home. Next they vented their fury on the mercantile establishment of Gilbert and Whitney, forcing their way into the store and demolishing the merchandise. Then they seized Edward Partridge and Charles Allen, dragged them to the public square, and demanded of them a repudiation of the Book of Mormon. When the two men refused to renounce their faith, the angry mob stripped them of their clothes and smeared their bodies with burning tar, sprinkled with feathers.[6]

Hostilities were renewed on July 23 when a mob compelled a number of Latter-day Saint leaders to assemble in the public square and tried to force them to sign an agreement to leave the county. One group of Saints must leave before January 1 and the other before the following April, they were told. John Corrill and Sidney Gilbert could remain in Jackson County temporarily to sell the property of those who had been unable to dispose of their land prior to the expulsion from the area.

The agreement to emigrate was signed by some of the Church members, resulting in a temporary calm in Jackson County. This suspension of hostilities provided the Saints with the time they needed to notify Joseph Smith of conditions in Missouri and to await instructions from Kirtland.[7]

Reactions in Ohio to the Violence in Missouri

When news of the attacks on the Saints in Jackson County became known in Ohio, both members and nonmembers denounced the atrocities. The most notorious anti-Mormon newspaper in Ohio, the *Painesville Telegraph*, summarized the news Oliver Cowdery had brought back, mentioning the destruction of the Latter-day Saint press, the tarring of Bishop Partridge, who had formerly resided in Painesville, and the promise to leave the county that the Saints had been forced to make under duress. The *Telegraph* stated that although the reports were presumably "mag-

nified and exaggerated," the citizens of Jackson County had
brought disgrace upon themselves by interfering with the legal
rights of their neighbors.[8]

Several other Ohio newspapers also condemned the Missourians. The *Cleveland Herald* reported that the circumstances were
to be regretted in part because groups sometimes became stronger
when they were subjected to persecution.[9] The *Ohio Argus*, published in Lebanon, reported that the "outrages" seemed to be "un-
congenial with the character of free institutions." This paper argued that "to say . . . that any class of free white citizens shall be
deprived of 'privileges and immunities' enjoyed by other citizens—To 'prohibit the free exercise' of religion and 'abridge the
freedom of speech and of the press' in this manner, is exercising a
prerogative altogether repugnant to the constitution and laws of
our country and contrary to the laws of civilized society." The article denounced the actions of the Missourians on the basis that
America was heralded as a land of liberty. "The great characteristic of the citizens of our free country should be universal tolera-
tion," the report continued, adding that although "Mormons may
have been troublesome and their doctrines may be obnoxious,"
the Missourians were still not justified in resorting to violent
measures. Finally, the paper recommended that if the Mormons
had participated in crimes in Missouri, the citizens of Jackson
County should seek legal means of redress rather than resorting to
the "outrages" they had committed.[10]

Supported by a general feeling in Ohio that the rights of the
Saints in Missouri had been violated, Church leaders in Kirtland
agreed that their fellow members should not vacate their lands in
Zion. Instructions were sent to the Missouri Saints that unless
they had specifically signed a document promising they would
leave, they should not emigrate nor should they sell their property
in Jackson County. They were also told to seek legal redress for all
crimes committed against them.[11]

Expulsion of the Saints in Missouri

While the Saints in Kirtland were waiting for further news
from Missouri, Orson Hyde and John Gould arrived with the

startling report that the Saints in Jackson County had been forced
to leave their homes and were fleeing across the Missouri River,
wandering in an unknown wilderness.[12] Elder Hyde vividly described some of the tragic events that led to the expulsion.

On Thursday, October 31, 1833, he reported, when the Missourians were convinced that the Mormons were not going to
leave in accordance with the terms of the manifesto, some forty or
fifty men attacked several homes of Latter-day Saints approximately ten miles west of Independence near the banks of the Big
Blue River, destroying about a dozen homes, then seizing two
Church members and beating them severely with stones and
clubs.[13]

Elder Hyde added that the following day, a mob broke into the
Gilbert and Whitney store in Independence and scattered the
merchandise in the street, while others destroyed Sidney Gilbert's
brick home and broke windows and tore down doors in many
homes of the Latter-day Saints. When Gilbert seized one of the
men who had been destroying his property and took him before a
local official, the man was immediately acquitted, while Gilbert
was unjustly accused of illegally holding him prisoner.

According to Elder Hyde's report, another series of atrocities
occurred on Saturday and Monday nights (November 2 and 4)
among the settlements near the Big Blue River. On Saturday, a
mob returned to that area to continue their ravages. They fired
five or six shots toward the Saints, who had armed themselves,
and members of the Church returned the fire and wounded one of
the mobsters. Although the mob withdrew in confusion, on Monday a crowd of two to three hundred gathered again in Independence and marched toward outlying settlements near the Big Blue
River. That night, in another encounter between the Mormons
and the Missourians, two or three mobsters were killed, several
were wounded, and about four Latter-day Saints were wounded.[14]

On Tuesday, November 6, Elder Hyde reported, as some
three hundred Missourians prepared to renew their hostilities
against the Saints, members of the Church agreed to vacate their
homes in Jackson County. But as they began their exodus, the
mobsters struck again. The last word he heard before he left the

region was that Mormon homes were being plundered, their crops were being ruined, and the Saints were fleeing for their lives, many of them penniless and without sufficient food, clothing, blankets, and other provisions.[15]

Elder Hyde's report concluded with the observation that he had read a report in a non-Mormon publication shortly after the skirmishes, and that the writer accused the Mormons of being the aggressors, arguing that they had fired the first shot. Such an accusation, Elder Hyde insisted, was deceptive misrepresentation, for he himself had personally observed the armed mob fire five or six times before the Saints returned fire.[16]

When they learned of the tragedy in Jackson County, the Kirtland Saints were overwhelmed with grief. Lucy Mack Smith said that when her son Joseph heard the news, "he burst into tears and sobbed aloud, 'Oh my brethren! my brethren. . . . Would that I had been with you, to have shared your fate. Oh my God, what shall I do in such a trial as this!'"[17]

Oliver Cowdery was deeply concerned about the welfare of his wife, Elizabeth, as well as other members of the Church in Missouri. He did not know if Elizabeth had been killed or beaten; and if she was alive, he did not know where she might have fled. In anguish, he wrote to her, "God only knows the feelings of my heart as I address a few lines to you." He told her that he did not know where to send the letter, and that he wished that she were with him in Ohio. "My prayers ascend daily and hourly to God that you and I may be spared, and yet enjoy each other's society, in this life, in peace." Then, expressing his continued trust in the Lord amid all this adversity, he advised her, "O be faithful to the Lord."[18]

The fears and concerns of the Saints in Ohio for their friends and loved ones in Missouri were not immediately alleviated. On December 5 a letter arrived from one of the exiled Saints, William W. Phelps, describing the exodus from Jackson County and including information not previously related by Orson Hyde. He reported that on Tuesday, November 5, after a mob of about three hundred men had gathered and threatened the Saints, the Church members agreed to leave the county. They were also forced to surrender their arms, leaving them defenseless. Then, Elder Phelps continued, "a party of the mob . . . began to whip, and even murder" members of the Church as they began the exodus from Jackson County. [19] Although this letter substantiated Orson Hyde's report, it did not identify those who had been killed nor did it describe the status of the refugees. Details concerning the expulsion were still unknown, leaving the Kirtland Saints with much anxiety and many unanswered questions.

Responding to the Phelps letter, Joseph Smith wrote to Edward Partridge, William W. Phelps, and John Whitmer in Missouri and noted that since he had received conflicting and unsubstantiated accounts of the tragedy there, it was difficult to advise them. "We can only say," he said, "that the destinies of all people are in the hands of a just God." He then told them to "collect every particular, concerning the mob, from the beginning" and to send to Kirtland a "correct statement of facts, as they occurred," in order that Church officials in Ohio could present to the public "correct information on the subject." He further requested that the leaders in Missouri apprise the Kirtland Saints of the conditions under which the refugees were living, including "their means of sustenance." He advised the exiled Saints not to retaliate against their aggressors by renewing hostilities. Instead of fighting, they were to try to purchase land in Clay County and to live there during the emergency. "It is your privilege," he suggested, "to use every lawful means in your power to seek redress for your grievances from your enemies, and prosecute them to the extent of the law." Although the Prophet desired to send monetary help to the oppressed Saints in Missouri, he concluded that members of the Church in Ohio could not at that time do so, for they were "deeply in debt" and did not know the means by which they could extricate themselves. [20]

The first news from Missouri that brought some relief to the troubled minds of the members in Kirtland arrived on December 10. In a letter mailed from Liberty, Missouri, on November 19, Edward Partridge, John Corrill, and William W. Phelps wrote that they knew of only one Latter-day Saint, Andrew Barber, who had been killed during the mobbing in Jackson County, and one other member, Philo Dibble, who had been seriously wounded.[21]

Upon learning there had not been a mass slaughter of the Saints in Missouri, Joseph Smith immediately prepared another letter to the members there. "O brethren, let us be thankful," he wrote, "that it is as well with us as it is, and we are yet alive." Nevertheless, he lamented, word of the sufferings of the Saints in Missouri "awakens every sympathy of our hearts; it weighs us down; we cannot refrain from tears." Again he asked the Saints to seek redress through legal channels and instructed William W. Phelps to write a reliable history of their persecution in Jackson County. "We must be wise as serpents," the Prophet admonished, "and harmless as doves."[22]

Although Joseph Smith admitted in his letter of December 10 that he did not know why God had suffered so great a calamity to strike Zion, on the sixteenth of that month he received a revelation that partly explained the reasons the Lord did not intervene and assist the Saints during the crisis in Missouri. This revelation informed the Saints that the Lord "suffered the affliction to come upon them . . . in consequence of their transgressions." Some of the failings of the Saints were then identified: "Behold, I say unto you, there were jarrings, and contentions, and envyings, and strifes, and lustful and covetous desires among them; therefore by these things they polluted their inheritances." Since the afflicted Saints "were slow to hearken unto the voice of the Lord," the revelation continued, the Lord was "slow to hearken unto their prayers, to answer them in the day of their trouble. In the day of their peace they esteemed lightly [his] counsel; but, in the day of their trouble, of necessity they feel after [him]."[23] Church members also learned from the revelation that even though the Saints had been driven from Jackson County and had been scattered abroad, the location of Zion had not been changed. They were instructed to settle in other areas, but they were also told that eventually the "pure in heart" would return and establish Zion in Jackson County.[24]

One year before Joseph Smith recorded this revelation, he

had written to the members in Zion and warned them not to pollute their inheritance. "If Zion will not purify herself," he predicted, the Lord "will seek another people; . . . they who will not hear His voice must expect to feel His wrath. Let me say unto you," the Prophet continued,

> seek to purify yourselves, and also all the inhabitants of Zion, lest the Lord's anger be kindled to fierceness. Repent, repent, is the voice of God to Zion; and strange as it may appear, yet it is true, mankind will persist in self-justification until all their iniquity is exposed, and their character past being redeemed. . . .
>
> Our hearts are greatly grieved at the spirit which is breathed both in your [William W. Phelps's] letter and that of Brother Gilbert's, the very spirit which is wasting the strength of Zion like a pestilence; and if it is not detected and driven from you, it will ripen Zion for the threatened judgments of God.

In conclusion, he reminded the Saints that "God sees the secret springs of human action, and knows the hearts of all living."[25]

Confirmation of the Earlier Reports

As Church members in Ohio continued to gather information concerning the expulsion of the Saints from Jackson County, they learned that while the reports of Orson Hyde and William W. Phelps contained some errors, their general descriptions of the oppression that had occurred in Jackson County were confirmed. They learned that on Thursday, October 31, about ten homes in the Whitmer settlement west of the Big Blue River had been demolished by a mob of some forty or fifty persons and that border ruffians had brutally whipped several Latter-day Saints. The new reports also confirmed the mobbings in Independence on Friday, November 1, when insurgents stoned houses, broke windows, and tore down doors of many Latter-day Saint homes and partly demolished the Gilbert and Whitney store. When one of the mobsters had been taken before the justice of the peace, Samuel Weston, he was immediately released. Since local officials had refused to protect the Saints, the members in Kirtland were convinced that Elder Hyde was correct when he said that Saints in Zion had armed themselves to defend their lives and property.[26]

The Kirtland Saints were also able eventually to reconstruct events that had occurred on November 4, 5, and 6. On Monday, November 4, after a hostile group had captured a Mormon ferry on the Big Blue River, Missourians rode to the Wilson store about one mile away and began intimidating women and children. At sunset, armed Saints encountered the ruffians and a pitched battle ensued. The mob fled with the Latter-day Saints in rapid pursuit. In this battle, two non-Mormon Missourians were killed, one Latter-day Saint, Andrew Barber, died, and four members were wounded: Henry A. Cleveland, Jacob Whitmer, William Whitney, and Philo Dibble. A surgeon told Elder Dibble that he would not survive, but after Newel Knight performed a faith-healing ordinance on his behalf, his body discharged a ball and buckshot and the pain suddenly left. Although he recovered, he was crippled for the remainder of his life.[27]

Following the battle of November 4, Mormons were accused of being the aggressors in that skirmish, and some of the men who had routed the mob near the Blue River were accused of murder. A rumor was circulated that Latter-day Saints were attacking non-Mormons, while another story said the Saints planned to join forces with Indians to drive all non-Mormons from Jackson County. When a militia arrived in the area, supposedly to establish and maintain peace, the commanding officer, Colonel Thomas Pitcher (who was later accused of being one of the mobsters), commanded the Saints to relinquish their guns and leave the state. The Saints assumed that the militia would also seize the arms of their enemies and protect them as they emigrated from the county.[28] But the next day, armed mobocrats attacked defenseless Saints in many sections of Jackson County, and hundreds were forced to flee from their homes. The disorganized exodus continued on November 7. Men, women, and children fled in every direction; husbands were separated from their wives and children from their parents, as the Missouri River was lined on both sides with destitute emigrants. While rain descended in torrents, the refugees clustered in tents and around fires or tried to rest on the rain-soaked earth. Some members escaped with their household goods, while others lost nearly everything they owned. Though only one Latter-day Saint had been killed by mobsters, others were beaten and molested by the ruthless assailants.[29]

Disturbing news continued to flow to Ohio from western Missouri in 1834. Philo Dibble reported that all his household furniture, hogs, cows, and crops had been destroyed or stolen, and he failed to recover any of these possessions.[30] Parley P. Pratt described how all of his provisions for the winter were stolen or destroyed, some of the grain he had left in his fields was harvested by his enemies, his home was burned to the ground, and his fruit trees and other improvements were ruined. He reported that many other Saints in Jackson County experienced similar losses and that the bandits boasted they had burned 203 homes belonging to members of the Church.[31]

As Latter-day Saints in Kirtland pieced together information about the tragic expulsion of their compatriots in Jackson County, they also attempted to learn what action those in Missouri were taking to receive recompense for the crimes committed and what steps were being taken for them to return eventually to their homes in Jackson County. In a letter dated December 15, 1833, William W. Phelps notified the Prophet that Missouri Governor Daniel Dunklin had been informed about the plight of the Saints and had indicated that he intended to conduct a court of inquiry. Until the Saints secured protection, however, they felt they could not attend this hearing, Elder Phelps added, for if they returned, they faced death at the hands of the mob. A militia in the upper counties was ready to move upon the order of the governor; however, Elder Phelps concluded, "The Governor is willing to restore us, but as the constitution gives him no power to guard us . . . we are not willing to go."[32]

In a letter written in December to Oliver Cowdery and published in Kirtland in the January issue of the *Evening and the Morning Star*, John Corrill, a counselor to Bishop Edward Partridge, reported that the governor had manifested a willingness to restore the Mormons to their lands if they requested such help, but such assistance would be "of little use unless he could leave a force there to protect us." The mob has sworn that "three months shall not pass before they will drive us [out] again," he noted, adding that permanent protection could not be provided unless the governor secured such authorization from the state legislature, which would require the calling of a special session of that body, or unless the president of the United States ordered an army into the area. John Corrill also stated that he did not believe a grand jury could resolve the problems that afflicted the Missouri Saints. An impartial grand jury could probably not be formed, he surmised, and even if such a body were created and the insurgents convicted and imprisoned, others would undoubtedly tear down the jails and liberate them. He concluded his lengthy treatise with a persuasive recommendation: The Latter-day Saints could return to their homes if they were "organized into independent companies" and were "armed with power and liberty" to defend themselves. To accomplish this objective, he advised that the numerical strength of the Saints be increased. The enemy was twice as numerous as those whom they expelled, and if the Saints could not effectively protect themselves after returning to their homes, their return would merely lay the "foundation for another scene of murder and bloodshed."[33]

This letter and similar ones convinced members of the Church in Kirtland that Governor Dunklin would probably help the Saints return to their lands from which they had been driven. "Intelligence from the west informs us that there was a prospect that the governor of Missouri was about to reinstate the brethren upon their lands," Oliver Cowdery wrote on January 7, 1834.[34] Six days later, Lyman Cowdery wrote that he had been "informed that the governor of that state [had] offered to reinstate" the Mormons on their lands and had issued a proclamation to call out three hundred men from adjoining counties in order that a court of inquiry could be conducted. Although Lyman apparently believed this account, he admitted the report had not been confirmed.[35]

A Plan of Action Evolves

When Parley P. Pratt and Lyman Wight arrived in Kirtland on February 22, 1834, members of the Church there learned that no definite action had yet been taken by Governor Dunklin. Two days later, the recently organized high council assembled in Joseph Smith's home along with other bearers of the priesthood to listen to the reports of these men and consider the requests of the Missouri Saints for help.[36] As they reviewed the reports, they apparently recognized that an impartial court of inquiry could not be conducted at that time in Jackson County, thereby hindering an attempt to insure reconciliation by legal channels. For three months no progress had been made toward securing protection for the Saints if they returned to their lands, they concluded, so unless an army of the Saints was sent to Missouri to provide the necessary protection, within a brief period the members in Missouri would again be driven from their homes.[37] Thus the leaders in Kirtland realized that they had a responsibility to assist their afflicted brethren. In the revelation that had identified the reasons the Lord was slow to hearken to the prayers of the Saints, a parable described how a nobleman's vineyard, which had not been sufficiently protected, was invaded by an enemy, and the nobleman's servants subsequently fled. The nobleman, after rebuking his servants for failing to comply with all his instructions, commanded one of his men to gather the remainder of the servants, to take "all the strength" of his house, which consisted of his warriors, and to then redeem his vineyard.[38]

After hearing the reports of Elders Pratt and Wight, Joseph Smith arose and announced that he was going to Zion to assist in its redemption. He then requested the council to approve his decision, and the priesthood bearers sanctioned the resolution without a dissenting vote. When he called for recruits to travel with him, about thirty or forty men immediately volunteered. The elders considered whether they should follow a land route or travel primarily on canal barges and river boats, and they determined to travel by land. They also unanimously agreed that Joseph Smith should serve as the "commander-in-chief of the armies of Israel," an army that was to be called "Zion's Camp."[39]

Chapter 11

Zion's Camp Marches West

On February 24, 1834, the same day members of the Church in Kirtland decided to send an army west to assist the Saints in Missouri, Joseph Smith received a revelation concerning the recruitment and size of this army. Eight men were called by revelation to gather young and middle-aged male members and also to raise money to help the oppressed members in Missouri. One of these elders, Joseph Smith, was compared in the revelation to the servant who had been instructed by the lord of the vineyard to gather the strength of his house for the recovery of his lands. Another missionary, Sidney Rigdon, was specifically commanded to inform members in the east to keep the commandments relating to the restoration and redemption of Zion. Two other missionaries, Parley P. Pratt and Lyman Wight, were told not to return to Missouri until an acceptable army had been organized.[1]

By revelation, members of the Church also learned what the Lord considered a satisfactory force. The army ideally was to consist of five hundred volunteers; if five hundred men could not be recruited, an army of three hundred was to be organized; and if three hundred could not be found, then an army of at least one hundred was to be formed. The revelation further instructed the Saints to organize into companies of tens, twenties, fifties, and one hundreds.[2]

While the Saints were receiving specific instructions by revelation concerning the organization of Zion's Camp, they were also
warned that the "redemption of Zion" would be delayed if the
Saints continued to "pollute their inheritance." Though members
in the East were to be granted an opportunity to assist the exiles in
the West, the successful completion of this mission was predi-
cated upon their living in harmony with the commandments of
the Lord. The revelation further specified that Zion would not be
redeemed until after much tribulation, at which time the Lord
would manifest his power. "I say unto you," the revelation read,
"Mine angels shall go up before you, and also my presence, and in
time ye shall possess the goodly land."[3]

Organizing the Army of Israel

For two and a half months, leaders of the Church recruited
men in the East to march in Zion's Camp and concurrently
gathered contributions of money and goods to help destitute
members in Missouri. In the latter part of February the eight missionaries called by revelation left Kirtland and headed east.
Traveling two by two, they followed different routes, "visiting the
churches and instructing the people." On March 13 Orson Pratt
and Orson Hyde held a meeting in New York with members of the
China branch and informed them of the "necessity of obeying the
parable in the revelations." According to Elder Pratt, three or
four young to middle-aged men agreed that if they could arrange
their business affairs, they would join this army.[4] Joseph Holbrook
recorded in his journal that the missionaries instructed the volunteers to be in Kirtland no later than May 1. He sold his property in
New York for what he considered as one-third of its real value;
then he, his brother Chandler, and Solomon Angel, with their
families, left New York in March so that the three men could participate in the journey of Zion's Camp.[5]

On March 17, a conference was held at Alva Beaman's home
in Avon, Livingston County, New York, with six of the eight missionaries present. While preaching to members in New York,
Joseph Smith talked about the expedition that was being organized and the anticipated results of this action. "The object of

the Conference," he later wrote, "was to obtain young and middle-aged men to go and assist in the redemption of Zion, according to the commandment; and for the Church to gather up their riches, and send them to purchase lands according to the commandment of the Lord."[6]

After seeking recruits and contributions in central New York, the missionaries separated and continued preaching in different regions. Joseph Smith, Sidney Rigdon, and Lyman Wight traveled together as they returned to Kirtland, while Orson Pratt and John Murdock served as missionary companions, preaching along the way back to the Western Reserve. Accompanied by Henry Brown, Parley P. Pratt, who had traveled east with Joseph Smith, visited members of the Church in the Black River country of New York, where he continued recruiting, raising money, and preaching the gospel.[7] During this part of his mission Elder Pratt met Wilford Woodruff for the first time and told the young convert it was his duty to prepare to travel to Zion. Like many other volunteers, Wilford Woodruff settled his business affairs, said farewell to relatives in Richland, and traveled by wagon to Kirtland, arriving there on April 25.[8]

Although the initial request for volunteers was successful, Joseph Smith was not pleased with the response to the plea for help in redeeming Zion. In a letter dated April 7, 1834, and sent by the First Presidency to Orson Hyde, who had continued preaching in New York after the presidency had returned to Kirtland, the Prophet expressed his deep disappointment. "The fact is, unless we can obtain help," he lamented, "I myself cannot go to Zion, and if I do not go, it will be impossible to get my brethren in Kirtland, any of them, to go." He then suggested an economic incentive that might be coupled with a humanitarian motive to encourage the Saints to support the program. He suggested that the brethren in the East could "better themselves" by obtaining land in Missouri for "one dollar and one quarter per acre"; and by responding to this call, they could help the Missouri Saints "stand against that wicked mob." The Prophet also issued another warning to members of the Church: "Unless they do the will of God," he prophesied, "God will not help them. . . . If this

Church, which is essaying to be the Church of Christ will not help us, . . . God . . . shall prevent them from ever obtaining a place of refuge, or an inheritance upon the land of Zion."[9]

During the initial phase of recruiting, the missionaries had sought help from the Missouri Saints in eastern areas where the largest number of Latter-day Saints lived: Ohio, New York, and Pennsylvania, and eventually New England. While some of them continued to labor outside Ohio, throughout the month of April the First Presidency concentrated on efforts in northeastern Ohio. On April 17, Sidney Rigdon preached to Church members in Kirtland, urging them to continue supporting the temple project and at the same time help the distressed members in Missouri. Following these remarks, Joseph Smith asked the Kirtland Saints to contribute all they could for the deliverance of Zion, and they responded with contributions amounting to $29.68. A few days later, while presiding at a conference in Norton, Medina County, Ohio, the Prophet again asked members to sacrifice, and donations totaled $66.37 for the "benefit of the scattered brethren in Zion," and a few additional men volunteered to march to Zion.[10]

Although most of the Kirtland Saints who participated in the march to Zion enlisted on the day the Prophet announced his decision to travel to Missouri, a few others volunteered during the two and a half months of ardent recruiting. When the initial call came, Joseph Young was engaged in a short-term mission; upon his return to Kirtland, he was encouraged by Brigham Young to enlist. Having recently married and having already served in the mission field, he hesitated to accept the new assignment. Shortly thereafter, he and his brother Brigham discussed the subject with Joseph Smith. "I want you to go with us," the Prophet told Joseph. When Brigham interrupted and said that his brother had not yet decided to join those who were marching west, Joseph Smith said, "Brother Brigham and brother Joseph if you will go with me in the camp to Missouri and keep my counsel, I promise you, in the name of the Almighty, that I will lead you there and back again, and not a hair of your heads shall be harmed." As a result of this promise, Joseph Young agreed to participate in the march to Zion and, according to Brigham Young, the three men clasped hands as a sign of confirming this covenant.[11]

Some of the elders sought recruits for Zion's Camp in Michigan, Indiana, and Illinois. On April 21, Hyrum Smith and Lyman Wight left Kirtland and followed a northern route westward, with instructions to lead those who joined them to a designated place in eastern Missouri. Traveling by wagon, they visited branches of the Church in northern Ohio, Michigan, and Illinois, and contacted members living in many settlements of the Old Northwest. About sixteen men in the Pontiac (Michigan) Branch volunteered to join the march to Zion, and three of them took their wives with them. Since their wagons were filled, these pioneers walked most of the way. As they continued west, a few other recruits, including Charles C. Rich, joined them. After crossing the Mississippi at Quincy, Illinois, this company of Zion's Camp, known as Hyrum's division, traveled to the Salt River, where they joined the much larger company directed by Joseph Smith.[12]

Preparations in Kirtland

Though Joseph Smith was disappointed because some members did not support the call to help the beleaguered Saints in Zion, he must have been pleased with the early response of the Kirtland Saints. Nearly every able-bodied priesthood holder in that community volunteered to march to Zion. Only a few elders, including Oliver Cowdery and Sidney Rigdon, were left behind; these men were to supervise the construction of the temple and direct the affairs of the Church in Kirtland.[13]

The call to join Zion's Camp was issued six days after Brigham Young married Mary Ann Angell; yet he was one of the first to enlist. Before answering the Prophet's call, the new couple had been busy securing a house, planting a garden, and establishing a home for Brigham's two daughters, who, following the death of his first wife, had been cared for by Vilate Kimball, wife of Heber C. Kimball. Now Mary Ann assumed these responsibilities and began preparing for the absence of her husband.[14]

Since many of the men had to leave their families with little or no money and there would be no income while they were away, members planted gardens so the women and children could harvest corn and other crops during the army's absence. They were also busy gathering supplies for the army and for the Saints in Missouri, including clothing, bedding, food, and arms, as well as teams to transport the supplies to Missouri.

Some Saints were almost destitute at the time the armies organized to march west. Some had been serving on missions; others were still recovering from the expense of moving to Kirtland, and still others were young men who had never possessed many material goods. George A. Smith was one such person. His father furnished him with a musket, a pair of pantaloons made of bed ticking, several cotton shirts, a straw hat, a cloth coat and vest, a new pair of boots, and a blanket. He packed his blanket and extra clothes in a knapsack made of heavy checked cloth. Soon after he began the journey west, his new boots wore blisters on his feet so severe that his feet began to bleed. Recognizing his distress, Joseph Smith gave him a pair of his own boots, which provided great relief. [15]

The March Toward Zion

On May 1, 1834, the first volunteers for the redemption of Zion marched from Kirtland. This strange group of approximately twenty soldiers, clad in a variety of homespun clothes, were armed with muskets, pistols, swords, bayonets, and dirks (daggers), and accompanied by four baggage wagons. Although May 1 had been designated as the day when the army of Israel was to begin the one-thousand-mile journey to Missouri, most of the men in Kirtland were not ready to begin the march. Consequently, the Prophet instructed the advance party to proceed south to New Portage, where they were to wait for others to join them. [16]

Four days after the first volunteers departed for New Portage, the Saints in Kirtland gathered to listen to their Prophet. Standing in the shade of the new school, which was under construction, Joseph Smith addressed most of his remarks to the men who had enlisted in Zion's Camp. According to George A. Smith, the

Prophet "bore testimony of the work which God had revealed through him" and impressed upon the members of Zion's Camp "the necessity of being humble, exercising faith and patience and living in obedience to the commands of the Almighty." He also promised them that if they "were united and exercised faith, God would deliver them out of the hands of their enemies" and all would "safely return." He warned the men not to murmur like the children of Israel against the Lord and His servants, for he said that if they forgot God and treated His commandments lightly, the Lord "would visit them with His wrath and vex them in His sore displeasure."[17]

On Monday, May 5, the Prophet assumed his new role as commander-in-chief of the armies of Israel and led about eighty-five men (which, coupled with the twenty who had departed on May 1, was the minimum number set by revelation) from Kirtland. About half of this segment of the army consisted of Kirtland Saints; the others had been gathered from the eastern branches of the Church. Most of these men and others who later joined them were young. George A. Smith and Benjamin Winchester were but sixteen. The average age of the men of the army was about twenty-nine, the same age as their leader, Joseph Smith. A few of the men were much older. Samuel Baker from Norton, Ohio, was nearly eighty; Martin Harris and Freeman Nickerson were in their fifties; and Frederick G. Williams was forty-six.[18]

While some of the men feared that they might never again embrace their wives and children, others marched briskly in anticipation of an exciting and rewarding adventure. Wilford Woodruff, who had departed with the group that left on May 1, pitched his tent following the first day's journey, then climbed a hill overlooking the camp of Israel and knelt in prayer. He recalled, "I rejoiced and praised the Lord that I had lived to see some of the tents of Israel pitched, and a company gathered by the commandment of God to go . . . and help redeem Zion."[19]

Although the men marched from Kirtland with mixed emotions, they were united in the belief that not only would they aid the stricken Saints in Missouri with money and supplies, but also they would help them regain their land in Jackson County. These two objectives were announced in a letter from Oliver Cowdery and Sidney Rigdon, dated May 10, 1834, and addressed to the membership of the Church. They informed the Saints that the money carried west by the army would help the exiled members in Missouri purchase wheat and supplies. They also wrote that after Zion's Camp had joined the exiled Saints, members of the Church in Missouri would inform the governor that they were prepared to return to their lands. The governor, they suggested, would then be bound to call out the militia to protect them as they returned to their homes in Jackson County. Other members of the Church would subsequently immigrate to Zion so that the Saints there would be sufficiently strong to protect themselves. Since the members of Zion's Camp would eventually return to their families in the East, Elders Cowdery and Rigdon instructed the members in Kirtland to begin preparing immediately, as circumstances permitted, to move to the West.[20]

After staying overnight in a barn in Streetsboro, Joseph Smith led the main segment of Zion's Camp to New Portage, about fifty miles south of Kirtland, arriving there late in the day on May 6. Here he reorganized the army. In addition to instructing the men concerning safety, comfort, and discipline, he divided them into companies of approximately twelve each. Then he told each company to elect a captain, who was to assign each man his responsibilities. In most companies there were two cooks, two firemen, two tentmakers, two watermen, two wagoneers and horsemen, one runner, and one commissary. Captains were appointed to command not only groups of from ten to twelve, but also groups of fifty and eventually one hundred men, according to the ancient order of Israel.[21]

At New Portage, the men agreed to consolidate their money into a general fund. Frederick G. Williams was appointed paymaster, with responsibility for managing the fund. Though contributions of members to the Missouri Saints were also placed in the general fund, accounts of these contributions were kept separately. Detailed records of expenses were kept during the journey of Zion's Camp, and at the time the army was disbanded, $233.70 remained, to be redistributed among the veterans.[22]

Route of Zion's Camp

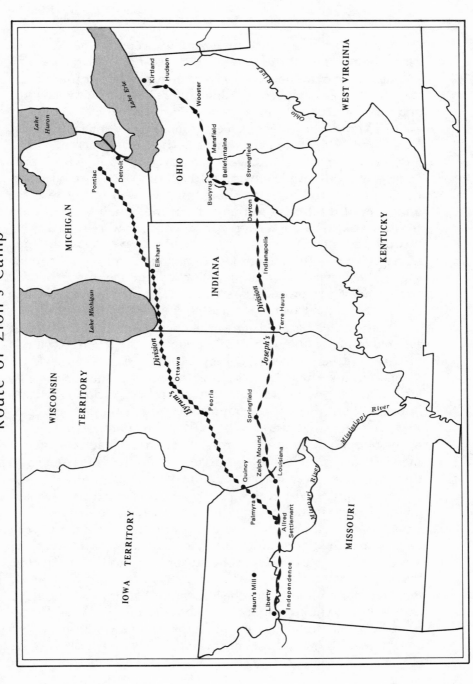

Recruits traveling with their families were instructed not to place their money in the general fund. Most of these men anticipated settling in Missouri and were therefore accompanied during the long march by their wives and children, who did the cooking and washing and performed other similar services.[23]

On May 8, the army of Israel resumed their long march west. Volunteers had continued to arrive at the encampments south of Kirtland, enlarging the number of troops to over 130, with twenty baggage wagons. After moving through the heavily wooded sections of northern Ohio stretching from Wooster to Bucyrus, the army passed the Indian settlements on the Sandusky Plains. As they proceeded through a long range of beech woods, their wagons became mired in mud, but, aided by heavy ropes, the men managed to pull the wagons along the muddy trails. Continuing south, they passed Bellfontaine, marched through the fertile Mad River Valley, and proceeded to Dayton. On May 17, after wading across the Miami River, they crossed the state boundary.

As the army marched across the open plains of Indiana, they suffered from the blazing heat of the sun and the relentless pain of blistered, bleeding feet. On May 21, they passed through Indianapolis, and three days later they crossed the Wabash River by ferryboat. May 30 found them marching through Springfield, Illinois, and on June 4, they camped near the banks of the Mississippi. Though they were aware of the threats that Missourians would not permit a Mormon army to enter their state, the men of Zion's Camp spent two days ferrying across the Mississippi and then continued west across the rolling fields of Missouri.[24]

As Joseph's division of Zion's Camp continued its relentless march, it was gradually strengthened with additional volunteers, arms, stores, and money. Recruiting officers continued to seek help from Latter-day Saints living in the states where the army was traveling. One of these recruiting officers was Parley P. Pratt. Instead of marching with other members of the army, he rode from one farmhouse to another, locating Latter-day Saints and asking them to help their oppressed brethren in the West. Sometimes he would ride all day and night to remain near the army, and on occasions he would ride into camp, enjoy breakfast with the other troops, secure a fresh horse, and then resume his recruiting activities.[25] As a consequence of the efforts of various recruiters, about fifty additional men joined this division of Zion's Camp.[26]

On June 7, Joseph's division encamped in some woods near a spring at the Allred Settlement, where the Salt River Branch of the Church was located. The next day, a Sunday, as the men were resting and attending to their religious duties, they were joined by Hyrum Smith and Lyman Wight, who were leading the other company of about twenty men. Zion's Camp had reached its maximum numerical strength; the army of Israel now numbered about 207 men, 11 women, and 11 children.[27] They now had twenty-five baggage wagons. After the two divisions combined, the Prophet continued as commander-in-chief, with Lyman Wight now serving as second officer. Following another reorganization, in harmony with the pattern established at New Portage, the army proceeded west.[28]

In many respects the daily routine of Zion's Camp was similar to that of other armies. Since the wagons were loaded with supplies, nearly every able-bodied person walked along the muddy and dusty trails, many of them carrying knapsacks on their backs and guns in their arms. They marched from morning till late afternoon or early evening, when they would make camp, generally near a body of water. Guards would be posted around the encampment at night. There was little time for relaxation, for when the men were not busy marching, caring for their animals, or preparing meals, they were drilling and preparing for action when they reached their destination.

Their diet was also monotonous. They purchased flour along the trail, baked their own bread, and cooked their own food, "generally, which was good," observed Heber C. Kimball, "though sometimes scanty." In addition to flour bread, they sometimes had johnnycake and corn dodgers.[29]

In other respects, Zion's Camp was not like an ordinary army. These men were heading west in compliance with what they believed to be a commandment of the Lord, and they were being led by a prophet of God. During the journey their commander-in-chief preached the doctrines of the kingdom to them. Every morning and evening the soldiers offered prayers in their tents. On Sunday, the men would usually rest and hold meetings, where they would hear sermons and partake of the sacrament. Moreover, many members of this army had implicit faith that the Lord was accompanying them. As recorded in Joseph Smith's history, "God was with us, and His angels went before us, and the faith of our little band was unwavering. We know that the angels were our companions, for we saw them."[30]

Parley P. Pratt recalled that on one occasion, while recruiting men for the army, he had traveled all night. About noon the following day he stopped to rest and turned his horse "loose from the carriage to feed on the grass" growing on a broad, level plain. He fell into a deep sleep, he said, and "might have lain in a state of oblivion till the shades of night had gathered" about him. "I had only slept a few moments till the horse had grazed sufficiently," he reported, "when a voice, more loud and shrill than I had ever before heard, fell on my ear, and thrilled through every part of my system." This voice said, "Parley, it is time to be up and on your journey." Shocked into a sudden awareness that he had fallen asleep on an isolated plain, he sprang to his feet, located the horse, and continued his journey. When he rejoined Zion's Camp later and informed Joseph Smith of the incident, the Prophet testified that he had been awakened by "the angel of the Lord who went before the camp."[31]

According to Heber C. Kimball, during the journey the Prophet not only reported that angels accompanied the camp, but he also told the men about an unusual vision he received. On June 2 the army crossed the Illinois River at Phillips Ferry; and while encamped on the west bank of the river the next day, Joseph and some of the brethren climbed to a high mound on the bluffs above the river. Some of them dug into the mound and discovered a large skeleton with an arrow lodged between its ribs. As the men continued their journey, some desired to know more about the person who had been killed by that arrow. After inquiring of the Lord, Joseph Smith learned by means of vision that he had been an officer who fell in battle, in the last destruction among the Lamanites, and his name was Zelph. "This caused us to rejoice much," Heber C. Kimball commented, "to think that God was so mindful of us as to show these things to his servant."[32]

While the march was tedious, the participants were constantly on the alert due to threatening rumors and reports. When they learned that antagonists in Indianapolis had boasted that Zion's Camp would not pass through that community, the Prophet assured his followers that the army would proceed through Indianapolis without anyone being aware of their passage. He divided the men into small groups, and some of them hid in the baggage wagons while others walked leisurely through the town, taking different routes. After they regrouped on the other side of town, the Prophet noted that their enemies were still awaiting an approaching army.[33]

Fearing that others might organize and attack the Saints if they learned the reasons they were marching to Missouri, the members of Zion's Camp generally tried to conceal their identity and objective. Sometimes spies approached the army in an attempt to learn about their mission, and when they asked the Saints where they were from, the soldiers, who were not in uniform, would reply, "Some are from Maine, others are from Massachusetts, New York, and Ohio." Sometimes they were even less specific and would say, "We are from the East." When asked where they were going, they would reply, "We are heading west." Sometimes strangers would also inquire concerning their leader, and the men would respond, "We have no one in particular." When this question was pursued, members of the camp would answer ambiguously, "Sometimes one and sometimes another takes charge of the company so as not to throw the burden upon any one in particular.[34]

As Zion's Camp continued its long march west, many factors combined to create internal disorder. Many of the men were fearful of the many possible dangers ahead. Some grumbled because of changes in their accustomed life-style, and a few questioned the decisions of the leaders. There were also personality clashes. For forty-five days the men lived and marched together, covering twenty-five to forty miles most days, and suffering from thirst, hunger, and fatigue. Many complained of "sore toes, blistered feet, long drives, scanty provisions, poor quality bread, bad corn dodger, 'frowsy' butter, strong honey, [and] maggoty bacon and cheese." The grumblers often complained to Joseph Smith and blamed him for their discomfort. George A. Smith observed that "even a dog could not bark at some men without their murmuring at Joseph."[35]

One member of Zion's Camp who exhibited a complaining disposition was Sylvester Smith. On May 14, two days after George A. Smith noted that for the first time in his life he ate raw pork and bread for breakfast, the army ran out of its supply of bread. The commissary had anticipated purchasing bread at Bucyrus but was unable to do so, and the army had no baking utensils. While some men were sent ahead of the army to purchase additional provisions, Zion's Camp was temporarily short of food, and Sylvester Smith grumbled because of what he considered to have been a failure in making proper preparations for the journey.[36]

Several weeks later Sylvester Smith threatened to kill Joseph Smith's dog because it had kept him awake during the night. Since the Prophet was deeply attached to the watchdog, which had been given to him by Samuel Baker, he was alarmed by Sylvester's threats. One verbal exchange followed another until Joseph accused Sylvester of being possessed of a wicked spirit. Then according to George A. Smith, Joseph prophesied "in the name of the Lord that if [Sylvester] did not get rid of that spirit, the day would come when a dog would bite him, and gnaw his flesh and he would not be able to resist it." Sylvester retorted, "You are prophesying lies in the name of the Lord."[37]

Sylvester Smith was not the only member of Zion's Camp who murmured and quarreled with others. On June 3 the Prophet stood on the back of a wagon and scolded the men for their lack of humility, their murmuring and fault-finding, and their "fractious and unruly spirits." Because of these transgressions, he said that some of them would die like sheep with the rot. However, if they humbled themselves before the Lord and repented, the scourge would be alleviated, though not entirely nullified. Concluding his chastisement, the Prophet said, "As the Lord lives, this camp will suffer for giving way to their unruly tempers."[38]

The problems of Zion's Camp were compounded as the men continued their march across the state of Missouri. While at Salt River, Joseph Smith had sent Parley P. Pratt and Orson Hyde to Jefferson City, the capital of Missouri, to ascertain if the governor "was ready to fulfill the proposition which he had previously made to the brethren to reinstate them on their lands in Jackson county, and leave them there to defend themselves."[39] When the two men arrived at the capital, Governor Dunklin expressed concern over reports that the citizens of Jackson County were armed and were prepared to attack the Mormons if they returned to that county. In his first direct communication with Latter-day Saints, he advanced a position concerning his executive authority from which he refused to deviate. In a letter addressed to the leaders of the Church in Missouri, dated February 4, 1834, he had argued that the Latter-day Saints had the right to arm themselves, to organize a militia for their protection, and to return to their homes in Jackson County. Nevertheless, he said, "as to the request for keeping up a military force to protect your people, and prevent the commission of crimes and injuries, were I to comply, it would transcend the powers with which the Executive of this state is clothed." Moreover, he reasoned that the U.S. Constitution gave Congress the power to call the militia to assist the state executive in cases of "actual or threatened invasion, insurrection or war, or public danger, or other emergency . . . as [the president] may deem expedient." But, he insisted, "none of these, as I consider, embraces this part of your request." In other words, Governor Dunklin concluded that military force could be used legally to quell mobs but not to restore justice. Therefore, he suggested that Latter-day Saints use the courts to secure redress for any crimes committed against them.[40]

When they learned that Governor Dunklin would not militarily intervene to help the Saints in the repossession of their Jackson County property, many Church members believed that they had been betrayed. Parley P. Pratt asserted that the governor had refused to carry out the duties of his office because he feared such action would lead to civil war. As he left the governor's office, Elder Pratt mumbled, "The poor coward ought, in duty, to resign; he owes this, morally at least, in justice to the oath of his office."[41]

Governor Dunklin not only dealt a serious blow to the hopes of the Latter-day Saints by refusing to call out the militia, but he also put another impediment in their path by announcing on June 6 that Mormons had "no right to march to Jackson county in arms," a direct contradiction of his letter of February 4. According to his executive pronouncement, unless men received an order from or were given permission by the commander-in-chief, they did not have the right to "'levy war' in taking possession of their rights, any more than others should in opposing them" while they returned to their lands.[42]

Without the protection of a militia and without a strong armed force of Latter-day Saints to defend them as they crossed the Missouri River, there was apparently no hope that the Saints would be able to return peacefully to their homes. The Saints recognized that an armed enemy was waiting to destroy all Mormons who dared immigrate into Jackson County. Angered and frustrated by the governor's decisions, the men of Zion's Camp resumed their march.[43] As they traveled, they learned that their enemies were not only prepared to repulse any Saints who crossed the Missouri River, but were also planning a surprise attack on Zion's Camp. On June 19, shortly after entering Clay County, the army encamped near a hill overlooking Fishing River. While they were setting up camp, five men approached on horseback and swore that the Mormons would "see hell before morning." They warned that sixty men from Richmond and seventy from Clay County were coming to join with an army from Jackson County, and that this force would utterly destroy the Mormons.

According to one observer, when this alarm was sounded, there was not a cloud in the sky; but as the sun set, clouds quickly gathered and a violent thunderstorm struck the region. Some of the members of Zion's Camp sought shelter in a log Baptist meetinghouse near their encampment. The fury of the storm broke branches from trees, destroyed crops, and disrupted the plans of the mob to crush the Saints. Rain soaked the gunpowder of the enemy, and the swollen and turbulent Missouri River prevented the mob from crossing to the Saints' encampment. Latter-day Saints were not harmed, though they did get wet and some of their tents were blown down. However, members of the mob did not fare so well. Some of them "had holes made in their hats," some suffered damage to their rifle stocks, and many of their horses fled in fright and pain.[44] Charles C. Rich recorded that the storm exceeded in severity any storm he had ever witnessed,[45] while Heber C. Kimball concluded, "It was evident the Almighty fought in our defense." Elder Woodruff added that following the storm, Joseph Smith informed Zion's Camp that "God is in this storm." Another observer, Nathan Baldwin, wrote in his autobiography that "all were conscious that God was engaged in the conflict, and thankful that they were under his special care and kind protection."[46]

Attempts to Reconcile the Land Disputes

The difficulties of the Latter-day Saints in Missouri became even more apparent when they failed to work out a satisfactory compromise with representatives from Jackson County at a meeting in Liberty, Missouri, on June 16. A committee from the county proposed to purchase within thirty days all property owned by Latter-day Saints in that area. The value of the land was to be determined by disinterested arbiters, with one hundred percent of the valuation to be added on condition that Latter-day Saints agreed never to settle within the limits of the county. An alternative plan was also proposed, under which the Latter-day Saints could purchase all the land of the non-Mormons in the county on the same financial terms.[47] This proposal, however, was unrealistic for the Latter-day Saints, since they were not willing at that time to sell their land in Zion, and members of Zion's Camp had not brought sufficient funds west to purchase even a fraction of the non-Mormon land.

Church leaders in Missouri prepared a counterproposal. They suggested on June 23 that a disinterested committee of Mormons and non-Mormons determine the value of the property of those who refused to live with Latter-day Saints, and the Saints would pay full value of this land within one year of the adoption of this proposal. Moreover, the Saints promised that they would not return to their lands until payment had been made. The committee was also to determine the damages incurred by the mobs and deduct this amount from the land to be sold by the non-Mormons.[48]

While representatives of the Latter-day Saints were involved in what proved to be futile negotiations with citizens from Jackson County, Joseph Smith received a revelation explaining that Zion could not at that time be redeemed. This revelation, received in Clay County near the Fishing River, stated:

> Behold, I say unto you, were it not for the transgressions of my people, speaking concerning the church and not individuals, they might have been redeemed even now.
>
> But behold, they have not learned to be obedient to the things which I required at their hands, but are full of all manner of evil, and do not impart of their substance, as becometh saints, to the poor and afflicted among them;
>
> And are not united according to the union required by the law of the celestial kingdom;
>
> And Zion cannot be built up unless it is by the principles of the law of the celestial kingdom; otherwise I cannot receive her unto myself.
>
> And my people must needs be chastened until they learn obedience, if it must needs be, by the things which they suffer. . . .
>
> Therefore, in consequence of the transgressions of my people, it is expedient in me that mine elders should wait for a little season for the redemption of Zion.[49]

After the Prophet informed Zion's Camp that the Lord had accepted their sacrifices and they would not have to fight the Missourians to help the Saints in Missouri regain their lands, some of the men expressed deep disappointment. According to Nathan Tanner, some were so frustrated that they vented their feelings by attacking bushes with their swords and cutting the plants to shreds. Because Zion's Camp had marched west not only to transport money and supplies to the oppressed Saints in Missouri but also with the intention of redeeming Zion, a few immediately apostatized. As a result of the insurrection, the Prophet again

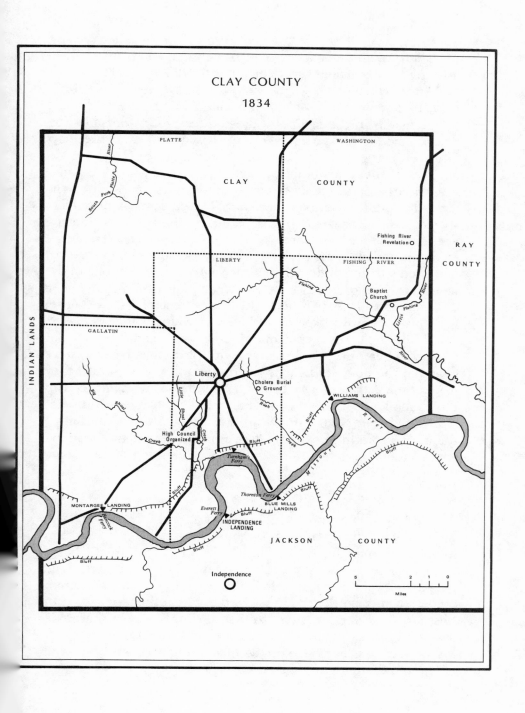

CLAY COUNTY
1834

warned the men that as a consequence of their complaints, a dev-astating scourge would strike the army.[50]

After experiencing fatigue, fear, discouragement, and frustra-tion, participants in Zion's Camp suffered a tragedy at the end of the march in the form of a dread disease. On June 21, Ezra Thayer and Joseph Hancock became ill with cholera. Three days later, while the army was encamped on the bank of Rush Creek, about two miles east of Liberty, some of the men who were stand-ing watch were suddenly struck by the disease and fell to the ground as though they had been shot. The epidemic continued to spread, causing severe diarrhea, vomiting, and cramps. On the evening of June 26, three of the afflicted died. Before the epidemic ended, about seventy persons, including Joseph Smith, had been stricken and twelve of the soldiers as well as one of the women traveling with Zion's Camp, Betsy Parrish, had died. The epidemic spread also to some of the Missouri members, and Newel K. Whitney's business partner, Algernon Sidney Gilbert, died.[51]

While the cholera epidemic raged, Joseph Smith traveled to Liberty. There, on July 2, he met with other members of Zion's Camp at the home of Lyman Wight and told them that "if they would humble themselves before the Lord and covenant to keep His commandments," the plague would be "stayed from that hour," and there would "not be another case of the cholera among them." The brethren, with uplifted arms, covenanted to keep the commandments, after which the Prophet certified, "The plague was stayed."[52]

Zion's Camp Is Disbanded

On July 3, two months and two days after the first members of Zion's Camp left Kirtland for Missouri, the army disbanded when Joseph Smith authorized General Lyman Wight to discharge every member of the camp who had faithfully served during the long march west. After securing their releases, the men scattered. Some returned to their families in the East, others remained in Missouri, and some returned to the mission field. On that same day the Prophet organized a high council in Missouri to assist Bishop Edward Partridge in administering the affairs of the Church in that part of the country.[53]

Accompanied by sixteen other men who had marched to Missouri, Joseph Smith began his journey back to Kirtland on July 9. The party had two horse-drawn wagons, a buggy, and several extra horses, and during the journey they camped at many of the same sites where they had stayed while traveling west. While crossing Indiana, Joseph, Hyrum Smith, William Smith, and Frederick G. Williams secured passage on a stage, leaving the wagons and horses with George A. Smith and other members of the group. The Prophet arrived in Kirtland about August 1, after a journey of some eighteen hundred miles. George A. Smith and his companions arrived home on August 4.[54]

Anxieties in Kirtland

During the three months that the men of Zion's Camp were away from their families, their wives worked in the fields, cared for their children, and anxiously awaited news concerning the welfare of their husbands. Their fears were quickened when Roger Orton rode into Kirtland in early July and announced that cholera had struck Zion's Camp and many were dying. Since he had left western Missouri shortly after the epidemic began, he did not know how many men were victims of the plague. On July 25 the *Painesville Telegraph* reported that seventeen men (there were actually twelve) attached to the "crusading army" of Joseph Smith had died of cholera and that "the whole division was on the retreat back to this country." The article also stated that a former merchant of Painesville, A. S. Gilbert, was among those who had died from the disease.[55]

In mid-July, Emma Smith and other members of the Church were shocked by the news that Joseph Smith had been killed in Missouri. According to a report in the *Chadron Spectator and Geauga Gazette*, which was widely circulated in northeastern Ohio and other states, the Prophet had led a body of well-armed Mormons into Jackson County, but his army had been repulsed by citizens from that county. As a consequence of this skirmish, the communique continued, Joseph Smith was wounded in the leg. Although his leg was amputated in an attempt to save his life, the report concluded, the Mormon Prophet had died three days after the operation.[56] Since this report did not indicate a date for the supposed battle, Roger Orton might not have been able to alleviate all the fears of the Saints. But as news continued to come from the west, members learned that the announcement of Joseph Smith's death was not correct. On July 18 the *Painesville Telegraph* declared that, based upon the latest information (dated June 18) from Liberty, Missouri, fighting had not erupted. Consequently, the paper concluded, the rumor that Joseph Smith had been killed was without foundation.[57]

The Legacy of Zion's Camp

In some respects Zion's Camp left a searing legacy. The *Painesville Telegraph* referred to this event as one of the wildest "goose chases" in history. Although only a few persons apostatized in 1834 because the army had failed to redeem Zion, as the years passed and as people viewed developments in the history of the Church, some claimed that this episode was an example that Joseph Smith was not a true prophet. Without recognizing that the revelation calling men to participate in the march included a warning that Zion would be built only upon the principles of righteousness, many of those in the army thought that with the help of the Almighty, they would be able to lead the exiled Saints back to Jackson County. Since Zion's Camp failed to redeem Zion, some critics accused Joseph Smith of being a false prophet and of "prophesying lies in the name of the Lord."[58]

The march to Missouri also failed to lessen the problems of the Saints living there. Spurred to action by rumors that the Saints were planning an invasion and then a massacre of the citizens of Jackson County, some of the Missourians prepared for war, thereby intensifying antagonism against the Latter-day Saints. Moreover, the spread of cholera in Clay County by members of Zion's Camp did not lessen the hatred generated in western Missouri against the Mormons. As the antagonisms increased, the hope of a fair trial for the Saints diminished.

After Zion's Camp disbanded, the Saints in Missouri continued to follow the instructions of the governor and of Church leaders in Ohio by seeking redress in the courts of the land. But the trials proceeded slowly, and the legal machinery maneuvered

the cases across the Missouri River. But after they had paid attor-
neys and waited for court action for three years, the Latter-day
Saints left Clay County and settled farther north. They continued
to seek restitution through legal channels, and their efforts continued to be unsuccessful. When Governor Dunklin attempted to
assess the reasons for the plight of the Saints, in one succinct sentence he wrote, "I am fully persuaded that the eccentricity of the
religious opinions and practices of the Mormons is at the bottom
of the outrages committed against them."[59]

The march west also created problems in Kirtland. After the
soldiers returned to their homes, some disrupted the renewed serenity of the community by recalling the internal problems that
had plagued the camp. In insulting and abusive language, Sylvester Smith accused the Prophet of improper conduct during the
march, of lying, and of issuing false prophecies. Responding to
these accusations, leaders of the Church convened a Church
court the last week of August, consisting of Bishop Newel K.
Whitney and members of the Kirtland high council. At the trial,
the court reviewed accusations and problems that had erupted
during the march of Zion's Camp, including the barking of Joseph
Smith's dog, Sylvester Smith's failure to share a portion of his
bread with Parley P. Pratt, disagreements concerning the selection of a site for a night's encampment, and other such incidents
that had created cancerous feelings. Ten men who participated in
Zion's Camp testified that Joseph Smith was not guilty of improper conduct, and witnesses disagreed with the defaming charges of
Sylvester Smith. After reviewing the evidence, Sylvester admitted that he had been in error and had behaved improperly. In October he published in the Messenger and Advocate a statement
clearing the Prophet of improper conduct during the march of
Zion's Camp; however, his accusations created discord in Kirtland and provided enemies of the Church with additional propaganda against the Church. While Sylvester wrote that he hoped
his confession would quell "the evil reports" that had originated
from his complaints, the damage had been done.[60]

Though Zion's Camp failed to help the Missouri Saints regain
their lands and was marked by some dissension, apostasy, and un-

favorable publicity, many members of the Church recognized positive results from the journey. Through the act of volunteering, the members demonstrated their faith in a living prophet and their earnest desire to harmonize their way of life with latter-day revelations. They showed their interest and concern for the exiled Saints in Missouri by traveling to their assistance and taking them money and supplies. Perhaps the history of the Church would have been different if all the members who had gathered in Zion and all of the participants of Zion's Camp could have lived a celestial life and if members in the East could have secured additional funds for the relief of Zion. Brigham Young recalled that the Prophet informed him that because of their lack of unity and humility, the men of Zion's Camp were not worthy to enter Jackson County.[61]

The journey to Missouri also proved to be a test to determine those who could best serve in positions of ecclesiastical leadership. On Sunday, February 8, 1835, Joseph Smith invited Brigham Young and Joseph Young to meet with him in his Kirtland home. There he informed them of a vision he had received relating to the men of Zion's Camp who died of cholera. He said, with tears in his eyes. "Brethren, . . . if I get a mansion as bright as theirs, I ask no more." According to Joseph Young, "When [the Prophet] had relieved himself of his feelings, in describing the vision, he resumed the conversation" and told Brigham Young that he was to be one of the twelve special witnesses who were "to open the door of the Gospel to foreign nations." Then he said to Joseph Young, "Brother Joseph, the Lord has made you President of the Seventies." He further instructed these men to call a meeting of all the brethren within a reasonable distance from Kirtland.[62]

The following Saturday, February 14, members of the priesthood crowded into the new schoolhouse next to the rising temple and listened to instructions from the Prophet. He told the men of Zion's Camp who were present that God had not "designed" all their trials and suffering "for nothing." "It was the will of God," he stated, "that those who went to Zion, with a determination to lay down their lives, if necessary, should be ordained to the ministry, and go forth to prune the vineyard."[63]

A few days later, the Prophet again informed members of
Zion's Camp that there was a significant purpose in their mission.
He admitted that some of the men had been angry with him when
he had notified the Saints that they would not cross the river into
Jackson County. "But let me tell you," he said, "God did not want
you to fight. He could not organize His kingdom with twelve men
to open the Gospel door to the nations of the earth, and with seventy men under their direction to follow in their tracks, unless He
took them from a body of men who had offered their lives, and
who had made as great a sacrifice as did Abraham."[64]

In February 1835, two new quorums, the Quorum of the
Twelve Apostles and the First Quorum of the Seventy, were organized, with many of the men who had sacrificed by marching
west called to serve in these priesthood bodies. In fact, nine of the
original twelve apostles called in 1835, all seven presidents of the
First Council of the Seventy, and all other sixty-three original
members of that quorum had served in the army of Israel that
marched to western Missouri in 1834.[65]

The most enduring legacy of Zion's Camp was that it provided
valuable training and experience for members of the Church.
That the leaders benefited from this experience is evident by their
application of principles they learned while marching west under
the direction of a latter-day prophet. When the Saints later organized militias for their protection and united for their mass
exodus across the plains to the Rocky Mountains, they adopted
many of the organizational patterns formalized by the Prophet
during the march of Zion's Camp in 1834.[66] Upon his return to
Kirtland, Brigham Young was asked by a skeptic, "What have you
gained by this journey?" He promptly replied, "Just what we went
for," adding, "I would not exchange the knowledge I have received this season for the whole of Geauga County; for the property and mines of wealth are not to be compared to the worth of
knowledge."[67]

The practical training and knowledge derived from participating in Zion's Camp was not considered by many of the men as
valuable as the spiritual benefits they received during the march
to Missouri. Since participants in this army had been gathered

from different parts of the young nation, many had not previously seen a prophet of God. Many declared that they were blessed abundantly as they traveled under the direction and tutelage of such a man. Shortly before his death, Marshall Hubbard told his wife, Caroline, that he knew Joseph Smith was a prophet of God, and that he would not exchange the experience he had had on the journey to Missouri for all that the world could offer.[68] Joseph B. Noble declared that prior to his participation in Zion's Camp, he had never experienced such "manifestations of the blessings of God."[69] Wilford Woodruff supplemented these testimonies with his own recognition of the benefits of this march when he said, "We gained an experience that we never could have gained in any other way. We had the privilege . . . of traveling a thousand miles with him [the Prophet], and seeing the workings of the Spirit of God with him, and the revelations of Jesus Christ unto him. . . . Had I not gone up with Zion's Camp I should not have been here today" (as an apostle of the Lord).[70]

For some participants, Zion's Camp was a failure. For many others, it was one of the most challenging, rewarding, and faith-promoting experiences of their journey through life.

Chapter 12

An Attempt to "Unvail" Mormonism

During the construction of the Kirtland Temple, enemies of the Church sought to destroy Mormonism by subverting Joseph Smith's reports of visions and revelations. At a public meeting held in Kirtland early in 1834, angered citizens complained that the Prophet had gathered in that township an impoverished group that threatened the entire region with "an insupportable weight of pauperism." A committee of the aroused citizenry announced to the public, in an article in the *Painesville Telegraph*, that their only hope of future security was to expose Joseph Smith's claims of "self-pronounced" divine authority. They reported that they had therefore employed Doctor Philastus Hurlbut "to ascertain the real origin of the Book of Mormon, and to examine the validity of Joseph Smith's claims" of revelation. That this was not to be an objective fact-finding mission is strongly hinted at in Hurlbut's commission. The committee admitted that he had been hired to collect data that would "prove the 'Book of Mormon' to be a work of fiction" and would "completely divest Joseph Smith of all claims to the character of an honest man." They further declared that in the near future a book would be published that would prove the Book of Mormon had been written over twenty years before in New Salem, Ashtabula County, Ohio, by Solomon Spaulding.[1]

An examination of several incidents in the life of Doctor Philastus Hurlbut (Doctor was a given name rather than a professional title) reveals that the man hired by the Kirtland committee to expose Mormonism was a vindictive apostate of the Church. In 1833 Philastus Hurlbut had been excommunicated by a Church council for immoral conduct. Following his excommunication on June 3, 1833, a council of high priests listened to his confession and decided that he should be reinstated. Three weeks later, on June 23, another tribunal was called into session, and this body agreed that Hurlbut's repentance was not genuine. He was therefore excommunicated a second time.[2] After he was employed to collect damaging information against the Prophet, Hurlbut publicly threatened the life of Joseph Smith. This led to his arrest and a subsequent trial on March 31, 1834, in Chardon, county seat of Geauga County. The court issued an order restraining Hurlbut for six months from injuring the person and property of Joseph Smith. He was also ordered to post a bond of two hundred dollars to pay the costs of the proceedings, which amounted to $112.59.[3]

In an attempt to gather information that would discredit the character of the Prophet, Hurlbut traveled to western New York, where the Smith family had resided. Prior to leaving for New York, he apparently wrote or obtained a series of affidavits that contained many common phrases and similar vocabulary, though they were signed by various individuals. A number of the affidavits specifically stated that Joseph Smith and members of his family were "indolent," "lazy," "intemperant," "money diggers," "adicted to various habits," and "entirely destitute of moral character."[4]

Although those who signed the purported affidavits lived in the townships of Palmyra and Manchester, it is questionable whether any of them could be considered an authority on the character of Joseph Smith or his family. During most of their residence in western New York, the Smiths lived in a sparsely settled section of Genesee County. While they probably traveled periodically to Palmyra and Manchester, they probably gained only a casual acquaintance with inhabitants of those communities. After Joseph began reporting about his First Vision and subsequent visitations from heavenly messengers, in all probability the number of those who were formerly "intimate friends" diminished; furthermore, many who met the Prophet after 1821 had previously formulated opinions concerning his character based on vicious rumors. The affidavits gathered by Hurlbut, therefore, seem to serve as evidence of the "evil" stories circulated about the Smiths rather than as reliable assessments of their characters.[5]

A legal investigation of the accusations of the Palmyra settlers exposed many inconsistencies in the affidavits. Most of the accusations were vague, undocumented, and unsubstantiated. The so-called witnesses relied on hearsay information or assumptions. For example, Joseph Smith was accused of being immoral, but no evidence was cited; in addition, such a charge conflicts with the teachings regarding morality that were published under Joseph's jurisdiction in the Book of Mormon.[6] Moreover, some who charged Joseph Smith with being lazy contended also that he wrote the Book of Mormon,[7] a contradiction in fact, since the writing of such a work would have been an exhausting task.

Critics of the Smith family also failed to produce evidence that Joseph was intemperate or an alcoholic. An acquaintance of Joseph Smith, a Mr. Bryant, declared in a Michigan newspaper that the young man was "a lazy, drinking fellow, loose in his habits every way." When William Bryant was interviewed shortly after the account was published, he admitted that he had seen Joseph only once or twice. In answer to the question, "Were they [the Smiths] drunkards," he replied, "Everybody drank whiskey in them times," and denied that he had uttered the statement that had been attributed to him.[8]

In addition to gathering derogatory information about the character of Joseph Smith, Hurlbut was hired to collect data that would support the theory that the Book of Mormon was a fictitious work based on the writings of Solomon Spaulding. The individual whom he sought to identify as the architect of the Book of Mormon was born in Ashford, Connecticut, in 1761. After graduating from Dartmouth College in 1785, Spaulding served as a

Congregational minister for a few years in New England. He sub-
sequently moved to Cherry Valley, New York, where he engaged
in land speculation and in a mercantile business with his brother,
Josiah Spaulding. He also became principal of the Cherry Valley
Academy and occasionally preached in the local Presbyterian
church. After his business enterprises failed, he moved in 1809 to
New Salem (now Conneaut), Ohio, where, with the assistance of
Henry Lake, he established an iron foundry.[9]

While living in New Salem, Spaulding became interested in
the Indian mounds located near his foundry, earthworks that had
excited residents of the region. During the War of 1812 his business venture failed, but in the midst of financial ruin and broken
health, he found solace in writing about the early inhabitants of
this land. He also entertained his friends by reading to them portions of his romance.[10] His story recounted the adventure of a
group of Romans, led by Fabius, who during the age of Constan-
tine (fourth century A.D.) headed for Britain. As they were sailing
to the British Isles, they encountered a violent storm and were
blown off course. They sailed across a large body of water and
traveled up a mighty river. After they arrived in this new land, the
refugees made no attempt to return to their homes but settled
among the aborigines they found there. This novel then related
the conflicts that divided the various tribes—the Delawares, Ohi-
ons, Kentucks, Sciotons, and Chiaugans. The leaders of these
early Americans were also identified, including Bombal, powerful
prince of the Kentucks (a nation that lived on the south side of the
Ohio River); Kadokam, King of Sioto; Labaska; Hamboon;
Ulipool; and Lamesa.[11]

Following his failures and disappointments in Ohio in 1812,
Spaulding moved to Pittsburgh, Pennsylvania, where he probably
sought a recovery from some of his debts by publishing his romance. The work was not printed, however, and Spaulding settled in Amity, near Pittsburgh, where he died on October 20,
1816.[12]

Learning that Spaulding had written a work that contained a
description of a migration to America, a history of the early inhabitants of this land, and an account of their conflicts, Hurlbut

sought affidavits that would reveal parallels in the Book of Mormon and the Spaulding romance. Like the affidavits collected in western New York, the new documents, reportedly signed by people who knew Solomon Spaulding, seem to have a common authorship. Eight individuals presumably signed statements to the effect that they had been introduced to the Spaulding manuscript through either reading the work or listening as Spaulding read it to them, and after examining the Book of Mormon, they affirmed that there seemed to be parallels in the two works. Three of the eight persons specifically stated that the "historical parts" of the two works were the same, while one said the "historical matter" was nearly the same. One person said that he found "many of the same passages" in the two works, while another claimed "many of the passages" in the two works to be verbatim. [13]

Two of these witnesses, John Spaulding, the brother of Solomon, and John's wife, Martha, specifically stated that the Spaulding romance revealed that the American Indians were descendants of the Jews or the lost tribes of Israel, a theory that was supposedly held by Solomon Spaulding and other Americans of the early nineteenth century. John and Martha Spaulding further said that the Spaulding manuscript described the journey of these Israelites from Jerusalem by land and sea under the command of two men, whose names were Nephi and Lehi. The emigrants, as a result of quarrels and contentions between them, then divided into two nations, the Nephites and Lamanites. [14]

Four of the eight individuals whose names are attached to the affidavits collected by Hurlbut stated that some names found in each of the two works were the same. This accusation was made twenty-two years after the individuals had read or had listened to Spaulding's fanciful story. The names found in the Book of Mormon would have been fresh on their minds, while they would have to dip back in their memories to recall the names mentioned by Spaulding. Possibly some of the names seemed similar after a lapse of two decades, for in Spaulding's manuscript there was a Moonrod (cf. Moroni); a Mammoon (cf. Mormon), a native term for woolly mammoth; a Lamesa (cf. Laman), who was a woman in the Spaulding romance; and a Hamelick (cf. Amaleki or Amalickiah). Although about three hundred possible names could have been selected from the Book of Mormon for comparison with the Spaulding manuscript, Hurlbut's witnesses used but a few specific examples. Four mentioned the name Nephi and three mentioned Lehi as names common to both histories. Only three additional names (plus Nephites and Lamanites) were given as examples of the common use of names in the two records, and these were Laban, Zarahemla, and Moroni. "Despite the elapsed decades, all recalled identical spellings for these odd-sounding names, spellings which matched exactly those found in the Book of Mormon."[15] Even though Hurlbut's witnesses mentioned only five proper nouns found in the two works, Hurlbut concluded that "most of the names and leading incidents contained in the Book of Mormon, originated with Solomon Spalding."[16]

The daughter of Solomon Spaulding, whose married name was Matilda McKenstry, recalled that she first became aware of parallels in the names appearing in the Book of Mormon and in her father's manuscript when several individuals asked her if she "did not remember" that the names were the same. After others had brought this similarity to her attention, she said she "thought" they were similar. Asked how she remembered after such a long time had elapsed since she had seen the names in her father's manuscript, she replied that she specifically remembered that one of the names, Lehi, began with an L and she recalled the name because of the fanciful manner in which her father made this capital letter. Although she claimed a similarity in the names of the two records, she admitted she had not read the Book of Mormon.[17]

Another apparent defect in the Spaulding affidavits collected by Hurlbut was that five of the eight witnesses distinctly stated that the religious matter in the two books was different. Yet Hurlbut and E. D. Howe concluded that the principal source of the Book of Mormon was the Spaulding manuscript, despite the fact that the Book of Mormon is a religious record and religious concepts permeate nearly every page.[18]

While gathering information to discredit the Church, Hurlbut searched widely for Spaulding's manuscript. In 1834, he traveled to Monson, Massachusetts, where Spaulding's widow, Mrs. Matilda Davison, resided. She told him she did not know where the manuscript had been deposited, but that it might have been left in Pittsburgh or in a trunk left in Harwick, New York. Hurlbut secured Mrs. Davison's permission to take the manuscript if he could locate it. He discovered it in Harwick, New York, and delivered it to Eber D. Howe, the anti-Mormon editor of the *Painesville Telegraph.*

Undoubtedly the two men were disappointed that there were no significant parallels between Spaulding's manuscript and the Book of Mormon—no reference to Israelites migrating to America and no names that matched those in the Book of Mormon. Moreover, they had not succeeded in gathering evidence that connected the writings of Joseph Smith with those of Solomon Spaulding.[19] Nevertheless, they were prepared to launch a major attack against the Church.

Since Philastus Hurlbut's excommunication from the Church and his conviction at the trial at Chardon had discredited him, the information he gathered was not published under his name. Instead, it was published in 1834 under the authorship of Eber D. Howe. The book, titled *Mormonism Unvailed* [*sic*], was the first book of significance printed with the design of destroying the Church.[20]

In *Mormonism Unvailed,* Hurlbut and Howe popularized their contention that most of the names and major incidents in the Book of Mormon originated with Solomon Spaulding. They admitted that they had found a manuscript written by Spaulding that was a romance written in modern style. They also briefly recounted the novel's plot about Romans who settled in America. Without producing any evidence, however, they also contended that Spaulding must have written another manuscript that paralleled the story in the Book of Mormon. Again without providing any sources, they claimed also that Sidney Rigdon must have secured the other Spaulding manuscript while he was living in Pittsburgh and then used this work as the basis of the Book of Mormon. They concluded, "We, therefore, must hold out Sidney Rigdon to the world as being the original 'author and proprietor' of the whole Mormon conspiracy, until further light is elicited upon the lost writings of Solomon Spaulding."[21] This conclusion contradicted the historical portions of the book they produced, for in *Mormonism Unvailed* is an account based upon articles from the *Painesville Telegraph* of Sidney Rigdon's conversion to The Church of Jesus Christ of Latter-day Saints in Ohio in November 1830, seven months after the Book of Mormon was published in Palmyra, New York. Moreover, Hurlbut had neglected to include in the affidavits any reference to more than one Spaulding manuscript.[22]

The first 175 pages of *Mormonism Unvailed* included articles from the *Painesville Telegraph* describing the Book of Mormon and the early history of the Restoration movement. These articles were frequently cited without any reference to sources and without the use of quotation marks (not an uncommon practice in that period). The Ezra Booth letters, initially published in the *Ohio Star*, were then reproduced in the volume, followed by Hurlbut's affidavits concerning the Smith family. The last major section of the book included the eight affidavits designed to substantiate the theory that Sidney Rigdon had written the Book of Mormon, using Solomon Spaulding's romance novel as a principal source.

Although few persons purchased copies of *Mormonism Unvailed* immediately following its publication, the information in the book became the basis for innumerable anti-Mormon books. Within a few years after its publication, newspapers in the country announced "it appears that Mormonism owes its origins to an individual named Solomon Spaulding; who wrote the historical part of the Book of Mormon."[23] For more than half a century, beginning in the early 1840s, nearly every major anti-Mormon work contained this theory, even though no one ever found substantial evidence linking Sidney Rigdon with the Spaulding manuscript and then with Joseph Smith. Moreover, the parallels in the Spaulding novel and the Book of Mormon continued to be advanced even though no one was able to produce a manuscript like the Book of Mormon.[24]

One of the Latter-day Saints living in Kirtland who decided to investigate the claims of Hurlbut and Howe regarding the origin of the Book of Mormon was Orson Hyde, a close associate of Sidney Rigdon who had lived with the Rigdon family in 1829. Based on his experiences with and knowledge of Sidney, Orson Hyde concluded that his former pastor would not have been involved in a scheme that included forgery and deception. He also recalled that when he had preached in New Salem in the spring of 1832 and had organized a branch of the Church there, he had met no one who claimed to have found parallels in the Book of Mormon and the Spaulding romance. After *Mormonism Unvailed* was published, Orson returned to New Salem and asked a number of people there if they had read Spaulding's novel and if there were similarities in that work and the Book of Mormon. Several who recalled hearing Spaulding read his manuscript insisted they were most surprised that anyone would claim the romance resembled the Book of Mormon.[25]

Sidney Rigdon also vehemently denied throughout his life that he participated in the coming forth of the Book of Mormon. He insisted that while he was living in Pittsburgh, he neither saw nor obtained the Spaulding manuscript, and that he had never heard of such a romance until Hurlbut announced his theory. Throughout his life, Elder Rigdon maintained that he was converted to the Church after reading the Book of Mormon.[26]

Another Latter-day Saint who investigated the charges regarding the Spaulding manuscript and the Book of Mormon was Benjamin Winchester. In a review of the controversy, he published the testimony of a man named Jackson who claimed that he had been a neighbor of Spaulding, that he was acquainted with the Spaulding manuscript, and that he had also read the Book of Mormon. Jackson insisted that the Spaulding manuscript contained a story about a group of Romans, and that there was no similarity in the two books.[27]

After critics of the Church had propounded the Spaulding theory for half a century, his manuscript was located in 1884 in Hawaii among the papers of L. L. Rice, who had purchased Howe's business in 1839 and had taken the manuscript to Hawaii. Included with this manuscript was the following statement: "The writings of Solomon Spalding, proved by Aaron Wright, Oliver

Smith, John N. Miller and others. The testimonies of the above gentlemen are now in my possession. [Signed] D.P. Hurlbut." The three persons whose names appeared on the certificate, which was written on a previously blank page of the manuscript, were among the eight individuals who had testified to parallels in the Book of Mormon and the Spaulding manuscript. [28]

The manuscript discovered in Hawaii was Spaulding's Roman story and bore no significant resemblance to the Book of Mormon. The styles of the two manuscripts are completely different, and there are no common names and no historical similarities except for the fact that each account tells a history of a migration to America (by different peoples and at different periods of time), and each mentions conflicts that divided the native inhabitants. [29]

Even after the Spaulding manuscript was located and printed, critics continued to insist that there must have been another Spaulding manuscript. In recent years, however, most critics have rejected this theory as well as the affidavits Hurlbut collected among Spaulding's friends and relatives. Nevertheless, the controversy is periodically revived, and some non-Mormons who have rejected the Spaulding affidavits continue to publish the affidavits Hurlbut collected in New York. [30]

Chapter 13

Unfolding the Doctrines of the Kingdom

I n the history of the restoration movement, one of the most productive periods
in the disclosure of principles of the everlasting gospel was the
1830s. When The Church of Jesus Christ of Latter-day Saints was
organized on April 6, 1830, the Book of Mormon had been available in print for less than two weeks, and there was no Doctrine
and Covenants nor Pearl of Great Price to aid members in their
understanding of the doctrines of God's kingdom. The basic beliefs of the first converts in New York and Pennsylvania were
primarily the religious concepts described in the Book of Mormon, such as the first principles of the gospel, the resurrection of
the body, a future state of happiness or misery, and a distinct belief concerning the antiquity of the gospel, the fall of Adam, and
the atonement of Christ. As a consequence of Joseph Smith's
early visions and revelations, members also shared a unique belief
concerning the priesthood: that the power and authority to act in
the name of God had been restored to the earth by the laying on of
hands by angelic messengers.[1]

An Unprecedented Era

As Latter-day Saints matured in their capacity to comprehend
the doctrines of the kingdom of God, additional doctrines were

unfolded to them. Many doctrinal disclosures were made in response to questions that the Prophet asked the Lord; at other times the Prophet was moved to petition the Lord by members of the Church who recognized a problem or did not understand a theological principle. During the 1830s, more revelations that currently appear in the Doctrine and Covenants were given than during any other period, and more of these revelations were recorded in Ohio than in any other state. Of the 138 sections in the current edition of the Doctrine and Covenants, almost half, or 65 (47 percent), were recorded in Ohio; and of the 65 Ohio revelations, 54 (83 percent) were recorded between February 1831 and January 1834.[2]

Many of the revelations of the early thirties were received while Joseph Smith was working on his translation of the Bible. While reading and studying the Old and New Testament, he was stimulated to seek counsel from the Lord. One leading contemporary authority on this new translation of the Bible has written:

> The real *purpose* of the Bible Translation was not so much to have a new corrected edition of the Bible, but rather, to bring the Prophet to a greater understanding of the gospel. Consequently, the real *product* is not so much a new Bible itself, but the doctrines that were revealed in the process. Consequently, the Prophet's work with the Bible is an indispensable element in the unfolding of the gospel and the building of the dispensation of the fulness of times—much of which occurred while the Prophet lived in the vicinity of Kirtland, Ohio.[3]

As doctrines of the restored gospel were gradually unfolded to the Prophet, he unveiled them to others. Sometimes when he received a revelation, he immediately told others what he had learned. He dictated some of the revelations in the presence of others. On occasions, however, he withheld from the Church members information he received through divine communication, often for months or even years. In an address to the Saints in the Kirtland Temple in 1837, he said that "if the Church knew all the commandments," they would condemn half of them "through prejudice and ignorance."[4] Six years later he said, "I could explain a hundred fold more than I ever have of the glories of the kingdoms manifested to me in vision, were I permitted, and were the people prepared to receive them."[5] The Prophet knew that when he unfolded concepts that were very different from popular beliefs of his age, some members would refuse to embrace the truth and would leave the Church. Consequently, he experienced the challenge of deciding what he should disclose and what he should withhold from the membership at any given time.[6]

Joseph Smith not only had the challenge of deciding when some doctrines should be disclosed, but he also had the responsibility of determining the best methods of revealing to others principles of the everlasting gospel. Some doctrines were initially made known to individuals during private conversations, and sometimes religious truths were unfolded while members were attending schools in Kirtland or were listening to the Prophet's public discourses. Church publications such as the *Evening and the Morning Star* and *Messenger and Advocate* were established to help the Saints to better understand doctrines and responsibilities of the Church.

Historical Background of the Doctrine and Covenants

Since the revelations given through Joseph Smith contained pertinent information concerning Church doctrines, procedures, and government, members of the Church desired to have access to them. Many of them copied down the early revelations, and copies were carried by missionaries into the mission field. Errors crept into these writings as they were copied and recopied. Some of the revelations were also read by the Prophet and others at gatherings in Kirtland, and some were published in Church periodicals as well as non-Mormon newspapers.[7]

In 1833 a mob destroyed most of the sheets of the Book of Commandments as it was being printed in Independence, Missouri. By the mid-1830s Joseph Smith had received many new revelations that had not been recorded when the Book of Commandments was being compiled for publication. Forty-one revelations, nearly all of which were received while the Prophet was living in Ohio, were copied in a manuscript titled Kirtland Revelation Book.[8]

Recognizing a need to extend the availability of the revelations, it was agreed at a conference in Kirtland on September 24, 1834, that Joseph Smith, Oliver Cowdery, Sidney Rigdon, and Frederick G. Williams should serve as a committee to select and prepare for publication revelations received by the Prophet.[9]

In preparing the revelations for publication, Joseph Smith edited them, sometimes to correct errors that had been made by scribes, and sometimes to add information not included in the initial recording of the communications from the Lord. For example, he added surnames in some of the inspired writings; he also added words of instruction, clarification, and enlightenment. Some of the words that were changed related to Church organization. For example, before certain priesthood offices were made known in some of the early revelations, the term *elder* was used to designate all who had priesthood responsibility. As the organization expanded, revelations were edited to replace the general term of *elder* with a more specific office.[10] This type of editing is illustrated by comparing the following sentences as they appeared in the Book of Commandments and in the Doctrine and Covenants (changes are in italics):

Book of Commandments (*chapter 44, verse 26*)	Doctrine and Covenants (1835) (*section 13, verse 8; now 42:31*)
They shall be laid before the bishop of my church, and two of the elders, such as he shall appoint and set apart for that purpose.	*And* they shall be laid before the bishop of my church and *his counselors,* two of the elders, *or high priests,* such as he shall appoint *or has appointed* and set apart for that purpose.
(*chapter 44, verse 29*)	(*section 13, verse 10; now 42:34*)
And the residue shall be kept in my storehouse, to administer to the poor and needy, as shall be appointed by the elders of the church and bishop.	*Therefore,* the residue shall be kept in my storehouse, to administer to the poor and *the* needy, as shall be appointed by the *high council* of the church *and the* bishop *and his council.*

When this revelation was initially recorded early in 1831, there were no counselors to the bishop and a high council had not yet been constituted.[11]

Some persons left the Church because they did not understand the process of recording communications from the Lord.

Oliver Cowdery recognized that Joseph Smith was editing the revelations and undoubtedly knew that some members would be concerned when they detected differences in the revelations as printed in Missouri and in Ohio. In fact, various changes had already appeared in the revelations when they were reprinted in Kirtland in 1835 in the *Evening and the Morning Star*. Twenty-four revelations had been printed in the *Star* while that paper was being printed in Missouri, and those revelations, along with forty others, were printed (with only a few typographical errors) in the Book of Commandments.[12] When those same writings were reprinted in Kirtland with modifications, Oliver Cowdery explained some of the reasons for textual variations in the printed versions:

> On the revelations we merely say, that we were not a little surprised to find the previous print so different from the original. We had given them a careful comparison, assisted by individuals whose known integrity and ability is uncensurable. Thus saying we cast no reflections upon those who were entrusted with the responsibility of publishing them in Missouri, as our own labors were included in that important service to the church, and it was our unceasing endeavor to have them correspond with the copy furnished us. We believe they are now correct. *If not in every word, at least in principle.* For the special good of the church we have also added a few items from other revelations.[13]

Although Joseph Smith did not describe the precise method used to receive communications from the Lord (except to note that he received the revelation during a vision or through the instrumentality of the Urim and Thummim, and so on), two revelations directed to Oliver Cowdery in April 1829 seem to indicate that the Prophet's responsibility was to understand the ideas he received from the Lord and then to place the concepts into coherent wording.[14] Nothing in the Doctrine and Covenants suggests that he was given perfect, final language as he recorded the word of God. Rather, he was inspired in fundamental thoughts.[15] While Joseph Smith testified that the revelations were of God and were correct, the preface of the Doctrine and Covenants reads: "Behold, I am God and have spoken it; these commandments are of me, and were given unto my servants in their weakness, after the manner of their language, that they might come to understanding."[16]

Brigham Young, who received one of the revelations included in the current edition of the Doctrine and Covenants (section 136), asserted that when messages were conveyed from God to man, the words were in the language of the recipient. "The revelations of God," he said, "contain correct doctrine and principle, so far as they go; . . . the Almighty . . . has to speak to us in a manner to meet the extent of our capacities. . . . If an angel should come into this congregation, or visit any individual of it, and use the language he uses in heaven, what would we be benefited? Not any, because we could not understand a word he said. When angels come to visit mortals, . . . they have to descend to our capacities in order to communicate with us."[17]

One of the most succinct but comprehensive summaries of the Prophet's activities while arranging the revelations for publication was written by Orson Pratt. In an article published in the *Millennial Star*, he aptly described his observations:

Joseph, the Prophet, in selecting the revelations from the Manuscripts, and arranging them for publication, did not arrange them according to the order of the date in which they were given, neither did he think it necessary to publish them all in the Book of Doctrine and Covenants, but left them to be published more fully in his History. Hence, paragraphs taken from revelations of a latter date, are, in a few instances, incorporated with those of an earlier date. Indeed, at the time of compilation, the prophet was inspired in several instances to write additional sentences and paragraphs to the earlier revelations. In this manner the Lord did truly give 'line upon line, here a little and there a little,' the same as He did to a revelation that Jeremiah received, which, after being burned by the wicked king of Israel, the Lord revealed over again with great numbers of additional words. (See Jeremiah XXXVI;32)[18]

In 1835 Joseph Smith completed editing and compiling the revelations that were to be published. On August 17 these writings were presented for approval of the Church at a general conference held in Kirtland. Leaders of the various priesthood quorums testified that the revelations received and compiled by the Prophet were true. William W. Phelps also read the testimony of the Twelve Apostles concerning the veracity of the revelatory writings. The Twelve bore witness to the world that the Lord had manifest to them through the Holy Ghost that "these Command-

Kirea on Broken wings,
How will I know about all these things?
Siera & Nikita, sing
while Russians play and dance and fling.

Rick and Hulk & Rambo think,
While cyndi, George and Julian sink,
Bruce and phil and Rocky roll
while whitney, Elton and Bryan Bowh

I don't need no money,
I don't need no Fame,
Dont need no credit card to ride this train.
Thats the power of love.

How will I know
If he really LOVES me?
If he loves me NOT
If he loves me NOT

ments were given by inspiration of God, and are profitable for all men, and are verily true." Following these testimonies, "all of the members present, both male and female," with uplifted hands, unanimously voiced their approval of the revelations, and by this procedure the revelations became binding upon the membership of the Church. [19]

The first edition of the Doctrine and Covenants, published in 1835, had 101 revelations. [20] The committee that had helped prepare them for publication introduced the work in a preface that stated that the writings contained "the leading items of the religion we have professed to believe." The first part of the book contained seven lectures on faith that had been delivered in Kirtland during the winter of 1834-35 to members of the priesthood. The second part contained one hundred revelations under the heading "Covenants and Commandments of the Lord to his Servants of the Church." The last part was an appendix that included a revelation dated November 3, 1831 (now section 133), a statement regarding marriage, a description of the beliefs of the Church regarding government and laws in general, and the minutes of two general assemblies of the priesthood. The first assembly authorized the publication of the Doctrine and Covenants, and the second recorded its approval of this work. At this time, the membership of the Church accepted only the one hundred revelations as inspired communications from the Lord; the statements on marriage, government, and laws were not endorsed as revelations but were accepted as correct expressions of the belief of the Saints on those subjects for that period. [21]

Some of the revelations received by Joseph Smith before 1835 were not included in the first edition of the Doctrine and Covenants but were published in Church periodicals. For example, all of the writings that now constitute the Book of Moses in the Pearl of Great Price had been recorded by the Prophet before March 1831, and except for chapter 8 of Moses, these writings had been recorded before he moved to Ohio. Portions of this segment of Joseph Smith's translation of the Bible—Moses 5:1-16; 6:43-68; 7:1-69; and 8:13-30—were printed in the *Evening and the Morning*

Star between August 1832 and the end of April 1833.[22] One chapter from Joseph Smith's translation of the New Testament, chapter 24 of Matthew, recorded in 1831, was also published (probably in Kirtland) before 1839.[23] Moreover, some of the revelations copied in the Kirtland Revelation Book, such as section 88 (the Olive Leaf), dated December 1832, were not included in the first edition of the Doctrine and Covenants.[24]

The Writings of Abraham

In the same decade that Joseph Smith began publishing selections from his translation of the Bible, he purchased four mummies and some ancient papyri that contained the writings of the patriarch Abraham and his great-grandson Joseph. These mummies, along with others, had been discovered on the west bank of the Nile River across from the ancient city of Thebes (now Luxor) by Antonio Lebolo, an Italian who was licensed by the French government. Following his death in Castellamonte, Italy, on February 19, 1830,[25] eleven of the mummies, along with some of the ancient writings on papyri, were shipped to the United States, where, in the spring of 1833, they were claimed by Michael H. Chandler. Chandler, who lived in Philadelphia and claimed that he was Lebolo's nephew, displayed the artifacts for a fee in various eastern cities.[26] In the summer of 1835, he arrived in Kirtland with four mummies and some ancient scrolls. When Joseph Smith learned about Chandler's inheritance, he decided to purchase the objects. In the summer of 1835, with financial assistance from Joseph Coe, Simeon Andrews, and others, the Prophet secured the mummies and papyri for $2,400.[27]

Describing the incidents preceding the Prophet's acquisition of the mummies and the rolls of papyrus, Orson Pratt said that Chandler had

obtained from learned men the best translation he could of some few characters, which however, was not a translation, but more in the shape of their ideas with regard to it, their acquaintance with the language not being sufficient to enable them to translate it literally. After some conversation with the Prophet Joseph, Mr. Chandler presented to him the ancient characters, asking him if he could translate them. The prophet took them and repaired to his room and inquired of the Lord concerning them. The Lord told him they were sacred records. . . . And he also enquired of the Lord concerning some few characters which Mr. Chandler, gave him by way of a test, to see if he could translate them. The Prophet Joseph translated these characters and returned them, with the translation to Mr. Chandler; and who, in comparing it with the translation of the same few characters by learned men, that he had before obtained, found the two to agree.[28]

After Joseph Smith had provided Michael Chandler with a translation of some of the characters, Chandler gave the Prophet a certificate that included the following statement:

Kirtland, July 6, 1835

This is to make known to all who may be desirous, concerning the knowledge of Mr. Joseph Smith, Jun., in deciphering the ancient Egyptian hieroglyphic characters in my possession, which I have, in many eminent cities, showed to the most learned; and, from the information that I could ever learn, or meet with, I find that of Mr. Joseph Smith, Jun., to correspond in the most minute matters.

MICHAEL H. CHANDLER,
Traveling with, and proprietor of,
Egyptian mummies.[29]

Early in July 1835, a few days after purchasing the ancient scrolls from Michael Chandler, Joseph Smith commenced translating the papyri, with William W. Phelps and Oliver Cowdery serving as his scribes. He wrote that "much to our joy [I] found that one of the rolls contained the writings of Abraham, another the writings of Joseph of Egypt." He also wrote in his diary that after further examination, he would unfold to others a more complete account of what he learned while translating the records. "Truly we can say," he said, "the Lord is beginning to reveal the abundance of peace and truth."[30]

Since Joseph Smith had not learned to read Egyptian characters in July 1835 when he used the term *translation* in connection with this record, he probably meant at least in part an explanation or the rendering of ideas from one language to another. Thus through revelation or inspiration from God, he dictated to a scribe the writings of ancient prophets. After he left the Church, Warren Parrish, a close associate of the Prophet in the mid-1830s, wrote that he had served as Joseph Smith's private secretary, had kept his journal, and had sat "by his side and penned . . . the translation of the Egyptian Hyeroglyphics [sic] as he claimed to receive it by direct inspiration from heaven."[31] Orson Pratt also said he observed Joseph Smith as he translated the writings found in the Book of Abraham in the Pearl of Great Price: "I saw his countenance lighted up as the inspiration of the Holy Ghost rested upon him, dictating the great and most precious revelations now printed for our guide. I saw him translating, by inspiration, the Old and New Testaments, and the inspired book of Abraham from Egyptian papyrus."[32]

During Joseph Smith's remaining years of residence in Kirtland, he maintained an interest in translating the papyri he had purchased from Chandler. In the latter part of July 1835, he reported that he "was continually engaged in translating an alphabet to the Book of Abraham, and arranging a grammar of the Egyptian language as practiced by the ancients."[33] On October 1, he wrote that while laboring on the Egyptian alphabet, he learned the principles of astronomy as understood by Abraham.[34] One week later, he recorded in his diary that he had "re-commenced translating the ancient records."[35] In November he spent a great deal of time working on this project; and in December, while discussing the Egyptian records with Brigham Young, Jared Carter, and William E. McLellin, he explained "many things concerning the dealing of God with the ancients, and the formation of the planetary system."[36] By the fall of 1837, the Prophet had completed the translation of a portion of the ancient records and was preparing to publish it.[37]

While Joseph Smith was translating the ancient Egyptian records, the mummies and some of the scrolls were shown to many persons, both members of the Church and nonmembers. Frederick G. Williams and his sons exhibited them from one community to another around Kirtland, and others took ancient objects to Hiram and other parts of Portage County, where they were shown to many settlers. Following the completion of the Kirtland Temple, the mummies were exhibited in the upper story of this building. And later, after the Saints became established in Nauvoo,

Joseph Smith and other members of his family showed the mummies and ancient parchments to a constant stream of visitors. [38]

Patterns of Thought and Behavior

Many themes were touched upon in the revelations and instructions that were constantly being unfolded by the Prophet to members of the Church. Many of the revelations confirmed contemporary Christian conduct, dealing with such transgressions as pride, selfishness, idleness, dishonesty, stealing, killing, and committing sexual perversions. [39] The Saints were also commanded to observe the Sabbath, identified as the first day of the week or the Lord's day. [40]

Some of the principles revealed were not emphasized by most Christian ministers in that age. Every member had the responsibility of teaching the gospel to others, with priesthood holders directed to serve as traveling elders, preaching from community to community and from house to house. [41] Members were also challenged to become acquainted with good books and to study history, geography, languages, and other disciplines. [42] A number of revelations emphasized that the Saints were to impart of their substance to the poor and consecrate their material goods and talents for the building of God's kingdom. [43]

The Age of Accountability

During the 1830s Latter-day Saints also learned the age at which children should be baptized and the reason for performing this ordinance when a child reached a particular age. While translating the Bible, the Prophet received instructions from the Lord concerning the age of accountability. Sometime between February 4, 1831, and April 5, 1831, while translating chapter 17 of Genesis (which describes the law of circumcision), the Prophet learned that children, when properly taught, are responsible before the Lord for their actions and are to be baptized when eight years old. [44] This concept was later included in a revelation recorded in November 1831 and initially printed in the Evening and the Morning Star in October 1832. According to this revelation, parents have a responsibility to teach their children the principles of the gospel and to prepare them for baptism when they are eight years old, the age of accountability.[45]

The Antiquity of the Gospel

Selections from Joseph Smith's translation of the first chapter of Genesis now constitute the Book of Moses in the Pearl of Great Price. When these selections were initially published in the *Evening and the Morning Star*, the Saints' understanding of the antiquity of the gospel was enhanced. From the Book of Mormon, they learned that the Nephites and Jaredites understood long before his birth in mortality that Jesus Christ is the Redeemer, and that prior to the meridian of time, repentant believers were baptized by water and "of fire and of the Holy Ghost." They further learned that the plan of salvation was preached from the beginning and that all the holy prophets spoke about the Savior of mankind.[46] Joseph Smith's translation of the Bible enlarged upon the doctrine of the antiquity of the gospel by explaining in greater detail the gospel as understood by Adam, Enoch, and Noah. When the earliest selections from the revised Bible were printed, the Saints learned that Adam, after being cast out from the garden of Eden, and subsequent patriarchs (including Enoch and Noah) understood the basic principles of the gospel, including faith in the Lord Jesus Christ, repentance for one's transgressions, and baptism in the name of the Only Begotten Son, Jesus Christ, "the only name which shall be given under heaven, whereby salvation shall come unto the children of men."[47]

From the revelation now included in the Book of Moses, the Saints also learned that Adam and Eve were the first to offer "the firstlings of their flock for an offering to the Lord." The King James Version of the Bible has no reference to Adam's offering a sacrifice. In the article in the *Evening and the Morning Star*, members learned that this symbolic sacrifice was in "similitude of the sacrifice of the Only Begotten of the Father."[48]

The writings of Moses confirm and add to biblical and Book of Mormon teachings concerning Melchizedek. According to the Bible, Melchizedek, the king of Salem and the "priest of the most high God," received tithes from Abraham. The Book of Mormon enlarges upon this by teaching that after he preached the doctrine of repentance to the people, Melchizedek helped establish peace in the realm and was subsequently called the Prince of Peace. Expanding upon these teachings, Joseph Smith's translation of the Bible asserts that Melchizedek received the office of the high priesthood, according to the holy order of God. This priesthood "holds the keys of the mysteries of the kingdom of God, even the keys of the knowledge of God, and has power to pronounce blessings according to the will and commandment of the Lord."[49] The excerpts from the new translation vividly demonstrated to the Saints that the gospel they were striving to live was not new, but had been taught to the children of God in every dispensation, beginning with the first man, Adam.

Premortal Life

During the 1830s Joseph Smith learned many principles relating to the eternal nature of man, but as with many other doctrines, the full scope of this belief did not become common knowledge for the Saints until after they later moved to Illinois. During the time Kirtland was a headquarters of the Church, the Saints did not publish any articles describing man's premortal existence. Parley P. Pratt wrote that he gained a new insight into his relationship to God during the winter of 1839-40 after the Prophet taught him the nature of the eternal family organization. When he learned that his wife might become his eternal companion and that the result of their eternal union could be offspring as numerous as the stars of heaven, Elder Pratt rejoiced and exclaimed, "I felt that God was my Heavenly Father indeed; [and] that Jesus was my brother."[50]

Although Joseph Smith probably did not preach in public before 1839 the doctrine of man's premortal existence, he received many revelations that referred to this subject during the thirties. While working on the revision of the Bible, he learned that the Lord created all things spiritually before they were created naturally upon the face of the earth.[51] In a revelation received in September 1830 (D&C 29), he learned that before the devil tempted

Adam in the garden of Eden, he rebelled against God, saying,
"Give me thine honor, which is my power." After leading one-
third of the hosts of heaven against God, Satan was defeated. According to this revelation (and information published in the Book
of Moses), Satan's rebellion included his effort to destroy the
agency of man.[52] The Prophet's understanding of this conflict was
also enhanced when he learned (as recorded in August 1830) that
the angel Michael was Adam; in the book of Revelation, John
specified that Michael was one of those who waged war against
Satan. Years probably passed before the Latter-day Saints connected Adam with the war that was waged prior to his temptation
in the garden of Eden. Nevertheless, in the 1830s some of them
learned that Adam was the angel Michael and that Noah was
Gabriel. In a letter dated January 1, 1834, Oliver Cowdery included information that identified these two angelic messengers
and added, "I just drop this because I supposed you would be
pleased to know, and I have no disposition to keep back anything
from my brethren that I am privileged to know."[53]

Other references to man's premortal existence are found in
the revelations received by Joseph Smith. A revelation received
in Kirtland on May 6, 1833, and printed in the 1835 edition of the
Doctrine and Covenants states that "man was also in the beginning with God. Intelligence, or the light of truth, was not created
or made, neither indeed can be."[54] While translating the Book of
Abraham, the Prophet also learned that "intelligences . . . were
organized before the world was; and among all these there were
many of the noble and great ones," and that Abraham was one of
the righteous spirits chosen before his birth in mortality to be a
leader. These later writings, however, were not published until
1842.[55]

Eschatology

The understanding of the Latter-day Saints concerning the
doctrine of last things and man's ultimate destiny was enhanced
during the thirties. The Book of Mormon served as a guide, helping the Saints to interpret properly many Bible passages relating to
the second coming of Christ, the Millennium, the resurrection,

and the future state of mankind. Before migrating to Ohio, the Saints understood that catastrophic developments would precede the Second Advent, that Israel would be gathered in Palestine, and that others would be gathered in a holy city (a place of refuge, a city of God, a New Jerusalem) in America. From the Book of Mormon they also learned that America was the place where the city of New Jerusalem would be built.[56] Moreover, they learned that Christ would usher in a millennial era, a thousand years of peace during which Satan would have no power because of the righteousness of the people.[57]

The Book of Mormon further instructed the Saints that there would be a universal resurrection; that as a result of the atonement of Christ, the body and spirit would be reunited; that the resurrected body would be a tangible, corporeal body; and that there would be two resurrections, the first a resurrection of the just and the second, of the unjust.[58] This record also described the condition of the spirit between death and the resurrection. At death the righteous enter paradise, a state of rest and peace, and the wicked enter a spirit prison where the unrighteous suffer mental anguish.[59]

The Last Days

The revelations that Joseph Smith recorded in the early 1830s gave the Saints an increased understanding of events that would occur in the future. In addition to learning that Independence, Jackson County, Missouri, was the location of the New Jerusalem that would be established in America, they learned that the city of Enoch, which was caught up into heaven, would descend and unite with the city of Zion in America. According to an excerpt from Joseph Smith's translation of the Bible, "The Lord said unto Enoch: Then shalt thou and all thy city meet them there, and we will receive them into our bosom, and they shall see us, and we will fall upon their necks, and they shall fall upon our necks, and we will kiss each other."[60]

While Joseph Smith received many revelations in the thirties that confirmed biblical and Book of Mormon teachings concerning the wickedness and destruction that would occur in the last days, he received additional knowledge concerning the destructive forces that would plague mankind and the relationship between the abominations of the people and the catastrophic events. He learned that because mankind would not repent, the Lord would "take vengeance upon the wicked." These destructions would be so extensive, the revelations said, that the earth would be transfigured. Elements would melt with fervent heat. Mountains would be broken down. Valleys would be exalted. The earth would return to its state as it was before it had been divided, and a new earth and a new heaven would be created.[61]

The Civil War Prophecy

The devastating forces that would plague mankind prior to the Millennium were emphasized in a prophecy recorded by the Prophet on December 25, 1832: "The inhabitants of the earth shall mourn; and with famine, and plague, and earthquake, and the thunder of heaven, and the fierce and vivid lightning also, shall the inhabitants of the earth be made to feel the wrath, and indignation, and chastening hand of an Almighty God, until the consumption decreed hath made a full end of all nations."[62]

Describing events that were occurring in the world at the time he received this prophecy, the Prophet wrote that a "rebellion" had erupted in South Carolina.[63] The people of South Carolina at that time were experiencing a deteriorating economy; while cotton planters were faced with declining prices and exhausted soil, settlers in Charleston were finding it difficult to compete with more powerful trading centers in New York and other port cities. Meanwhile, many in South Carolina were concerned about increased agitation in the North against slavery. They also feared the growing political power of the North, which in time would enable that section of the country to impose its will over the South. Discontent in South Carolina eventually focused on protective tariffs that apparently favored the North at the expense of the South. Both the Tariff of 1828 and the Tariff of 1832 included provisions that, according to many southerners, channeled the wealth of the South into the hands of their political opponents. In November 1832, leaders of South Carolina, meeting in convention, declared the hated Tariff of 1832 null and void in their state beginning February 1, 1833.[64]

With threats of nullification and possibly secession, President Andrew Jackson maneuvered forces in the nation's capital to try to prevent the citizens of South Carolina from carrying out their objectives. In December, after calling on Americans to demonstrate their loyalty to the Union, he asked Congress to pass an act permitting him to enforce the revenue laws in South Carolina by any means necessary. Congress responded by granting the President authority to use the national army and navy to crush the rebellion in South Carolina.[65]

While Joseph Smith's prophecy on war was recorded during a period of crisis in American history, at a time when there was talk of war, there was no immediate threat of major civil war in 1832. No other state was willing to support South Carolina at that time. It is possible that if war had erupted at that time, the confrontation would have been between South Carolina and the combined forces of all other states. After Joseph Smith received the revelation on war, the crisis in South Carolina was temporarily resolved when Congress met in January 1832 and discussed lowering the tariff, and settlers in South Carolina suspended their nullification ordinance. In the spring of 1832 Congress enacted a compromise tariff, providing for a genuine downward revision of the tariff, after which South Carolinians rescinded a nullification ordinance that was never enacted.[66]

When the prophecy on war is placed in its historical setting and statements in it are coupled with Joseph Smith's interpretation of what he learned from the Lord, it emerges as one of the most remarkable predictions recorded by the Prophet. He wrote that on December 25, 1832, while "praying earnestly on the subject," he learned that "the commencement of the difficulties which will cause much bloodshed previous to the coming of the Son of Man will be in South Carolina."[67] In addition to learning through revelation that there would be a rebellion in South Carolina, the Prophet learned that the northern states would be divided against the southern states (in 1832-33 no other state supported South Carolina in the nullification controversy); that the civil war would lead to the death and misery of many souls; that the South would call on other nations for help, even the nation of Great Britain (which South Carolinians were not considering in the early thirties); that the slaves would be marshaled and disciplined for war; and that following this irrepressible conflict, war would be poured out upon all nations.[68] All these prophecies were later fulfilled to some extent.

Though nearly all of the predictions recorded in the prophecy on war have been realized, it also contains instructions to those who will be living during the turbulent days preceding the Second Coming of Christ. In the midst of the sorrow, suffering, death, and destruction that will occur in the last days, followers of the Lord are admonished, "Stand ye in holy places, and be not moved."[69]

One year after this revelation was recorded, Joseph Smith received another revelation that explained, in part, the significance of the Lord's instructions. Latter-day Saints were to gather to the places appointed by the Lord, according to the parable of the wheat and the tares, in order that the wheat (the followers of Christ) might be secured in the granaries "to possess eternal life, and be crowned with celestial glory," when Christ rewards every man according to his works.[70]

The Second Coming and the Millennium

While members of the Church in the latter days are urged by the revelations to live in harmony with the teachings of Christ at a time when wickedness is most evident and destructive forces will strike the earth, they have also learned through the revelations that when Christ returns, He will appear to those who have gathered in Zion (America) and Jerusalem. Moreover, the ten tribes of Israel will participate in this gathering and will come down from the land of the north, will be crowned with glory, and will receive special blessings from the children of Ephraim.[71]

As he was working on the translation of the Bible, Joseph Smith learned the interpretation of various concepts recorded by John in the book of Revelation. These concepts teach many important doctrines concerning the last days and the Millennium.

For example, through revelation, the Lord has revealed that the seven seals mentioned in Revelation refer to the seven thousand years of the earth's temporal existence, and that "in the beginning of the seventh thousand years" the Lord will "sanctify the earth, . . . and complete the salvation of man, and judge all things."[72] Moreover, the resurrection of the just will usher in the Millennium, there will be a separation of the righteous and wicked, and only the righteous will inhabit the earth during the thousand years of peace.[73] At the time of judgment, the apostles who were with Him during His ministry in Jerusalem will stand by His side "to judge the whole house of Israel."[74] After returning to the earth, He will make "a full end of all nations," become the king and lawgiver, and rule mankind from His two world capitals.[75] Then, while Satan is bound, children will be born and will "grow up without sin unto salvation." When they become old they will die, but instead of sleeping in the dust, they will be "changed," or resurrected, "in the twinkling of an eye."[76]

Through revelation the Prophet also learned that the restored Church, which possesses the priesthood and keys of the priesthood, is the kingdom of God on earth, the stone that, according to Daniel, is to roll forth gradually until it fills the whole earth. Eventually all living persons on the earth are to come to a "knowledge of the Lord." This truth is inseparably connected with the priesthood of God, for the knowledge of God is derived through the power of the priesthood.[77] In fact, by revelation the Saints learned that during the Millennium there will be a significant expansion of knowledge and truth never before disclosed to mankind.[78]

Early revelations recorded by the Prophet further instructed the Saints concerning events that will occur at the end of or following the Millennium. Satan is to be loosed for a brief season, after which the devil and his armies will again be defeated by the Lord and "cast away into their own place" where they will have no power over the Saints. A new heaven and a new earth will be created. After this earth becomes a celestial abode, "crowned with glory, even with the presence of God the Father," and the meek will inherit this kingdom.[79]

The Heavenly Mansions

Primarily as a result of the vision of glories Joseph Smith and Sidney Rigdon received in Hiram, Ohio, in February 1832, and as a consequence of a revelation the Prophet recorded nearly a year later in Kirtland, the understanding of the Latter-day Saints regarding the resurrection and the mansions in heaven has been increased significantly. Through revelation they have been taught that there are four classifications of resurrected bodies and four destinations for mankind. Those who develop a sanctified body in this life through obedience to the principles and ordinances of the gospel will be resurrected in the first resurrection, receive a celestial body, and inherit a celestial glory. They will receive the fulness of the Father; they will become kings and priests of the Most High and "gods," even the sons of God," and will dwell in the presence of the Father.[80]

A second group will be resurrected with terrestrial bodies. These include individuals who were not valiant in their testimony of Christ. "These are they who are honorable men of the earth," but who have been "blinded by the craftiness of man." They will receive of the Son's glory but not the fulness of the Father.[81]

A third group of resurrected beings will be resurrected with telestial bodies. According to the revelations, these individuals will participate in the second resurrection, which will take place at the end of the Millennium. "These are they who are liars, and sorcerers, and adulterers, and whoremongers, and whosoever loves and makes a lie." Although these children of God will not be caught up to meet Christ when He returns, and they will suffer everlasting punishment, meaning God's punishment, they will inhabit a kingdom of glory. While the glory of the celestial kingdom is likened in brightness to the sun, the telestial is likened to the stars.[82]

A fourth group of resurrected beings is composed of the sons of perdition. These are individuals who have denied the power of the Holy Ghost after having received it, who have known the power of God but have denied it, and who therefore form an alliance with Lucifer. Following their resurrection, they will be cast into outer darkness with the devil and his angels. The revelations, however, do not reveal in detail the nature of their punishment. [83]

Salvation for the Dead

Four years after Joseph Smith beheld the vision in which he learned about the three degrees of glory, he beheld another vision in which he gained his initial understanding of the principle of salvation for the dead. In this vision of the celestial kingdom, received in the Kirtland Temple on January 21, 1836, he learned that all who would have accepted the gospel in this life had they been granted an opportunity are heirs of the celestial kingdom. In light of this concept, he wrote in his diary that he also learned that children who died before they arrived at the age of accountability would be saved in the celestial kingdom. [84]

In an article in the *Messenger and Advocate* in March 1837, Warren Cowdery stated that the gospel was preached to the dead, as described in 1 Peter 4:6, so that man might be granted the privilege of embracing or rejecting the gospel. "We feel," the article read, that the Lord will "condemn no one until he hears, and refuses to obey the mandates of heaven." And all "who love and obey him, will be received with this pleasing plaudit, well done [thou] good and faithful servant."[85]

The Godhead

For some members of the Church, including Joseph Smith, some of the original members of the School of the Prophets, and some bearers of the priesthood who were in Kirtland at the time of the dedication of the temple, knowledge of the Godhead was in part based on visionary experiences during which individuals beheld God. [86] In a conversation with Robert Matthias, also known as "Joshua the Jewish minister," a visitor to Kirtland in 1835, Joseph Smith described his first vision. He said that while he was engaged in a quest for religious truth, he called upon the Lord and beheld a glorious vision. "A pillar of fire appeared above my head," he explained, "and filled me with unspeakable joy. A personage appeared in the midst of this pillar of flame, which was spread all around and yet nothing consumed. Another personage

soon appeared like unto the first: he said unto me thy sins are forgiven thee."[87] During the 1830s the Prophet identified in his writings the two personages who appeared to him in the spring of 1820
as the Father and the Son.[88] In addition to Joseph Smith, at least
three other early members of the Church, Sidney Rigdon,
Zebedee Coltrin, and Lyman Wight, testified that they not only
beheld Jesus Christ in vision, but also saw God the Eternal
Father.[89] Thus, members of the Church in the 1830s understood
that the Father and Son are two separate and distinct personages.[90]

   The Lectures on Faith, published in the 1835 edition of the
Doctrine and Covenants, not only identified the Father and Son
as two personages, but also stated that the Godhead consists of the
Father, the Son, and the Holy Ghost and implied that the Father
and Son are material beings in a form like created man. These lectures declared that man is formed after the image and likeness of
God and that Jesus Christ is a personage "of tabernacle" who is
"the express image and likeness of the personage of the Father."[91]
Joseph Smith undoubtedly understood in the 1830s that spirit is
matter and that the resurrected body is a spiritual body. A revelation recorded on May 6, 1833, declared that "man is spirit. The
elements are eternal, and spirit and element, inseparably connected, receive a fulness of joy."[92] The anthropomorphic nature
of God was more clearly explained by the Prophet in the early
1840s, when he taught the Saints that "all spirit is matter, but it is
more fine or pure." He further stated that while the Holy Ghost "is
a personage of Spirit," the Father and the Son have tangible
bodies of flesh and bones.[93]

   The Reverend Truman Coe, a Presbyterian minister in Kirtland, recognized that one of the distinct teachings of the Latter-
day Saints was a belief that God was a material being who created
man in his physical likeness. After living among the Saints in
Kirtland for about four years, he wrote a brief history of the Saints
that included a description of some of their most unusual beliefs.
"They contend that the God worshipped by the Presbyterians and
all other sectarians is no better than a wooden god," he said.

"They believe that the true God is a material being, composed of body and parts; and that when the Creator formed Adam in his own image, he made him about the size and shape of God himself."[94]

Another concept relating to the Godhead that Joseph Smith disclosed in the 1830s was that Jesus is Jehovah, the God of ancient Israel. The Book of Mormon strongly affirms that Jesus was the God of the Old Testament, and when Joseph Smith worked on the inspired translation of the Bible and translated the Book of Abraham, he learned that the ancient patriarchs Abraham, Isaac, and Jacob knew the Lord by the name of Jehovah.[95]

Plurality of Gods

With the printing in 1832 of the vision of the degrees of glory that Joseph Smith and Sidney Rigdon beheld in the John Johnson home, Latter-day Saints were introduced to the concept of plurality of gods. According to this revelation, individuals exalted in the celestial kingdom will receive the title of "gods." In commenting on this vision in 1844, the Prophet said, "Every man who reigns in celestial glory is a God to his dominions. . . . They who obtain a glorious resurrection from the dead, are exalted far above principalities, powers, thrones, dominions and angels, and are expressly declared to be heirs of God and joint heirs with Jesus Christ, all having eternal power."[96] He admitted that this might appear as a very strange doctrine to the Christian world; and in the 1830s, a large percent of the members of the Church probably did not fully understand the significance of the sentence in this revelation that related to this concept.[97]

After the concept of the plurality of gods had been introduced to the Saints in February 1832, Joseph Smith received additional revelations disclosing information relating to this doctrine. In one dated September 22 and 23, 1832, members of the Church learned that Jesus Christ promised His Father's kingdom to those who receive His Father. "Therefore," the revelation read, "all that my Father hath shall be given unto him."[98] Three months later, another revelation identified the blessings that await the righteous resurrected saints: they "shall be filled with his [God's] glory, and receive their inheritance and be made equal with him."[99]

Lorenzo Snow observed that some Latter-day Saints were acquainted with the doctrine of plurality of gods in the mid-1830s. Shrotly before his baptism in 1836, he attended a patriarchal blessing meeting in the Kirtland Temple. Following the service, he was introduced to Joseph Smith's father, the patriarch to the Church, who prophesied that Lorenzo would be baptized. Elder Smith told him, "You will be as great as you can possibly wish— even as great as God, and you cannot wish to be greater."[100]

At least one non-Mormon understood that the Latter-day Saints embraced an unusual belief concerning blessings that would be extended to the righteous following their resurrection. In *Mormonism Exposed and Refuted,* published in 1838, LaRoy Sunderland accused the Saints of blasphemy for teaching that some of God's children would be filled with Christ's glory "and be equal with him."[101] Parley P. Pratt responded to these accusations, defending his belief concerning the propriety of referring to resurrected saints as gods, "even the sons of God." He stated that the Bible taught this type of equality. Referring to Christ's petition that the saints might become one even as He and His Father were one, Elder Pratt suggested that there was a relationship between oneness, equality, and becoming gods. He noted that the Bible stated that the saints would become "joint heirs" with God and that the spirit would guide them into all truth. According to Elder Pratt, "knowledge is power," and when the saints were blessed to know the many truths that God knows, they would possess God's power and would therefore become gods.[102]

The Word of Wisdom

While Joseph Smith was unfolding to the Church guidelines for behavior and patterns of belief, he recorded a unique revelation that became known as the Word of Wisdom. When the Word of Wisdom was revealed to the Prophet on February 27, 1833, many members of the Church used tobacco, drank hard liquor, and regularly partook of tea and coffee. Many Americans recognized in the early nineteenth century that these stimulants were injurious to the body, and crusaders were campaigning against their consumption. The temperance crusade was rapidly gaining momentum in various parts of the United States, including the Western Reserve. Like many other revelations, the Word of Wisdom was given in response to a recognized need for additional insight on a specific subject. Brigham Young later commented on the events leading to Joseph Smith's inquiry that brought forth this revelation:

> I think I am as well acquainted with the circumstances which led to the giving of the Word of Wisdom as any man in the Church, although I was not present at the time to witness them. The first school of the prophets was held in a small room situated over the Prophet Joseph's kitchen in a house which belonged to Bishop Whitney, and which was attached to his store, which store probably might be about fifteen feet square. In the rear of this building was a kitchen, probably ten by fourteen feet, containing rooms and pantries. Over this kitchen was situated the room in which the Prophet received revelations and in which he instructed his brethren. The brethren came to that place for hundreds of miles to attend school in a little room probably no larger than eleven by fourteen. When they assembled together in this room after breakfast, the first they did was to light their pipes, and, while smoking, talk about the great things of the kingdom, and spit all over the room, and as soon as the pipe was out of their mouths a large chew of tobacco would then be taken. Often when the Prophet entered the room to give the school instructions he would then find himself in a cloud of tobacco smoke. This, and the complaints of his wife at having to clean so filthy a floor, made the Prophet think upon the matter, and he inquired of the Lord relating to the conduct of the Elders in using tobacco, and the revelation known as the Word of Widsom was the result of his inquiry.[103]

Brigham Young noted that although Joseph Smith asked the Lord specifically regarding tobacco, he received not only an answer to that inquiry but also to many other concerns relating to health. The revelation includes prohibitions against the consumption of tobacco, wine, strong drinks, and hot drinks, as well as affirmative provisions regarding the use of wholesome herbs, fruits, grains, and meat. Fruits are to be used in their seasons "with prudence and thanksgiving," and grain is recommended as "the staff of life." The revelation promises that those who observe this word of wisdom will be blessed physically, mentally, and spiritually. It was given to the Saints "not by commandment or constraint, but by revelation and the word of wisdom, showing forth the order and will of God in the temporal salvation of all saints in the last days."[104]

While many of the same principles related to health were being taught by others in the 1830s, the Word of Wisdom was unique in that Latter-day Saints were given a law of health through revelation. Sylvester Graham and many other reformers of the 1830s taught views that today are recognized either as incorrect or highly controversial. The Prophet Joseph Smith, however, recorded through revelation provisions relating to health that by and large have been substantiated in the twentieth century by leading authorities in this field of research.[105]

Many of the religious concepts unfolded through Joseph Smith during the 1830s were distinct theological concepts taught by no other religious leader in the United States at that time. While some critics have suggested that he created a religion by copying from his contemporaries, a careful comparison of the Prophet's teachings with the theology advanced by others in that period clearly reveals that he could not be considered a popularizer. Through revelation, he restored many religious principles that had been forgotten during the long years following the disruption of the primitive Church of Christ. Thus the Lord was fulfilling his promise to the faithful that they would be given "line upon line, precept upon precept,"[106] as the heavens continued to open and new principles were given. Truly the heavens resounded during the Saints' sojourn in Kirtland!

Chapter 14

Church Policies, Programs, and Administration

O ne of the important and enduring developments in the 1830s related to the structure of Church government. In the early 1840s, Joseph Smith wrote, "We believe in the same organization that existed in the primitive Church, viz.: apostles, prophets, pastors, teachers, evangelists, etc." This basic pattern of church government was constituted before 1836.[1] When the Church was organized on April 6, 1830, Joseph Smith was called to serve as first elder and Oliver Cowdery as second elder. The names and principal responsibilities of the three offices of the Aaronic Priesthood—priests, teachers, and deacons—were also known at that time. Although there was not a Quorum of the Twelve Apostles, Joseph Smith was designated not only as a prophet, seer, and revelator, but also as an apostle.[2]

As the Church increased rapidly in membership, the Prophet continued to unfold through revelation the ordained offices in the priesthood. Within five years, he directed the calling and ordination of bishops and their counselors, high priests, a First Presidency, assistant presidents, a patriarch, high councils, seventies, and a Quorum of the Twelve Apostles, as well as organized in Kirtland the first stake of the Church. By 1835 a well-developed ecclesiastical judicial system had also emerged, and while its emphasis has changed in some respects, this basic judicial pattern has continued to the present day.[3]

During this formative period in the history of the restoration, many members learned that some of their presumptions regarding the role and conduct of a prophet were incorrect. Before they joined the Church, the only acquaintance that converts generally had with prophets was through reading the Bible; and in the view of some, Joseph Smith appeared and acted in a manner very different from their ideas of ancient prophets. He did not have a long, flowing beard and did not wear a long robe. Instead, he looked like his contemporaries. While laboring in the fields he wore the work clothes of the period; he played with his children; he wrestled with the strongest men in the communities where he lived; and he joked with friends. He was a man with imperfections as well as a prophet who recorded the word of God, and some early converts found it difficult to recognize or accept his dual role. When some claimed revelations pertaining to basic principles affecting the entire Church, Joseph Smith informed them that he alone had the authority to receive such messages. It was difficult for some of the early converts to accept this restricted form of revelation from an individual who appeared so human in some respects and yet whose spiritual authority encompassed the whole Church.[4]

While the Saints were learning about the functions and responsibilities of a prophet and their relationship to him, Joseph Smith also taught them about many other offices in the Church, which created various new challenges for the membership. In addition to learning about the duties of the new officers, the Saints had to become acquainted with the relationship of one office to another and to the place of each position in the broadening channel of jurisdiction and authority.

Office of Bishop

The first new office in the priesthood to be revealed shortly after Joseph Smith moved to Kirtland was that of a bishop. On February 4, 1831, the Prophet received a revelation directing that Edward Partridge be ordained a bishop, sell his merchandising interests, and devote all of his time to service in the Church. Five days later, the thirty-eight-year-old merchant from Painesville, who had been a Latter-day Saint for only two months, was given the responsibility of directing the Church's temporal affairs, including the law of consecration and stewardship, and was instructed to use the Saints' contributions and surplus properties to assist the needy and the poor.[5]

On June 6, 1831, two men were called to assist Bishop Partridge—Isaac Morley as his first counselor and John Corrill as second counselor. Soon thereafter Edward Partridge journeyed to Missouri with Joseph Smith and other elders. There, with the assistance of various counselors, he served the Saints until they were expelled from that state during the winter of 1838-39. Since the law of tithing was not revealed until 1838, during most of the thirties Bishop Partridge used primarily the general free-will offerings and consecrations of the Saints to administer the financial affairs of the Church in western Missouri.[6]

On December 4, 1831, a second bishop, Newel K. Whitney, was called to direct the temporal affairs of the Church in the East. At the time of his call, he was given additional knowledge through revelation concerning the responsibilities of a bishop. He was told to "keep the Lord's storehouse; to receive the funds of the Church in this part of the vineyard," and to assist the poor and the needy. By revelation, every elder was told to give an account of his stewardship to the bishop, while the bishop was instructed to issue certificates recommending those whom he deemed prepared and worthy to gather to Zion.[7]

Hyrum Smith and Reynolds Cahoon were set apart on February 10, 1832, as counselors to Bishop Whitney, and the three men met frequently as a bishopric to discuss problems of the Saints and to consider actions that should be taken to help impoverished families. They visited and administered to the sick and counseled those who needed assistance. They also occasionally preached to the Saints, reminding them of their responsibility to identify and provide help for those in need. All these duties were filled while the men continued to labor to support their families.[8]

The responsibilities of the bishoprics of Kirtland and Missouri increased as new revelations were received. In August 1831 the Prophet recorded a revelation in Missouri that stated the bishop was to "judge the people" according to the "laws of the kingdom . . . given by the prophets of God."[9] In September 1832, Bishop Whitney was instructed to travel "among all the churches, searching after the poor to administer to their wants by humbling the rich and the proud."[10] Another revelation, dated November 1831, stated that unless a bishop was a literal descendant of Aaron, he was to be chosen from the High (Melchizedek) Priesthood. In addition to his temporal responsibilities and service as a judge in Israel for those who transgressed the laws of the Church, the bishop was also to preside over the Aaronic Priesthood and serve as president of the priests quorum.[11]

Office of High Priest

In the summer of 1831, four months after the first bishop was called, twenty-three priesthood bearers were ordained high priests or, as the office was initially designated, "to the high priesthood." At a general conference in Kirtland June 3 to 6, Joseph Smith ordained five of the men to the high priesthood and Lyman Wight ordained eighteen others. According to John Whitmer, who was then serving as Church historian, at the time of the ordinations the Spirit of the Lord fell upon Joseph Smith and Lyman Wight "in an unusual manner." Both men were blessed with the gift of prophecy, he said. "Joseph Smith prophesied that John the Revelator was then among the Ten Tribes of Israel," and Lyman Wight "prophesied concerning the coming of Christ." Elder Wight then "saw the heavens opened and the Son of Man sitting on the right hand of the Father, making intercession for his brethren, the Saints." At this conference, Satan exhibited his power, but the Prophet, recognizing his presence, commanded him in the name of Christ to depart. After the evil influence had left, John Whitmer declared, the Saints rejoiced and were comforted.[12]

As Joseph Smith continued to receive revelations relating to Church government, high priests gained an increased understanding of their office and their responsibilities. In November 1831, a revelation declared that a high priest of the Melchizedek Priesthood "has authority to officiate in all the lesser offices" of the priesthood.[13] In September 1832, another revelation told high priests of their responsibility to travel to preach the gospel.[14]

In an important revelation on the priesthood dated March 1835, the Saints learned that there are in the Church two priesthoods—Aaronic, which includes the Levitical, and the Melchizedek, and that all offices in the Church are appendages to these priesthoods. The Melchizedek Priesthood holds the right of presidency and the authority to administer in spiritual concerns, while the Aaronic or lesser priesthood has power to administer in "outward ordinances." The revelation also taught that the office of a high priest was the highest ordained office the Melchizedek Priesthood, and that high priests "have a right to officiate . . . in administering spiritual things."[15]

The First Presidency

The highest or supreme council in the Church, the First Presidency, was organized in the early 1830s. At a conference held in Amherst, Lorain County, Ohio, on January 24, 1832, Joseph Smith was sustained and ordained as "President of the High Priesthood," meaning president of the priesthood.[16] The following March, he learned (in an unpublished revelation) that the office of President of the High Priesthood is vested with the authority to preside, with the assistance of counselors, over all the concerns of the Church.[17] On March 8, 1831, the Prophet selected and ordained Jesse Gause and Sidney Rigdon as his counselors.[18] Sidney Rigdon probably served as first counselor and Jesse Gause as second counselor. After the latter, a convert from the Shaker religion, denied the faith and was excommunicated on December 3, 1832, Frederick G. Williams was called to serve as counselor in the presidency.[19]

Various revelations recorded by Joseph Smith in the early 1830s clearly identified the First Presidency (a term used in 1835 to identify the presidency over the entire Church and not just the priesthood) as the supreme authority in the Church. In a revelation recorded in March 1832, the Saints learned that the keys of the kingdom belong always to "the Presidency of the High Priesthood."[20] One year after the presidency of the High Priesthood had been organized, the Prophet received a revelation, dated March 8, 1833, asserting that this body was "to preside in council, and set in order all the affairs" of the Church.[21] The revelation on priesthood recorded in 1835 further identified the authority and responsibilities of the First Presidency. "Three Presiding High Priests, chosen by the body, appointed and ordained to that office and upheld by the confidence, faith, and prayer of the church, form a quorum of the Presidency of the Church."[22] The First Presidency "have a right to officiate in all the offices in the church, . . . for this is the highest council of the church of God," with authority to render "a final decision upon controversies in spiritual matters."[23] The Church also learned by revelation that bishops must be approved by the First Presidency and shall be tried for alleged offenses before this quorum.[24]

Although Joseph Smith was told by revelation that the quorum of the First Presidency was to be comprised of three men, prior to that date he had established a precedent of calling, in addition to the first and second counselors, "assistant presidents" and other counselors. This practice continued after the revelation was received, indicating that he, Brigham Young, and other presidents of the Church recognized the propriety of occasionally calling more than two counselors to assist the President. On December 5, 1834, for example, Oliver Cowdery was called to serve as "assistant president," and the following day Joseph Smith, Sr., and Hyrum Smith were appointed as counselors. Oliver Cowdery's role was typified as one of "joint leadership," and all three men served as counselors to the Prophet.[25]

The First Patriarch to the Church

The first Patriarch to the Church in this dispensation was also called and set apart while the Saints were in Kirtland. On December 18, 1833, Joseph Smith, Sidney Rigdon, Frederick G. Williams, and Oliver Cowdery ordained Joseph Smith, Sr., to that office. According to Oliver Cowdery, Joseph Smith held all the keys of authority in the Church including the right to bestow on others patriarchal blessings; and he conferred the authority which he held upon his father. While Joseph Smith, Sr., was presiding patriarch, or Patriarch to the Church, John Young, the father of Brigham Young, was also ordained a patriarch, but he had limited jurisdictional authority.[26]

One of the unusual teachings of the Prophet relating to Church government was his explanation of the meaning of evangelist. While Christians of the 1830s referred to evangelists as revivalists or itinerant preachers, he taught that an evangelist is a patriarch. "Whenever the Church of Christ is established in the earth," he explained, "there should be a Patriarch for the benefit of the posterity of the Saints, as it was with Jacob in giving his patriarchal blessing unto his sons."[27]

The Prophet also taught that the patriarch was "the oldest man of the blood of Joseph or of the seed of Abraham." Consequently, Joseph Smith, Sr., received his authority "by blessing and by right." He was not only ordained to that position, but he was also the oldest son of Ephraim (who was the head of the house of Israel) holding the priesthood in this dispensation.[28]

Through revelation the Prophet learned of the order of the patriarchal priesthood, instituted during the time of Adam and passed from father to son until the days of Noah. According to this order, the presiding church officer was a high priest and a patriarch. This characteristic of ancient priesthood government was restored when Joseph Smith, Sr., was ordained Patriarch to the Church. He had previously been ordained a high priest, and now he was given a special patriarchal authority that was to pass from father to son. While patriarchs ordained in various stakes are not chosen on the basis of that ancient law of primogeniture, the right to the office of presiding patriarch, or Patriarch to the Church, is inherited. It belongs to the literal descendants of Joseph Smith, Sr.[29]

Following his ordination as Patriarch to the Church, Father Smith began conferring patriarchal blessings upon Latter-day Saints, setting the pattern for patriarchal blessings that have been bestowed upon members of the Church since the time he received his calling. The blessings he gave to members designated their lineage from one of the twelve tribes of Israel, counseled them, and informed them of their potential and their future activities.[30]

Though many Saints received their patriarchal blessings in Kirtland, others received these blessings from Father Smith in many other areas of North America. Edward Stevenson remembered the powerful spirit that penetrated a meeting held in 1834 in Pontiac, Michigan, during which Father Smith blessed the Saints in that region.[31] On June 22, 1836, Father Smith, accompanied by John Smith, the Prophet's uncle, left Kirtland for a mission in the eastern states to confer patriarchal blessings upon members there. For almost five months, Joseph Smith, Sr., visited branches of the Church in New York, New Hampshire, Vermont, and Pennsylvania, bestowing blessings upon hundreds of Latter-day Saints. During this 2,400-mile journey, he and John Smith also preached to thousands, baptized many converts, and visited friends and relatives.[32]

The First Stake and High Council

While the Saints were witnessing many changes in the pattern of Church government, the first stake was organized in Kirtland. As used in the Church the word *stake* probably originates from the poetic imagery of the prophet Isaiah. "Enlarge the place of thy tent," Isaiah wrote, "and let them stretch forth the curtains of thine habitations: spare not, lengthen thy cords, and strengthen thy stakes [or tent pins]."[33] The Book of Mormon also refers in symbolic terms to the church or Zion as a tent supported by cords and stakes. This ancient American scripture informs us that by lengthening the cords and strengthening the stakes, the tent (or church) can be enlarged, and spirituality and righteousness enhanced.[34] Kirtland was designated as one of the locations where a stake of Zion would be established,[35] and in the summer of 1833, the Saints were commanded "to commence a work of laying out and preparing" a "stake of Zion" there, in harmony with the pattern that had previously been revealed to the Prophet.[36]

Less than a year later, a more formal organization of the first stake of the Church occurred with the creation of the first high council. On February 17, 1834, approximately sixty members of the Church gathered at the home of Joseph Smith to attend a special meeting. Following the invocation, the Prophet announced that the purpose of the meeting was to select twelve high priests to serve as members of a high council. The high council, he said, was to help settle difficulties arising in the Church that could not be resolved in a bishop's court or by other procedures. In preparation for the meeting, the Prophet had instructed the Saints five days earlier that no man was capable of judging others unless "his heart was pure." "We frequently are so filled with prejudice, or have a beam in our own eye," he warned, "that we are not capable of passing right decisions."[37]

Under the direction of Joseph Smith forty-three members at the meeting (nine high priests, seventeen elders, four priests, and thirteen others) formed a council, and this body approved the twelve high priests, as well as the First Presidency, who were called to serve as members of this first high council.[38]

The procedures for filling vacancies in the high council and for conducting trials were described in the meeting and recorded in the minutes, which were later included in section 102 of the Doctrine and Covenants. At least seven men and one of the presidency of the Church were to form a quorum of the high council, and these members had the power to appoint other worthy high priests to serve when members of the council were absent. Vacant offices were to be filled by the nomination of the president or the presidency and approval of the council of high priests.[39]

The Kirtland high council was a unique body in the history of the Church, not only because it was the first—and for a while the only—high council, but also because the First Presidency served as the stake presidency of this "standing" high council. Later the Quorum of the Twelve Apostles was formed as a "traveling" high council, and on July 7, 1834, the Prophet organized a second high council in Clay County, Missouri, with David Whitmer as president and William W. Phelps and John Whitmer as counselors. These first two high councils were constituted before there were wards and before stake presidents presided over bishops and quorums of high priests.[40]

No single offense was consistently considered by the Kirtland high council; members were tried for a variety of improprieties of behavior. One member was accused of speaking (possibly praying) so loud during a prayer meeting that he disturbed others living in the vicinity and of not articulating so that he could be understood by those in attendance. His loud cries were considered by his accusers as disturbing rather than edifying.[41] One man was excommunicated for abandoning his family and leaving his wife and children destitute and without sufficient food or firewood.[42] Several persons were tried for breach of contract, two for lack of charity, and one for failing to attend meetings and to fulfill his promise to serve as a missionary.[43] In 1836 one of the seventies was charged with "singing songs or ditties" in a store in Kirtland that were considered incompatible with the dignity of his office and calling; this same member was also accused of smoking his pipe and drinking rum, wine, and other alcoholic beverages in the Johnson tavern.[44] Several persons were charged with publicly condemning the behavior of Joseph Smith. One person claimed that Joseph Smith was possessed of an evil spirit when he chastized a new convert, but the court ruled that the Prophet was justified in his criticisms.[45]

Most individuals tried by the Kirtland high council were members of the priesthood, but a few women and some couples were asked to appear before this ecclesiastical body. Several women were charged with injuring the character of others by spreading malicious gossip.[46] One brother and sister were found guilty of "unlawful matrimony."[47] Most religious communities in America at that time believed that dancing was improper; since the Prophet had not published a revelation relating to that subject, it seemed natural that, while he was on a trip to Missouri in 1837, the high council would consider the actions of some of the Saints who had attended a ball and would rule that dancing "with the world," in which they had been engaged, was improper.[48]

Some who appeared before the high council court were charged with teaching incorrect doctrines. One person was accused of rejecting the revelations and commandments received by Joseph Smith; another, of preaching "heretical" doctrines; and one small group, of embracing revelations allegedly received by one of the Saints who did not have the authority to receive revelation for the entire Church.[49]

A high percent of those who were accused of transgressions and were asked to appear before the Kirtland high council complied with the request, and in nearly all instances members confessed their faults during the trial and agreed to correct their failings. Only a few members were excommunicated from the Church by this court, generally individuals who were found guilty of what were considered the most serious offenses, such as "unlawful matrimony" and apostasy.[50] In nearly all instances the court ruled that fellowship would be withdrawn from those who had been found guilty until satisfaction had been made, and generally the accused persons, after admitting their mistakes and promising to correct them, retained their standing in the Church. The high council courts attempted to help rather than condemn individuals. The high councilors sought to correct the improper behavior patterns of the Saints, to reconcile contesting members, and to establish greater harmony in the Church. Disciplining members by exposing problems and withdrawing the hand of fellowship was considered necessary as a means of helping the Saints to better understand their failings and prompting changes that would enable them to strive more diligently for perfection.

The first high council of the Church was not merely a judicial body; it had administrative responsibilities as well. Acting under the direction of the presidency of the Church, the Kirtland high councilors approved men for ordination to the Melchizedek Priesthood, assigned missionaries to labor in various parts of North America, and recommended that some members settle in Kirtland and that others migrate to Missouri.[51] They agreed to encourage Emma Smith to proceed with the publication of a hymnal in compliance with a revelation that Joseph Smith had received.[52] They recommended that Joseph Smith, Sr., be paid ten dollars a week plus expenses for his services as Patriarch to the Church, and that Frederick G. Williams be paid the same for serving as his scribe.[53] And in October 1837, the high council appointed a committee to ask John Johnson, Jr., to desist from selling spiritous li-

quors to those who were in the habit of becoming intoxicated and
to report to Church authorities the names of any Mormons who
drank alcoholic beverages in his tavern.[54]

The Quorum of the Twelve Apostles

Almost a year before the organization of the Church, Joseph
Smith and Oliver Cowdery were ordained and confirmed apostles
and special witnesses of Christ by Peter, James, and John.[55]
Shortly thereafter, in June, 1829, Joseph received a revelation
that not only declared that Oliver Cowdery and David Whitmer
had received the same calling as that of the ancient apostle Paul,
but also commissioned these men to select the original Twelve
Apostles in this dispensation.[56] Later Martin Harris was called to
assist Elders Cowdery and Whitmer in this selection; this meant
the three special witnesses to the Book of Mormon as a group were
given the responsibility of choosing the Twelve Apostles. Oliver
Cowdery said that the Three Witnesses constantly stretched their
minds and frequently fasted and prayed, seeking the advice of the
Lord concerning those who should be selected to serve as His
twelve special witnesses.[57]

After receiving a series of visions and revelations relating to
the pattern of Church government, the Prophet invited the
former members of Zion's Camp and many others living in and
near Kirtland to a special meeting on Saturday, February 14,
1835, in the schoolhouse next to the rising temple. There he informed them that the meeting was being held in harmony with a
commandment of the Lord. He reminded the congregation of the
trials and sufferings of the members of Zion's Camp, explaining
that their sacrifices had not been in vain. Then he noted that
these men were now to "go forth to prune the vineyard." He
promised the Saints that they would be involved in great accomplishments, would be blessed by the "whisperings of the Spirit of
God," and would be "endowed with power from on high."[58]

Following the Prophet's discourse and the customary prayers
and singing of hymns, the meeting was adjourned for an hour.
When it was reconvened, the Quorum of the Twelve Apostles
was organized. The presidency laid their hands on the heads of the

Three Witnesses and blessed them, after which the names of the Twelve whom they had been selected were read in the following order:

1. Lyman E. Johnson
2. Brigham Young
3. Heber C. Kimball
4. Orson Hyde
5. David W. Patten
6. Luke S. Johnson
7. William E. McLellin
8. John F. Boynton
9. Orson Pratt
10. William Smith
11. Thomas B. Marsh
12. Parley P. Pratt

Three of the newly appointed apostles—Lyman E. Johnson, Brigham Young, and Heber C. Kimball—were ordained as apostles by the Three Witnesses, who took turns in offering the ordination prayers and blessings. The presidency then confirmed the ordinations and blessings, and also predicted "many things which should come to pass."[59]

Nine of the Twelve Apostles were ordained soon after the February 14 meeting. The next day, Oliver Cowdery ordained Orson Hyde, David W. Patten, and Luke S. Johnson, after which William E. McLellin, John F. Boynton, and William Smith received similar blessings. At a meeting held February 21, Joseph Smith, David Whitmer, and Oliver Cowdery ordained Parley P. Pratt.[60] The last two men to be set apart were serving in the mission field at the time of their call and were subsequently ordained to the apostleship after they returned to Kirtland. Thomas B. Marsh was probably ordained on April 25 by Oliver Cowdery, and Orson Pratt was ordained on April 26. These last two elders were also blessed with a confirmatory ordinance by David Whitmer.[61]

Like so many other individuals called to serve in the 1830s, the original Twelve Apostles knew very little about their responsibilities, and it is likely that Joseph Smith himself did not fully understand in 1835 all of the duties of these new officers. Consequently, the presidency periodically instructed the men concerning their new assignment.

After nine of the Twelve Apostles had been ordained, Oliver Cowdery delivered a general charge to them that is sometimes referred to as the "Oath and Covenant of the Apostleship." He read to the apostles a selection from a revelation received by the Prophet in June 1829 that specified that apostles were to take upon themselves the name of Christ "with full purpose of heart" and were "to go into all the world to preach" the everlasting gospel. President Cowdery encouraged them to cultivate humility; to avoid "worldly objects," to establish their ministry as a first priority in their lives; to gain a powerful conviction of the divinity of the Savior; and then, after receiving an endowment of power from God, to go forth as special witnesses of Christ into all the world. Then he grasped the hand of each of the apostles in turn and said to each one, "[Will] you with full purpose of heart take part in this ministry, to proclaim the Gospel with all diligence, with these your brethren, according to the tenor and intent of the charge you have received?" Each of them responded affirmatively.[62]

Shortly after the calling of the apostles, a question arose concerning the jurisdiction of the Twelve in relationship to that of the two high councils that had recently been constituted. Joseph Smith considered this subject at a priesthood meeting in Kirtland on May 2, 1835. After the Twelve had taken their seats according to their age (with Thomas B. Marsh, who was then the oldest apostle, called as the first apostle to preside over that body), the Prophet instructed the priesthood that the apostles were to serve as a traveling high council and were to preside in areas outside of the stakes where there were standing high councils. He also stated that "no standing High Council has authority to go into the churches abroad, and regulate the matters thereof, for this belongs to the Twelve." Moreover, he said that high councils should be organized only in regions where stakes were formed.[63]

Early in 1836 the Prophet instructed the apostles that they had an authority above that of the high council. At a meeting on January 16, the Prophet again explained to the Twelve their duties and emphasized that the authority of the Twelve Apostles was next to that of the First Presidency and was subject to them and to no other body in the Church.[64]

In keeping with the initial guideline that the apostles were to regulate affairs of the Church outside the stakes, the Prophet called the Twelve in 1835 to preach, teach, and administer the affairs of the Church in Canada and the northern states. One evening, shortly before the Twelve departed for their missions, they met with the Prophet and asked him to inquire of the Lord whether it would be in harmony with His will to receive a revelation relating to their duties. They explained that such a revelation would be a means of comforting them and brightening their hopes while they were away from home. In response, the Prophet inquired of the Lord and received the first fifty-eight verses of what is now section 107 of the Doctrine and Covenants. In addition to identifying the distinctions between the Aaronic and Melchizedek priesthoods, the revelation explains many of the duties of the various quorums and of the Church's presiding officers.[65]

After receiving a charge to go forth and build up the kingdom of God, all of the original members of the Quorum of the Twelve Apostles left Kirtland in May 1835 to preach and regulate the affairs of the Church in the East. Over the next six months, they conducted conferences in New York, Massachusetts, New Hampshire, and Maine, and helped determine boundaries for conferences (geographical regions) and branches. They counseled and instructed the presiding officers in these areas and attempted to resolve problems that had developed. They also encouraged the Saints to contribute to the building of Zion in Missouri and appointed others to continue promoting this program after they had departed. During their busy schedule, the apostles called individuals to serve as local leaders of the Church, preached at conferences, baptized and confirmed new members, administered the sacrament, and taught many members and nonmembers the basic principles of the gospel.[66]

The Twelve returned to Kirtland for additional schooling and to receive their endowments in the temple. At a meeting in the temple on March 30, 1836, the Prophet said, "The Twelve are at liberty to go wheresoever they will, and if any one will say, I wish to go to such a place, let all the rest say amen."[67] During the summer of 1836 most of the apostles served missions in the East. The following winter, ten preached in Ohio, while Thomas B. Marsh labored in Missouri. In 1837 two of the apostles were sent to England to introduce the gospel in that land and between 1839 and 1841 all but two of the apostles served in foreign lands.[68]

The First Quorum of Seventy

Two weeks after the organization of the Quorum of Twelve Apostles, the Prophet began to form the First Quorum of Seventy. Prior to this meeting, while discussing the vision he had received relating to the structure of Church government, the Prophet said to Joseph Young, "Brother Joseph, the Lord has made you President of the Seventies." Joseph Young was startled by the Prophet's remarks. He said that he knew about Moses and the seventy elders of Israel and that Jesus had appointed other seventies, but he had not known that seventies would serve in the restored Church. He also marveled when the Prophet informed him that he was to serve as one of the presidents, as though the event had already transpired.[69] The first seventies in this dispensation were called on Saturday, February 28, 1835, from among those who had served in Zion's Camp. Some of them were ordained that day, and others were ordained at a meeting the following day.[70]

Although some early members of the Church referred to the seventies as seventy elders who had received a special missionary call,[71] specific information concerning the quorum of seventy appeared in the revelation on the priesthood dated March 28, 1835. This revelation stated that the seventies (referring to the First Quorum of Seventy) formed a quorum "equal in authority to that of the Twelve special witnesses or Apostles." Decisions made by each quorum were to be unanimous. Under the direction of the Twelve, the seventies were to preach the gospel throughout the world and to build up and regulate the affairs of the Church. Seven presidents selected from the seventies would preside over them. The revelation, printed in the 1835 edition of the Doctrine and Covenants, further stated that other officers of the Church were "not under the responsibility to travel among all nations," but were "to travel as their circumstances" allowed. Though the revelation did not identify all the responsibilities of the seventies and other bearers of the priesthood, it concluded that every man should learn his duty and act in all diligence in the office to which he was appointed.[72]

The Prophet identified the seventies as a distinct quorum when, at various meetings, officers of the Church sat together according to their callings. At a general assembly in Kirtland on August 17, 1835, the seven presidents of the seventy elders occupied one section and twenty-seven of the seventy elders sat together. When some of the presidents were absent during special priesthood meetings, others were appointed to take their place, and alternates participated in the business conducted during the meetings. Under the direction of the Prophet, the seventies also met as a quorum in the Kirtland Temple in 1836 and received special blessings.[73]

As the number of priesthood bearers called to serve as seventies increased, additional quorums were formed, with seventy members comprising each of the full quorums. On Sunday, February 7, 1836, the Prophet met with the presidency of the First Quorum of Seventy in the loft of the printing office and organized the Second Quorum of Seventy.[74] Less than a year later, on December 20, 1836, the Third Quorum of Seventy was constituted in Kirtland.[75]

Following the calling of the seventies, a controversy developed between the seventies and high priests concerning which group had preeminence. Joseph Smith resolved the difficulty in the spring of 1837 by reorganizing the seventies and asking the presidents of the seventies who had been ordained high priests prior to their ordination as seventies to unite with the high priests quorum. Then he called others to serve as presidents of the seventies. Five of the seven presidents were thereby released, and five other bearers of the priesthood were called and ordained presidents of the First Council of the Seventy.[76]

The First Aaronic Priesthood Quorums

During the same decade that the offices of the Melchizedek Priesthood were revealed and presiding quorums were formed, members of the Aaronic Priesthood were also organized into quorums in harmony with information in the revelation on the priesthood, section 107 of the Doctrine and Covenants. The revelation stated that deacons, teachers, and priests were to be directed by presidencies and that there was to be a limited number in each quorum or organized body of priesthood holders. The president of the deacons quorum was to preside over twelve deacons, the teachers' president over twenty-four teachers, and the priests' president over forty-eight priests.[77] While the bishop was to preside over the Aaronic Priesthood, including the priests quorum, during the 1830s presidents who were not bishops helped direct the activities of the priests.[78]

By 1835, the first known deacons, teachers, and priests quorums had been organized in Kirtland. At a general conference on August 1, 1835, at which members approved the revelations included in the first edition of the Doctrine and Covenants, Ira Ames acted as president of the priests quorum; Erastus Babbitt, the teachers quorum and William Burgess, the deacons quorum.[79] One year later, on the day of the dedication of the Kirtland Temple, leaders of the Aaronic Priesthood sat in the pulpits located on the east end of the chapel. The bishop of Kirtland and his counselors sat in the three highest pulpits, the bishopric of Zion in the second tier down, the presidency of the priests quorum in the third tier, and the presidency of the teachers quorum in the lowest level. Meanwhile, the presidency of the deacons quorum sat near the pulpits adjacent to the high councilors of Zion.[80] Deacons, teachers, and priests also participated in the ordinances performed in the temple and received a special endowment.[81]

No records are available indicating whether or not Aaronic Priesthood quorums were organized in the 1830s in branches or conferences outside the stakes of Zion. Since so few men were called to serve in the offices of the Aaronic Priesthood at that time, quorums were probably not formed, and regular meetings of those holding this priesthood were not held in the regions where few Latter-day Saints lived.[82]

During this early period, there seems to have been no relationship between age and ordination to offices in the Aaronic and Melchizedek priesthoods. Although mature men were generally ordained to the priesthood, there were exceptions to this practice. Don Carlos Smith, the youngest brother of the Prophet, was ordained to the lesser priesthood at fourteen years of age, and before he was twenty, he was called to serve as president of the high priests. Some of the younger members of Zion's Camp were also ordained to offices of the Aaronic Priesthood before marching to Missouri, and one father was ordained to the office of deacon while his son was ordained to the office of priest. [83]

During the 1830s there apparently was no regular procedure for advancement from one office in the priesthood to another. Some converts were ordained to the office of elder on the day of their baptism. Others were ordained to the office of deacon, teacher, or priest on the day they were confirmed members of the Church. Some were ordained to the office of teachers and later advanced to elder or high priest, while others were initially ordained to the office of deacon and a few years later to elder. Some of these advancements occurred shortly after the initial ordinations, while others took place a number of years later. Orrin Porter Rockwell, for example, was baptized in 1830 but was not ordained a deacon until July 1838. [84]

Members seemed to have been ordained to particular offices according to the needs of the Church as well as the guidance leaders received from the Holy Ghost. [85] Though there seems to have been no established time between ordinations, there is no evidence that any member was ordained to a lower office in the priesthood after having received his first higher priesthood ordination, or that bearers of the Aaronic Priesthood, even those who served in the mission field, were authorized to ordain others to the priesthood. [86]

Church Courts and Secular Governments

While the various priesthood quorums were being formed, the basic pattern of the judicial system of the Church was developed and the beliefs of the Saints concerning the relationship between religion and the state were clarified. By mid-1835 the three standing courts in the Church had been created: the bishop's court, the stake high council, and the council of the First Presidency. While the bishop's court was a court of original jurisdiction, the stake high council became not only a court of original jurisdiction, but also an appellate court to hear appeals from the bishop's court. According to the revelation on priesthood, the highest court in the Church is the council of the First Presidency. This body, coupled with twelve other high priests appointed by the First Presidency, forms a council with authority to consider any case arising in the Church; it may also review appeals from any other Church court and register decisions from which there is no appeal.[87]

As the judicial system of the Church was expanding, so too were the beliefs of the Saints concerning government and law and the relationship between church and state. These were codified and set forth at the meeting on August 17, 1835, when the Saints approved the revelations published in the first edition of the Doctrine and Covenants. At that meeting, Oliver Cowdery read a statement of belief describing the attitude of the Church toward civil government. This declaration was included in the appendix of the Doctrine and Covenants and is now section 134. According to this affirmation, "governments were instituted of God for the benefit of man," constitutional laws are designed to protect the rights and privileges of all, and the Latter-day Saints are obligated to obey and sustain the law of the land. Although this document declares that religious influences should not be mingled with civil government, it does not advocate total separation of church and state; rather, religion has the right to secure protection from the state. On the other hand, the secular government has no right to interfere with the religious beliefs of its citizens so long as such beliefs do not incite crime or infringe upon the rights of others. Concerning the relationship between civil and ecclesiastical courts, the declaration asserts that religious societies have the right to try members for infringing upon the rules and regulations of the religious community and to withdraw the hand of fellowship from disobedient members, but they do not have the right to inflict death or physical punishment upon their members nor deprive anyone of his property. Such actions fall under the jurisdiction of civil government.[88]

The Name of the Church

During this formative era, the Latter-day Saints considered various names for their church organization, which had generally been referred to as the Church of Christ. Although the Book of Mormon states that the Church should be named after Christ, confusion developed because many religious communities in America and various local congregations also identified themselves as members of the Church of Christ or the Church of Jesus Christ.[89] To differentiate the new church from others, some nonmembers began referring to it as the "Mormonites" (because of the Saints' belief in the Book of Mormon). After expressing displeasure at being identified in this way, members of the Church agreed at a conference in Kirtland on May 3, 1834, that the Church be known by the name of "The Church of the Latter-day Saints," and that this title be used in minutes of meetings.[90] Although some members began using this new title, they continued to refer to the Church as the Church of Christ. Before 1838, many other names were used in records to identify the restored Church, such as Church of Christ of the Latter-day Saints.[91] On April 26, 1838, shortly after he moved to Far West, Missouri, the Prophet received a revelation that identified the official name of the Church as The Church of Jesus Christ of Latter-day Saints.[92]

The Word of Wisdom

Since new revelations were being received frequently in the new church, the Saints were constantly challenged to interpret correctly and then apply in their lives the principles revealed to them. One revelation that created such a challenge was the Word of Wisdom. The administration of this principle demonstrates not only the procedures used to guide the membership and clarify Church policy, but also the gradual process by which members integrated into their lives teachings that sometimes demanded substantial changes in their pattern of living.

There seems to have been no question among the Saints that strong drink meant alcoholic beverages, and members of the 1830s interpreted hot drinks as tea and coffee. Elizabeth Tanner, who lived in Kirtland, wrote that after learning about the revelation known as the Word of Wisdom, she and her husband discarded "tea, coffee, and spirituous liquors."[93] When William W. Phelps wrote to his wife and informed her that the Saints in Kirtland were observing the Word of Wisdom, he specifically stated that they refrained from drinking tea and coffee.[94] According to Joel H. Johnson, five months after the Word of Wisdom was revealed, Joseph Smith asked a congregation, "Now, what do we drink when we take our meals? Tea and coffee. Is it not?" Answering his own question, he said, "They are what the Lord meant when He said 'Hot drinks.'"[95] Hyrum Smith and Brigham Young also defined hot drinks as tea and coffee, explaining that these two stimulants were the hot beverages that were most popular among Americans when the revelation was received.[96] Zebedee Coltrin recalled that while many members gradually discontinued using tobacco, the Saints' fellowship "was jeopardised" if they did not immediately discontinue using tea and coffee; and in March 1838, those who desired to migrate west with the seventies in a group called Kirtland Camp signed their names to a constitution that included the following rule: each person would keep the commandments and heed the Word of Wisdom, "that is, no tobacco, tea, coffee, snuff, nor ardent spirits of any kind taken internally."[97]

Although the Saints understood that the revelation proscribed smoking and chewing tobacco and drinking alcoholic beverages, tea, and coffee, questions arose concerning the relationship between Word of Wisdom observance and Church membership and service. Since many members were addicted to these habit-forming substances, observance of the law was sometimes gradual and sporadic.

In February 1834, one year after the Word of Wisdom was announced, a dispute occurred among members in Erie County, Pennsylvania. Some of them refused to partake of the sacrament because the elder who administered it did not observe the Word of Wisdom. Lyman Johnson, who was visiting the branch at the time, argued that because of the transgression of the elder the members were justified in not partaking the sacrament. However, Orson Pratt, another traveling elder who was also visiting the branch, disagreed. He argued that members were entitled to receive the sacrament from a bearer of the priesthood as long as the priesthood bearer retained his office and license. The issue was referred to Church officials in Kirtland. The Kirtland high council was at the time considering another related problem. On February 20, 1834, they discussed whether or not disobedience to the Word of Wisdom was a sufficient transgression to deprive a person who understood the revelation from holding a Church position. Following the discussion, Joseph Smith, as president of the high council, declared, "No official member in this Church is worthy to hold an office, after having the Word of Wisdom properly taught him, and he, the official member, neglecting to comply with, or obey" it. The council confirmed this decision. [98]

Many members scattered throughout the country did not know about the high council's decision and consequently wrote letters to Kirtland for clarification of the revelation. In response to these inquiries, Church leaders printed the high council's decision in the November 1836 issue of the *Messenger and Advocate*. [99] The essence of this decision was repeated in an editorial printed in the same periodical in May 1837:

> If, as the Lord has said, strong drinks are not to be taken internally, can those who use them thus be held guiltless? We ask, if hot drinks are not to be used, if those who make use of them do not transgress his commands, or at least set at nought his counsel? Most assuredly they do.
>
> Have not the authorities of the church in council in this place, decided deliberately and positively that if any official member of this church shall violate or in any wise disregard the words of wisdom which the Lord has given for the benefit of his saints, he shall lose his office? What official member does not know this? Brethren, either we believe this to be a revelation from God, or we do not. [100]

While Church leaders encouraged the Saints to refrain from undesirable habits, many members continued to struggle in their attempts to discontinue habits that were difficult to control. During their first extended mission in 1835, the apostles instructed the Saints to incorporate in their lives the principles outlined in the Word of Wisdom revelation. Upon their return to Kirtland, they reported that some members failed to have the Spirit because they neglected to observe the Word of Wisdom. [101] Mary Ann Stearns Winters recalled that her mother, Mary Pratt, habitually used snuff before she learned about the Word of Wisdom. But after she learned about the revelation and also after she was told in her patriarchal blessing that she should observe the Word of Wisdom, she accepted the challenge to discontinue this troublesome habit. When she was tempted, especially in the evenings, she would read the Book of Mormon until the desire had passed. According to Mary Winters, it was only after years of struggle that her mother overcame the habit. [102]

In 1837 there was a renewed effort to encourage the Saints to live in harmony with the Word of Wisdom. In April and July, the seventies agreed that they would not fellowship (by recognizing their right to preach) any member of the quorum who indulged in the "use of ardent spirits."[103] In May the First Presidency, the high council of Missouri, two of the twelve apostles, and ten seventies held a priesthood meeting in Far West, Missouri, and resolved unanimously that they would not fellowship any ordained member who did not observe the Word of Wisdom "according to its literal reading."[104] In October, the First Quorum of Elders agreed unanimously that all traveling elders who preached the gospel were "to observe and teach the Word of Wisdom." They further agreed to revoke the licenses of elders who did not comply with the policy.[105] And on November 7, at a priesthood meeting in Far West, the congregation "voted not to support stores and shops selling spirituous liquors, tea, coffee, or tobacco."[106]

Except for the offense of habitual drinking of hard liquors, the policies adopted by the priesthood in 1837 regarding Word of Wisdom observance were not rigidly enforced. Some persons justified the occasional use of tea and other stimulants for medical purposes or as stimulants in cases of stress or unusual fatigue. Sidney Rigdon proposed in December 1836 that the Saints discontinue using liquor during periods of sickness,[107] but there apparently was little or no significant change in the habits of the Saints as a result of this proposal. In fact, so many writings of members in the thirties casually mention the drinking of wine that it is apparent a sizeable number of members did not consider moderate wine drinking in the same category as the use of strong drinks.[108] Sometimes members justified their own breaking of the Word of Wisdom by pointing out that some Church leaders failed to observe all aspects of that revelation. One such case was brought before the high council in Kirtland, and the person who had used this as his excuse for not keeping the Word of Wisdom was rebuked and instructed to "observe the Word of Wisdom, and commandments of the Lord in all things."[109]

Except for excessive drinking, members of the Church in the thirties were generally not disfellowshipped or excommunicated for violating provisions in the Word of Wisdom. In all cases in which the Word of Wisdom was mentioned as a factor leading to an excommunication, other more serious infractions were cited as reasons for expelling the members from the Church. One elder in New York was expelled "for breach of covenant and not observing the Word of Wisdom."[110] Another elder was removed from office because he neglected his family and used strong drink.[111] One of the accusations that led to the excommunication of David Whitmer in 1838 was that he violated the Word of Wisdom. Included among the more serious problems of Elder Whitmer was his refusal to acknowledge the Word of Wisdom as a revelation.[112]

In 1913 President Joseph F. Smith reviewed the gradual embracement of the Word of Wisdom by many members of the Church, stating, "The reason undoubtedly why the Word of Wisdom was given—as not by 'commandment or restraint' was that at that time, at least, if it had been given as a commandment it would have brought every man, addicted to the use of these noxious things, under condemnation; so the Lord was merciful and gave them a chance to overcome, before he brought them under the law."[113]

In the 1830s, Joseph Smith received many revelations related to various gospel principles, moral conduct, patterns of ecclesiastical government, and Church programs. As they were instructed, the Saints had the challenge of embracing these new patterns of religious thought, of altering some of their opinions and habits, of accepting new calls of leadership and service, and of magnifying their callings. As they harmonized their actions with the new directions they received from the Prophet, they were promised that they would reap joy, find great treasures of knowledge, obtain internal peace, and receive a special blessing in the House of the Lord.[114]

Chapter 15

Life among the Early Saints

The Saints in Kirtland lived in an agrarian society. Not all of their time, however, was spent in plowing, planting, harvesting, cutting wood, making clothes, preparing foods for the winter, and constructing buildings. During the 1830s they also found time for study, attending school, worship, and prayerful meditation. Their daily lives were generally centered around the family, and families enjoyed long evenings together.

In some respects life in the 1830s was very different from that of individuals in the twentieth century, but in other respects the pattern of living was similar to that encountered by later generations. Like people of today, the early Saints experienced sorrow and suffering, faced constant challenges, and felt joy in working, worshiping, learning, relaxing, and partaking of the beauties of the world in which they lived.

Educational Opportunities

During the 1830s, Kirtland became an educational center, providing schools for missionaries, members in general, and non-members, for men and women, young and old alike. Educational opportunities for many persons in the early nineteenth century were meager. Joseph Smith wrote that while he was living in Manchester, New York, he was unable to attend school as often as most teenagers because of the poverty of his family. His early formal education was limited, he said, to a study of the rudiments of reading, writing, and arithmetic.[1] Brigham Young attended school for approximately eleven days before joining the Church.[2] Others who settled in Kirtland had received more formal education. For example, Oliver Cowdery, Orson Hyde, Sidney Rigdon, and William E. McLellin had all taught school before learning about the restoration.[3]

Many of the revelations Joseph Smith received in Ohio not only commanded Church leaders and missionaries to study various subjects, but also emphasized the importance of education for all members. In June 1831, William W. Phelps and Oliver Cowdery were commanded by revelation to select and write books that could be used in the schools established to provide a general education for the Latter-day Saints.[4] In a revelation received in 1833, the Prophet learned that "the glory of God is intelligence."[5] This same revelation instructed the Saints to "bring up [their] children in light and truth," with truth being defined as "knowledge of things as they are, as they were, and as they are to come."[6] Another revelation taught that "it is impossible for a man to be saved in ignorance." Some members of the Church concluded from this that salvation itself depended on education of the spirit, if not of the mind as well.[7]

In 1838, Church leaders explained that one of the principal reasons for gathering to Kirtland was to provide members with educational advantages. "Intelligence is the great object of our holy religion," the Saints were told. Therefore, "It is of all things important, that we should place ourselves in the best situation possible to obtain it. . . . Intelligence is the result of education, and education can only be obtained by living in compact society; so compact, that schools of all kinds can be supported." They were assured that it did not matter how much they had learned before joining the Church, for it would always be a major challenge to everyone to increase his intelligence and enlarge his knowledge and understanding of all things relating to his peace and happiness.[8]

Latter-day Saints were not the only Christians in Ohio in the 1830s who promoted education among their members. All advanced schools (those going beyond the training received in public and private elementary and secondary schools) were controlled to a large extent by religious groups. Since there was no state aid for education at that time, each community was responsible to provide schools for its citizens. With the influx of thousands of Latter-day Saints into Kirtland, a definite need arose for the Church to provide educational opportunities for the converts who gathered in that area.[9]

A few schools were scattered about the township of Kirtland when the first Latter-day Saints began gathering there. One of these was located on a hill north of the Isaac Morley farmhouse. Another school was situated on the flats east of the Newel K. Whitney store, on the south side of the road near the creek that ran into the east branch of the Chagrin River. These schools provided an elementary education for the children of all faiths living in Kirtland township.[10]

The School of the Prophets

The first school established by Latter-day Saints—and the forerunner of all formal educational efforts by the Church—was a seminary for missionaries and Church leaders called the School of the Prophets.

On December 27, 1832, Joseph Smith received a revelation, known as the "Olive Leaf," which commanded the Church to organize this school and provided instructions concerning the curriculum, the operation of the school, the student body, and the blessings to be derived from complying with the commandment.[11]

The revelation specified that the Saints should not only learn the doctrines of the kingdom by seeking wisdom "out of the best books," but that they should also study "things both in heaven and in the earth, and under the earth; things which have been, things which are, things which must shortly come to pass; things which are at home, things which are abroad; the wars and perplexities of the nations, and the judgments which are on the land; and a knowledge also of the countries and of kingdoms."[12] The Olive

Leaf revelation emphasized that individuals were to "teach one another" and to learn by "study and also by faith."[13] Knowledge was to be derived not only by reason, but also by revelation. A few weeks later, Joseph Smith recorded another revelation in which members of the Church were told to "become acquainted with all good books, and with languages, tongues, and people."[14]

Not all priesthood members were invited to participate in the first session of the School of Prophets. Only those who were considered "the first laborers in the last kingdom" gathered for this instruction. While these men assembled in Kirtland for a season, other missionaries were told to continue laboring "in the vineyard."[15] When the School of the Prophets was officially organized in January 1833, fourteen individuals—twelve high priests and two elders—attended. Orson Pratt was admitted to the school a few weeks later. Zebedee Coltrin, one of the original fourteen students, later recalled that when the Word of Wisdom was initially read to this group, twenty-one elders were in attendance.[16]

Although most rules governing the actions of those who attended the School of the Prophets were gospel principles that all Latter-day Saints were expected to follow, some policies of the school marked it as a distinct educational system. The students frequently gathered at sunrise in the spirit of fasting and prayer. The teacher preceded the students into the classroom and, after offering a personal prayer, admitted the others into the room. When the students had gathered, the instructor saluted them with uplifted hands and cited an oath that had been received by revelation. The students repeated this oath, which included a promise that they were keeping all the commandments of God. The classes often continued until about four o'clock in the afternoon. The students usually fasted during the day and broke their fast before leaving for home by partaking of the sacrament together, eating some bread (often freshly baked, about the size of a man's fist according to Zebedee Coltrin), and drinking a glass of wine, in harmony with the pattern practiced by Jesus and his disciples.[17]

Another unusual aspect of the School of the Prophets was that members were admitted only after participating in the ordinance of washing of feet. On January 23, 1833, a select group of elders assembled in Kirtland and, "after much speaking, singing, praying, and praising God, all in tongues," followed the procedure outlined in the thirteenth chapter of John's Gospel and participated in this sacred ordinance. According to Joseph Smith, "Each Elder washed his own feet first, after which I girded myself with a towel and washed the feet of all of them, wiping them with the towel with which I was girded." Before washing the feet of his father, the Prophet requested and received a father's blessing. Frederick G. Williams washed Joseph Smith's feet, after which the Prophet pronounced the elders "clean from the blood of this generation." The meeting continued throughout the day and concluded after all present had partaken of the Lord's Supper.[18]

Describing one of the major objectives of the School of the Prophets, Orson Pratt said that the men gathered so that they might learn about "the operations of the Spirit upon the mind of man."[19] John Taylor reported that Joseph Smith counseled the elders not to hesitate in expressing their thoughts, for, the Prophet said, "it was very common for the Holy Spirit to reveal some things to obscure individuals" that were not known to others. Consequently, an exchange of ideas and reflections was considered profitable to all.[20] Joseph noted in his history that because of "the things revealed, and our progress in the knowledge of God," great joy and satisfaction enriched the lives of the members of the school.[21]

One of the blessings promised to members of the School of the Prophets was a knowledge of the Savior. When the students went forth to preach, they were endowed with a special witness of the living Christ. In a letter written in January 1833 to William W. Phelps in Independence, Missouri, Joseph Smith referred to the Olive Leaf revelation and then stated that if the members complied with the commandments included in that revelation, they would receive unusual blessings, "even a visit from the heavens." They would be honored, he wrote, with God's presence.[22] This promise was partially realized in March 1833. Two months after the School of the Prophets was organized, the Prophet instructed the students to prepare themselves for a day of "revelation and vision." After the students gathered at sunrise, Joseph Smith counseled them to prepare their minds, for "the pure in heart should see a heavenly vision." For a brief period, the elders offered personal prayers. Then a powerful spiritual experience occurred. According to minutes kept by Frederick G. Williams, which were later included in the *History of the Church,* "Many of the brethren saw a heavenly vision of the Savior, and concourses of angels, and many other things, of which each one has a record of what he saw.[23]

In addition to Joseph Smith and Frederick G. Williams, two other persons, Zebedee Coltrin and John Murdock, testified that Christ appeared to members of the School of the Prophets. Elder Coltrin declared that while the men in the school were praying, he saw a personage pass through the room. Joseph Smith asked if the men knew who had appeared to them. Before anyone could answer, the Prophet replied that it was "Jesus, our elder brother, the Son of God." The men resumed praying, and once again, Elder Coltrin said he beheld a person in the room "whose glory and brightness was so great" that he likened it to the burning bush Moses saw. "Its power was so great," he said, "that had it continued much longer I believe it would have consumed us." After this second personage disappeared, Zebedee Coltrin recalled, Joseph Smith announced that they had just seen "the Father of Jesus Christ."[24]

John Murdock, who was boarding with the Prophet during the spring of 1833, described in his journal the experience he had while attending one of the meetings in the Prophet's home:

> The Prophet told us if we could humble ourselves before God, and exercise strong faith, we should see the face of the Lord. And about midday the visions of my mind were opened, and the eyes of my understanding were enlightened, and I saw the form of a man, most lovely, the visage of his face was sound and fair as the sun. His hair a bright silver gray, curled in most majestic form. His eyes a keen penetrating blue, and the skin of his neck a most beautiful white and he was covered from the neck to the feet with a loose garment, pure white, whiter than any garment I have ever before seen. His countenance was most penetrating, and yet most lovely. And while I was endeavoring to comprehend the whole personage from head to feet it slipped from me, and the vision was closed. . . . But it left on my mind the impression of love, for months, that I never felt before to that degree.[25]

For approximately three months, members of the priesthood gathered in Joseph Smith's home to attend the School of the Prophets. At that time he was living in an apartment built in the Newel K. Whitney store, and the school met in a room above the kitchen. There the men were taught the doctrines of the kingdom by the Prophet. It is probable that Sidney Rigdon, Orson Hyde, and other students attending the school also instructed the students in areas in which they had special knowledge. [26]

The School for the Elders

During the winter of 1834-35, one year after the School of the Prophets was organized, the Church sponsored two educational institutions in Kirtland: the School for the Elders and the Kirtland School. The School for the Elders, organized in November 1834, replaced the School of the Prophets. Although Joseph Smith sometimes referred to this new school as the School of the Prophets, there is no evidence that members of the priesthood involved in it participated in the footwashing ordinance. [27] As with the School of the Prophets, a major purpose of this institution was to train the men who were enrolled to be more effective missionaries and ministers of the gospel. [28] Another important function was to prepare the men to receive an endowment in the temple after its completion. [29] The school was initially held in a thirty- by thirty-eight-foot room below the printing shop in a building on the lot west of the temple. [30]

The School for the Elders convened during the winter months, when there was not as much work to be done on the farms and when the elders were not as actively involved in missionary work. The first term ran from November 1834 through March 1835, after which the elders were instructed to go forth and proclaim the gospel. [31] Another session began on November 3, 1835, and continued in the schoolroom below the printing office until January 18, 1836, when the school moved into rooms on the third floor of the temple. [32] About April 1, as the priesthood bearers again began to prepare to return to the mission field, the second session terminated. [33]

Those who attended the school studied such subjects as English grammar, writing, philosophy, government, literature, geography, and ancient and modern history. Among the texts they used were Richard Watson's *Theological Institutes or a View of the Evidences, Doctrines, Morals, and Institutions of Christianity* (1834) and Royal Robbins's *The World Developed in its History and Geography Embracing a History of the World* (1832). Although the students explored a variety of disciplines, religious topics received the main emphasis. Under the date of December 1, 1834, the Prophet recorded that the School for the Elders was well attended and lectures on theology were delivered regularly. He also said that the school absorbed nearly all the time of the students.[34]

Seven of the lectures on theology that were delivered to the School for the Elders during the winter of 1834-35 were published in the first edition of the Doctrine and Covenants, under the title "Lectures on Faith." These discussions contained information on such Church doctrines as faith, miracles, sacrifice, the existence of God, the attributes and character of the Father and the Son, and the gift of the Holy Ghost. From 1836 to 1921 this information was included in all editions of the Doctrine and Covenants published by the Church. Though lectures were not regarded as equal in authority to the revelations, they were considered profitable for the gaining of a better understanding of the doctrines of the kingdom.[35]

In harmony with the commandment to teach one another words of wisdom, several individuals served as instructors in the School for the Elders. Joseph Smith presided over the school and taught various subjects, including theology. Sidney Rigdon was also one of the principal teachers. Frederick G. Williams and William E. McLellin also probably assisted in directing the studies of the elders in what was one of the first schools for adults organized in the United States.[36]

As priesthood bearers gathered in Kirtland in the fall of 1835 to receive an endowment and attend dedicatory services of the temple, the numbers who attended the School for the Elders increased rapidly. Accommodations were so crowded in Kirtland that some persons stayed in nearby communities or farms and traveled to Kirtland to attend classes or meetings in the temple.[37]

After the Kirtland Temple was completed, various educational organizations of the Church began to meet there, some concentrating on theological subjects and others on secular knowledge. In 1836 the School for the Elders was reorganized under the name School of the Prophets. Within the walls of the temple, the students participated again in the ordinance of washing of feet, partook of the sacrament, received counsel from the Prophet, and obtained a special endowment or gift of knowledge and power. Then many of them went forth to serve as missionaries of the Church.[38]

Hebrew School

On January 4, 1836, Church leaders separated from the elders' school a Hebrew class that had been included in that body and created a new educational institution, which they named the Hebrew School. Students attending the new school met in the translating room or presidencies room on the west end of the third floor of the temple, while those attending the elders' school gathered in an adjoining room.[39]

In the fall of 1835, Church leaders searched for a scholar who could teach this subject. When Oliver Cowdery was sent to New York to purchase a book bindery, he was told also to secure Hebrew textbooks. Returning to Kirtland in November 1835, he brought a Hebrew Bible, lexicon, and grammar, plus a Greek lexicon. Joseph Smith immediately commenced studying Hebrew, and his desire to secure help in learning the language intensified as he read. Dr. Daniel Piexotto, a professor at the Willoughby Medical College, was hired, but he failed to arrive in Kirtland on the date he was expected to begin teaching. The search continued for a suitable Hebrew scholar.[40]

At that time Eliza R. Snow was living with the Prophet's family in Kirtland, and she had been corresponding frequently with her brother Lorenzo, a student at Oberlin College. In the fall of 1835 Lorenzo had studied Hebrew privately with a visiting professor, Joshua Seixas, who had an excellent reputation as a teacher and scholar. The first week of January, Joseph Smith sent Orson Hyde and William E. McLellin to Hudson, Ohio, some twenty-eight miles southwest of Kirtland, to meet with Professor Seixas. They returned and reported that they had hired the scholar at a fee of $320 to teach forty students for seven weeks.[41]

While members of the school were waiting for Professor Seixas to arrive in Kirtland, Joseph Smith attempted to teach the Hebrew class, but progress was slow. The first day of the Prophet's instruction, he engaged in a heated debate with Orson Pratt over the correct pronunciation of a Hebrew letter. The next day was spent in resolving the problems.[42] Their studies were also interrupted one day when class members spent their time discussing some powerful spiritual manifestations in the temple. The students were more interested in discussing the visions they had witnessed than trying to learn to read Hebrew. Nevertheless, while the men were working during the day to complete construction of the temple and holding meetings in the evenings, they spent many hours each week studying Hebrew.[43]

Enthusiasm to learn Hebrew reached a new peak on January 26, 1836, when Joshua Seixas arrived in Kirtland. Although the scholar was young, only a few years older than Joseph Smith (who was thirty at that time), he was an experienced teacher. He had previously taught Hebrew, Spanish, and Portuguese in New York; had studied and taught in Andover, Massachusetts; and had taught Hebrew at Oberlin College and at the Western Reserve College in Hudson, Ohio.[44]

Soon after Professor Seixas commenced teaching the forty enrolled class members, others expressed an interest in attending his classes. Consequently, three other classes were formed, each with from thirty to forty students, so that this young Hebrew scholar taught about 120 persons. Since the enrollment in the Hebrew School was much larger than anticipated, there were not sufficient textbooks for everyone. Therefore, some of the Hebrew Bibles were divided into sections, and students studied different portions of the Old Testament. In addition to reading from a Hebrew Bible, the classes studied Moses Stuart's A Grammar of the Hebrew Language (1835), A Hebrew Grammar (1821), and a Supplement to J. Seixas' Manual of Hebrew Grammar (1836), which contained a preface written by Oliver Cowdery. While classes were held daily from 10:00 to 11:00 A.M. and from 2:00 to 3:00 P.M., members often gathered before and after class to read to one another. According to Lorenzo Barnes, a student at the school, tuition was approximately six dollars.[45]

Hebrew classes were held for almost three months under the tutelage of Joshua Seixas. Following the first three weeks, a few persons were selected by Professor Seixas to receive advanced instruction to this subject, including Joseph Smith, Oliver Cowdery, Sidney Rigdon, Orson Hyde, Orson Pratt, William W. Phelps, William E. McLellin, Edward Partridge, and Sylvester Smith. Professor Seixas stated that the elders were the most forward of any class he had instructed for the same length of time.[46]

Although no women were enrolled in the Hebrew School, some of them decided to learn the language and studied with their husbands. Caroline Crosby recalled that after her husband returned home each day, he taught her what he was learning, and eventually she learned to read Hebrew.[47]

After Professor Seixas left Kirtland, some persons continued to study Hebrew and periodically applied some of the language skills they had developed. William W. Phelps occasionally included in letters to Brigham Young a translation of chapters from a Hebrew Bible that were of particular interest to the Saints. Orson Pratt also maintained his interest and studies in Hebrew and received a certificate from Professor Seixas stating that he was capable of teaching the language. Joseph Smith also never lost his interest in this or in other languages. "My soul delights in reading the word of the Lord in the original," he wrote. "I am determined to pursue the study of the languages, until I shall become master of them, if I am permitted to live long enough."[48]

Other Kirtland Schools

While members of the priesthood attended the School for the Elders, other persons, both young and old, male and female, attended another school established by Church leaders. Originally called the Kirtland School, this institution was similar in many respects to the first high school organized in America (in Boston, twelve years earlier) as well as some of the academies and private schools organized in various parts of the nation. When the winter term began in December 1834, students of all ages were invited to attend; but after the enrollment increased to 130, the trustees realized that the facilities were inadequate, and they dismissed the younger and less advanced students. In February 1835, some one hundred students attended the school, which was taught by William E. McLellin. They studied geography, writing (penmanship), arithmetic, and English grammar. In addition to using Noah Webster's dictionary as a text, they studied Samuel Kirkham's *Grammar*, J. Olney's *Geography*, and T. Burdick's *Arithmetic*. Tuition and fees were comparable to those at other educational institutions in the area. Tuition for a term of English grammar (about six weeks) was one dollar, while the cost of studying other subjects ranged from two to four dollars. Young men and women living outside that community obtained room and board with "respectable families" for one dollar or so per week.[49]

Because they were needed to work on the farms during the summer, the children and many adults received most of their formal education during winter time. When the Kirtland School began its second winter term in November 1836, classes were held in the attic of the temple. About 140 students were enrolled. The school was divided into three departments: languages were taught in the department of classics, English grammar, geography, mathematics, and arithmetic in the department of English, and basic courses in the "juvenile department." H. M. Graves, professor of Greek and Latin languages, was principal of the school, and he was assisted in the teaching by two other instructors. George A. Smith recalled that when he was twenty, he attended school in the upper story of the temple and studied Samuel Whelpley's *Compend of History*, Kirkham's *Grammar*, Olney's *Geography*, and Jacob's *Latin Grammar*. He received free tuition and was given the responsibility of teaching for one hour a day a beginning grammar class in Greek and Latin.[50]

Additional Educational Opportunities

In addition to the formally organized schools in Kirtland, the Saints had various other opportunities to learn. Benjamin F.

Johnson recalled attending a geography class one evening. William W. Phelps wrote to his wife that he had attended a writing school. Eliza R. Snow stated that during the spring of 1836 she "taught a select school" for young ladies in Kirtland.[51] Debating was a popular activity in America at that time, and many of the Saints studied the art of persuasion and techniques of communication. They often participated in debates that lasted for three hours or more. Joseph Smith attended one of these long verbal confrontations in which some young elders discussed the question "Was it, or was it not, the design of Christ to establish His Gospel by miracles?" Following the debate, the judge ruled in favor of those who argued for the negative position, which, according to the Prophet, was "a righteous decision." Although the Prophet noted that much congeniality was displayed during the evening, he was concerned that some were determined to argue a case whether it was right or wrong. "I therefore availed myself to drop a few words upon this subject, by way of advice," he said, that they might "improve their minds and cultivate their powers of intellect." He cautioned the elders not to incur the displeasure of heaven when they discussed sacred topics, that whatever they did should always be "with an eye single to the glory of God."[52]

Another educational opportunity for the Saints in Kirtland was a singing school. A committee was appointed on January 4, 1836, to organize it. Shortly thereafter, members began to gather in the temple two evenings a week to learn to improve their singing. During the first year, M. C. (probably Marvel Chapin) Davis served as instructor. The next year, Luman Carter and Jonathan Crosby provided instruction on principles of vocal music. Since singing was a regular part of services conducted by the Church, participants in this school had many opportunities to sing in meetings in the House of the Lord.[53]

Several schools were established in Kirtland where Church members studied elementary subjects. On December 2, 1835, for example, Orson Pratt delivered a lecture on English grammar and afterwards proposed to teach a grammar school from one to four evenings per week. Because of his involvement in other activities, this school was closed after being in session only fifteen days.[54] Lorenzo Barnes refers in his journal to another grammar school that was taught by Sidney Rigdon and Vinson Knight in December 1835.[55]

Though there were a number of schools in Kirtland, the home was the basic institution for learning religious and secular truths. While they worked long hours together to provide for their families, Latter-day Saint parents heeded the counsel of their leaders to teach their children. Some families also invited others into their homes to help direct the studies of their young ones. For example, while she was living with the Prophet's family in 1837, Eliza R. Snow taught his children.[56]

Early Latter-day Saint Meetings

The Saints in Kirtland not only spent many of their waking hours earning a living and attending school; they also participated regularly in worship and Church meetings. In 1831 Joseph Smith learned through revelation that the Lord's day—which was Sunday, the first day of the week—was to be a day of rest: a day for the Saints to "go to the house of prayer and offer up [their] sacraments," and to pay their "devotions unto the Most High."[57] In preparation for the Sabbath, members sometimes collected wood and endeavored to complete other routine activities on Saturday, so that Sunday would be a day devoted to religious activity. One convert remembered that as a youth, before his family joined the Church, he was instructed not to play with his knives, whistles, balls, and other such objects on Sunday, and to be as sober and serious as possible. Many Christian families in the early 1800s spent their time together on the Lord's day, reading, relaxing, conversing, and attending meetings.[58]

As Church membership in Kirtland grew during the 1830s, the locations of meeting places changed. The first converts gathered on the Morley farm to worship. After Joseph Smith arrived in Kirtland, meetings continued to be held on the Morley farm, but the homes of other settlers (including John Smith's residence), and schoolhouses were also used. Sometimes, when weather permitted, the Saints gathered out-of-doors to worship. Soon after the Church purchased the lot on which the temple was to be built, meetings were held there. As the temple walls began to rise, worshipers took advantage of the shade. On Sunday, May 4, 1834, the Prophet preached to members meeting in the shade created by the new schoolhouse under construction west of the temple.[59]

Before the temple was completed, some meetings were being held in it. Nancy Tracy recalled attending a Sunday service there. Members and visitors often had to sit on the center pews and on workmen's benches, while the floors were covered with wood shavings.[60]

Even after the temple was finished and available for full use, members continued to hold meetings in homes, in the school-room below the printing office, and in the schoolhouse on the flats. And since the temple was the only house of worship built by the Saints during the 1830s, members who lived in branches out-side of the Kirtland area met in homes throughout the 1830s.[61]

By the mid-1830s a basic pattern had been established in Kirt-land for Sunday worship. Members gathered at 10:00 A.M. for their morning meeting. The service opened with congregational singing and a vocal prayer. This was usually followed by one or two sermons. Then the congregation sang another hymn, and one of the members offered benediction. A second service was usually held in the afternoon. In addition to following the pattern of the morning meeting, the afternoon service generally included the ordinance of the Lord's Supper. On occasion, this ordinance was also administered between the Sabbath services, on Sunday evenings, and during the week in the homes of the Saints. Ini-tially the emblems of the sacrament were bread and wine. The first reference in Joseph Smith's history to members receiving bread and water was recorded under the date April 6, 1837.[62]

Sunday services sometimes included confirmations of new members or marriage ceremonies. On January 17, 1836, Joseph Smith married three couples during the afternoon service; since the congregation was unusually large that day, creating an un-pleasant crowded condition, following the marriage and the ad-ministration of the sacrament the Prophet dismissed the congre-gation.[63] Individuals who had recently been baptized were often

*Top, early photograph of Joseph Smith, Sr., home in Kirtland;
bottom, Smith home as it appears today*

confirmed at Sunday meetings. William Burgess recalled that during the week in which he was baptized, about thirty other individuals received this ordinance. The following Sunday, the converts occupied the first three rows, and one by one they were confirmed members of the Church.[64]

Meetings held on week nights in Kirtland often occupied the time of the Saints. In 1835 a weekly meeting was held on Tuesday evenings in the schoolhouse on the flats, where Joseph Smith, Sidney Rigdon, and other leaders expounded the principles of the gospel. On one occasion the Prophet spoke for a reported three hours, but sermons that lengthy were the exception.[65] Sometimes members attended patriarchal blessing meetings. On Tuesday, December 29, 1835, for example, a large group crowded into Oliver Olney's home, and following an opening hymn and prayer, Joseph Smith, Sr., bestowed patriarchal blessings upon fifteen individuals.[66] A few days later, on Thursday, January 7, 1836, a similar meeting was held in the home of Bishop Newel K. Whitney. The meeting opened with singing and prayer, after which Father Smith blessed Bishop Whitney's parents and a few others who had requested a patriarchal blessing. Before adjourning, the group sang more hymns. Then "a bountiful refreshment" was served. Summarizing the events of that day, the Prophet recorded in his diary, "Our hearts were made glad."[67]

Occasionally, special meetings were held in the homes of the Saints. Brigham Young recalled that during the week he was visiting Kirtland to become acquainted with Joseph Smith, meetings were held nearly every night. The first evening he was in Kirtland, in early November 1832, some of the brethren gathered in the Prophet's home to discuss "the things of the kingdom." After Joseph called upon Brigham to pray, the young convert from Mendon commenced speaking in tongues. When the men arose from their kneeling position, some asked the Prophet his opinion concerning this gift. Some thought he would condemn the manifestation, but, according to Brigham Young, he told the brethren that "it was of God," and that Brigham had spoken "the pure Adamic language." Later that same evening, while Brigham Young was absent, the Prophet prophesied, "The time will come

Four buildings of Latter-day Saints
in Kirtland in 1830s: top left,
William Marks home; left, Sidney
Rigdon home (center portion);
bottom left, John Johnson home;
below, John Johnson tavern

when bro. Brigham Young will preside over this church."[68]

After the Kirtland Temple was dedicated, many different types of meetings were held there. In addition to the Sunday morning and afternoon services, special meetings were sometimes held on Sunday evenings. The youth of the Church not only attended school in the temple during the week, but also participated in a Sunday School.[69]

On the first Thursday of each month a fast and testimony meeting was held in the temple. Joseph Smith, Sr., who presided over these fast meetings in 1837, regularly entered the temple about sunrise to prepare himself through prayer. The meeting usually commenced at ten o'clock in the morning and continued until four in the afternoon. During most of these meetings, the white cloth curtains were lowered, dividing the main floor of the temple into four compartments. Consequently, what had been one meeting became four, each presided over by an elder. Members sang, prayed, and bore their testimonies, describing manifestations of the power of God in their lives and exhorting others to live the gospel. Usually at about three o'clock, the curtains were raised and all in attendance would continue worshipping under the direction of Father Smith. According to Mary Ann Stearns Winters, it was generally known that on Thursday "Father Smith, the Patriarch, would not break his fast and partake of food til the sun went down."[70]

On weekdays, the Kirtland High School met in the rooms on the third floor of the temple. On Tuesday evening, the seventies met in the temple, and on Wednesday evenings, the elders gathered there. Occasionally, but not on a regular basis, the high council and apostles also met in the temple.[71] The priesthood meetings generally followed a common pattern. After an opening prayer and the singing of a hymn, quorum leaders, especially the presidents of each quorum, instructed the men in Church doctrines and procedures. The meetings then ended, as they began, with a song and a prayer.[72]

Music was an important part of the worship of the Kirtland Saints. They sang at the beginning and end of nearly all their meetings, organized a choir that sang in the temple, and, in 1835, published a hymnal that contained a collection of hymns "adapted to their faith and belief in the gospel."[73] In July 1830, five years before the publication of the hymnal, Emma Smith was commanded by revelation to select hymns to be included in this work. "My soul delighteth in the song of the heart," the revelation read; "yea, the song of the righteous is a prayer unto me, and it shall be answered with a blessing upon their heads."[74]

By the spring of 1832, Emma Smith had selected a number of hymns considered appropriate for enriching Later-day Saint services. On May 1, Joseph Smith instructed William W. Phelps to correct and print the hymns she had collected. The first (June 1832) and subsequent editions of the *Evening and the Morning Star*, printed in Missouri, included hymns considered appropriate for use by the Saints. The publication of a hymnal at that time, however, was delayed by the printing of the Book of Commandments and the destruction of the press in July 1833.[75]

Following the expulsion of Latter-day Saints from Jackson County in November 1833, William W. Phelps traveled to Kirtland, where he continued to assist Emma Smith in preparing the hymnal for publication. The *Evening and the Morning Star* resumed publication in Kirtland in December 1833 and was succeeded in September 1834 by the *Latter-day Saints' Messenger and Advocate*. Hymns continued to be printed in that paper, indicating that the program of gathering hymns was continuing.

On September 14, 1835, the high council urged Emma to fulfill the responsibility she had been given by revelation and appointed William W. Phelps to revise and arrange for publication the items she selected.[76] Later that year a small book, measuring three inches by four inches, was printed in Kirtland. The hymnal had ninety selections (text only), of which thirty-nine had previously been printed in the *Star* or the *Messenger and Advocate*. More than half of the poems included in the hymnal were by members of the Church, including William W. Phelps, Eliza R. Snow, and Parley P. Pratt. Other hymns were selected from popular Protestant hymnals of that age, especially hymnals of Presbyterian, Congregational, Methodist, and Eastern Christian (a Protestant faith) congregations. Fifteen of the hymns selected were compositions of Isaac Watts, a Congregational minister who served as pastor in London, England, from 1702 until his death in 1748. The authors of the hymns were not credited for their contributions. Since there was no musical score, the hymns were sung to borrowed tunes, and congregations sometimes adopted different tunes for the same hymns. The hymnal currently used in the Church contains twenty-eight hymns from the 1835 collection. [77]

Occasionally, the daily life of the Latter-day Saints was interrupted by funerals and weddings. On November 24, 1835, Joseph Smith solemnized the marriage of Newel Knight and Lydia Bailey Goldthwaite. Friends of the couple gathered in the home of Hyrum Smith. Following an invocation, Joseph Smith asked the couple to stand and to join hands. Then he spoke to them concerning the importance of marriage, an institution, he said, that is ordained by heaven and should be solemnized by the authority of the priesthood. "You covenant to be each other's companions through life, and discharge the duties of husband and wife in every respect," he said. When they responded affirmatively, he declared them husband and wife, after which he pronounced upon them the blessings the Lord had conferred upon Adam and Eve in the garden of Eden, told them to multiply and replenish the earth, and further blessed them that they would experience a long and prosperous life. [78]

Leisure Hours

Though the Kirtland Saints were involved almost daily in physical labor, studying, and attending meetings, they also found time to enjoy recreational pursuits. Among the most popular leisure activities were hunting, fishing, swimming, sleighing, skating, wrestling, horseback riding, and riding in carriages. There was generally a close association among members of the family, and parents and children spent many evenings together conversing, singing, studying, and playing. The children had few toys, but they enjoyed playing with balls, marbles, whistles, and homemade dolls. In the wintertime they played in the snow, building forts and figures and having snowball fights. [79]

Since Joseph Smith had not outlined in detail what might be considered proper or improper leisure pursuits for members of the Church, the Kirtland Saints generally retained the same attitudes on this subject as they had had prior to joining the Church. Most religious denominations in New England, western New York, and Ohio at that time denounced dancing, card playing, horse racing, and attending the theater. In Kirtland, the Saints seem to have shared these beliefs with members of other Christian faiths.[80]

In the 1830s, holiday observances were not nearly as important as they later became. The annual parades, holiday feasts, and family outings so popular in the twentieth century were absent in most nineteenth-century settlements. There were few national, state, or even regional holidays. Even Christmas was little more than a routine day. Seldom did Joseph Smith refer in his diary to special activities on December 25, though in 1835 he did note, "Enjoyed myself at home with my family, all day, it being Christmas, the only time I have had this privilege so satisfactorily for a long period."[81]

Mary Ann Stearns Winters remembered being with her family in New York City on Christmas day. As she walked down the hall in the apartment where she was staying, she met a neighborhood friend who asked her, "What did Santa Claus bring you?" Mary, confused by this question since she had never heard of such a person, replied, "Nothing." "Didn't you hang up your stocking?" the friend asked. Still perplexed, Mary asked her friend to explain the meaning of her questions. She soon learned that all the children in that area who had hung up their stockings on Christmas Eve awoke the next day to find them filled with toys and other wonderful presents. Mary admitted that at that time she could not understand why Santa Claus would enter one home and fill the stockings, while in other homes where stockings had not been left out for him, he would neglect to leave any presents for the children.[82]

Chapter 16

A Pentecostal Season

K irtland was crowded in 1836. In addition to the constant stream of Latter-day Saint immigrants settling there, hundreds of visitors were gathering for the dedication of the temple. Leaders of the Church from Missouri were there, as well as many other members of the priesthood from other parts of the country. The newcomers crowded into the small homes of the Saints, and when the homes and the boarding houses near the temple were filled, the visitors sought accommodations in adjacent communities. But whether the Saints lived in Kirtland or were there for the dedication, they shared much of the same kind of anticipation. Because of their offerings and sacrifices during the building of the temple, they were told, the Lord would bestow upon them "great and choice blessings," including a special gift or "endowment with power from on high."[1]

Recalling the events that transpired during the period of the temple's dedication, Orson Pratt declared:

> God was there, his angels were there, the Holy Ghost was in the midst of the people, the visions of the Almighty were opened to the minds of the servants of the living God; the veil was taken from the minds of many; they saw the heavens opened; they beheld the angels of God; they heard the voice of the Lord; and they were filled from the crown of their heads to the soles of their feet with the power and inspiration of the Holy Ghost. . . . In that Temple, set apart by the servants of God, and dedicated by a prayer that was written by in-

spiration, the people were blessed as they never had been blessed for generations and generations.[2]

During a fifteen-week period, extending from January 21 to
May 1, 1836, probably more Latter-day Saints beheld visions and
witnessed other unusual spiritual manifestations than during any
other era in the history of the Church. There were reports of
Saints' beholding heavenly beings at ten different meetings held
during that time. At eight of these meetings, many reported seeing angels; and at five of the services, individuals testified that
Jesus, the Savior, appeared. While the Saints were thus commun-
ing with heavenly hosts, many prophesied, some spoke in
tongues, and others received the gift of interpretation of tongues.

The Kirtland Endowment

Most of the unusual spiritual manifestations occurred in the
Kirtland Temple at meetings in which members of the priesthood
were receiving or were preparing to receive the endowment.
Joseph Smith taught that the endowment was a gift of knowledge
derived from revelation, a gift of power emitting from God. This
gift consisted of instructions relating to the laws of God, including
the principle of obedience, and was partially designed to help missionaries to serve with greater power and to give them greater protection. The Prophet said that many would not comprehend the
endowment, but that bearers of the priesthood should prepare for
this gift by purifying themselves, by cleansing their hearts and
their physical bodies. "You need an endowment, brethren," he
said, "in order that you may be prepared and able to overcome all
things." After instructing the Saints for about three months, the
Prophet concluded that the brethren of the priesthood had received "all the necessary ceremonies" relating to that endowment. He then challenged those who had received the gift to "go
forth and build up the kingdom of God."[3]

A Washing Ceremony

While unfolding principles of the endowment, Joseph Smith
introduced a number of ordinances designed to purify those who
would receive it. The first known preparatory rite unfolded in

1836 was the ordinance of washing the body. Under the date of Saturday, January 16, Oliver Cowdery noted in his diary that he and John Corrill had met in the home of Joseph Smith, where the three men had washed and perfumed (with cinnamon) their bodies, confessed their sins, and covenanted to be faithful to God. Elder Cowdery remarked that they had participated in the ordinance so that they would be clean before the Lord for the Sabbath. Before they completed this purification, he added, Martin Harris entered the Prophet's home and was also washed.[4]

A similar purification occurred five days later. On Thursday afternoon, January 21, the Presidency gathered in the attic of the printing office adjacent to the Kirtland Temple, and there they washed their bodies with pure water and perfumed them in the name of the Lord, preparatory to receiving their anointings.[5]

The Ordinance of Anointing

Some of the reports of communion with heavenly beings in Kirtland occurred while bearers of the priesthood were participating in a second ordinance revealed through the Prophet in January 1836, the ordinance of anointing with sacred or consecrated oil. This ceremony, like the washing of the body, was designed to purify the Saints in preparation for receiving the endowment; it was performed in the temple after they had cleansed their bodies in their own homes or in other buildings in the community. When the first group in this dispensation to receive their anointings gathered on Thursday, January 21, 1836, little did they realize that that night, one of the great visions of the ages would be unfolded, and many would commune with the hosts of heaven.[6]

As the sun was setting that evening, approximately forty men entered the large doors of the nearly completed Kirtland Temple. The outside plastering of the building had been finished, but masons were still at work on the interior. The men passed the entrance of the large unpainted room on the main floor and began climbing the winding stairs. They passed by the second floor, which resembled the first, with four tiers of pulpits on either end of the room, and continued climbing to the third floor, or attic, which was divided into five rooms. About sixteen of the men gathered in the west room, which was being used as a classroom for the study of Hebrew. Called the translating room by Joseph Smith and the president's room by Oliver Cowdery, it had been dedicated on January 4 by Joseph Smith, Sr., as a place of learning.[7] Those assembled in this room included the Presidency of the Church, members of the two bishoprics (Kirtland and Missouri), and the Prophet's scribe, Warren Parrish. The twenty-four members of the high council gathered in two adjoining rooms.[8]

While members of the high council waited and prayed, the others participated in an ordinance of anointing their heads with holy oil. As the Presidency encircled Joseph Smith, Sr., the Prophet held a bottle of oil in his left hand and raised his right hand toward heaven. Then the Presidency raised their right hands, and the Prophet blessed and consecrated the oil in the name of Jesus Christ. After the oil had been consecrated, the Prophet anointed his father with it and invoked the blessings of heaven. All of the presidency, according to age, then laid their hands upon Father Smith and asked that the blessings of heaven be poured upon him. The Prophet then prayed to the Lord, requesting an acceptance of the anointing, after which the Presidency, according to Edward Partridge's account, raised their right hands toward heaven and said, "Amen."[9]

Following this initial ordinance, others were anointed. Father Smith placed his hands on the heads of each of the Presidency, beginning with the oldest, and anointed and blessed them. When he blessed his son Joseph, he sealed upon him "the blessings of Moses, to lead Israel in the latter days" and "the blessings of Abraham, Isaac and Jacob." "All of the Presidency laid their hands upon me," the Prophet said, "and pronounced . . . many prophecies and blessings." Edward Partridge added that after the Presidency had received their anointings, Bishop Whitney and his counselors, Bishop Partridge and his counselors, and Warren Parrish participated in the ordinance and were subsequently given blessings by the laying on of hands.[10]

A Vision of the Celestial Kingdom

After the men had received their anointings, Joseph Smith testified that "the heavens were opened upon us," and he "beheld the celestial kingdom of God, and the glory thereof." He saw "the blazing throne of God, whereon was seated the Father and the Son." He saw "the beautiful streets of that kingdom, which had the appearance of being paved with gold." He saw "Fathers Adam and Abraham" and others who were then living or who had recently died, including his father (who was with him at that time), his mother, and his deceased brother, Alvin. He saw the twelve apostles who had recently been called, sustained, and ordained to that office, and Jesus was standing in their midst. He also saw in his vision all of the Presidency and many others who were present with him there in the temple. The Prophet wondered how his brother, Alvin, who had died before the Church was restored and before he had had an opportunity to be baptized for the remission of sins, could have obtained an inheritance in that kingdom. In answer to his question, he received a remarkable revelation concerning salvation for the dead and for children.

The Prophet reported that during this vision angels ministered not only to him but also to many others who had received their anointings. "The power of the Highest rested upon us," he said, and "the house was filled with the glory of God." He further declared (in an account that he dictated and that was written in his Kirtland diary by his scribe, Warren Parrish), "My scribe . . . saw, in a vision, the armies of heaven protecting the Saints in their return to Zion, and many things which I saw."[11]

Before this remarkable series of visions ended, the high councilors of Kirtland and Missouri entered the west room of the temple. Since some of the original members of these quorums had died, had been called to other positions, or were not in Kirtland in January 1836, other leaders had been selected to fill the vacancies. A major reorganization had occurred between January 6 and January 13, so on that day (January 21), there were in Kirtland two full quorums of twelve men each who were acting as high councilors. Members of the high council of the Missouri stake were Simeon Carter, John Hitchcock, Levi Jackman, Peter Whitmer Jr., George M. Hinkle, Elias Higbee, Elisha H. Groves, Calvin Beebe, Newel Knight, Lyman Wight, Alva Beaman, and Isaac McWithy (the latter two were representing Solomon Han-

President's room in temple, where Joseph Smith received the Vision of the Celestial Kingdom (D&C 137)

cock and John Murdock, who were absent). The standing high council of Kirtland consisted of John Smith, John Johnson, Orson Johnson, Martin Harris, Samuel H. Smith, Jared Carter, Joseph Coe, Samuel James, Noah Packard, Joseph Kingsbury, Thomas Grover, and John P. Greene.[12]

After joining the other Church leaders in the translating room, the high councilors received their anointings. Hyrum Smith anointed the head of John Smith, president of the high council of Kirtland; and David Whitmer anointed Simeon Carter, president of the high council of Missouri. Then the presidents of the two high councils anointed the heads of the members of their respective councils, beginning with the oldest individuals.[13]

Following this ordinance, Joseph Smith said, "the visions of heaven were opened to them also. Some of them saw the face of the Savior, and others were ministered unto by holy angels, and the spirit of prophecy and revelation was poured out in mighty power." He added, in conclusion, "We all communed with the heavenly host."[14]

In addition to Joseph Smith and his scribe, Warren Parrish, other witnesses recorded the spiritual manifestations of that night. Edward Partridge wrote: "A number saw visions. Others were blessed with the outpouring of the Holy Ghost." Oliver Cowdery also bore his testimony of the experience. "The glorious scene" was "too great to be described," he wrote. "I only say that the heavens were opened to many, and great and marvelous things were shown."[15]

During this spiritual feast, the silence that usually permeated the winter darkness of the unfinished rooms of the Kirtland Temple was periodically pierced with vibrations emanating from the west room of the third floor. The men who gathered that night not only communed with the heavenly hosts, but on several occasions they joined in shouting, "Hosanna! Hosanna! Glory to God in the highest!" The meeting ended in the same manner in which it began—with singing and prayer. The head of each quorum offered prayers at the beginning of the meeting, and Joseph Smith offered the invocation and final benediction. The solemn assembly probably continued until after midnight, for the Prophet recorded in his diary that he retired between one and two o'clock in the morning.[16]

Friday, January 22, the day after the vision of the glories of heaven, was another memorable day in the history of the Church. Some of the men who were studying Hebrew gathered in their classroom at the usual hour, but instead of pursuing their lessons, they spent the morning discussing the visions of the preceding night. That evening the same leaders who had met the previous night again assembled in the temple, joined by members of the Quorum of Twelve Apostles, presidents of the First Quorum of the Seventy, and Don Carlos Smith, who had been called to preside over the high priests. After the apostles, the seventies, and Elder Smith had received their anointings, the heavens were again opened and many saw visions. The Prophet declared, "The gift of tongues fell upon us in mighty power, angels mingled their voices with ours, while their presence was in our midst, and un-

West side of Kirtland Temple, showing upper windows
of the president's room

ceasing praises swelled our bosoms for the space of half-an-hour."
Edward Partridge wrote, "During the evening more especially at
the time of shouting a number saw visions as they declared
unto."[17]

These rich outpourings of the Spirit continued as additional
members of the priesthood received their anointings and as
Joseph Smith unfolded principles relating to the sealing of the
anointing. After instructing the high priests and elders on Thursday, January 28, the Presidency anointed the leaders of these
groups, who in turn anointed the men over whom they presided.
The scribe who kept the minutes for the elders wrote, "The Lord
poured out His spirit and some spoke in tongues and
prophecied."[18]

While the high priests and elders were receiving their anointings, Joseph Smith met with the apostles and seventies and told
them that they should call upon God with uplifted hands to seal

the blessings that had been promised them during their anointings. He also declared that others had professed seeing heavenly
beings at the same time that he was beholding a glorious vision.
Sylvester Smith, who was temporarily serving as scribe because of
the illness of Warren Parrish, proclaimed that he beheld a pillar of
fire resting upon the heads of the apostles. Roger Orton reported
that he saw "a mighty angel riding upon a horse of fire, with a
flaming sword in his hand, followed by five others, [who] encircled
the [temple], and protected the Saints, even the Lord's anointed,
from the power of Satan and a host of evil spirits." Zebedee Coltrin stated that he saw the Savior "crowned with glory upon his
head above the brightness of the sun."[19]

Others who attended this meeting verified the descriptions of
visions recorded in Joseph Smith's diary and later in the *History of
the Church*. Zebedee Coltrin, for example, substantiated the
Prophet's account by testifying that he also beheld the Savior in
the Kirtland Temple. He said that he saw in the temple "the
power of God as it was in the day of Pentecost," including the
speaking in tongues as the Spirit gave men utterance.[20] William
Harrison Burgess was probably also referring to this meeting when
he recalled that the Spirit of the Lord rested upon him. It seemed
as though the interior of the temple had been illuminated by a
power from God, he said, adding that the Prophet, his brother
Hyrum, and Roger Orton seemed to have been engulfed in this
light. Then, he wrote, Joseph Smith exclaimed aloud that he beheld the Savior; Hyrum Smith said that he saw the angels of
heaven; and Roger Orton testified that he saw the chariots of Israel. Concluding his description of this solemn assembly, Elder
Burgess affirmed that the power of God was manifest, and many
prophesied.[21]

After these visions had ended, Joseph Smith instructed the
seven presidents of the seventies to anoint the other members of
their quorum. He then returned to the room where the high
priests and elders were meeting and instructed them concerning
the sealing of their anointings.[22] Describing the ceremony in
which he participated, Heber C. Kimball wrote that the First
Presidency laid their hands upon his head and sealed his anoint-

LDS

Zebedee Coltrin

ing. After the members of the Quorum of Twelve Apostles had received this blessing, they responded in unison with a loud "Amen," repeated three times.[23]

Sealing Their Blessings

Another series of remarkable visions occured in the Kirtland

Temple on February 6 while Joseph Smith was again instructing the priesthood concerning sealing. On this occasion, the high priests and elders met again in the west room of the temple's top floor, the seventies and the twelve in the second room, and bishops in the east room. On that night the Prophet told the priesthood members the precise order God had shown him concerning the sealing of their blessings. First, he said, the men should engage in solemn prayer. President Sidney Rigdon was to offer the sealing prayer, after which "all the quorums were to shout with one accord a solemn hosanna to God and the Lamb," followed by three amens. Then all were to "take seats and lift up their hearts in silent prayer to God." If anyone beheld a vision or received a prophecy, that individual, he advised, should "rise and speak" so that all might rejoice and be edified.

Some of the elders did not comply with these specific instructions, evidently believing that the precise order and wording were not essential. Consequently, the Prophet observed, "This caused the Spirit of the Lord to withdraw," depriving the quorum members of blessings they otherwise might have received. Members of other quorums followed the instructions and enjoyed a great flow of the Holy Spirit. "Many arose and spoke, testifying that they wer filled with the Holy Ghost, which was like fire in their bones, so that they could not hold their peace, but were constrained to cry hosanna to God and the Lamb, and glory in the highest," the Prophet declared. He also affirmed that William Smith saw in vision the Twelve Apostles laboring in England; Zebedee Coltrin saw a vision of the Lord's host; and others, filled with the Spirit of God, spoke in tongues and prophesied. "This was a time of rejoicing," he concluded, "long to be remembered."[24]

The Dedicatory Service

Not all the spiritual manifestations that occurred in Kirtland in 1836 followed the administration of ordinances. Some of the most memorable events occurred on Sunday, March 27, the day the temple was dedicated. On the preceding day, Joseph Smith, Sidney Rigdon, Oliver Cowdery, Warren Cowdery, and Warren Parrish met in the president's room on the third floor of the temple to make final preparations for the solemn assembly to be held on Sunday. Oliver Cowdery reported that during this meeting he assisted the Prophet "in writing a prayer for the dedication" of the Lord's House.[25]

On the morning of the dedication, long before the doors of the temple were opened, a large crowd gathered. Joseph Smith estimated that by 7:00 A.M. more than five hundred persons were waiting near the temple doors. Between seven and eight o'clock a number of Church leaders and ushers entered the building, after which Joseph Smith, assisted by other members of the priesthood, dedicated the pulpits and consecrated them to the Lord.[26]

At eight o'clock the temple doors were opened, and, as members of the First Presidency helped to seat the congregation, perhaps eight hundred or more people gathered in the main hall of the temple. The public sat in pews on the main floor of the temple, with Church leaders occupying benches and pulpits at the eastern and western ends of the hall. Presidents Frederick G. Williams, Joseph Smith, Sr., and William W. Phelps sat on the highest tier of pulpits at the east end. Directly below them sat Joseph Smith, Hyrum Smith, and Sidney Rigdon, with presidents of the high priests quorum occupying other seats in the Melchizedek Priesthood pulpits. Members of the Quorum of the Twelve, the presidency of the elders quorum, members of the high council, and Warren Cowdery and Warren Parrish, the two scribes assigned to keep minutes of the meeting, occupied the front seats on the east end of the building. At the west end, where the Aaronic Priesthood pulpits were located, were the bishoprics of Zion and Kirtland and the presidencies of the Aaronic Priesthood quorums (priests, teachers, and deacons).[27]

After every available seat had been occupied, the Presidency instructed the ushers to close the massive doors of the House of the Lord. Hundreds, including some who had sacrificed much of their time and material wealth for the building of the temple, were unable to crowd into it. Recognizing the disappointment of those who were standing outside, Joseph Smith recommended that they hold a meeting in the schoolhouse west of the temple. Many promptly gathered there in the room where the School of the Elders often met, but soon that hall also was filled to capacity, and many persons remained outside. Since so many had been unable to attend the solemn assembly, the service was repeated the following Thursday, March 31.[28]

The dedicatory service began at 9:00 A.M. with President Sidney Rigdon conducting. After he read Psalms 96 and 24, the choir, led by M. C. Davis, raised their voices in the four corners of the temple to sing "Ere Long the Veil Will Rend in Twain," a hymn by Parley P. Pratt. Following the invocation by President Rigdon, the choir sang a hymn composed by William W. Phelps, "O Happy Souls, Who Pray."[29]

President Rigdon then spoke eloquently for two and a half hours, using as a text Matthew, Chapter 8, verses 18 to 20, especially verse 20, which reads, "And Jesus saith unto him [a scribe], the foxes have holes, and the birds of the air have nests; but the Son of Man hath not where to lay his head." According to the Prophet, Elder Rigdon spoke "in his usual logical manner" and complimented the Saints for sacrificing amid privations and persecution to build a house for the Lord. Then he reminded the congregation of the trials of Jesus, including the rejection of His teachings by most of the people who lived in the meridian of time. Today, he said, people continue to reject His revelations and power. President Rigdon also explained that while people of various faiths had built many spacious buildings where they could worship God, this temple was different from all other houses of worship. It was the only building on earth, he declared, "that was built by divine revelation." He concluded by saying that if the Redeemer appeared "in this day of science, this day of intelligence," he might repeat to those who deny his revelations, the same phrase he uttered while he walked the earth, "The foxes have holes, and the birds of the air have nests; but the Son of Man hath not where to lay His head."[30]

Referring to President Rigdon's discourse, Eliza R. Snow commented that "he drew tears from many eyes, saying, these were those who wet those walls with their tears, when in the silent shades of the night, they were praying to the God of heaven to protect them, and stay the unhallowed hands of ruthless spoilers,

Lower auditorium of temple,
showing curtains that could be lowered from ceiling

who had uttered a prophecy when the foundation was laid that the walls should never be erected."[31]

Following his long discourse, President Rigdon called upon the respective quorums of the priesthood to acknowledge Joseph Smith as "Prophet and Seer" and to support him with their prayers. The quorums unanimously accepted the motion by rising, after which President Rigdon called upon the congregation to stand and indicate their acceptance of this motion. Everyone in the congregation stood. Then the choir and congregation sang another hymn by William W. Phelps, "Now Let Us Rejoice in the Day of Salvation."[32]

Following an intermission of about fifteen or twenty minutes, during which most people remained in the building (except mothers who left to care for their infants), the service continued with the congregation singing "Adam-ondi-Ahman" by William W. Phelps. The Prophet made a few brief remarks, after which he presented the names of officers of the Church for the sustaining vote of the priesthood quorums and the congregation. He first presented the Twelve Apostles, who were sustained by standing vote as prophets, seers, revelators, and special witnesses of Christ. Next he presented the presidents of the seventies; the high councils of Kirtland and Zion; the bishops of Kirtland and Zion and their counselors; the presidency of the elders; and finally the presidencies of the priests, teachers, and deacons in the Aaronic Priesthood. In each case the vote was unanimous in the affirmative. "I prophesied to all," the Prophet later said, "that inasmuch as they would uphold these men in their several stations, (alluding to the different quorums in the Church), the Lord would bless them; yea, in the name of Christ, the blessings of heaven would be theirs."[33]

After the congregation sang a hymn written by Isaac Watts, "How Pleased and Blest Was I,"[34] Joseph Smith offered the dedicatory prayer, which had been revealed through revelation. After expressing gratitude to God for His mercy, he asked the Lord to accept the temple, which had been built in obedience to His commandment and through great tribulation. "We have given of our substance," he said, "to build a house to Thy name, that the Son of Man might have a place to manifest Himself to His people." The Prophet prayed that the Lord would bless the Saints in attendance at the solemn assembly as well as those who would worship in the temple. He prayed for many others, including the leaders of the Church and all other Latter-day Saints, the leaders of nations, the children of Judah, and all of Israel.[35]

Following the dedicatory prayer, the choir sang a hymn that had been written for that occasion by William W. Phelps, "The Spirit of God Like a Fire Is Burning." The Prophet then asked the individual priesthood quorums, then the congregation, if they accepted the dedication prayer. After the congregation had manifested its approval, Don Carlos Smith blessed the bread and wine, and elders passed the sacrament to members of the Church.[36]

As the dedication services continued, the Prophet testified of his prophetic mission and of his being blessed with visitations from angelic beings, after which several others bore their testimonies. Don Carlos Smith bore witness of the truth of the Book of Mormon and of the work of the Lord in which he was engaged. Frederick G. Williams testified that during the dedicatory service he had seen a heavenly messenger enter the temple and sit between himself and Father Smith. David Whitmer testified that he also had beheld heavenly beings during the services. [37]

Some who attended the solemn assembly declared that the Savior was present. Truman O. Angell recorded in his journal that as Elder Rigdon was offering the opening prayer, "a glorious sensation passed through the House," and many felt a sensation that elevated their souls. During the afternoon meeting, he reported, Joseph Smith arose and informed the congregation that the personage whom President Williams had seen was the apostle Peter, who had come to accept the dedication. [38] Heber C. Kimball also declared that apostle Peter attended and accepted the dedicatory service. He declared that the heavenly being who had sat near President Williams and Father Smith was a tall personage with white hair who wore a long garment that extended to his ankles. [39]

Following some closing remarks by Hyrum Smith and Sidney Rigdon and a short prayer by President Rigdon, the congregation sealed the proceedings of the meeting with the Hosanna Shout, shouting "Hosanna! Hosanna! Hosanna to God and the Lamb" three times, and sealing each series of hosannas with three amens. [40]

After the congregation had participated in the Hosanna Shout, Brigham Young arose and spoke briefly in an unknown tongue, which was interpreted by David W. Patten, after which Elder Patten also delivered a short exhortation in tongues. Then the Prophet blessed the congregation, and at about four o'clock the seven-hour dedicatory service was concluded. [41]

The unusual outpouring of the Spirit manifest during the dedicatory service continued that evening at a priesthood meeting in the temple at which several men saw visions, prophesied, and spoke in tongues. George A. Smith declared that during this assembly he saw the temple filled with the hosts of heaven. He also recalled that David Whitmer reported that he saw three angels proceed along the south aisle of the temple. [42]

In addition to these reports of visions, prophesying, and

speaking in tongues within the walls of the temple, many persons described other unusual developments that took place during the period of the dedication. Several witnesses reported that they saw an unusul light on the top of the temple. Others mentioned that they heard heavenly singing coming from the roof of the building. [43] Several Latter-day Saints who were in Kirtland that night observed that angels were seen hovering around the outside of the temple, and that during the priesthood meeting a vibrant sound was heard, like a mighty rushing wind, that penetrated the House of the Lord. [44]

It was a challenge for Latter-day Saints who attended the meetings to express in words the feelings of joy and spiritual ecstasy that overpowered them. William Hyde wrote that "this was, by far, the best meeting I had ever attended." The gifts of the gospel, he added, were enjoyed in a marvelous manner. [45] Benjamin Brown recalled that the Spirit of God was poured out profusely, as on the day of Pentecost. "We had a most glorious and never to be forgotten time." [46] When Eliza R. Snow recorded her impressions of the dedicatory service, she wrote that "no mortal language" could "describe the heavenly manifestations of that memorable day." The congregation, she said, felt the "sweet spirit of love and union," "a sense of divine presence," and "each heart was filled with joy inexpressible and full of glory." [47] Nancy Alexander Tracy wrote that this was one of the happiest days in her life. Heavenly influences, she said, rested upon the Lord's House and heavenly beings appeared to many. [48]

The Ordinance of Washing of Feet

The season of unusual spiritual manifestations continued as Joseph Smith unfolded the last of the ceremonies connected with the Kirtland endowment, the ordinance of washing of feet. Like the anointing and the sealing of the anointing, this rite was originally performed in the temple and was restricted to members of the priesthood. Joseph Smith declared that one reason for the construction of the temple was so that members of the Church could "attend to this ordinance aside from the world." The rite, he taught, was as necessary in the latter days as when the Savior walked the earth. The Latter-day Saints needed to receive the ordinance to make the foundation of the Church complete and permanent and to prepare them for various blessings. "It is calculated to unite our hearts, that we may be one in feeling and sentiment, and that our faith may be strong, so that Satan cannot overthrow us, nor have any power over us," he said.[49]

Two days after the temple dedication, on Tuesday, March 29, the presidency met with the bishops and their counselors in the temple to participate in the ordinance of washing of feet. When they had gathered, Joseph Smith informed them that since they would spend the night there, they should send for anything they needed. He further said that the men were to cleanse their feet and partake of the sacrament in order that they might be qualified to participate in this ordinance when other elders of the Church assembled the following day. They then cleansed their faces and feet and proceeded to wash one another's feet. After they had partaken of the sacrament of bread and wine, the Prophet attested, "the Holy Spirit rested down upon us, and we continued in the Lord's House all night, prophesying and giving glory to God." Edward Partridge noted that they prophesied and some "spoke in tongues and shouted hosannas."[50]

At nine o'clock the next morning, some three hundred men gathered in the temple. Preaching from one of the pulpits in the main hall, the Prophet instructed them concerning the ordinance they were preparing to receive. Some of the curtains were lowered, creating several large compartments, with the priests, teachers, and deacons meeting in one corner of the temple and other members of the priesthood occupying the remainder of the hall. Tubs, water, and towels were placed in the chambers. Then the Presidency washed the feet of the apostles, "pronouncing many prophecies and blessings upon them in the name of the Lord Jesus." Throughout the morning, the presidency moved from one section of the hall to the other, instructing the men and supervising the administration of the ordinance. By noon all had participated in this ceremony. In the afternoon, Joseph Smith and Edward Partridge later reported, many began to prophesy and speak in tongues, with shouts of hosanna and amen.

In the evening, after a day of fasting, the men partook of bread and wine. Then they testified concerning the gifts of the spirit which they enjoyed. Although Joseph Smith retired to his home at about nine o'clock that evening (having already spent more than twenty-four hours in the temple) and did not witness all of the proceedings of that night, he summarized in his diary some of the developments that transpired after the men had partaken of the sacrament. "The Savior made His appearance to some," he said, "while angels ministered to others, and it was a Pentecost and an endowment indeed, long to be remembered."[51]

Restoration of Keys of the Priesthood

One of the most significant visions of the ages took place in the Kirtland Temple seven days after its dedication, on Sunday, April 3, 1836. In the morning, a congregation of more than eight hundred heard sermons delivered by Thomas B. Marsh and David W. Patten. That afternoon the Presidency and the apostles participated in administering and passing the sacrament. Then Joseph Smith and Oliver Cowdery retired behind the curtains, which had been lowered near the pulpits, and knelt in prayer, and the heavens were opened. The Prophet testified that they beheld a series of glorious visions. Jesus Christ appeared to them and accepted the temple and the sacrifices of the people. He told them that some members had been blessed by an endowment, and that the Saints would continue to receive blessings if they kept His commandments and did not pollute that sacred house. Then, Moses appeared and conferred upon the two men the keys of the gathering of Israel and the leading of the ten tribes from the land of the north. Elias appeared and conferred upon them the dispensation of the gospel of Abraham, after which Elijah appeared in fulfillment of the prophecy of Malachi, committing to the men the keys he held, preparing mankind for the Second Coming of the Savior.[52]

Later, while Joseph Smith was living in Nauvoo, he explained to the Saints on a number of occasions the significance of the appearance of Elijah in the Kirtland Temple. Elijah, he said, holds "the keys of the authority to administer in all the ordinances of the Priesthood; and without [this] authority . . . the ordinances could not be administered in righteousness." Explaining Elijah's mission of turning children to fathers and fathers to children, the Prophet said that this binding or sealing could be accomplished by the Latter-day Saints serving as saviors on Mount Zion. He asserted that by building temples, erecting baptismal fonts, and performing "all the ordinances, baptisms, confirmations, washings, anointings, ordinations and sealing powers upon their heads, in behalf of all their progenitors who are dead," Latter-day Saints could redeem others so that they might come forth during the first resurrection.[53]

More Unusual Spiritual Manifestations

At two additional priesthood meetings held in the spring of 1836, members reported that they beheld the hosts of heaven and enjoyed various spiritual gifts. On both of these occasions, on April 6 and May 1, men who had recently been ordained as well as priesthood bearers who had arrived in Kirtland after the dedication of the temple gathered in the temple for the ordinance of washing feet. Those who received the ordinance on April 6 had been washed in their homes and had been anointed in the temple the preceding day, while the seventies and elders who gathered on May 1 attended to both the ordinance of anointing and that of the washing of feet in a solemn assembly in the temple.

Approximately four hundred priesthood members met throughout the night of April 6, and after those who had not previously participated in the ceremony of washing feet received this ordinance and were pronounced clean, Heber C. Kimball recalled, the "spirit of prophecy was poured out upon the assembly." "Angels ministered to many," he said, "for they were seen by many."[54]

Another witness of these proceedings, William Draper, testified that the Spirit of the Lord entered the temple "like a mighty rushing wind and filled the house." "Many," he explained, "spoke in tongues and had visions and saw angels and prophecied." It was a general time of rejoicing, he said, "such as had not been known in this generation."[55]

Ebenezer Robinson's description of the May 1 meeting re-
sembles in many respects accounts of the April 6 gathering and of
other meetings in the House of the Lord. After partaking of the
sacrament, he wrote, many anxiously awaited and received powerful spiritual experiences. While some professed the gift of
prophecy, others testified that the heavens were unveiled and
they beheld angelic messengers from God.[56]

Other contemporaries wrote in their diaries or journals general impressions of the gifts they received during the season of the
temple's dedication. Ira Ames, Luke Johnson, and Chapman
Duncan emphasized that when they received their endowments,
they were blessed by the Lord.[57] Warren S. Snow declared that
when he received his endowment, he heard clearly the voice of
God.[58] Nathan Tanner observed that during this period many felt
the Spirit of the Lord daily.[59] George A. Smith testified that while
he was in the temple he beheld a vision of the Millennium,[60] and
Parley P. Pratt wrote, "Many persons were carried away in the visions of the Spirit, and saw and heard unspeakable things; and
many enjoyed the ministering of angels."[61]

After reading Joseph Smith's account of this period (which
was recorded in his Kirtland diary and published in his history of
the Church), some contemporaries wrote their own verification
of his narrative. Brigham Young and Joel H. Johnson, for example, stated that they witnessed the powerful gifts of the Spirit described in the Prophet's history.[62] Newel Knight testified that he
was present in the temple when God's power was revealed to the
Saints.[63]

Not all manifestations of spiritual gifts mentioned by persons
in Kirtland in the spring of 1836 occurred within the walls of the
temple. Some affirmed that they witnessed the healing power of
God or experienced unusual blessings during meetings in their
own homes. Lorenzo Snow stated that in many instances "the sick
were healed—the deaf made to hear—the blind to see and the
lame to walk."[64] Some members remembered experiencing at that
time a "sweet heavenly communion with the Holy Ghost." Nancy
Alexander Tracy wrote that this joyful feeling occurred while
elders went from house to house, administering the sacrament

and blessing the Saints. While solemn assemblies were being held and some persons were receiving an endowment, Nancy said, several families met occasionally in one of their homes and ate and worshipped together.[65]

The spiritual feasts enjoyed by the Saints in Kirtland continued during fast and testimony meetings held in the temple on the first Thursday of each month. Lorenzo Snow testified that at many of these meetings, the Spirit of God "was poured out in copious effusion" and many Saints enjoyed pentecostal refreshings from on high. Many Saints, including Lorenzo Snow, Eliza R. Snow, and Elizabeth Ann Whitney, wrote that the gifts of healing, prophesying, speaking in tongues, and the interpretation of tongues were periodically manifest.[66]

During one of these monthly fast days, Prescindia Huntington, who had moved to Kirtland in May 1836 and was baptized the following June, was in her home when an excited young girl rushed to her door and in bewilderment said that a meeting was being held on top of the temple. "I went to the door," Prescindia declared, "and there I saw on the temple angels clothed in white covering the roof from end to end. They seemed to be walking to and fro; they appeared and disappeared. The third time they appeared and disappeared before I realized that they were not mortal men. . . . This was in broad daylight, in the afternoon." She said that a number of children in Kirtland saw this assembly of angels, and that when members of the congregation returned to their homes after the meeting, they reported that the power of God had been manifest both inside and outside the temple. According to Prescindia, Saints who attended the meeting reported that members were blessed with the gifts of prophesying and speaking in tongues, and that one person who was interpreting an unknown language said that angels "were resting" upon the building.[67]

Prescindia Huntington stated that on another Thursday fast day, she and her sister Zina were kneeling in the temple with the congregation in vocal prayer when she heard a "choir of angels singing most beautifully." Their voices seemed to have come, she observed, from one of the upper corners of the hall. Although she said that she and her sister did not see any heavenly beings on that occasion, they heard "myriads of angelic voices" that seemed to have been united in singing a song of Zion. She further reported that during another fast meeting conducted by Father Smith, the "Holy Ghost filled the house." While "the spirit of revelation, prophecy, and tongues" was being manifest, she said, a "sound of a mighty rushing wind" was heard by the Saints, and the spirit was so powerful that some thought the building had caught fire.[68]

Word circulated that pentecostal gifts were being manifest in the temple during the Thursday sacrament meetings, and many relatives and friends of the Saints traveled to Kirtland to attend the meetings. Once one of Prescindia's cousins visited Kirtland, anticipating that she would witness a hilarious and ludicrous scene. Accordingly, Prescindia continued, "We went with our cousin to the meeting, during which a Brother McCarter rose and sang a song of Zion in tongues; I arose and sang simultaneously with him the same tune and words, beginning and ending each verse in perfect unison, without varying a word. It was just as though we had sung it together a thousand times." Following the meeting, the cousin confessed that instead of laughing, "I never felt so solemn in my life."[69]

Another outpouring of pentecostal gifts occurred in the Kirtland Temple on Thursday, April 6, 1837, at a solemn assembly to commemorate the organization of the Church. Some members prepared for the meeting by fasting and praying for several days beforehand. Some priesthood members who had not been in Kirtland when the temple was dedicated received their washings and anointings on April 4.[70] On the morning of the solemn assembly, these men met in the upper story of the temple, where they were blessed with the ordinance of sealing the anointing; then they retired to the main floor of the temple. The curtains had been lowered, dividing the main hall into chambers, and some of the men retired behind the curtains to participate for the first time in the ordinance of washing of feet. Following the administration of these ordinances, Joseph Smith spoke to the congregation for about three hours. Oliver Cowdery and Sidney Rigdon then preached, after which the sacrament was blessed and passed to the congregation.[71]

*Kirtland Temple, drawn by Henry Howe in 1846. He identified the
building north of the temple as the "Teacher's Seminary"
(site of the Methodist church in the 1830s) and the building
south of the temple as "the old banking house of the Mormons"*

After the solemn assembly, members were invited to retire to
their homes or if they desired, to remain in the temple for the
night. That night Joseph Smith conducted a testimony meeting
at which some members were blessed with the gift of prophecy,
others spoke in tongues, and some received the gift of interpretation of tongues.[72]

Another meeting was held in the temple on the night of April
7. Wilford Woodruff attended the service and later wrote in his
diary that "the power of God rested upon us." "We were baptized
with the Holy Ghost," he said, "and the spirit of God immersed

our bodies like a consuming fire." He also testified that the spirit of prophecy and revelation was manifest, and that through the gift and power of the Holy Ghost, many precious things were revealed to him. "Our hearts were made glad," he added, "[and] we returned to our homes rejoicing."[73]

Elder Woodruff also reported that the "power, gifts, and graces of the gospel" were again manifest in the Kirtland Temple on Thursday, April 20. Many members spoke in tongues during this service, and one man sang in tongues while one of the sisters interpreted his message. Much of the discussion, Elder Woodruff observed, centered on the "fame of Joseph" and his magnificent accomplishments.[74]

Signs of Dissension

While the Saints rejoiced as they attended one pentecostal meeting after another for more than a year, the peace and serenity of that season were marred by some strife and friction. Wilford Woodruff wrote in his diary in February 1836 and again on April 28 that the spirit of murmuring, complaining, and mutiny was beginning to be manifest in Kirtland. Many persons, including some in positions of responsibility, were beginning to reject the leadership of the the Prophet and were "striving to overthrow his influence."[75]

Other Kirtland Saints observed that in the fall of 1836, six months after the remarkable spiritual manifestations and communion with the hosts of heaven in the temple, the Spirit of the Lord was withdrawn from some of the members. Daniel Tyler wrote in his diary that after the priesthood had received their endowments, Joseph Smith cautioned them, "Brethren, for some time Satan has not had power to tempt you. Some have thought that there would be no more temptation. But the opposite will come, and unless you draw near to the Lord you will be overcome and apostatize."[76] Six months later, three apostles were disfellowshipped; and within a year, three of the original seven presidents of the seventies had been released. Before two years had passed, eight of the twenty-five General Authorities who had witnessed some of the most remarkable events in the history of the Church had been excommunicated or released from their ecclesiastical responsibilities.

This episode, like so many other events in the history of Christianity, is difficult for historians to analyze. Why did the Saints who gathered in the Kirtland Temple in 1836 experience so many pentecostal gifts? Some critics have sought to discredit these events by suggesting that illusions occurred following the liberal consumption of wine.[77] However, Latter-day Saints, like so many other Christians of the 1830s, regarded intemperance as a serious transgression, and there is no evidence that any of the visions described by numerous witnesses followed the consumption of large amounts of wine. Contemporary testimonies of these events are so numerous that they cannot be dismissed with such an oversimplification.

One possible explanation is that bearers of the priesthood who gathered in the temple in 1836 had been promised and were anticipating special blessings, and for some, this meant an unusual spiritual experience. After dedicating their lives to the advancement of the restoration movement and after sacrificing much of their material wealth for the sake of building up a new kingdom on earth, many awaited a special gift of the Spirit. By following precisely the instructions of their prophet, many testified that they partook of spiritual blessings in a magnitude unlike anything they had previously experienced.

Nancy Tracy, reflecting on this experience, wrote that although she felt during this pentecostal season that heaven was on earth, she recognized that such special blessings would not continue. Nevertheless, she suggested that these blessings were to prepare the Latter-day Saints for the trials that awaited them. "We have opposing elements to contend with," she said, adding that the Saints "shall be made perfect through suffering."[78]

Chapter 17
Conflict at Kirtland

The year following the dedication of the Kirtland Temple saw a spirit of pride, selfishness, disaffection, and apostasy sweep through the quorums of the Church. In the summer of 1837, members of the Quorum of the Twelve Apostles, witnesses to the Book of Mormon, and other priesthood leaders met in the upper room of the Kirtland Temple. Though the preceding year many of these same individuals had witnessed in that building some of the most remarkable spiritual manifestations in the history of the restoration movement, now they were meeting to oppose the leadership of Joseph Smith. At this assembly, some persons who had once been faithful supporters of the Prophet recommended that he be replaced as president of the Church by David Whitmer. Others vehemently opposed this motion, including Brigham Young, Heber C. Kimball, and John Smith. Brigham Young, "in a plain and forcible manner," said that he knew that Joseph was a spokesman for the Lord, and though others "might rail and slander him [the Prophet] as much as they pleased," they "could not destroy" his appointment as a "Prophet of God." Their apostate actions, he declared, would destroy their authority, cut the thread that bound them to the Prophet and to God, and lead them to destruction. Many of the disgruntled members, enraged at Elder Young's efforts to thwart their recommendations, threatened to resolve the conflict with physical blows. The meeting finally ended without agreement on a course of action. According to Elder Young, "The knees of many of the strongest men in the Church faltered."[1]

On another occasion during this turbulent period, Warren Parrish, John F. Boynton, and other dissidents entered the temple on a Sabbath morning armed with pistols and bowie-knives and sat in the Aaronic Priesthood pulpits at the east end. Shortly after the morning service began, the men interrupted the meeting. Eliza R. Snow, who witnessed the interruption, called it "a fearful scene." Drawing their pistols and knives, the dissidents rushed from the stand into the congregation and attempted to gain control of the building. Amid great confusion and with screams of alarm, some persons tried to escape by jumping out the windows. Local officials were summoned, and finally, with the assistance of the police, members of the congregation succeeded in removing the belligerents from the temple. Though no one was injured, the incident was another in a disrupting chain of events leading to the expulsion of the Saints from Kirtland just a few months later.[2]

Economic Problems in Kirtland

The historical roots of apostasy among Kirtland Saints reach back to a policy of community improvement and expansion, followed by a period of improved economic conditions, followed in turn by a year of economic disasters. After the temple was dedicated, many Latter-day Saints concentrated on enlarging their homes, erecting new dwellings and shops, and beautifying their community. A master plan for the improvement of Kirtland was drafted by Joseph Smith in 1836. According to this model, Kirtland was to be divided into rectangular plots and square blocks, with streets bisecting each other at right angles.[3] Commenting on this plan, Wilford Woodruff wrote in April 1837:

It was given him [Joseph Smith] by vision. It was great, marvelous and glorious. The city extended to the east, west, north and south. Steam boats will come puffing into the city. Our goods will be conveyed upon railroads from Kirtland to many places and probably to Zion. Houses of worship would be reared unto the most high. Beautiful streets was [sic] to be made for the Saints to walk in. Kings of the earth would come to behold the glory thereof, and many glorious things not now to be named would be bestowed upon the Saints.[4]

Many contemporaries observed that in the fall and early

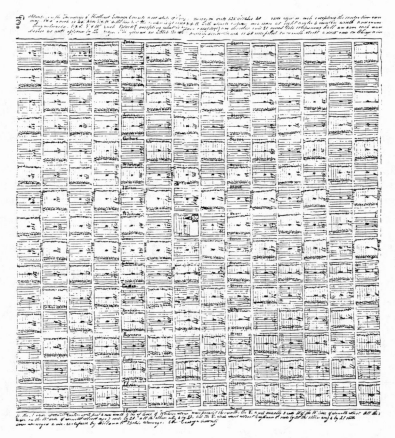

Plan of Kirtland, Ohio, 1836

winter of 1836 the Kirtland Saints were involved in various construction projects, seemed to be happy, and were participatng in a
vibrant program of community growth. "The noise of the ax and
the hammer" were heard everywhere, Wilford Woodruff wrote in
his diary, and "a cheerfulness beaming upon every countenance"
revealed a new sense of prosperity.[5] The *Messenger and Advocate*
reported in January 1837 that the streets of Kirtland were crowded
with teams loaded with provisions and with wood and other building materials, and that many visitors had come to Kirtland to view

the stately and magnificent temple. According to the paper, the recent growth of Kirtland was more remarkable than that of any other community of similar size situated so far from navigable water.[6]

During this era of rapid growth, Church leaders and other members were acquiring additional property in Kirtland. The land was needed to put into effect Joseph Smith's plan for an enlarged and beautified city of the Saints in the Western Reserve. After the temple was completed, many members who now had more time to devote to farming pursuits wanted enlarged farms to raise their standard of living and to adequately support their families. In the spring of 1836, Latter-day Saints were assessed land taxes on over twelve hundred acres in Kirtland, representing about 5.7 acres per family. The average farm size of non-Mormons in the township was about fifty acres per family, a minimal amount at the time for a satisfactory farm operation.[7] Although some of the Saints owned stores and shops and others worked as teachers, laborers, and craftsmen, property held by the members in 1836 was not considered sufficient to meet current needs and future plans. Additional land was needed not only for those who had settled in Kirtland, but also for others who would be immigrating there. Joseph Smith and other leaders of the Church undoubtedly viewed the future optimistically. Based upon recent developments, they might have expected a growth in the Kirtland membership of eighty to one hundred families annually for at least a few years.[8]

While members of the Church were increasing their property holdings in Kirtland, land prices rose sharply, and there was reason to believe inflationary conditions would continue.[9] Changes in the real price of land in the 1830s were determined primarily by changes in the general price level (inflation) and changes in population. Between 1830 and 1837 the annual average price of land in Kirtland rose from $6.54 to $44.48 per acre.[10] After the community was surveyed and divided into half-acre lots in the mid-1830s, some lots that had sold for $10.00 to $50.00 soon sold for many hundreds of dollars. According to an editorial appearing in the June 1837 issue of the *Messenger and Advocate*, the price of land in Kirtland during the preceding year had increased 800 percent.[11]

To secure the money needed for economic expansion, many of the Saints were forced to borrow. During the previous three years most of their resources had been used for the construction of the temple, and by the summer of 1836, many of the debts incurred while the temple was being built had not yet been liquidated.[12] Meanwhile, lenders were willing to extend credit to Saints seeking financial assistance. Land could be reclaimed, and creditors assumed that goods could be sold within a reasonable period for a profit. Since Kirtland was expected to continue growing, with land values increasing at a normal inflationary rate, Church leaders and creditors assumed that the Mormons could manage all the debts they had accumulated.[13]

The financial problems of the Saints in Kirtland were compounded after the temple was completed. During its construction, members of the Church in the East and other areas of North America had sent contributions to Kirtland, which temporarily bolstered the town's economy. These donations decreased after the temple was dedicated, at a time when the debts of the Kirtland Saints were mounting. Recognizing a cash-flow deficiency, Church leaders sought a means to transform into cash some of the assets they and other members possessed in land. One means to which they now gave consideration was the establishment of a bank in Kirtland.[14]

Banks played a significant role in the development of many American communities in the nineteenth century. As the nation's economic growth accelerated, the demand for credit and money increased, resulting in the establishment of banks in small as well as large communities throughout the country. Between 1830 and 1837, the period when the Latter-day Saints were headquartered in Kirtland, the number of banks in the United States increased from 329 to 634 and the number in Ohio from 11 to 31. Banks provided loans, a medium of exchange, and a safe depository for money. To meet public demand for a readily acceptable medium of exchange, banks would provide notes or currency in exchange for the promissory notes of individuals and businesses.

While a promissory note was not generally accepted as a medium of exchange to secure goods and services, bank notes could be used quite readily. Local bank currency was generally accepted only within a small geographical area served by the bank, and was heavily discounted by banks outside that area.[15] Prior to 1837, banks had already been established in several Ohio communities smaller than Kirtland, and based on the successful experience of these institutions, as one group of scholars recently reported, "Kirtland probably could have supported a modest bank."[16]

On November 2, 1836, leaders of the Church in Kirtland, probably with the help of a non-Mormon attorney, drafted an article of agreement providing for the organization of a banking institution to be called the Kirtland Safety Society Bank.[17] Orson Hyde then traveled to Columbus with a petition directed to the Ohio legislature, requesting approval for the incorporation of a banking institution. Church leaders, assuming that the legislature would grant the request, also sent Oliver Cowdery to Philadelphia to secure plates for the printing of currency. On January 1, 1837, Oliver Cowdery returned with the plates—but Orson Hyde returned with discouraging news.[18] The legislature had refused to consider the petition. "Hard-money" Democrats who were opposed to an expansion of banks in Ohio had gained control of the legislature; in 1835 all requests for bank charters had been rejected, and in 1836 only one of sixteen such requests had been accepted. Thus, Orson Hyde was unable to secure a charter granting the Saints the right to organize a bank in Kirtland.[19]

The Saints, disappointed by the rejection of their request to incorporate a bank in Kirtland, decided to reorganize and to create a private joint-stock company, the Kirtland Safety Society Anti-Banking Company.[20] They probably assumed that individuals had a legal right to organize a private company that engaged in banking activities, since other unchartered or unauthorized banks were organized in Ohio before and after the Kirtland Safety Society was constituted. Insurance companies, savings institutions, and even a literary firm assumed banking powers during that era, including issuing notes, loaning money, and providing a de-

Three money bills issued by the Kirtland Safety Society

pository for funds. Referring to the pre-Civil War era in Ohio, one modern historian has written that "all laws against unauthorized banks and bank paper seem to have been in vain."[21]

Many persons in the Western Reserve initially supported the formation of the Kirtland Safety Society. Church leaders served as officers, with Joseph Smith as treasurer and Sidney Rigdon as secretary. Both members and non-members bought stock in the company, most of the stock being purchased during the last three months of 1836 before the company was constituted. Two hundred investors purchased (primarily with gold and silver) 39,025 shares in the company, with subscriptions totaling about $20,000.00. Although the face value of the stock was $50.00 per share, the price per share varied from ⅓¢ to $3.93, with an average price being 26¼¢. The average investor bought $12.00 worth of stock, representing almost one week's income.[22]

On January 2, 1837, the Kirtland Safety Society opened its doors for business. Using the plates that Oliver Cowdery had secured, the company issued its first notes during the first week of January, stamping on some of the currency words that changed "BANK" to "antiBANKing Co." This first issue consisted of $1, $2, and $3 denominations and amounted to about $10,000. Possibly $15,000 had been invested in subscriptions, serving as backing for this first issue. Additional notes of denominations ranging from $1 to $100 were issued in February and March, bringing the total to perhaps $100,000.[23]

Shortly after the Kirtland Safety Society began to function, serious problems interfered with its successful operation. On January 23, Sidney Rigdon announced that the society could no longer redeem its notes with specie. Thereafter, its notes were subject to heavy discounts.[24] In February, Joseph Smith, Sidney Rigdon, and other leaders of this company were charged with violating an 1816 Ohio statute that prohibited the issue and circulation of unauthorized bank notes and fixed a penalty of $1,000 for officers of institutions that violated this law.[25] In June, Joseph Smith resigned as an officer in the company and withdrew his support of this institution.[26] In August, Warren Parrish was accused of defrauding the bank of funds and becoming involved in counterfeiting.[27] In October, a jury found Joseph Smith and Sidney Rigdon guilty of violating the Ohio statute of 1816, and a judgment amounting to $1,000 was assessed them.[28] Finally, in November the company closed its doors.[29]

As the Prophet struggled to prevent the Kirtland Safety Society from collapsing, his financial problems increased. His subscriptions to the society totaled 1,360 shares, more than any other investor except John Greene. He also paid more per share than 85 percent of the investors, and in February and March, when the company was experiencing financial difficulties, he increased his subscriptions. Apparently in an effort to help the business, in 1837 he secured three loans. On January 2, he borrowed more than $3,000 from the Bank of Geauga; on July 3, he secured $1,225 from the Commercial Bank of Lake Erie-Cleveland, and a loan from the Bank of Monroe, a Michigan bank in which members of the Church had a controlling interest. Meanwhile, because of financial difficulties, he also sold property in Kirtland at a price of more than $5,000.[30]

Many forces combined to destroy the Kirtland Safety Society. Success of any business at that time, especially banking institutions, depended upon public support. Many banks in the Western Reserve refused to accept the Kirtland Safety Society notes as legal tender, and anti-Mormon newspapers branded the currency as worthless "rags." Moreover, banks did not possess sufficient specie to satisfy large demands for redemption of their currency. Since the capital backing the Kirtland Safety Society was primarily in the form of land, in order for the society to continue as a successful business enterprise, supporters had to prevent individuals from securing large amounts of the Safety Society notes. Enemies of the Church, however, managed to obtain sufficient quantities of the notes to initiate a run on the institution, forcing the Safety Society to suspend payment in specie a few weeks after the first notes were issued.[31]

Another reason for the failure of the company was the lack of a charter. During the trials in which Joseph Smith and Sidney Rigdon were charged with violating the banking statute of 1816, their attorney argued that that law had been repealed by an act of

Table 3

Average-size Farms in Kirtland, Ohio, 1830-1839

	Latter-day Saints					Non-Latter-day Saints				
Year	Residents Assessed Taxes	Number Assessed P.P. Tax[1]	Estimated # of Families	Total Assessed Acres	Mean[2]	Residents Assessed Taxes[3]	Number Assessed P.P. Tax[1]	Estimated # of Families	Total Assessed Acres	Mean[2]
1830[4]	7	6	9	132	14.6	129	121	153	6,944	45.3
1832	9	7	20	84	4.2	151	132	170	7,692	45.2
1833	10	7	31	189	6.1	174	155	193	8,782	45.5
1834	36	32	73	438	6.0	169	148	184	9,111	49.5
1835	66	63	145	1,181	8.1	168	148	184	9,827	53.4
1836	105	96	218	1,236	5.7	195	159	203	10,021	49.4
1837	173	150	309	2,389	7.7	199	154	200	8,717	43.1
1838	167	78	364	2,961	8.1	201	142	200	7,749	38.7
1839[5]	111	14	18	1,718	95.4	241	188	246	8,879	36.1

Source: Geauga County Tax Records, 1830-1839

[1] P. P. Tax was a personal property tax—a tax on horses, cattle, and merchandise.

[2] To create the estimated acres owned by each family, the total number of acres was divided by the estimated number of families (LDS and non-LDS).

[3] The number of non-LDS residents who paid a land tax was determined by omitting all non-LDS who did not pay during the 1830s a personal property tax, assuming that those who did not pay such a tax were land speculators (who were not living in Kirtland). This list also includes those assessed a personal property tax.

[4] The 1830 LDS taxpayers are individuals who were living in Kirtland in 1830 and who joined the Church during the winter of 1830-31. (Tax records for 1831 have not been located.)

[5] A few of the 14 LDS personal property taxpayers and residents in 1839 had disassociated themselves from the Church and never joined the main body of Latter-day Saints.

1824. In fact, the February 16, 1837 issue of the *Painesville Republican* reported that the law of 1816 had been replaced by a general law of 1824 that declared that all notes "issued by unauthorized banking companies" were "null and void, without, however, annexing a penalty." The court did not sustain this interpretation. It ruled that the 1824 banking act amended provisions in earlier laws but did not replace these other statutes;[32] thus, the operations of the Kirtland Safety Society were in violation of the laws of Ohio. When Church leaders decided in January 1837 to charter a bank in Kirtland, they and their legal advisers had not understood that forming a company with banking powers would be considered illegal. Since other unauthorized institutions in Ohio during that era were engaged in similar banking activities, Joseph Smith and other members recognized that enemies abroad and apostates within were involved in the destruction of the Kirtland Safety Society.[33]

Demise of the Kirtland Safety Society intensified the economic problems of the Kirtland Saints. The two hundred individuals who invested in the bank lost nearly everything they subscribed; others secured notes issued by the company and redeemed their currency at heavy discounts. As the months passed, many still held bills that had no redeemable value. When the company failed, many persons lost their savings and a few were ruined financially.[34] It has been estimated that the financial loss approached $40,000, almost the total cost of building the Kirtland Temple. This loss was sustained by persons whose income averaged about $400 annually.[35]

Joseph Smith's economic losses from the failure of the Kirtland Safety Society were greater than those of any other individual. While seeking to establish and then sustain the company and at the same time purchase land in Kirtland and goods for his store, he had accumulated debts amounting to approximately $100,000.[36] Although he had assets in land and goods that were of greater value in some respects than his debts, he was unable to immediately transform these assets into a form that could be used to pay his creditors.[37]

The Saints' economic problems were compounded in the

spring of 1837 by a panic that spread west from New York into other parts of the nation. In May 1837, there was a general suspension of payment in specie by the banks of Ohio. Chartered banks did not discontinue business, however, and prior to the resumption of specie payment in August 1838, only one bank in the state is known to have failed.[38] But during the panic, money was scarce, and many creditors were unable to extend credit or postpone dates when debts were due. Unable to meet their financial obligations, Joseph Smith and other Church leaders were in an awkward and embarrassing position. While the Prophet's creditors pressured him to pay for supplies he had purchased at wholesale prices, he was unable to apply this same pressure on members of the Church who had purchased goods from him on credit. Brigham Young aptly described Joseph Smith's predicament while he was laboring as a merchant in Kirtland:

Joseph goes to New York and buys 20,000 dollars' worth of goods, comes into Kirtland and commences to trade. In comes one of the brethren, "Brother Joseph, let me have a frock pattern for my wife." What if Joseph says, "No, I cannot without the money." The consequence would be, "He is no Prophet," says James. Pretty soon Thomas walks in. "Brother Joseph, will you trust me for a pair of boots?" "No, I cannot let them go without the money." "Well," says Thomas, "Brother Joseph is no Prophet; I have found *that* out, and I am glad of it." After a while, in comes Bill and sister Susan. Says Bill, "Brother Joseph, I want a shawl, I have not got the money, but I wish you to trust me a week or a fortnight." Well, brother Joseph thinks the others have gone and apostatized, and he don't know but these goods will make the whole Church do the same, so he lets Bill have a shawl. Bill walks off with it and meets a brother. "Well," says he, "what do you think of brother Joseph?" "O he is a first-rate man, and I fully believe he is a Prophet. See here, he has trusted me this shawl." Richard says, "I think I will go down and see if he won't trust me some." In walks Richard. "Brother Joseph, I want to trade about 20 dollars." "Well," says Joseph, "these goods will make the people apostatize; so over they go, they are of less value than the people." Richard gets his goods. Another comes in the same way to so make a trade of 25 dollars, and so it goes. Joseph was a first-rate fellow with them all the time, provided he never would ask them to pay him. In this way it is easy for us to trade away a first-rate store of goods, and be in debt for them.[39]

"Vexatious Law Suits"

In the summer of 1837, in the midst of financial reversals, Joseph Smith was involved in what he called "malicious and vexatious law suits."[40] Enemies of the Church continually harassed him, indicting him on one charge after another. Grandison Newell, for example, one of the most outspoken critics of the Church in Geauga County, brought a suit against the Prophet, charging him with instructing two other members of the Church to kill Newell in harmony with the will of God. Joseph's actions, Newell alleged, were aimed at preventing him from prosecuting the Mormon leader for his involvement in the Kirtland Safety Society. The court convened in June, and after hearing various testimonies, the judge ruled that there was no reliable evidence substantiating Newell's complaint and suggested that his hatred toward the Mormon leader, not his fear of a threat on his life, had induced the prosecution.[41]

On July 27, 1837, Joseph Smith set out on a trip to visit the Saints in Canada, accompanied by Sidney Rigdon and Thomas B. Marsh. Brigham Young and a new convert, Albert P. Rockwood, were to accompany them part of the way. They got only as far as Painesville, where the Prophet was arrested. After a preliminary hearing, he was released by the court for lack of evidence. Within a short time he was again arrested by the sheriff, and again he was released. In fact, on that day he was arrested six times, charged with various offenses, and each time the case was dismissed for lack of evidence. After spending all day in Painesville, the Prophet and his companions returned to Kirtland. They commenced their mission again the next day.[42]

As he returned from Canada, Joseph was again detained in Painesville. According to an account by Mary Fielding, based on information she learned from the Prophet, he and Brigham Young were seized by a mob when they were about four miles from home. Taken to a tavern in Painesville, they escaped through the kitchen door, aided by a housekeeper who was a member of the Church. The mob, upon learning of their disappearance, took up the chase. Joseph and Brigham fled through dense woods and along muddy roads, hiding in swamps and behind trees and logs. At times their pursuers, carrying blazing torches, were so close that the two men feared their own heavy breathing might be heard. At dawn they finally reached Kirtland.[43]

Most of the legal proceedings against Joseph Smith in Ohio were cases involving debts. Between 1837 and 1837 seventeen lawsuits were filed against Joseph Smith in Geauga County for debts involving claims of more than $30,000. Four of the suits were settled; three were voluntarily withdrawn by plaintiffs; and ten resulted in judgments against the Prophet and others. Three of the ten judgments were fully discharged, three were partly satisfied, and available records indicate that four were not satisfied.[44]

The Roots of Apostasy Spread

During this period of economic distress and increasing opposition against the Church, many converts apostatized. Eliza R. Snow observed that following the temple dedication, many of the Saints who had received marvelous spiritual blessings anticipated that "prosperity was dawning upon them." As economic conditions improved, some became "haughty in their spirits" and were "lifted up in the pride of their hearts." And as individuals "drank in the love and spirit of the world," she added, the Spirit of the Lord withdrew, and "they were filled with pride and hatred toward those who maintained their integrity."[45]

Wilford Woodruff also pointed to pride as a factor leading to dissension within the Church. In January 1837, he wrote, Church leaders chastized some of the Saints assembled in the temple. "David Whitmer . . . warned us to humble ourselves before God lest his hand rest upon us in anger for our pride & many sins that we were runing into in our days of prosperity as the ancient Nephites did & it does not appear evident that a scourge awates this stake of Zion even Kirtland if their is not great repentance immediately."[46]

At the same time that pride was manifest among the Saints, a spirit of selfishness emerged. Heber C. Kimball wrote that as the Saints were anticipating the commencement of an era of prosperity, some developed an inordinate desire to become suddenly and vastly wealthy.[47]

In an article in the *Messenger and Advocate* in May 1837, editor Warren Cowdery suggested that the unbridled desire to accumulate worldly wealth led some of the Saints into mercenary and deceptive business practices in Kirtland. Unscrupulous brethren, he announced, were taking advantage of others and, after obtaining their money, deserting them. Such action, he said, was marring the peace of the community and causing distress among members of the Church, leading some to apostatize. He especially warned Church members who were planning to immigrate to Kirtland to beware of individuals who approached them shortly after their arrival and inquired concerning their financial status. Some persons were reportedly taking advantage of newcomers by describing unusual investment opportunities that would lead to financial gain and abundant blessings from the Lord, but that actually would deprive the investors of their savings. Elder Cowdery suggested that before anyone entered into a contract with a person with whom he was not acquainted, he should investigate the proposal and seek counsel from Church leaders and other reliable sources.[48]

A few Kirtland Saints identified in their writings practices of Mormons in Kirtland that they regarded as selfish and un-Christian, including land speculation that brought excessive profits to some at the expense of their brethren.[49] After some of the Saints lost their savings as a result of the failure of the Kirtland Safety Society, they complained about the lack of charity of their creditors. Ira Ames asserted that after he had lost nearly everything, including the land on which he was living, two creditors who were then serving as apostles tried to take his horse.[50] Describing the contention, Parley P. Pratt wrote that there were "jarrings and discords" in Kirtland, that "envyings, lyings, strifes, and divisions . . . caused much trouble and sorrow," and "many fell away," becoming apostates and enemies of the Church.[51]

In addition to pride and selfishness, a third major force leading to an apostasy in Kirtland was criticism of the Prophet Joseph Smith. According to Wilford Woodruff, even prior to the collapse of the Kirtland Safety Society some members complained about the leadership of Joseph Smith. Under the date of February 19, 1837, Elder Woodruff wrote that while Joseph was absent from Kirtland on business for the Church, some turned against him. He compared these members to the children of Israel who rebelled against Moses while he was on Mount Sinai. The Saints' discontent at that time was temporary, he said, for after the Prophet returned and spoke to the people in the temple, the complainers "saw that he stood in the power of a prophet."[52]

As the financial crises in Kirtland deepened, the Prophet was criticized for his business transactions, for excessive borrowing, for speculating in land, and for supporting a banking institution that was experiencing serious problems. Some critics blamed the Mormon prophet for the economic reversals of 1837, failing to recognize that Joseph Smith was a mortal, subject to the weaknesses of the flesh, and was not directed in all of his personal affairs by the Lord.[53] He became a scapegoat upon which many tried to unload their problems. A rumor was circulated that the Kirtland Safety Society had come about through revelation and that Joseph Smith had predicted the company would never fail, so some persons claimed that the demise of that institution was evidence he was a fallen prophet.[54] Recognizing that he had been misrepresented, Joseph testified before the Kirtland high council that he had never uttered nor authorized a statement concerning the infallibility of the banking company. He declared in September 1837 that he had always said that "unless an institution was conducted on righteous principles it would not stand."[55]

In mid-1837, many members living in Kirtland, including some who had been called to serve in the highest positions of responsibility, rejected the leadership of Joseph Smith, declaring that he was no longer a true prophet. While Joseph was lying in bed with a debilitating illness in June, apostates circulated a rumor that he was suffering because of his transgressions in leading the Church into a desperate financial condition.[56] When Heber C. Kimball began his mission that month to England, he said that John F. Boynton called him a fool for leaving home at the call of a "fallen prophet."[57]

Parley P. Pratt was among those who censured the Prophet and Sidney Rigdon for their "business transactions." He admitted that "under feelings of excitement, and during the most peculiar trials," he wrote a letter condemning the actions of the men.

After the letter was published by a non-Mormon in what Elder Pratt called a garbled form, he recognized his mistake and sought forgiveness from the Church and those whom he had offended. In his apology, Elder Pratt censured himself for his "rashness, excitement, imprudence, and many faults," adding that at no time, even during the period of his most intense anger, had he believed that the men were dishonest or held improper motives. "I have ever esteemed them from my first acquaintance," he said, "as men of God, and as mighty instruments in his hands to bring forth, establish, and roll on the kingdom of God. But I considered them like other men, and as the prophets and apostles of old liable to errors, and mistakes, in things which were not inspired from heaven; but managed by their own judgement."[58]

Another factor that precipitated an apostasy of members in Kirtland was immorality. Referring to priesthood leaders who left the Church in the fall of 1837, George A. Smith observed that after the "spirit of adultery or covetousness" had seized control "of their hearts . . . the Spirit of the Lord left them."[59] A few members in Kirtland possibly entered into the practice of plural marriage without authorization of Church leaders, justifying their actions by asserting that Joseph Smith had taken a plural wife. The Prophet had probably received revelations in Ohio relating to eternal and plural marriage in the early 1830s and may have been practicing plural marriage about 1835.[60]

One contemporary of the Prophet wrote that after they learned that Joseph was practicing plural marriage, Oliver Cowdery, Warren Parrish, and Jared Carter incorrectly assumed that prerogative for themselves and became involved in promiscuous relations.[61] Commenting on Oliver Cowdery's transgression, George Q. Cannon, who later served as a counselor to four nineteenth century presidents of the Church, wrote:

The Lord revealed to the Prophet Joseph in an early day, some points connected with the doctrine of celestial marriage. He was told that it was to obey God's will that His ancient servants had taken more wives than one; and he probably learned, also, that His servants in these days would be commanded to carry out this principle.

The Prophet Joseph, however, took no license from this. He was content to await the pleasure and command of the Lord, knowing that it was as sinful to enter upon the practice of a principle like this before being commanded to do so, as it would be to disobey it when required to carry it into effect.

Not so with Oliver Cowdery. He was eager to have another wife. Contrary to the remonstrances of Joseph, and in utter disregard of his warnings, he took a young woman and lived with her as a wife, in addition to his legal wife.

Had Oliver Cowdery waited until the Lord commanded His people to obey this principle, he could have taken this young woman, had her sealed to him as his wife, and lived with her without condemnation. But taking her as he did was a grievous sin, and was doubtless the cause of his losing the Spirit of the Lord, and of being cut off from the Church.[62]

Benjamin F. Johnson asserted that Joseph Smith's practice of plural marriage not only provided members with an excuse to justify their transgressions, but also caused others to leave the Church, undoubtedly because they did not understand the eternal principles involved in this marital law.[63]

A "Great Apostasy"

On September 3, 1837, at a conference in Kirtland, Joseph Smith was unanimously sustained as President of the Church, and Sidney Rigdon was sustained as a counselor in the Presidency. The conference failed, however, to sustain some of the leaders, including Martin Harris, John Johnson, Joseph Coe, and Joseph C. Kingsbury; and a few were disfellowshipped, including three apostles—Luke S. Johnson, Lyman E. Johnson, and John F. Boynton. Moreover, David Whitmer, Oliver Cowdery, and Leonard Rich were accused of transgressions, but these men and many other leaders who were charged with improper conduct apparently confessed their errors and sought forgiveness.[64] When the three apostles who had been disfellowshipped admitted their mistakes and indicated a desire to repent, they were received back into fellowship and retained their special calling as apostles.[65]

That fall, while Joseph Smith was visiting the Saints in Missouri, criticism of him was renewed and reached an ugly schismatic dimension. The selfishness, murmuring, lust, and contention that had been manifest among the Saints in Kirtland led to a "great apostasy." Repudiating the Prophet's leadership, about thirty priesthood bearers renounced the Church and organized a new church in Kirtland, under the leadership of Warren Parrish. They adopted the name "Church of Christ" and tried to seize control of the temple.[66]

Between November 1837 and June 1838, possibly two or three hundred Kirtland Saints withdrew from the Church, representing from 10 to 15 percent of the membership there.[67] Many of the apostates had served in major positions of responsibility. During a nine-month period, almost one-third of the General Authorities were excommunicated, disfellowshipped, or removed from their Church callings. Among those who left the Church during this stormy period were the three witnesses to the Book of Mormon (Oliver Cowdery, David Whitmer, and Martin Harris) four apostles (John F. Boynton, Lyman E. Johnson, Luke S. Johnson, and William E. McLellin), three of the original presidents of the First Quorum of Seventies (Hazen Aldrich, Leonard Rich, and Sylvester Smith), and two of the presidents of the seventies who were serving in 1837 (John Gould and John Gaylord). One president of the seventies (Salmon Gee) was disfellowshipped, and one member of the First Presidency (Frederick G. Williams) was released from his calling. Although some of these leaders were not excommunicated until after they had moved to Missouri, the roots of their apostasy stem back to transgressions that occurred in Kirtland.[68] (Almost half of those who were excommunicated, disfellowshipped, or dropped from their positions of responsibility in 1837 or 1838 later repented and returned to the Church.)[69]

Some of the apostates became bitter enemies of the Latter-day Saints and organized to expel them from Kirtland. Oliver B. Huntington wrote that "persecution commenced with an iron hand" in the fall of 1837 shortly after Joseph Smith and Sidney Rigdon left for Missouri. "It was the life and glory of the apostates," he said, "to hatch up vexatious law suits and strip the brethren of their property." He added that "it seemed as though all power was given them to torment the Saints," and that leaders of the Church "were hunted like rabbits and foxes." Some of the men whose lives were in danger, including Joseph Smith's father and two of his brothers, Samuel and Don Carlos, hid in Huntington's home and, while concealed there, planned their exodus west. "Even the mummies were secreted there," he concluded, "to keep them from being destroyed."[70]

Others testified that dissidents tried to seize the property of the Saints and threatened to kill members of the Church. Brigham Young said that apostates threatened to destroy him in December 1837 because he proclaimed in public and in private that he "knew, by the power of the Holy Ghost, that Joseph Smith was a Prophet of the Most High God, and had not transgressed and fallen as apostates declared."[71] Many contemporaries agreed that men who had once held the priesthood were responsible for the intense persecution that erupted in Kirtland and for the disruption of that community of Saints.[72]

Religious Intolerance in Ohio and America

While apostates played a significant role in forcing Latter-day Saints to abandon their homes in Kirtland, enemies outside the Church were also involved in oppressive actions. Though the number of anti-Mormon articles appearing in Ohio papers declined after 1833, antagonists expanded the range of tools used in their campaign from newspapers to magazines, periodicals, and books. Throughout that decade (and continuing for more than a century), members of the Church frequently complained that their history and beliefs were being misrepresented by others. Persecution of the Kirtland Saints during the thirties was not limited to the constant flood of negative and often inaccurate propaganda. They were also socially ostracized, were denied employment opportunities, faced economic boycotts, and occasionally lived in fear of attack on their lives and property.[73] While some members guarded the temple twenty-four hours a day, others slept near the Prophet, to preserve his life from his enemies.[74] Expressing his grave concern that the Saints would be driven from Kirtland as others had been expelled from Jackson County, the Prophet had written to Edward Partridge on December 5, 1833, "The inhabitants of this county [Geauga County] threaten our destruction, and we know not how soon they may be permitted to follow the example of the Missourians." Four years later, persecution approached the dimension that the Prophet feared.[75]

One of the major forces that helped precipitate intolerance against Latter-day Saints was the bigotry Americans inherited from their colonial ancestors. The earliest immigrants to America brought with them the behavioral patterns of western Europe. Among the religious concepts transplanted to America were the beliefs that there should be only one legal religion in each community; that heresy was a serious crime; that religious pluralism would lead to political anarchy; and that settlers should be required to pay a tax for the support of a religious establishment. Prior to 1634 there was strict religious uniformity in North American communities, solidarity that continued for a half century or longer in the colonies. During most of the seventeenth century, for example, there was but one legal religion in Virginia (Anglican) and in Massachusetts and Connecticut (Congregational in both colonies); and prior to 1664, the Reformed faith (primarily the Dutch Reformed Church) was the only legal religion in what is today New York.

When missionaries of the Society of Friends penetrated colonies where religious establishments existed in the midseventeenth century, they experienced cruel opposition. In Virginia and New York (then New Netherlands), Quakers were fined, imprisoned, and then banished. In Massachusetts, they were not only imprisoned and later banished but were also sometimes branded, whipped, or even put to death.[76]

Prior to the American Revolution, tax-supported religions existed by law in nine of the thirteen colonies. In all the South and in New York City, the Church of England was supported by public taxes; and in New England, except for Rhode Island, the Congregational Church was the tax-supported faith. Laws were also enacted in most colonies to prevent non-Trinitarian Protestants and Roman Catholics from voting, holding office, or worshiping in public. During the early 1770s, itinerant missionaries were imprisoned in Virginia for preaching without authorization of resident ministers, and Baptists and members of a Strict Congregational Church were fined and imprisoned for failure to pay ecclesiastical taxes.

Although a new birth of religious and political freedom did indeed accompany the emergence of a new nation, intolerance remained a serious problem. Those who were considered threats to the established order of society were socially ostracized, defamed, mobbed, and otherwise cruelly treated.

The angry moods and ugly passions that led to violent mob action were sometimes generated by inflammatory newspaper articles. Although it is impossible to assess the precise influence journalistic campaigns had on individuals, propaganda undoubtedly molded the attitudes of many, justifying, in some minds, intolerant behavior. As Alexis de Tocqueville noted in his *Democracy in America:* "I shall not deny that in democratic countries, newspapers frequently lead the citizens to launch together into very ill-digested schemes."[77] During the 1830s, pens became swords, individuals were joined by crowds, and crowds became menacing mobs in various parts of America, including the Western Reserve.

Latter-day Saints, therefore, were not the only Christians impugned by American journalists of the new nation. One of the most outspoken critics of the restored Church, Alexander Campbell, complained in the January 2, 1832, issue of the *Millennial Harbinger* that "never was there a more vigilant, determined, and untiring opposition to any religious paper, published on this continent . . . than at this time to this paper." He reported that his religious paper had been repeatedly "denounced from the pulpit and the press," and that some subscribers were being persecuted by ministers of various faiths.

Persecution had grown from seeds of ignorance, fear, revenge, jealousy, and other passions that instigated hatred. The tendency toward conflict was further stimulated as old standards were being discarded and new patterns of conduct were emerging. When these forces combined in a region where the arm of the law was weak, mobs sometimes became the ruling force. Occasionally, opinions of groups took precedence over the rights outlined in constitutions and laws. Robert Boyd, a missionary who labored in the Western Reserve during the 1830s, offered an interesting explanation for the lawlessness that sometimes became so distressing in that section of America. The New Englanders who settled there, he reasoned, had emerged from a religious environment that was as strict and somber as the physical climate. It was not surprising that some behaved "like freed prisoners." While in New England, he pointed out, many "walked the courts of God's house," but upon arriving in the West, they threw off the shackles of conformity that had previously disciplined their actions. [78] Boyd's theory needs amplification, however, for lawlessness was not limited to the Western Reserve or to parts of America settled by New Englanders. During the 1830s and 1840s mobbings occurred in the west, east, north, and south, in both rural and urban communities of the young nation.

When new elements appeared in communities, violence sometimes resulted. As Roman Catholic immigrants poured into America during the 1830s, confrontations reached ugly dimensions in some cities where they settled in large numbers. Roman Catholics challenged the prevailing views of religious orthodoxy, with some regarding them as enemies of America's democratic institutions. This added to the problems of poverty and unemployment in the cities.

In Ohio, various reform movements suffered from intolerance and mob action. The abolitionists of Ohio experienced especially cruel treatment from mobs during the 1830s. A report issued at the Ohio Anti-slavery Convention of 1836 states that during the previous year abolitionists had been attacked by mobs in thirteen Ohio towns, from Zanesville in the south to Willoughby and Painesville in the north. Mobs from Zanesville had attacked settlers in the neighboring town of Putnam on five or six different occasions, disturbing meetings, scattering people, attacking homes and other property, and ordering settlers to depart. At Painesville, a mob had pelted men and women with rotten eggs and tried to drown out the words of the abolitionists by beating on drums, blowing horns, and ringing sleigh bells. At Willoughby, an abolitionist was abducted, threatened with death if he returned to his home, and dropped off five or six miles down the road. One abolitionist, Theodore Weld, was greeted in Circleville and Granville with a barrage of eggs and stones. Two of his friends were attacked in Middlebury, Portage County, by a howling mob who threw glass and eggs at all who had gathered. [79]

In April 1836, abolitionists meeting in Granville mounted an

offensive against a group who threatened to interrupt their deliberations. Armed with clubs, the reformers rushed from their
meeting and dispersed the mob. The next day the mob returned
with new recruits, creating a force of about two hundred men. As
the abolitionists were returning to their homes, the mobsters engaged them in fist fights, and a number of abolitionists were
beaten mercilessly.[80]

Another abolitionist, Marius Robinson, was tarred in Trumbull County in June 1837. The night before he was to deliver a
lecture at Berlin, he was dragged from the home of his Quaker
host, beaten and tarred and covered with feathers, then transported in a wagon about ten miles to Canfield and dumped. He
wandered to a nearby farmhouse, where he was cared for and
given a suit of clothes. Then he walked back to Berlin and delivered a Sabbath evening sermon against the evils of slavery.[81]

While others who were considered a threat to existing institutions were being mobbed, the Latter-day Saints in Ohio, Missouri, and elsewhere were being persecuted partly because of their
unusual religious convictions. The Saints believed that because of
the disruption of the Primitive Church of Christ, all other faiths
were void of God's authority and advanced inaccurate doctrines.
They taught that the restored Church would continue to grow,
like the stone mentioned by Daniel, and would roll forth until it
eventually encompassed the earth. Opponents vigorously denounced the Latter-day Saint beliefs concerning a restoration of
"Christianity in its primeval purity," the Book of Mormon as a
new witness for Christ, latter-day visions and revelations, and the
restoration of the priesthood with its accompanying miraculous
powers. They condemned the Saints for worshiping a God who
was a material personage and who literally created man in His
own image; for calling others to repentance; and for teaching that
the Church had been restored in preparation for the Second
Coming and the millennial reign of Christ. The sacrifices of the
Saints in building a temple and supporting an expanding missionary program were criticized by their enemies, as was the Saints'
pattern of living in compliance with instructions and revelatory
writings from an authoritarian ecclesiastical leader.[82]

NORTHERN TIMES.

WHERE INTELLIGENCE DWELLS, THERE IS FREEDOM.

VOL. 1, NO. 28.   KIRTLAND, OHIO, FRIDAY, OCTOBER 9, 1835.   WHOLE NO. 28

NORTHERN TIMES.

Kirtland, Oct. 9, 1835.

NATIONAL NOMINATION!!

FOR PRESIDENT,

MARTIN VAN BUREN,
OF NEW YORK.

FOR VICE PRESIDENT,

Richard M. Johnson,
OF KENTUCKY.

"Union, harmony, self-denial, concession, —every thing for the cause, nothing for men, —should be the watchword, and motto of the democratic party."—*Benton's Letter.*

Appointment by the President.

GEORGE WASHINGTON MONTGOMERY to be Consul for the Port of St. John's, in the Island of Porto Rico, in the place of Sidney Mason.

Abolition.

Several communications have been sent to the Northern Times, for insertion, in favor of anti-slavery—or the abolition of slavery. To prevent any misunderstanding on the subject, we positively say, that we shall have nothing to do with the matter—we are opposed to abolition, and whatever is calculated to disturb the peace and harmony of our Constitution and country. Abolition does hardly belong to law or religion, politics or gospel, according to our idea on the subject.

The Contest.

Next Tuesday decides, for one year,

An announcement for the support of Martin Van Buren for president of the United States, superimposed on front page of an issue of the Northern Times

Political and Civil Issues

Another factor leading to Mormon persecution in Ohio stemmed from political issues. While most people in the Kirtland area supported candidates of the Whig party, a majority of the Latter-day Saints living there supported the Democratic party led by President Andrew Jackson.[83] Most Kirtland Saints not only supported Jackson's opposition to the national bank, but also felt that under Whig leadership, as one historian has written, "the evils of the Old-World aristocracy would emerge in America in the form of federal privileges and monopolies." They feared that the Whigs would grant political favors to the wealthy that would transform "the purest government . . . into the rankest aristocracy."[84] To publicize their political views and gain friends amid increasing opposition to the Church, the Saints established a newspaper in Kirtland, the *Northern Times*. The paper, edited initially by Oliver Cowdery and later by Frederick G. Williams, supported policies and candidates of the Democratic party. After the first issue was printed in February 1835, Whig papers in the Western Reserve denounced the Saints for their political stance and continued their tirade against the Church. One Whig editor responded to the appearance of the *Northern Times* by writing sarcastically:

> The Mormonites in this county, as if weary of dull monotony of dreams and devotion, of visions and vexation—of profitless prophecys, and talking in *tongues*,—have concluded to turn their attention to political matters. A paper entitled the *Northern Times* has made its appearance from their press in Kirtland, bearing the name O. Cowdery, one of their leaders and preachers, as Editor. The editor breaks forth with a flood of words, filling seven columns under his editorial head—pounces upon the dead carcass of the United States Bank with most Quixotic ferocity—talks about "WIGS"—praises the President—and says, the nomination of Van Buren "we still add, would meet our mind, and receive our warm support." As the editor professes to have communication with the spirits of the invisible world, and certifies that he has seen an Angel, and "hefted" the golden plates of the Prophet, he will be a political anomaly, if not a *dangerous opponent*.[85]

Non-Mormons not only denounced Latter-day Saints for supporting Jacksonian democracy, but also expressed concern because Mormons were an increasingly powerful political force in

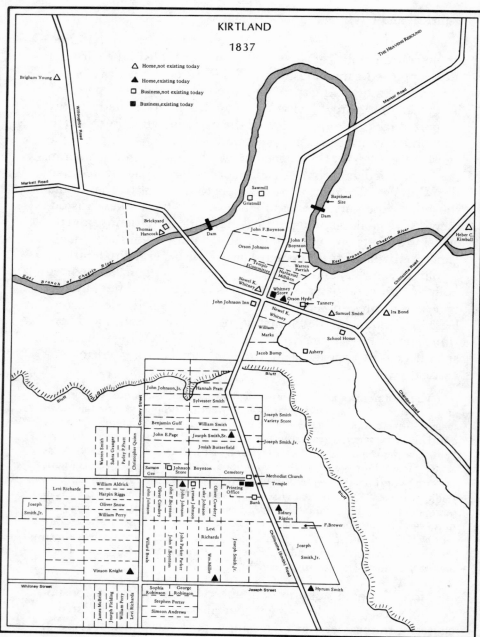

KIRTLAND

1837

△ Home, not existing today

▲ Home, existing today

□ Business, not existing today

■ Business, existing today

Brigham Young △

THE HEAVENS RESOUND

Willoughby Road

Mentor Road

Markell Road

Sawmill
Gristmill

Baptismal
Site

Dam

Brickyard
Thomas Hancock
Dam

John F. Boynton

Orson Johnson

John F. Boynton

East Branch of Chagrin River

Heber C. Kimball △

East Branch of Chagrin River

Temple Committee

Warren Parrish

Nathaniel Milliken

Chillicothe Road

Newel K. Whitney

Whitney Store

Orson Hyde

Tannery

John Johnson Inn

Newel K. Whitney

Samuel Smith △

Ira Bond △

William Marks

School House

Jacob Bump

Ashery

Bluff

Bluff

John Johnson Jr.

Hannah Pratt

Sylvester Smith

Cemetery Street

Joseph Smith Variety Store

Benjamin Goff

William Smith

Warren Smith

Sabra Granger

Parley P. Pratt

Christopher Quinn

John E. Page

Joseph Smith, Sr. ▲

Josiah Butterfield

Joseph Smith, Jr.

Samon Gee

Johnson Store

Boynton

Cemetery

Methodist Church

Temple

Printing Office

Bank

Levi Richards

William Aldrick

Harpin Riggs

Oliver Snow

William Perry

Joseph Smith, Jr.

John Johnson

Oliver Cowdery

John F. Boynton

John Johnson

Luke Johnson

Oliver Cowdery

Sidney Rigdon ▲

F. Brewer

Levi Richards

Joseph Smith, Jr.

Willard Boak

John F. Boynton

John Parker Parker

Wm. Miller

Joseph Smith, Jr.

Chillicothe (South) Road

Vinson Knight ▲

Whitney Street

James McBride

Joseph Fielding

William Perry

Levi Richards

Sophia Robinson

George Robinson

Stephen Porter

Simeon Andrews

Joseph Street

Hyrum Smith ▲

Chardon Road

Research by Keith Perkins

Kirtland. Members of the Church were elected to most township offices in 1837, and critics feared that if their membership continued to grow, they would soon gain control of county offices as well.[86]

In addition to being viewed as a threat to the political aspirations of others, Mormons were accused of interfering with the democratic process by voting according to instructions received from their ecclesiastical leaders. Moreover, the critics warned, if the growth of the Church were not soon halted, inhabitants of Kirtland would be governed by the revelations of the Mormon Prophet.[87]

Non-Mormons also accused the Latter-day Saints of violating the laws of Ohio by performing marriages, and refused to recognize Mormon elders as ministers who had the legal authority to solemnize marriages. The Prophet, however, claimed that he had received a commission from heaven not only to organize the Church but also to perform ordinances, including marriage. In 1835 Sidney Rigdon was tried before the court of common pleas at Chardon for "solemnizing marriages without a license," but since he had received the right to perform this rite while he was serving as a Baptist preacher and there were no records proving that he had been expelled from that faith, the case was dismissed. Although Latter-day Saint leaders continued to perform marriages and recorded in the *Messenger and Advocate* the names of those who had been married in Kirtland by Mormon elders, critics continued to question the "propriety" of elders solemnizing "matrimonial contracts."[88]

The Poverty of the Saints

Another cause for the disfavor with which enemies of the Church looked upon the Saints in Kirtland was their economic status and the conditions under which they lived. As a rule, the Saints in Kirtland were poorer than most of their neighbors. Whereas most pioneers in the new area concentrated on improving their economic and living conditions, the Latter-day Saints had been challenged by revelation to devote their time and talents to the building of the kingdom of God. Complying with this law of consecration, the Kirtland Saints gave generously to the construction of a temple. They also helped poorer members who had gathered to Kirtland, aided families whose husbands and fathers were serving in the mission field, and assisted oppressed Saints in Missouri who had been expelled from their homes.[89]

The economic problems of the Saints were compounded by inflationary conditions, as well as by an expanding population. Between 1830 and 1838, the population of Kirtland township increased threefold, increasing from one thousand to three thousand inhabitants. William W. Phelps, who lived in Kirtland during the winter of 1835-36 while his family resided in Missouri, wrote his wife, Sally, in December 1835 that he doubted he could support his family adequately in that community. "Everything is dear with us in Kirtland," he said. "Fresh pork costs from 5 to 6 cents per pound and beef from 2½ to 3½ cents per lb; wheat is $1.12½ centers per bushel and rising; corn 75 cents per bushel, cheese 9 cents per lb. by wholesale, butter 25 cents per lb., and hay and oats are also high. Without great business or plenty of money a family fares course in this part of the county. We have not had any butter for six or eight weeks."[90]

Jonathan Crosby, who settled in Kirtland with his wife in 1835, lived in the home of Parley P. Pratt. He recalled that not long after he arrived in Kirtland, Brigham Young, Heber C. Kimball, and Parley P. Pratt came to him for a loan. Shortly before that, Brigham Young had had nothing in his house to eat and no means with which to secure food. Parley P. Pratt approached Elder Young and informed him that he was also without food. Then he remembered that Jonathan Crosby had recently arrived in Kirtland with one hundred dollars, so the two men, accompanied by Heber C. Kimball, went to the new settler, who loaned them $25 each.[91]

Following the completion of the temple, members acknowledged that for three years they had neglected to improve their homes and beautify the community. In an article in the *Messenger and Advocate*, one person wrote that most homes built on the property that stretched from the river to the temple (land that the Church had purchased from Peter French) were "small and inelegant, evincive of anything but wealth." He noted that the

Table 4
Ratio of LDS and Non-LDS Town Officers
Kirtland Township, 1830–1839

| Year | All Officials Except Supervisors of Highways | | Supervisors of Highways | |
	LDS No. (%)	Non-LDS No. (%)	LDS No. (%)	Non-LDS No. (%)
1830[1]	0	12 (100%)	0	17 (100%)
1831[1]	0	11 (100%)	0	17 (100%)
1832[1]	0	12 (100%)	1 (5%)	17 (95%)
1833	0	12 (100%)	0	20 (100%)
1834	2 (15%)	11 (85%)	2 (8%)	22 (92%)
1835	2 (18%)	9 (82%)	7 (29%)	17 (71%)
1836[2]	4 (36%)	7 (64%)	5 (31%)	11 (69%)
1837	11 (65%)	6 (35%)	8 (44%)	10 (56%)
1838[3]	1 (8%)	12 (92%)	1 (4%)	24 (96%)
1839[4]	0	11 (100%)	0	26 (100%)

[1] In 1830, 1831, and 1832 one individual who later joined the restored Church was elected to a major office.
[2] In 1836 Oliver Harmon, Jr., was elected as Overseer of the Poor, as one of the two Fence Viewers, and as one of the Supervisors of the Highways.
[3] In 1838, five former Latter-day Saints were elected to one of the town offices.
[4] In 1839, no Latter-day Saints or former Latter-day Saints were elected to a town office.

dwellings had been built during a period when the Saints had "little control, and but feeble means to execute any plan with elegance or taste." Consequently, instead of establishing an orderly, planned community, they had constructed "rude dwellings" that were "scattered in all directions" from the river to the Lord's House and south of that building.[92]

At a conference in the fall of 1836, Church leaders declared that the Saints in Kirtland had been "poor from the beginning," and that their burdens had been compounded by the gathering there of many who needed economic assistance. The members were told that they should assume increased responsibility in caring for the poor, and that henceforth, branches of the Church in other areas were not to send their poor to Kirtland unless local leaders provided them with an adequate means of support.[93]

As early as 1833, the poverty of the Saints provided non-Mormon critics with an excuse to demand their removal. Shortly after they began gathering in Kirtland in large numbers, local authorities warned many of them to leave town, thereby relieving the local government of its responsibility to care for the poor. Such an order was in harmony with the laws of the state. According to early statutes of Ohio, if a person who had been warned to leave applied for assistance or became a public charge, the overseer of the poor had the authority to remove that person from that community to the township where he had last gained legal status. Though some families who were not members of the Church received the same orders, it appears that there was a conscious attempt by local politicians in 1833 and 1834 to issue this special warning to Latter-day Saints.[94]

As the Saints continued to gather, their enemies' complaints increased. One anti-Mormon group met in Kirtland in January 1834 and lamented that an undesirable element was spreading in the community. They charged that the Mormons were alienating other settlers and were threatening the town with an "insupportable weight of pauperism."[95]

Local businessmen also considered the Saints' presence in the town an economic liability. In 1830, entrepreneurs in Kirtland were anticipating significant economic expansion as a result of expected population growth. Although there was significant growth of the LDS population, the non-Mormon growth remained almost stationary during the mid-1830s. Meanwhile, Latter-day Saints settled on land that would have been occupied by non-Mormons and established businesses that competed with others. While some older settlers in the community engaged in normal business relations with the Saints, buying from the Mormons and providing them with goods and services, others refused to hire Latter-day Saints, would not mill their grain, and would not sell goods to them. One group was frustrated in 1835 when it imposed an economic boycott in order to force the Latter-day Saints from Kirtland. After demanding that the Saints leave that community, the businessmen agreed not to sell grain to them during a winter when there was a shortage of food. The owner of the Kirtland gristmill joined the boycott, forcing the Saints not only to locate food in another community but also to find a mill outside of Kirtland. Though their problems were increased by added transportation costs, the Saints located the grain they needed and decided to send it to a mill owned by a Church member in another town. The boycott failed to produce the desired results. Mormons did not abandon their homes, and the local merchants lost many customers.[96]

Thus, economic pressures, combined with religious, political, and social forces, led anti-Mormons to feel justified in oppressive actions against the Church and its members. Less than nine months after launching a new volley of attacks, they finally succeeded in forcing nearly all Kirtland Saints to abandon their homes, leave their sacred temple, and migrate to another section of the young nation.

Chapter 18

The Exodus from Kirtland

When Brigham Young described conditions existing in Kirtland on December 22, 1837, the day of his departure from that community, he said that he fled for his life because of the fury of the mob. After making hasty preparations for a journey of more than eight hundred miles, he left his wife and his three-year-old son and one-year-old twins, mounted his horse, and galloped southward.[1] His flight was the beginning of a mass exodus from Geauga County. Between the end of December 1837 and the middle of July 1838, probably more than sixteen hundred members of the Kirtland branch migrated west, abandoning their homes and beginning a new colonizing adventure in the wilderness of western America.

Three weeks after the first Latter-day Saints left Kirtland because of the "mobocratic spirit prevailing in the bosoms of the apostates." Joseph Smith, Sidney Rigdon, and George W. Robinson (clerk and recorder of the Church and Sidney Rigdon's son-in-law) also fled.[2] "Persecution became so violent," Lucy Mack Smith observed, that "Joseph regarded it as unsafe to remain any longer in Kirtland."[3] Eliza R. Snow also testified that the Prophet "had to flee" Kirtland because his life was in danger.[4]

Joseph Smith recorded in greater detail the circumstances that led to his flight from the community he had helped build. "A new year dawned upon the Church in Kirtland," he wrote, "in all the bitterness of the spirit of apostate mobocracy, which continued to rage and grew hotter and hotter, until Elder Rigdon and myself were obliged to flee from its deadly influence, as did the Apostles and Prophets of old." Quoting the Savior, the Prophet said that "when they persecute you in one city, flee to another." He and his companions rode from Kirtland on the night of January 12, 1838, "to escape mob violence."[5]

Describing another form of persecution that he feared, the Prophet asserted that the "hellish designs" of his enemies were colored under the disguise of legal processes. Luke S. Johnson, a former apostle who had left the Church but was opposed to the intolerant acts of others, believed that had Joseph not left Geauga County, he would have been involved in another expensive lawsuit for illegal banking and possibly faced imprisonment. Learning that the sheriff was planning on arresting the Prophet, Johnson intervened and placed Joseph in his custody "on an execution for his person, in the absence of property to pay a judgment of $50." After settling the judgment, the Prophet left for Missouri.[6]

Fleeing from disgruntled creditors, angry apostates, and civil authorities, Joseph and his companions rode southward under cover of darkness and arrived the next morning in New Portage, Norton Township, Medina County, about sixty miles from Kirtland. Three days later, after the Prophet's wife, Emma, and their children arrived in Norton, the group continued their journey in covered wagons. Though the weather was bitterly cold, the Prophet wrote that a mob, armed with pistols and guns, followed him for about two hundred miles. During the pursuit, his enemies once stayed in a home where the Saints were sleeping, with only a partition separating the Smith family from their pursuers. That night, the Smiths listened to "their oaths and imprecations, and threats" concerning actions they would take if they seized the Mormon leader. On other occasions members of the mob passed Joseph Smith and his family passing through small Ohio communities, but failed to recognize them.[7]

In Dublin, Indiana, the Smith party met Brigham Young, who was staying there with his brother Lorenzo. By this time Joseph and his companions had spent all of their money, and al-

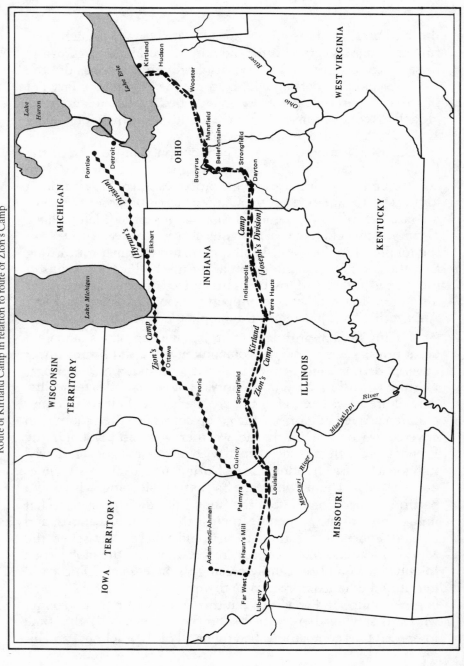

ROUTE of KIRTLAND CAMP

Route of Kirtland Camp in relation to route of Zion's Camp

though he secured employment in Dublin, cutting and sawing wood, he did not consider the money he earned sufficient to continue the journey. Thus he went to Brigham Young for assistance, telling him, "You are one of the Twelve who have charge [hold the keys] of the kingdom in all the world; I believe I shall throw myself upon you, and look to you for counsel in this case." Although Brigham was startled that a Prophet was seeking help from him, he agreed to help. One of the members in Dublin, Brother Tomlinson, had been trying to sell his tavern, and Brigham had instructed him that if he remained obedient to righteous counsel, he would soon receive a good offer on his property. Shortly thereafter, Brother Tomlinson told Brigham that he had been offered $500 in cash, a team of horses, and $250 in store goods for his property. Brigham advised him to sell and to help Joseph Smith. Consequently, Tomlinson sold his tavern and gave the Prophet $300 so he could continue his journey to Missouri.[8]

Joseph Smith and his family and traveling companions traveled through Indiana and Illinois, crossed the Mississippi River at Quincy, Illinois, and headed across the state of Missouri toward Far West. When they were within 120 miles of their destination, they were met by some Saints from Far West who had brought wagons, money, and provisions for them. When they were eight miles from the city, they were met by another escort group, and on March 14, as they reached the outskirts of Far West, a large number gathered to welcome them. The Prophet commented, "We were immediately received under the hospitable roof of Brother George W. Harris, who treated us with all possible kindness, and we refreshed ourselves with much satisfaction, after our long and tedious journey, the brethren bringing in such things as we had need of for our comfort and covenience."[9]

Other Church leaders were also forced to flee from Kirtland during the winter of 1837-38. In January 1838, Joseph Smith, Sr., was arrested for performing illegal marriages. Placed in the custody of Luke Johnson, he was taken to a small room next to the magistrate's office. There Johnson removed a nail from the window sash and left the room, locking the door behind him. With the help of Hyrum Smith and John Boynton, Father Smith slipped out the window. Luke Johnson then returned to the room, replaced the nail in the sash, and rushed back to the magistrate's office to report that the prisoner had disappeared. The officials rushed into the room and saw the window was securely locked from the inside. According to several contemporary accounts, a perplexed constable settled the disappearance problem by explaining, "It is another Mormon miracle."[10]

Father Smith hid in the homes of Oliver Snow (the father of Lorenzo and Eliza R. Snow) and William Huntington for approximately three weeks, while he prepared for the westward journey. On occasions he was joined in this Mormon underground by his sons Don Carlos and Samuel and by other members of the Church whose lives were in danger. To prevent the escape of the Patriarch from Geauga County, handbills were posted in public places and along the roads leading from Kirtland, and sentinels prepared to seize him and take him back for trial were stationed along the roads. Joseph Smith, Sr., however, evaded his pursuers; he managed to ride to New Portage, where he waited for his family before setting out for Missouri.[11]

Other members of the Smith family left Kirtland under distressing circumstances. A mob tried to seize Don Carlos, accusing him of the same crime his father had allegedly committed—performing marriages illegally. He fled to Norton Township, where he was joined by other members of the Smith family. On May 7, twenty-eight members of the family started for Missouri, including Joseph Smith, Sr., and his wife, Lucy; their children Don Carlos, William, Catherine, and Sophronia, and their families; and a few others. Don Carlos's wife, Agnes, was very weak from giving birth to a daughter only two weeks before. The group began the journey with fifteen horses, seven wagons, two cows, $75 in cash, tents, blankets, clothes, and a few other provisions.

The Smith family were delayed often on their journey westward. Shortly after crossing the Mississippi River, they stopped at a small wooden hut belonging to a black family and requested help for Catherine; shortly after being placed in this shelter, she gave birth to a son named Alvin. The next day she and the baby were transported on a lumber wagon four miles to another home, where she rested while her husband and sister Sophronia attended to her needs. Meanwhile, other members of the party continued their journey, but because the Prophet's mother was ill, they proceeded slowly. In Huntsville, Missouri, they stopped temporarily so she could recover. Eventually those who had stayed with Catherine joined the others in Huntsville, but Catherine became ill there, so they were again delayed while she regained her health and strength. Lucy Mack Smith reported that after the elders administered to Catherine she seemed better, so the company was able to resume its journey to Far West without further difficulties.[12]

The Persecution Continues

After many of the Church leaders had left Kirtland, the fury of the Saints' enemies was directed toward those who remained. This relentless persecution continued as the Latter-day Saints prepared to leave the community. One of the most vivid descriptions of conditions in Kirtland in 1838 was recorded in a series of letters written by Hepzibah Richards, a convert who had migrated to Kirtland shortly before persecution erupted. "For some days past the spirit of things has been rapidly changing," she wrote on January 18, 1838, "and to the view of all appears to be gathering blackness. A large number have dissented from the body of the Church and are very violent in their opposition to the President and all who uphold him." She reported that apostates had vowed to seize control of the temple even if such action led to "the shedding of blood."[13]

After the lives of members of the Kirtland high council had been threatened, Hepzibah wrote in another letter, "All our friends design leaving this place as soon as posssible. . . . The feeling seems to be that Kirtland must be trodden down by the wicked for a season. . . . Probably several hundred families will leave within a few weeks."[14] In February, she again noted that Latter-day Saints were being forced to abandon their homes: "They are driven out of this place as truly as the Saints were driven out of Jackson County 4 years ago, though in a different manner. There they were driven by force of arms, here by persecution, chiefly from the dissenters."[15]

A month later Hepzibah reported that the oppression of the Saints had not abated. "I have been wading in a sea of tribulation ever since I came here. For the last three months, we as a people, have been tempest-tossed, and at times the waves have well nigh overwhelmed us, but we believe there will yet be a way of escape."[16]

In July 1838, after nearly all the Latter-day Saints had left Kirtland, Zadoc Judd arrived with his family, anticipating settling there. Their plans were immediately altered after they assessed the situation, and their stay there was short. He wrote that "apostates and mobbers had caused nearly all the good and worthy people to leave the place." After deciding that Kirtland was not a favorable location for Mormons, the Judds continued west along the trail leading to Missouri.[17]

In addition to living in fear that they might be killed or beaten, Latter-day Saints reported that mobs had broken into their homes, shattered their windows, destroyed their property, stolen their goods, and threatened continued violence if they did not leave. According to the family records of Nathan Cheney, a mob stole four of his cows and some bedding. The following day Nathan was seized while searching for his animals and was held prisoner for two weeks. During his confinement, his wife, Eliza Ann, who did not know whether her husband was dead or alive, was menaced by ruffians who threatened to burn the Cheney home. Terrified, she took her two young girls and fled into the woods, where she hid until she thought it safe to return. When they returned home, she found her husband alive and uninjured. Because of the persecution, the Cheney family was driven from Kirtland, leaving behind a home and farm they had bought for $1,200, for which they received nothing.[18]

Daniel Wood testified that enemies of the Church were so "unrelenting in their persecution" that the Saints could not consider secure any property they possessed, even if they had personally contracted no debts. Sometimes, he explained, a constable would enter the home of one of the Saints and seize a large brass kettle, an iron pot, or some other item, and then would auction these goods. To justify such action, the constable would say that he was taking goods that belonged to Joseph Smith and was selling them to liquidate debts the Prophet had accrued. When Daniel Wood learned that the constable planned to take his wagon, he took it apart, placed the pieces on the back of a sled, covered the parts with hay, and had his younger brother transport the dissembled vehicle out of town, where he could later recover and rebuild it.[19]

Members of the Church were also unjustly accused of crimes and thefts. Sometimes enemies would place their clothes near Mormon homes, summon the law enforcement officials, lead the officers to the sites where they had deposited the clothing, and then accuse the Mormons of stealing.[20] Hepzibah Richards asserted in March 1838 that one of the objectives of enemies of the Church was to seize "all the property of the Church for little or nothing and drive the Saints out of the place." She testified that the house of her nearest neighbor had been ransacked by a mob on the pretense they were trying to recover goods stolen by the Mormons.[21]

Kirtland Saints further complained that their enemies frequently attempted to burn their homes and other buildings. According to Luman Shurtliff, dozens of fires were started in the basements of Mormon homes, and Hepzibah Richards said that mobsters tried to burn her neighbor's home while the family was sleeping.[22]

Shortly after midnight on January 16, Kirtland residents were awakened by men yelling, "Fire!" Caroline Crosby wrote that she looked out her window and "beheld the ground as light as day, while the sky was as black as a thundercloud." Rushing to an outside door, she threw it open and saw the printing office in flames. Many men had responded to the cries for help and were trying frantically to control the blaze but to no avail. The printing office with all its contents, including many copies of the Book of Mormon, was destroyed. The temple and other buildings near the printing office were scorched and sparks landed on many homes in that area, but these other buildings did not ignite.[23]

Members and nonmembers blamed each other for destroying the printing office. Since the Saints had sold the property the day before the fire, apostates accused them of burning the building, an accusation that was vehemently denied. The Mormons had been forced to auction the property because of charges of indebtedness brought against the Presidency by Grandison Newell. The Saints insisted that the building had been taken from them unjustly, that their enemies knew they could not retain title to the property, and that their enemies had wanted to stop Mormon publications.[24]

The next day, a meeting was held in Kirtland to discuss the mounting crisis and to prevent further destruction. A patrol of twenty-one men that was appointed to guard the city included both members and nonmembers. Their effectiveness was weakened, however, because of mutual distrust, for the two factions devoted much of their time to spying on each other. Eventually the patrol was dissolved, and the arsonist responsible for destruction of the printing office was never apprehended.[25]

Four months later, on May 22, arsonists set fire to the Methodist chapel a few feet north of the temple. That same night someone broke a window in the temple and threw a bundle of straw and shavings containing hot coals into the building. Presumably the arsonists intended that fire to be fed by the Methodist Church fire. Only a few straws caught fire, however, and they were quickly extinguished. Efforts of those who gathered to fight the fires were hampered because someone had cut the rope in one of the wells in the area, removed a bolt from the pump of another well, and hidden the buckets kept there for use in fighting fires. Therefore, the Methodist chapel burned to the ground. Though anti-Mormon factions claimed that the seventies had set fire to the Methodist church, the *Painesville Telegraph* asserted that the fire was probably started by individuals who were trying to destroy the nearby Mormon temple.[26]

Preparations for the Exodus

Even as the Saints were experiencing persecution, they were preparing for their exodus to western Missouri. Since many had lost their savings during the financial reversals of 1837, they were forced to sell most of their material goods to pay debts, and once the exodus began, land values declined sharply. Many were unable to obtain the teams, wagons, provisions, and money they'd need for the trek west. One nonmember Kirtland resident, Christopher Crary, summarized the situation of the Saints at that time:

When their bank failed, all their imaginary wealth vanished; their money was gone; their teams were gone; their provisions were gone; their credit was gone; their stores of goods disappeared. No community could be left in more destitute circumstances, and the only alternative was for them to leave—leave their Temple, their homes, all that they had held dear, and go to, they knew not where. And how to go was a serious question.[27]

Though Crary wrote that the Saints did not know where they would settle, most planned to go to Far West, Missouri. Nearly all of the Kirtland Saints had previously sold their farms in the eastern states in order to gather in Ohio, and now they were being forced to leave that area. William Huntington, for example, sold his farm of approximately two hundred acres in New York (with 130 acres cultivated) and his stock, barns, and home, to move to Kirtland in 1836. One year later he lost all of his property in Kirtland and was "reduced to a state of poverty," with no idea how he could transport his family a thousand miles to Missouri. He managed to obtain a pair of oxen from Oliver Snow, and a Sister Ives loaned him thirty-two dollars. He wrapped his tools in clothes and shipped them to Missouri, then put a few other clothes and blankets in the bed of a small wagon and, accompanied by his family, started walking toward Far West.[28]

John Tanner, who had also arrived in Kirtland in the mid-1830s with a wagon loaded with goods and with ample money to buy a farm in Geauga County, had given generously to the temple-building project, had loaned money to Joseph Smith so he could purchase goods in the East, had invested in the Kirtland Safety Society, and had supported other similar programs. By 1838 he had sold, loaned, lost, or given to others nearly all of his money and property, including the land, mills, cattle, and barns he had owned in New York and the farm he had purchased in Kirtland. Thus, at the time of the exodus he was so poor that he had to borrow some of the necessities for the journey. He and his wife and other family members began the long journey to the frontier with a dilapidated cart, pulled by a broken-down stage horse that collapsed during the journey, and with only a few dollars in cash.[29]

Some of the Saints were much better prepared for the westward migration than the Huntington and Tanner families. Though Luman Shurtliff lost the two-hundred-dollar down payment he had made on property in Kirtland, he owned land about ninety miles west of that community that he was able to sell in order to secure horses, harnesses, wagons, and money for the journey to Missouri. He also exchanged a large quantity of maple sugar for axes. During the latter part of March, in a company with several other families, he left the Western Reserve with two teams and two covered wagons loaded with provisions. "The blessings of the Lord attended us in our preparations to move," he later recalled.[30]

Throughout the spring and early summer of 1838, small groups of Mormons left Kirtland for the western frontier in Missouri. While some enjoyed the luxury of water transportation, most walked or traveled in wagons. Like other pioneers of that age, few Latter-day Saints were accustomed to walking or riding such long distances, day after day, suffering from illness, fatigue, blistered feet, biting cold, intense heat, and unquenched thirst. Wagons became mired in the mud, wagon wheels and tongues broke, and animals collapsed and died. Moreover, many women gave birth during the long journey, while other Saints grieved the loss of husbands, wives, or children buried in graves along the trail leading west.[31]

Organizing Kirtland Camp

Although most of the Saints went west in small groups of less than fifty, one company of more than five hundred persons traveled in a body that was called Kirtland Camp. Plans for the company were constituted by the seventies in a series of meetings in the temple between March 6 and 20, 1838. Initially, the seventies considered migrating together to the West and then locating in the same general area so that they could meet together regularly when they were not involved in full-time missionary service. At these meetings they considered the advantages and disadvantages of organizing a large traveling company. Some feared that such a group would attract attention, which might lead to persecution; others brought up the problems of securing adequate supplies for the people and forage for their animals. Proponents of the plan pointed out that by traveling together, they could more easily help members of the three quorums in Kirtland who were destitute and might not otherwise be able to transport their families to Missouri. Through pooling their talents and means, they could help one another; in addition, provisions and other necessities for such a large group could be purchased in quantities at reduced costs.[32]

The presidents of the seventies invited Hyrum Smith, a member of the Presidency, to meet with them on March 10 as they sought spiritual confirmation of their decisions from the Lord. At the meeting, "the Spirit of the Lord came down in mighty power, and some of the elders began to prophesy" that if they traveled together and kept the commandments of the Lord, the expedition would succeed. Following this outpouring of the Spirit, one of the presidents of the First Quorum of Seventy, James Foster, arose and, in the course of his remarks, testified that he beheld a vision in which he saw a company of about five hundred starting from Kirtland and traveling and camping together, concluding that it was the will of God that the seventies should travel as a body to Missouri.[33]

Recognizing that other Saints who were not seventies were in need of help for the journey west, and with the approval of President Hyrum Smith, the seventies agreed to invite to join this company all members who were willing to comply with the requirements they specified, and those who failed to comply strictly with the rules would be expelled from the group and "left by the wayside."[34] According to Zera Pulsipher, when other members of the Church heard that the seventies were going together and would help one another, "they wanted to join us and get out of the 'hell' of persecution. Therefore, we could not neglect them for all there was against them was that they were poor and could not help themselves."[35] John Pulsipher, Zera's son, who traveled with the Kirtland Camp, wrote that as the plans for the camp were being formulated, the church in Kirtland was "being broken up and the poorest of the poor were left, because they could not get away."[36]

Since Hyrum Smith had previously proposed that the Saints consider chartering a ship to transport them to Missouri, some members thought there was a conflict in that recommendation and the seventies' plans for an overland expedition. Hyrum resolved this problem by telling the Saints that his proposal had been based on "his own judgment without reference to the testimony of the Spirit of God. . . . He said further that the Saints had to act oftentimes upon their own responsibility without any reference to the testimony of the Spirit of God in relation to temporal affairs," explaining that he had not received a spiritual confirmation sanctioning his plan, which indicated to him that "God did not approve" of it. He then declared that he knew by the Spirit of God that the plan being formulated by the seventies "was according to the will of the Lord."[37]

On March 13, a general outline, or constitution, for the organization and policies of Kirtland Camp was endorsed by the seventies. The seven presidents of the First Quorum of Seventy were to serve jointly as leaders, and a treasurer was to be appointed to maintain an account of the money received and expended by the camp. "Tent-men" were to be appointed to preside over small groups, with responsibility to secure teams and tents for those under their jurisdiction and to execute instructions from the presidents of the seventies. They were also charged to encourage those under their jurisdiction to be clean and decent and to observe the commandments, including refraining from using "tobacco, tea, coffee, snuff, or ardent spirits of any kind." The head of every family was to see that members of his family abided by the rules of the camp. Laws of the company were to be amended by majority vote of the participants, and all participants were to pay a proportionate share of expenses incurred by the camp as soon as circumstances permitted.[38]

Initially a group of about five hundred was to leave Kirtland in the middle of May. Participants were to carry with them clothing, blankets, cooking utensils, and "light crick bedsteads" to avoid sleeping on the ground. Shelter would be provided by large tents of common sheeting or duck cloth, and it was assumed that many of the women and children would be able to sleep in the wagons. Two good teams and one tent would serve for every eighteen immigrants. Runners sent ahead of the wagon train were to purchase necessary provisions, which would then be distributed to the travelers. The seventies agreed that they would travel slowly five days a week and stop on Saturday to wash, bake, and engage in various other chores. Services were to be held on Sunday, and the seventies would invite non-Mormons in areas where they were camped to attend the meetings.[39]

Before the departure of the company, 177 heads of households subscribed to the camp's constitution, including three women—Nancy Richardson, Mary Parker, and Julie Johnson. Although seventies directed the program, only 30 percent of the constitution signers were members of one of the three quorums of seventies.[40]

After determining the camp's needs and identifying the equipment and animals available for the journey, the leaders discovered that not only were there too few wagons and tents, but also only ten teams were owned by camp participants, and few had any money with which to purchase supplies. Therefore, the presidents of the seventies instructed the Saints to secure work in nearby communities for a few months to obtain the animals, wagons, and necessary provisions. Some secured work in the fields, some labored for a canal company for fifty cents a day, and some manufactured stoves and sold them to settlers in nearby areas.[41]

Members of the Kirtland Camp were not ready to begin the long journey to Missouri until the first week of July, more than three months after the seventies decided to lead a company west. On July 5, participants gathered in a clover field behind Mayhew Hillman's former home, about one hundred rods south of the temple. That day many pitched their tents, and at night they slept near their wagons and teams. The next day, about noon, a stream of about fifty-nine wagons began rolling from Kirtland. Included in the first company and those who followed shortly thereafter were about 515 pioneers—249 males and 266 females—with 27 tents, 97 horses, 22 oxen, 69 cows, and 1 bull.[42]

ROUTE of KIRTLAND CAMP THROUGH OHIO

ASHTABULA

GEAUGA
● Kirtland
● Chester
● Russell
● Bainbridge
Aurora
PORTAGE
Hudson
Stowe Corners
Talmadge
Akron Middleburg
Coventry New Portage
Milton Chippewa

TRUMBULL

PENNSYLVANIA

WILLIAMS   HENRY   WOOD   SANDUSKY

LORAIN   CUYAHOGA

MEDINA

COLUMBIANA

PAULDING   PUTNAM   HANCOCK   SENECA

HURON

WAYNE

Wooster

STARK

VAN WERT   CRAWFORD

Little
Sandusky   Mansfield Haynesville
Ontario Petersburg Readsborough Jefferson
Antrim   Bucyrus   New Castle Jeromesville

ALLEN   HARDIN

Burlington
Goshen   Grand
Dudley   Prairie   MARION

RICH-
LAND

HOLMES

JEFFER-
SON

MERCER

Rush Creek
Rushsylvania
Bellefontaine
West Liberty
Salem
Urbana

DELAWARE   KNOX

COSHOCTON

TUSCARAWAS

SHELBY   LOGAN

HARRISON

DARKE   MIAMI

LICKING

GUERNSEY   BELMONT

CHAM-
PAIGN   UNION   FRANKLIN

NATIONAL ROAD

CLARK

MONROE

PREBLE   MONT-
GOMERY   Springfield

Richmond   Fairfield
Dayton August
Alexander   Encampment
Easton   Johnsville   GREEN   MADISON
FAYETTE

MUSKINGUM
PERRY   MORGAN

FAIRFIELD

INDIANA

BUTLER   WARREN   CLINTON   PICKAWAY
ROSS   HOCKING   ATHENS

WASHINGTON

VIRGINIA

HAMILTON   CLER-
MONT   HIGHLAND   PIKE   JACKSON   MEIGS

BROWN   ADAMS   GALLIA

SCIOTO

LAWRENCE

Research by Max Parkin

The emigrants left Kirtland with mixed feelings of gratitude, remorse, anxiety, and determination. John Pulsipher said he was grateful that though their enemies had threatened to block their departure, no one interfered with them as they started southward. He also expressed enthusiasm at being a participant in the "largest company of Saints that had ever traveled together in this genera-tion."[43] His brother Charles wrote, "We had made a covenant that we would go . . . to Missouri together or die in the at-tempt."[44] And Elias Smith, the quorum clerk and historian of the camp, recorded his impressions as the Saints abandoned their homes and left the temple they had built at such great sacrifice:

> The feelings of the brethren on leaving Kirtland and parting with those who were left behind were somewhat peculiar, notwithstanding the scenes they had passed through in Kirtland; but the consciousness of doing the will of their heavenly Father, and obeying His commandments in journeying to Zion, over balanced every other considerations that could possibly be presented to their minds, and buoyed up their spirits.[45]

After the company left, only a few Latter-day Saints remained in Kirtland. A portion of the town was almost desolate, with most homes near the temple abandoned. Jeremiah Willey, who partici-pated in the Kirtland Camp, said, "I was obliged to leave my house and lot unsold." Although he had sent some of his personal belongings west by water, he left some clothing, bedding, and fur-niture in his abandoned home.[46] William F. Cahoon wrote that he turned the key and locked the door of his house, leaving all his property and other possessions in "the hands of enemies and stran-gers," without ever receiving one cent for that which he left in Kirtland.[47]

The Journey of Kirtland Camp

The problems of the Saints who traveled with the Kirtland Camp were compounded because of the large numbers involved and because most of them were not as well equipped as other members of the Church who immigrated to the Missouri frontier. During the first month of travel, the group followed their initial plans without many alterations. A trumpet generally awakened the camp at 4:00 A.M., and at 4:20, prayers were offered in each tent, which housed about three or four families (approximately fifteen or twenty persons). The first of the four divisions generally left camp about 7:00 or 8:00 A.M., and for more than an hour wagons rolled from the encampment. During the first three weeks, after traveling an average of twelve miles a day, the pioneers stopped in the late afternoon on a farm where they could obtain water, graze their animals, and build fires to cook their evening meal. Usually the Saints placed their wagons in a square or circle, pitched their tents so that they formed a rectangular pattern within the circle of wagons, and stationed guards around the site. On July 10, for example, fifty men were assigned to guard the encampment and keep the horses and cattle from straying.[48]

From Kirtland the camp proceeded south through Hudson to Akron, then westward to Wooster, Mansfield, and Bucyrus. South of Bucyrus they passed through the fertile Mad River Valley and proceeded past Springfield toward Dayton. They followed many of the same roads taken in 1834 by Zion's Camp, and about ten members of this wagon train had participated with the Prophet Joseph Smith in that earlier march.[49]

Throughout the journey to Missouri, the presidents of the First Council of Seventy served as a governing council. Since two of the presidents, Levi Hancock and Daniel S. Miles, had previously departed for the west, Benjamin Wilbur and Elias Smith were called to replace them until the group arrived in Far West. Therefore, the seven men who were involved in decision-making processes were Joseph Young, James Foster, Josiah Butterfield, Henry Harriman, and Zera Pulsipher, the permanent members of the governing council, and Elias Smith and Benjamin Wilbur, the two temporary leaders. This group established daily schedules, made assignments, altered general procedures, and instructed, counseled, and disciplined the Saints.[50]

Jonathan Dunham, the camp engineer, traveled ahead of the four divisions to search for campsites and find forage for the animals. Jonathan H. Hale, the commissar, was responsible for buying food and provisions for the Saints. Every evening rations were issued to the various families according to their numbers. The Saints lived primarily on corn and cornmeal, wheat and flour, beans, pork, and dried apples; they shared the milk they obtained from their cows.[51] The number in Kirtland Camp swelled to about 620, as a result of other families joining them, and on July 23, Jonathan Hale was unable to buy sufficient provisions in Marion and Hardin counties, through which they were traveling. Seven and a half bushels of corn had to suffice for the entire camp for three days. Elias Smith reported that although some members "complained and murmured because they did not have that to eat which their souls lusted after, . . . none lacked for food."[52]

Since the seventies had received a special call to be involved in missionary work and other members of the Church had been challenged to teach the gospel whenever possible, participants of the Kirtland Camp sought opportunities to discuss religion with those who stopped them along the trail and to bear their testimonies to inquirers who visited their encampments. Most of the missionary activity was conducted on Sundays. During the first two months of the journey, the Saints held outdoor meetings every Sunday. Visitors were invited to attend these services, and on July 15 some two hundred non-Mormons gathered and listened to the elders. Special services were planned for the visitors, and those who spoke bore witness to the restoration, the teachings of the Bible and the Book of Mormon, and latter-day revelation. So many visitors attended the meetings the first two Sundays that the sacrament was not administered. On the third Sunday, the Saints had to move their encampment to another area five miles away because of insufficient forage for their livestock, and on that day they held a single meeting to worship and partake of the sacrament.[53]

Accidents and illness constantly afflicted the pioneers. Some persons were crushed under wagon wheels; other succumbed to disease. Many forces contributed to their suffering. They perspired by day and slept on cold and sometimes damp terrain by night. They forded streams, climbed up and down inclines, and followed rutted roads and trails, continually weakened by fatigue, a meager and changing diet, and polluted drinking water.

In the midst of their suffering and afflictions, they turned to their Heavenly Father for help. Throughout the journey, elders administered to the sick and the injured; and diarists reported that through the power of the priesthood, many of the afflicted were instantly healed. On July 23, for example, Martin Peck's son Edwin accidentally fell, crushing his leg under the wheel of a heavily loaded wagon. "When he was picked up," one witness observed, "the limb appeared to be flattened as if almost crushed to pulp, and the flesh was laid open." Elder Peck immediately administered to his son and placed him in the wagon. An hour later, the boy "was entirely well, the only sign of the injury left being a slight scar which had the dry and scaly appearance of an old sore, long since healed."[54]

Samuel Tyler testified that the day following this miracle, his own son, James, complained of an earache, and his wife was very sick, so he asked Elder Peck to administer to them. Immediately following the administration, he said, his son's pain ceased and his wife was healed. Moreover, he reported that on August 5 his wife was again healed following an administration, and on August 8 elders walked among the people "rebuking diseases and foul spirits," and some, including himself, were promptly cured.[55]

Death periodically struck the camp, especially the young children. On the sixth day of the journey, the infant son of Benjamin Wilbur died. Within three hours, a funeral service was planned, a grave was dug in an orchard, a graveside prayer was offered, and those in that division resumed their journey and rejoined the other divisions. Seven other children were buried in the fields of Ohio. On September 3, while crossing Indiana, the first adult, Bathsheba Willey, died. Since the young son of E. P. Merriam had died the day before, a joint funeral was held that afternoon. Four days later, two other children passed away and were interred in one grave. One of these children was the thirteen-year-old daughter of Otis Shumway, who had buried another daughter just nine days earlier. Before the Saints arrived in Far West, fourteen children and one adult had been buried along the trail to the Missouri frontier.[56]

The non-Mormon response to this large movement of Saints varied from curiosity and amazement to criticism and threats. Hundreds sometimes gathered along the public roads and watched as they passed by. The camp was sometimes compared to

Table 5
Migration Patterns of Kirtland Saints
Who Were Members of the Kirtland Branch 1837–1838

Selected Locations Where LDS Were Living after 1838	Probable Kirtland Saints	Possible Kirtland Saints	Total[1]
Missouri	69%	76%	71%
Nauvoo and vicinity	76	51	69
Missouri or Nauvoo and vicinity or both	83	87	84
Kirtland (1840)[2]	4	1	5
Plains or Utah[3]	45	22	39
Total (names appearing on any one of the above lists)	88	86	87

[1]Percentage of 456 heads of families.

[2]Includes a few members who migrated to Missouri in 1838 and then returned to Kirtland. This and other lists do not include those who had left the Church, but their names are included in the 456 heads of families.

[3]Includes those who died en route to Salt Lake City or were in Iowa or Nebraska during the Mormon trek west.

This study by Milton V. Backman, Jr., and Mark Grandstaff is based on the migration patterns of 456 heads of families. The "probable" Latter-day Saints (329 heads of families, or 72 percentage of the total) were members who were undoubtedly living in or near Kirtland in 1837 or 1838. The "possible" Latter-day Saints (127, or 28 percent of the total) were members who were living in or near Kirtland during these years or were traveling through Kirtland. Most of these "possible" Saints were individuals who signed the Kirtland Camp Constitution, but their names do not appear on tax records, deed books, biographies, or similar records. This study reveals that a high percentage of the Kirtland Saints remained faithful to the gospel that they embraced and followed the general migration patterns of other Latter-day Saints.

the children of Israel, who, under the direction of a prophet, crossed a vast wilderness and headed toward a promised land. Many onlookers were "astonished . . . at seeing so large a body moving together." While some spectators expressed feelings of encouragement and warmth, others jeered and swore or expressed pity for those whom they called "the deluded believers in modern revelation."[57]

The ridicule was sometimes combined with threats of violence. On July 16, as the Saints approached Mansfield, Ohio, a sheriff arrested and imprisoned Josiah Butterfield, Jonathan Dunham, and Jonathan H. Hale for alleged involvement in the

Kirtland Safety Society. Meanwhile, the Saints were told that they would not be permitted to pass through Mansfield. Later that afternoon, however, the camp traveled through the town without interference or commotion except for the firing of a cannon. The next day the three brethren who had been imprisoned were discharged by the court.[58] Two weeks later, Jonathan Dunham was ordered off a farm near Springfield, Ohio, as he tried to purchase feed for the cattle. The irate farmer swore that he would shoot the first Mormon who stepped on his property.[59]

Many of the difficulties of Kirtland Camp were caused by internal strife and discontent. Periodically, the presidents of the seventies chastized the pioneers for their selfishness, murmuring, and failure to work congenially with others. Samuel Tyler wrote that on July 20 the presidents told the Saints that "God was angry" with them because of their "ingratitude," their "hardness of heart," their "slowness to keep his commandments," and their "iniquities," and warned them that God "would scourge" them if they did not repent. Occasionally, families or persons who persisted in violating the camp's constitution, who continually complained about decisions of the governing council, or who were unable to live harmoniously with others were excluded from the camp. The presidents of seventies devoted so much of their time to resolving internal problems that on August 3 they formed a lesser or assistant council to discipline recalcitrants.[60]

The task of feeding and renting campsites for such a large group was apparently greater than the seventies had anticipated. By the end of July, three weeks after they left Kirtland, the company had spent nearly all of their money, though they had traveled only 250 miles, less than one-third of the distance to Far West. While they were camped on the outskirts of Dayton, Ohio, some of the men were offered work on a road under construction between Dayton and Springfield. Because of their need for money, the company made camp, and throughout August, some of the men worked on the road while others secured employment in Dayton. Meanwhile, those who remained in the encampment organized four schools, one for each of the four divisions, and the women taught the children in an unusual summer session.[61]

The number traveling with the Kirtland Camp continued to change, with families frequently joining and leaving the company. While some were ordered to leave, others departed because of sickness or because they were unable to repair their wagons. Samuel Tyler estimated that in the early part of August the number of participants ranged from about 530 to 550.[62]

By late August, the men who had been working on the turnpike completed their contract, earning twelve hundred dollars for their labors. Although the Saints were asked to build another segment of the road, the governing council decided to resume the journey to Far West.[63] Therefore, on August 29, the trumpet sounded at 3:00 A.M., and by 9:00 A.M. the encampment had been vacated. Kirtland Camp crossed the state line into Indiana on August 31, proceeded along the national road through Indianapolis and Terre Haute, and entered Illinois on September 8. After traveling through Springfield, they ferried across the Mississippi River about fifty miles below Quincy and, on the evening of September 20, pitched their tents one mile west of Louisiana, Pike County, Missouri.[64]

In September the governing council altered some of their plans. Instead of traveling no more than fifteen miles per day (unless circumstances absolutely required it), resting on Saturday, and holding worship services on Sunday, they decided to travel nearly every day and to increase the distance covered each day. Therefore, during the last phase of the journey, Kirtland Camp traveled an average of almost twenty miles a day. On September 8 they covered twenty-five miles, the longest distance to that date, and four days later they set a record of twenty-nine miles. They also rested for a full day on only a few occasions. On Sunday, September 2, they covered twenty-one miles because feed for their livestock was scarce. The next Sunday they traveled two miles, and on September 23 and 30, they continued traveling because of the shortage of funds. On only one Sabbath in September did they remain in camp and conduct Sabbath meetings.[65]

Due to the lack of funds, the governing council also requested some of the participants in the immigrant train to leave the camp. On September 9, shortly after they reached Illinois, the presi-

dents of the seventies asked nine or ten families to secure employment in the area of Amboy, Illinois, and join the Saints later in
Missouri. At that time a few other families also left the camp because of illness.[66] Less than one week later, on September 15,
about fifteen or sixteen additional families departed and secured
employment in the area of Springfield. Joel H. Johnson remained
with this group and presided over the branch of the Church.[67]

Describing the hardships of the Saints during their trek across
Illinois, Samuel Tyler wrote that they were often short of food for
themselves and their animals. They frequently ate boiled corn
and corn pudding and fed the cobs to their horses so that nothing
was wasted. He found the corn pudding to be delicious when
mixed with milk, butter, fat, and any kind of sweetening. He also
wrote under the date of September 14 that the size of the company
had been greatly depleted. "Our number is now about 260," he observed, which was about half the size of the group that had started
from Kirtland. He concluded that one reason the camp was smaller was that some members had failed to live the celestial law.[68]

Shortly before the pioneer company crossed the Mississippi
River, the Saints encountered another problem that persisted
during most of the remaining 260 miles of their trip. This new affliction was fear that they would be attacked by mobs if they tried
to cross the state of Missouri. They were warned that a war had
erupted in western Missouri between the Saints and non-
Mormons, that all Mormons would soon be driven from the state,
and that if they continued their journey, they would be attacked
and would suffer a similar fate. Intimidated by these threats, nine
additional families left this company in Illinois.[69]

Threats of violence continued as Kirtland Camp continued
west across the rolling prairies of Missouri. On September 20,
while Samuel Tyler was looking for a stray cow, he met a Missou-
rian who asked him if he belonged to that "gang of Mormons."
When he responded in the affirmative, the stranger said that he
was a fool to let the Mormons lead him into danger. "Don't you
know the Missourians are raising armies to cut you all to pieces?"
he was asked.[70]

Four days later, as the camp passed through Madisonville, they were told that several armies, including a military force led by Governor Lilburn W. Boggs, were located east of Far West and that if they continued their journey they would be attacked.[71]

One of the presidents of the seventies, James Foster, became so concerned about the threats that on September 26 he recommended that the camp be dissolved and that each family continue alone so they would not be identified as Mormons. The other presidents rejected the proposal, and following a vote, the company resumed traveling together. Later that day a group of Saints from Far West met them and assured them they could complete their journey to Far West without being mobbed.[72]

On October 2, the wagons of Kirtland Camp rolled into Far West, 870 miles from Kirtland. As the party of about two hundred Saints neared the end of their journey, they were met by Joseph Smith, his brother Hyrum, Sidney Rigdon, and a few other Church leaders, who escorted them during the last five miles. They stopped at the public square about 5:00 P.M. and pitched their tents near the site designated for a temple. There they visited with old friends and accepted their hospitality. Isaac Morley, one of the first persons to join the Church in Kirtland, donated some beef, and Sidney Rigdon provided supper for many of the weary travelers.[73]

Responding to an earlier request by the Prophet, members of Kirtland Camp resumed their travels on October 3, and the next day they settled twenty-two miles north of Far West on land that had not yet been offered for public sale. Under the date of Thursday, October 4, Samuel Tyler concluded his journal describing his experiences as a participant of Kirtland Camp, noting that "this is a day long to be remembered." As the Saints pitched their tents at sunset that evening, he reported that one of the brethren proclaimed in a loud voice, "Behold, your long and tedious journey [is] now ended; you are now on the public square of Adam-ondi-Ahman,"[74] the place that Joseph Smith had identified, through revelation, as the location where Adam blessed his children and predicted what would befall his posterity.

The trials of the Kirtland Saints did not end when they reached the Missouri frontier. On October 27, less than one month after Kirtland Camp arrived there, Governor Lilburn W. Boggs issued one of the most intolerant decrees uttered by an executive in the history of the United States. After telling General John B. Clark of the Missouri militia that the "Mormons must be treated as enemies," the governor ordered him to exterminate or drive members of the faith from that state.[75] Some of the participants in the Kirtland Camp had settled in a community called Haun's Mill, and on October 30, Missouri militiamen suddenly attacked the Saints living there. The threats of death that they had heard while crossing Missouri became a reality: seventeen Saints were killed and thirteen others were wounded.[76]

Throughout the long winter of 1838-39, hundreds of Latter-day Saints fled again from persecutors. Many had been forced to abandon Kirtland in 1838, and now they were being driven from the state of Missouri. Fortified by their faith, many of the former Kirtland Saints settled in Iowa and Illinois and helped build a new city, Nauvoo, on the banks of the Mississippi River. Within a few years, they would once again have to abandon their homes, cross a vast wilderness, and begin a new life in the great basin of western America.

Although few Americans experienced as a consequence of their religious beliefs such agonizing and overt oppression as did the early Latter-day Saints, many members of the Church testified that during their trials they were sustained by their faith. Oliver Huntington wrote in his autobiography that although his parents lost all of their worldly wealth in Kirtland and subsequently suffered poverty and persecution, he never heard them complain nor question the divine calling of Joseph Smith.[77] George Q. Cannon summarized the Prophet's perseverance, integrity, and courage as manifest amid great trials and persecution when he said:

Think of what he passed through! Think of his afflictions, and think of his dauntless character! Did any one ever see him falter? Did any one ever see him flinch? Did any one ever see any lack in him of the power necessary to enable him to stand with dignity in the midst of his enemies, or lacking in dignity in the performance of his duties as a servant of the living God? God gave him peculiar power in this respect. He was filled with integrity to God; with such integrity as was not known among men. He was like an angel of God among them. Notwithstanding all that he had to endure, and the peculiar circumstances in which he was so often placed, and the great responsibility that weighed constantly upon him, he never faltered; the feeling of fear or trembling never crossed him—at least he never exhibited it in his feelings or actions. God sustained him to the very last.[78]

Chapter 19
The Aftermath

When the long line of the Kirtland Camp teams and wagons moved south from the temple on July 6, 1838, along the old Chillicothe road toward Chester, few Latter-day Saints remained in Kirtland. Probably more apostates lived there than active members of the Church, but these dissenters divided into many factions and consequently were unable to unite under a common religious banner. A few Saints traveled with this large migrating company the first seven miles to Chester and then returned to their homes.

Two days after the camp left Kirtland, Joseph Smith received a revelation in Far West directing William Marks, a member of the Kirtland high council, and Bishop Newel K. Whitney to settle their business affairs as quickly as possible and leave for Missouri.[1] Complying with these instructions, the two men left Kirtland in the fall of 1838. Before they reached western Missouri, however, they learned of the expulsion of the Mormons from that state. Therefore, like a number of other Kirtland Saints, they did not reach the Missouri frontier, but settled temporarily in other areas and then gathered in Nauvoo.[2]

While nearly all of the faithful Kirtland Saints abandoned that community in 1838, a few members were still living there in November 1839 when Brigham Young and Heber C. Kimball stopped there while en route to the British Mission. Brigham Young wrote that he met "a good many friends and brethren who were glad" to see him. Many of these persons, he added, lacked the energy or the disposition to move to Missouri in 1838. The

Kirtland Temple was still available for use by the Latter-day Saints at that time, for on Sunday, November 17, Elder Young preached in a meeting in the morning and John Taylor preached in the afternoon. That evening, after Elder Taylor had "washed himself in pure water with castile soap," members of the priesthood gathered in the temple, and Elder Young anointed Elder Taylor "with pure sweet oil, and pronounced such blessings as the Spirit gave utterance." They also participated in the ordinances of sealing the anointing and of washing of the feet.[3]

A Second Gathering

In the early 1840s there was a temporary growth of the Church in Kirtland through conversions and renewed migration. In April 1840, Hiram Kellogg, a leader of the Kirtland Branch, reported that as a result of recent baptisms, membership in the congregation had increased to about 125.[4] Six months later, leaders of the Church in Nauvoo called Almon W. Babbitt to preside over the Saints in northeastern Ohio and again designated Kirtland as a gathering place for members of the Church living in the eastern states. Immediately following this announcement, Latter-day Saints commenced a new migration to the Western Reserve, and by the spring of 1841 membership of the Kirtland branch had increased to between three hundred and four hundred members.[5]

During this renewed migration, the Kirtland Stake was reorganized. In May 1841, Almon W. Babbitt was sustained as president of the stake, which consisted of branches in ten towns in northeastern Ohio. He selected as his counselors Lester Brooks and Zebedee Coltrin. Many other leaders were sustained during this conference, including Thomas Burdick as a bishop, with Hiram Winters and Reuben McBride as counselors; Hiram Kellogg as president of the high priests quorum, with John Knapp and Joseph Pine as counselors; and Amos Babcock as president of the elders quorum, with Otis Hobart and Thomas Green as counselors. Nehemiah Greenhalgh was called to preside over the lesser priesthood, with James Crumpton and John Craig as his counselors.[6]

For two years, from 1841 to 1843, Kirtland continued to be a

gathering place for the Saints. In October 1841, President Babbitt wrote to Joseph Smith informing him that the Kirtland
Branch had about five hundred members, that other branches in
the Kirtland Stake were growing, and that the House of the Lord
was in good condition as a result of recent repairs. Of the five
hundred members in the Kirtland Branch, about one hundred
were converts from England who were staying in Kirtland during
the winter before continuing on to Nauvoo.[7] Though many members of the Church left Kirtland in the spring of 1842 to gather
with the Saints in Illinois, others moved to Kirtland, replacing
those who had emigrated, so that the membership was sustained.
When Lyman Wight visited Kirtland in October 1842, he reported that he preached to a congregation of from 500 to 700, that
he ordained 30 elders, and that he baptized 203 individuals.[8]

That Kirtland was to be a temporary gathering place for the
Saints in the East is clearly evident from a revelation recorded by
Joseph Smith in January 1841 and from a prophecy uttered by
Hyrum Smith. In the January revelation, William Law, who was
called to be a counselor in the First Presidency, was told not to
take his family to Kirtland. "Nevertheless," the commandment
continued, "I, the Lord, will build up Kirtland, but I, the Lord,
have a scourge prepared for the inhabitants thereof."[9] Hyrum
Smith's prophecy harmonized with this revelation. While serving
as Patriarch to the Church, he sent the following instructions to
members in Kirtland:

> All the Saints that dwell in the land are commanded to come away, . . .
> 'Thus saith the Lord;' therefore pay out no moneys, nor properties for houses,
> nor lands in that country, for if you do you will lose them, for the time shall
> come, that you shall not possess them in peace, but shall be scourged with a
> sore scourge; yet your children may possess them, but not until many years shall
> pass away. . . . Then I will send forth and build up Kirtland, and it shall be
> polished and refined according to my word.[10]

The Waning

In 1843 Latter-day Saints participated in a major exodus from
Kirtland for the second time. They were not fleeing amid apostate
mobocracy and increasing threats from other enemies. Rather
they abandoned their homes because they were instructed by

Church leaders to gather in Illinois. At a conference in the Kirtland Temple on April 6, 1843, Lyman Wight, an apostle who presided over this conference, announced that the time had come for the Saints in the Western Reserve to migrate to Nauvoo. "I . . . told you not to leave this place until you were instructed so by revelation," he said, adding that the season had arrived when the Saints were to be instructed more perfectly and that one of the objects of that conference was "to devise means to effect a removal of the church [from Kirtland] to the city of Nauvoo" in harmony with the revealed word of God. He advised the Saints to leave as soon as possible while they had "a chance to go in peace." The Saints attending the conference voted unanimously to support this program of removal, and they began immediately to plan their migration to Nauvoo.[11]

Apparently not all Latter-day Saints in Kirtland complied with the instructions concerning the gathering. In 1845 members living there were again reminded in a directive from Brigham Young to move west, "leaving neither man, woman or child behind that desires to come up here with a pure heart, leaving Kirtland to the owls and the bats for a season."[12] At a conference held in the Kirtland Temple on April 5, 1845, attended by more than one hundred Saints, members again agreed to sustain the General Authorities, to assist in building the temple in Nauvoo, and to gather with the body of the Church in Illinois.[13]

During the latter half of the 1840s and the early 1850s, a small branch of the Church was generally maintained in Kirtland, while groups of apostates sought to restore that community to its former position as a major church center. In January 1845, William E. McLellin, Leonard Rich, Jacob Bump, and others organized a new religious group called the Church of Christ. This group grew to about one hundred, then began to dissolve within a few years. Another group during the late 1840s adopted the name Church of Christ and attempted to establish Kirtland as a headquarters, but this faith, which later became known as Brewsterites, also began to decline in 1849. In 1851, Elder James W. Bay summarized conditions in Kirtland in a letter to President Brigham Young:

There have been all kinds of false prophets here in Kirtland, but I have found a few that begin to feel that west is the place, and the authority is there. Bro. Isaac Bullock and I succeeded in getting an organization here, and they begin to have the gifts, and are blessed, and calculate to gather west to the valley.[14]

During the latter part of the 1840s, after most members of the Church had permanently left Kirtland, apostates seized the temple, and the Latter-day Saints never regained possession. The building was used by various groups for religious, educational, and civic purposes. In fact, shortly after the Saints' major exodus in 1838, the Reverend Nelson Slater obtained a five-year lease on the second and third stories, and that September classes were conducted there under the direction of trustees of the Western Reserve Teachers' Seminary. This school was maintained throughout the 1840s and part of the 1850s and was regarded as an important educational institution in that area.[15]

After the Western Reserve Teachers' Seminary was dissolved, the population of Kirtland continued to decline, the temple was abandoned, and for years no one maintained the building.[16] The Reorganized Church of Jesus Christ of Latter Day Saints took possession of the building in 1880, and in the twentieth century it was restored to it original beauty.[17]

The population of Kirtland Township declined from 1,778 in 1840 to 909 in 1890, the latter census recording fewer inhabitants than when the missionaries introduced the gospel in the Western Reserve in October 1830.[18] During the first half of the twentieth century, the population remained sparse, with only 2,663 residents reported in the census of 1950. When Richard W. Young visited Kirtland in 1882, he found a community thinly settled and a temple in poor repair. "Much of the interior wood work has been taken away for fire wood," he observed, "and sashes contained more broken than undamaged panes of glasses. Paint it has not seen for a generation at least."[19]

A Wondrous Past

For 130 years, from 1850 to 1980, few Latter-day Saints resided in Kirtland. During this long era, however, Kirtland and its towering temple stood as a symbol reminding those who visited the site of the faith and dedication of the early Saints, of their response to the call of repentance and baptism, of their gathering in Ohio, of their missionary zeal, of their attempts to help those who gathered in western Missouri, of their sacrifices in building a house for the Lord, of the powerful spiritual manifestations that many witnessed in the temple, and of the resolute faith of those who experienced poverty and persecution. Rather than deny the reality of the restoration, these and other pioneers abandoned their homes and searched for a site where they could worship in peace.

In 1839 an early convert of the Church visited Kirtland and recorded his impressions of the Saints who had lived there. As he and his traveling companions passed through the community, en route to join the main body of the Saints farther west, they found a sparsely settled community with many abandoned houses. He wrote:

> We entered the Temple, and beheld the fixtures, the curtains, the seats, etc., with astonishment, being so different from anything we had before seen, and being, as we believed built by revelation and commandment of God. Here the Saints though few in number and poor, in the infancy of the Church surrounding with opposition, nevertheless, rich in faith and in knowledge of God, united their efforts, some toiling for a whole year together, without pay and with scanty food until this fine edifice was completed, being the first in the 19th century, and at the time the only building on the face of the earth built by revelation from Heaven. Our hearts were filled with gratitude to God, that we were thus highly favored to live in the day when the voice of the Lord was again heard out of the heavens, and with bosoms burning with the intelligence of God, we still prosecuted our journey westward in order to join the Presidency and main body of the Church with whom the oracles of God had been entrusted. [20]

More than 140 years after nearly all Latter-day Saints had left Kirtland, a new glory appeared. Through renewed sacrifice and persistent labor, Saints living in northeastern Ohio built a spacious meetinghouse there. On October 17, 1982, Ezra Taft Benson, president of the Council of the Twelve Apostles, dedicated that sacred building. He prayed that the Lord would accept the humble offerings of those who through faith and devotion had built that sacred house in a sacred area on sacred ground. He also expressed gratitude to the Lord for the prospect of growth and development in Kirtland, where so many inspirational experiences had transpired and where so many truths of the gospel had been restored. The dedication of the Kirtland Ward inaugurated a new era in the history of the restoration movement. While the glory of Kirtland lies in the past, a renewed glory shines in the present and awaits the future.

Appendixes

Notes

Bibliography

Index

Appendix A

Members of Zion's Camp

Latter-day Saints have compiled various lists containing the names of participants of Zion's Camp. Although most of the lists are similar, all contain variations in the spelling of names and differences regarding those who participated in this march to Missouri. Joseph Smith included a list of fifty-six participants in his history, which was published in the *Millennial Star* (March 26, 1853), 2:205. A more complete list, containing more than two hundred names, was compiled by Thomas Bullock (see Zion's Camp Roll, 1864, Church Archives) and published in the *Deseret News*, October 19, 1864. (See also Journal History, October 10, 1864.) Solon Foster, a participant in the march, prepared another list, a copy of which is included in the Church Archives. Andrew Jenson published still another list in the *Historical Record* (June 1889, 8:940), and B. H. Roberts included a roll of the participants in the first edition of Joseph Smith's *History of the Church*, published in 1902 (HC 2:183-85).

In many instances, the spellings of names below are those used in records kept by the seventies or other contemporary records. Other marked differences in spellings and variations of names that are probably associated with the same individual have been placed in brackets. Footnotes identify individuals whose names appear on few of the listings, and an asterisk (*) identifies participants who were recruited from Michigan by Hyrum Smith and Lyman Wight or who traveled with them in what is sometimes referred to as Hyrum's division. This listing includes 207 men, 11 women, and 11 children, 5 of the children not being identified by name.

Aldrich, Hazen
Allen, Joseph S.
Allred, Isaac
Allred, James
Allred, Martin C.
Andrus, Milo
Angell [Angel], Solomon
Avery, Allen A.
Babbitt, Almon W.
Badlam, Alexander
Baker, Samuel
Baldwin, Nathan Bennett
Barber, Elam
Barlow, Israel
Barnes, Lorenzo D.
Barney, Edson
Barney, Royal
Benner, Henry
*Bent, Samuel
Blackman, Hiram
Booth, Lorenzo

Brooks, George W.
Brown, Albert
Brown, Harry
Brown, Samuel
Brownell, John
Buchanan, Peter
Burdick, Alden
Burgess, Harrison
Byur [Byers], David
Cahoon, William F.
Carpenter, John
Carter, John S.
Cathcart, Daniel
Champlin, Alonzo
Chapman, Jacob
Cherry, William
Chidester, John M.
Childs, Alden
Childs, Nathaniel
Childs, Stephen
Clements, Albert[1]

Colborn, Thomas
*Colby, Alanson
Cole, Zera S.
Coltrin, Zebedee
Coon, Libeus T.
Cowan, Horace
*Curtis, Lyman
*Curtis, Mecham
Denton, Solomon W.
Doff [Dopp], Peter
*Dort, David D.
Duncan, John
*Dunn, James
Duzette, Philemon
Elliot, Bradford W.
Elliot, David
Ettleman, Philip
Evans, David
Field, Asa
Fisher, Edmund
Fisk, Alfred
Fisk, Hezekiah
*Fordham, Elijah
*Fordham, George
Forney, Frederick
Fossett, John
Foster, James
Foster, Solon
Gates, Jacob
Gifford, Benjamin
Gifford, Levi
Gilbert, Sherman
Glidden, True
Gould, Dean C.
Grant, Jedediah M.
Green, Addison
Griffith, Michael
Griswold, Everett
Groves, Elisha H.
Hancock, Joseph
Hancock, Levi W.
Harmon, Jesse [Joseph]
Harriman [Herriman], Henry
Harris, Martin
Hartshorn, Joseph
Hayes, Thomas
Higgins, Nelson
Hitchcock, Seth

Hodges, Amos
Holbrook, Chandler
Holbrook, Joseph
Holmes, Milton
*Houghton, Osmon [Ornan]
Hubbard, Marshal
Humphrey, Solomon
Huntsman, Jesse [Joseph]
Hustin, John
Hutchins [Hutchings], Elias
Hyde, Heman T.
Hyde, Orson
Ingalls, Warren S.
Ives [Ivie], Edward
Ivie, James Russell
Ivie, John Anderson
Ivie, William Shelton
Jessop [Jessup], William
Johnson, Luke S.
Johnson, Lyman E.
Johnson, Noah
Johnson, Seth
Jones, Isaac
Jones, Levi
Kelley, Charles
Kimball, Heber C.
Kingsley, Samuel
Lake, Dennis
Lawson, Jesse B.
Lewis, L. S.
*Littlefield, Josiah
*Littlefield, Lyman O.
*Littlefield, Waldo
Lyman, Amasa M.
Martin, Moses
Marvin, Edmond [Edward] W.
McBride, Reuben
McCord, Robert
Miller, Eleazer
Miller, John
Morse, Justin
Murdock, John
Nicholas, Joseph
Nickerson, Freeman
Nickerson, Levi Stillman
Nickerson, Uriel [Uriah] C.
Noble, Joseph B.
North, Levi [Ur.]

Orton, Roger
Parker, John D.
Parrish, Warren
Patten, David W.[2]
Pratt, Orson
Pratt, Parley P.
Pratt, William D.
*Rich, Charles C.
Rich, Leonard
Richardson, Darwin
Riggs, Burr
Riggs, Harpin
Riggs, Nathaniel
Riley, Milcher[3]
Ripley, Alanson
Robbins, Lewis
Rudd, Erastus
Sagers, Wm. Henry Harrison
Salisbury, Wilkins Jenkins
Sherman, Henry
Sherman, Lyman
Shibley, Henry
Smalling, Cyrus
Smith, Avery
Smith, George A.
Smith, Hyrum
Smith, Jackson
Smith, Jesse B.[4]
Smith, Jezeniah [Zechariah] B.[5]
Smith, Joseph, Jr.
Smith, Lyman
Smith, Sylvester
Smith, William
Snow, Willard
Snow, Zerubbabel

Stanley, Harvey
Stevens [Stephens], Daniel
Stratton, Hyrum [Hiram]
Strong, Elias [Elial]
Tanner, John Joshua
Tanner, Nathan
Thayer, Ezra
Thomas, Tinney
Thompson, James L.
Thompson, Samuel
Tippetts [Tibbetts], Wm. P.
Tubbs, Nelson
Vaughn, Joel
Warner, Salmon
Weden, William
Wells, Elias
Whitesides, Alexander
Whitlock, Andrew W.
Wight, Lyman
Wilcox, Eber
Wilkinson [Wilkerson], Sylvester B.
Williams, Frederick G.
Winchester, Alonzo
Winchester, Benjamin
Winchester, Stephen [Lupton]
Winegar, Alvin
Winegar, Samuel
Winters, Hiram
Wissmiller, Henry
Woodruff, Wilford
Yale, Gad[6]
Young, Brigham
Young, Joseph
Zobriskie, Lewis[7]

Women in Zion's Camp
*Alvord, Charlotte
Clements, Ada
Chidester, Mary, wife of John M.
*Curtis, Sophronia
Drake, Diana
Gates, Mary Snow, wife of Jacob
Holbrook, Eunice, wife of Chandler
Holbrook, Nancy Lambson, wife of Joseph
*Houghton, Aurelia, wife of Osmon
Parrish, Betsy, wife of Warren
Ripley,———, wife of Alanson

Children in Zion's Camp
*Chidester, Eunice, daughter of John M. and Mary
*Chidester, John P., son of John M. and Mary
Holbrook, Charlotte, daughter of Joseph and Nancy
Holbrook, Diana, daughter of Chandler and Eunice
Holbrook, Sarah Lucretia, daughter of Joseph and Nancy
———, daughter of Alvin Winegar
Pulsipher, Sarah, daughter of Zera Pulsipher
Four sons of Charlotte Alvord

[1]Albert Clements appears on the list that was included in the first edition of Joseph Smith's history (edited by B. H. Roberts), but he does not appear on the Bullock, Foster, or Jenson listings.

[2]David W. Patten and William D. Pratt were sent from Kirtland in advance of the army, carrying dispatches to the Saints in Missouri. Both men are included in a list of fifty-six participants identified in in Joseph Smith's history and appear in most listings of members of Zion's Camp. When Joseph Smith's scribes or historians referred in his history to the "205" men who comprised Zion's Camp on June 8, 1834, they undoubtedly did not include these two men. (See HC 2:87.)

[3]Milcher Riley appears on the Jenson and Roberts listings but not on the rolls compiled by Bullock and Foster.

[4]The name Jesse J. Smith appears on the Bullock list but not on the lists prepared by Foster, Jenson, and Roberts. On the other hand, Jesse B. Smith appears on the Foster and Jenson lists but was excluded by Roberts and Bullock. Possibly Jesse J. Smith and Jesse B. Smith refer to the same individual. Joseph Smith or those who wrote that portion of his history referred to Jesse Smith dying of cholera while burying one of the members of Zion's Camp in Missouri. (HC 2:115.) The Prophet also identified Jesse B. Smith as one of the participants in the march. (Millennial Star 15 [March 26, 1853]: 205.)

[5]The "J.B." often referred to in various records of Zion's Camp was probably Jezeniah B. Smith, whose name was spelled Jazariah, Jozeniah, and Zechariah in various listings.

[6]Gad Yale, a member of the second quorum of seventy, appears on the Bullock and Foster lists but not on the rolls compiled by Jenson and Roberts. In the Kirtland Council Minute Book (p. 196), there is a reference to Gad Yale having traveled to Missouri in relief of the Saints.

[7]Lewis Zobriskie also appears on the Bullock and Foster rolls and not on the lists compiled by Jenson and Roberts. Although his name appears in early records of the Church with more than thirty different spellings, contemporary records inform us that "Captain" Lewis Zobriskie participated in a mock battle with other members of Zion's Camp during the march to Missouri. (HC 2:75.)

Two names appear on the roll prepared by Thomas Bullock but not on any other listing cited above: Horace Evans and Thomas Turner. Except for the Bullock listing, there is no other evidence that these men participated in the march; and following the name of Thomas Turner in one of the manuscripts compiled by Bullock is a large question mark. Two Latter-day Saints, Joseph C. Kingsbury and John Riggs, volunteered to march with Zion's Camp to Missouri, but they were counseled by the Prophet to remain in the East and were told they would receive the same blessings as those who participated in the march. (Journal History, October 10, 1864, p. 1.) One of the marchers, Dean C. Gould, traveled during part of the journey west as a nonmember; on June 15, 1834, he was baptized by Lyman Wight in the Chariton River in Missouri. (HC 2:95.)

Appendix B

Callings of Participants in Zion's Camp

A broadside printed in Kirtland in April 1836 identified members of the Quorum of the Twelve Apostles and the first and second quorum of seventies. This broadside has been reproduced below in the same format as the original. Members of these priesthood bodies who participated in the march to Zion have been identified by an asterisk, a mark that the author of this volume has added to the printed page.

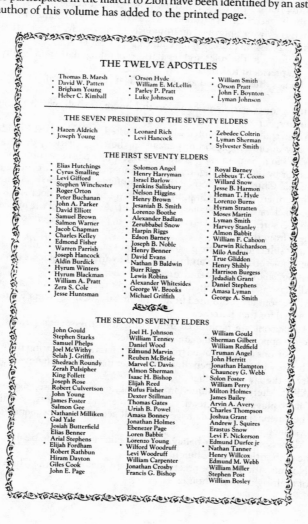

THE TWELVE APOSTLES

Thomas B. Marsh
David W. Patten
Brigham Young
Heber C. Kimball

Orson Hyde
William E. McLellin
Parley P. Pratt
Luke Johnson

William Smith
Orson Pratt
John F. Boynton
Lyman Johnson

THE SEVEN PRESIDENTS OF THE SEVENTY ELDERS

Hazen Aldrich
Joseph Young

Leonard Rich
Levi Hancock

Zebedee Coltrin
Lyman Sherman
Sylvester Smith

THE FIRST SEVENTY ELDERS

Elias Hutchings
Cyrus Smalling
Levi Gifford
Stephen Winchester
Roger Orton
Peter Buchanan
John A. Parker
David Elliott
Samuel Brown
Salmon Warner
Jacob Chapman
Charles Kelley
Edmond Fisher
Warren Parrish
Joseph Hancock
Aldin Burdick
Hyrum Winters
Hyrum Blackman
William A. Pratt
Zera S. Cole
Jesse Huntsman

Solomon Angel
Henry Harryman
Israel Barlow
Jenkins Salisbury
Nelson Higgins
Henry Brown
Jesaniah B. Smith
Lorenzo Boothe
Alexander Badlam
Zerubbabel Snow
Harpin Riggs
Edson Barney
Joseph B. Noble
Henry Benner
David Evans
Nathan B Baldwin
Burr Riggs
Lewis Robins
Alexander Whitesides
George W. Brooks
Michael Griffith

Royal Barney
Lebbeus T. Coons
Willard Snow
Jesse B. Harmon
Heman T. Hyde
Lorenzo Burns
Hyram Stratten
Moses Martin
Lyman Smith
Harvey Stanley
Almon Babbit
William F. Cahoon
Darwin Richardson
Milo Andrus
True Gliddon
Henry Shibly
Harrison Burgess
Jedadiah Grant
Daniel Stephens
Amasa Lyman
George A. Smith

THE SECOND SEVENTY ELDERS

John Gould
Stephen Starks
Samuel Phelps
Joel McWithy
Selah J. Griffin
Shedrach Roundy
Zerah Pulsipher
King Follett
Joseph Rose
Robert Culvertson
John Young
James Foster
Salmon Gee
Nathaniel Milliken
Gad Yale
Josiah Butterfield
Elias Benner
Arial Stephens
Elijah Fordham
Robert Rathbun
Hiram Dayton
Giles Cook
John E. Page

Joel H. Johnson
William Tenney
Daniel Wood
Edmund Marvin
Reuben McBride
Marvel C. Davis
Almon Sherman
Isaac H. Bishop
Elijah Reed
Rufus Fisher
Dexter Stillman
Thomas Gates
Uriah B. Powel
Amasa Bonney
Jonathan Holmes
Ebenezer Page
Loren Babbit
Lorenzo Young
Wilford Woodruff
Levi Woodruff
William Carpenter
Jonathan Crosby
Francis G. Bishop

William Gould
Sherman Gilbert
William Redfield
Truman Angel
John Herritt
Jonathan Hampton
Chauncey G. Webb
Solon Foster
William Perry
Milton Holmes
James Bailey
Arvin A. Avery
Charles Thompson
Joshua Grant
Andrew J. Squires
Erastus Snow
Levi F. Nickerson
Edmund Durfee jr
Nathan Tanner
Henry Willcox
Edmund M. Webb
William Miller
Stephen Post
William Bosley

Appendix C

Rules and Regulations to Be Observed in the House of the Lord in Kirtland

On January 13, 1836, a committee consisting of Joseph Smith, Jr., Sidney Rigdon, Hyrum Smith, W. W. Phelps, and David Whitmer was appointed to draft rules for the regulation of the house of the Lord in times of worship. Two days later, Joseph Smith presented to the high council in Kirtland the rules that had been drafted by this committee, after which they were approved unanimously by that body. (See Kirtland Council Minute Book, p. 203, and *History of the Church* 2:368-69.)

I. It is according to the rules and regulations of all regularly and legally organized bodies to have a president to keep order.

II. The bodies thus organized are under obligation to be in subjection to that authority.

III. When a congregation assembles in this house, it shall submit to the following rules, that due respect may be paid to the order of worship, viz.:

1st. No man shall be interrupted who is appointed to speak by the Presidency of the Church, by any disorderly person or persons in the congregation, by whispering, by laughing, by talking, by menacing gestures, by getting up and running out in a disorderly manner, or by offering indignity to the manner of worship, or the religion, or to any officer of said Church while officiating in his office, in anywise whatsoever, by any display of ill manners or ill breeding, from old or young, rich or poor, male or female, bond or free, black or white, believer or unbeliever. And if any of the above insults are offered, such measures will be taken as are lawful, to punish the aggressor or aggressors, and eject them from the house.

2nd. An insult offered to the presiding Elder of said Church shall be considered an insult to the whole body. Also, an insult offered to any of the officers of said Church, while officiating, shall be considered an insult to the whole body.

3rd. All persons are prohibited from going up the stairs in times of worship.

4th. All persons are prohibited from exploring the house, except waited upon by a person appointed for that purpose.

5th. All persons are prohibited from going into the several pulpits, except the officers who are appointed to officiate in the same.

6th. All persons are prohibited from cutting, marking or marring the inside or outside of the house with a knife, pencil, or any other instrument whatever, under pain of such penalty as the law shall inflict.

7th. All children are prohibited from assembling in the house, above or below, or any part of it, to play, or for recreation, at any time: and all parents, guardians, or masters, shall be amenable for all damage that shall accrue in consequence of their children's misconduct.

8th. All persons, whether believers or unbelievers, shall be treated with due respect by the authorities of the Church.

9th. No imposition shall be practiced upon any members of the Church, by depriving them of their rights in the house.

Appendix D

The Constitution of the Kirtland Camp

(The constitution of the Kirtland Camp was drafted and approved on March 13, 1838. See *History of the Church* 3:90-91. This manuscript is located in the Church Archives, and spelling and punctuation have been preserved as in the original document.)

The council of the seventies met this day in the attic story of the Lord's House and took into consideration the propriety and necessity of the body of the seventies going up to the land of Zion, in a company together, the present season; and adopted the following resolutions. Viz—Resolved. That we, as a body do agree to put our strength, our properties, and monies together, for the accomplishment of this work, and that we adopt the following rules, & laws, for the organization, and government, of the Camp.

1st That the Presidents of the Seventies, seven in number, shall be the counsellors [i.e., leaders] of the camp, and that there shall be one man appointed as treasurer, who shall by the advice of the counsellors, manage the financial concerns, during the journey, and keep a just and accurate account of all monies received, and expended for the use of the camp.

2nd That there shall be one man appointed to preside over each tent, to take charge of it, and that from the time of their appointment they [the tentmen] shall make all necessary arrangements for the providing of teams, and tents, for the journey, and they shall receive counsell and advice from the counsellors, and furthermore shall see that cleanliness, and decency are observed in all cases, the commandments kept, and the word of wisdom heeded, that is, no tobacco, tea, coffee, snuff or ardent spirits of any kind, taken internally.

3rd That every man shall be the head of his own family, and shall see that they are brought into subjection, according to the order of the camp.

4th That all those that shall subscribe to these resolutions, rules, and regulations, shall make every exertion, and use all lawful means to provide for themselves, and their families and for the use and benefit of the Camp to which they belong. And also, to hand over to the Seven Counsellors all monies appropriated for that purpose, on or before the day the camp shall start.

5th That the moneys shall be retained in the hands of the counsellors, being divided proportionably among them for safety, and shall be paid over to the Treasurer, as circumstances may require.

6th That any faithful brethren wishing to journey with us, can by subscribing to, and observing these rules and regulations.

7th That every individual shall at the end of the journey, when a settlement is to be made, pay their proportional part of the expenses of the journey, or as soon thereafter as their circumstances will admit. By expenses it is understood all that is necessarily paid out for the use of the Camp, after it starts: and that no individual is to receive any thing for services, nor for the use of a team, wagon or cow, if they safely arrive at the place, where the camp shall finally break up.

8th That these rules and laws shall be strictly observed, and every person who shall behave disorderly and not conform to them, shall be disfellowshipped by the Camp and left by the wayside.

9th That this shall be the law of the camp in journeying from this place up to the land of Zion and that it may be added unto or amended as circumstances may require, by the voice of those who shall subscribe to it. And we whose names are hereunder written do hereby bind ourselves to pay our proportional part, or the expenses of the Camp and to observe, and see that our families observe during the journey, the above rules, and regulations. In witness whereof we hereunto affix our names. [The names and number in each family who signed this constitution have been arranged in the list below at the end of this appendix in alphabetical order (with the signatures inserted above each printed name) and an asterisk has been placed in front of each individual who was ordained a seventy before the camp left Kirtland.]

Additional Regulations Which Were Adopted on July 10, 1838
(See *Millennial Star* 16 [1854]: 184)

1st. The Engineer shall receive advice from the Counsellors concerning his duties.

2nd. At four o'clock, A.M., the horn shall blow for rising, and at twenty minuts past four for prayers, at which time each overseer shall see that the inmates of his tent are ready for worship.

3rd. The head of each division shall keep a roll of all his able bodied men to stand guard in turn, as called for by the Engineer, one half in the former, the other half in the latter, part of the night.

4th. Each company of the camp is entitled to an equal proportion of the milk whether it owns the cows or not.

5th. Thomas Butterfield shall be appointed herdsman, to drive the cows and stock, and see that they are taken care of and call for assistance when needed.

6th. That in no case at present, shall the Camp move more than fifteen miles per day, unless circumstances absolutely require it.

Signers of the Kirtland Camp Constitution

Names	Number in Family	Names	Number in Family
Daniel Allen, Jr.	4	*Truman O. Angell	4

Names	Number in Family	Names	Number in Family
Benjamin Baker	4	Richard Brasier	4
Jesse Baker	2	Zephaniah Brewster	9
Amos Baldwin	12	•George W. Brooks	4
Charles N. Baldwin	2	Alfred Brown	2
•Nathan B. Baldwin	2	James Brown	
Samuel Barnet	5	Jason Brunett	7
Charles Bird	7	Benjamin Butterfield	7
Asaph Blanchard	1	•Josiah Butterfield	4
Daniel Bliss	2	Thomas Butterfield	3
Justin Blood	5	Hiram H. Byington	4
Abram Bond	3	•Anson Call	3
•William Bosley	2	Alexander Campbell	
•Daniel Bowen	7	William Carey	
Abram Boynton	7		

Names	Number in Family
*Dominicus Carter	6
John Carter	2
*William Carpenter	5
Aaron Cheney	6
Amasa Cheney	6
Elijah Cheney	2
Nathan Cheney	4
Orin Cheney	9
Joseph C. Clark	6
Adonijah Cooley	5
Joseph Coon	4
*Jonathan Crosby	2
Munro Crosier	2

Names	Number in Family
Austin Cowles	9
Reuben Daniels	7
*Hiram Dayton	12
David C. Deming	
Isaac Dewitt	8
Thomas Draper	
William Draper, Sr.	2
Zemira Draper	6
Joel Drury	5
*Jonathan Dunham	4
David K. Dustin	2
*Lewis Eager	3
William Earl	11
William Field	5

Names	Number in Family	Names	Number in Family
Cyrus B. Fisher	6	*Jonathan H. Hale	5
Jonathan Fisher	5	Samuel Hale	3
Thomas G. Fisher	4	Benjamin K. Hall	
John R [or B] Sawyer [or Folger]	4	John Hammond	6
*James Foster	6	*Jonathan Hampton	4
Samuel Fowler	8	Martin Hanchet	5
*Amos B. Fuller	3	*Jesse P. Harmon	6
E. [Elijah] B. Gaylord	6	Joel Harvey	5
*Sherman A. Gilbert	3	*Henry Harriman	2
David Grey	8	Arnold Healey	3
John Gribble	8	Stephen Headlock	2
William Gribble	3	Reuben Hedlock	8
Hiram Griffith	3	Bro. Hitchcock	5
*Michael Griffith	6	*James S. Holmon	7

Names	Number in Family	Names	Number in Family
*Joshua S. Holman	8	James Lethead	2
*Jonathan H. Holmes	3	*Duncan McArthur	9
*Amos Jackson	6	Joseph McCauseland?	4
Aaron Johnson	4	Michael McDonald	5
*Joel H. Johnson	6	Edwin P. Merriam	3
Julia Johnson	8	Elijah Merriam	2
Joel Judd	3	Josiah Miller	10
Eleazer King, Sr.	7	Ethan A. Moore	8
Eleazer King, Jr.	3	Laban Morri	2
John M. King	4	Samuel Mulliner	5
Nathan K. Knight	9	Henry Munro	3
Jabez Lake	5	Thomas Nickerson	4
Andrew Lamoreaux	7	*J. B. Noble	7
John Lamoreaux	6	Daniel M. Repshire	3

Names	Number in Family	Names	Number in Family
*Oliver Olney	9	Daniel Pulsipher	4
Levi Osgood	5	Elias Pulsipher	8
Noah Packard	9	John Pulsipher	2
*J. [John] D. Parker	3	*Zerah (Zera) Pulsipher	7
Mary Parker	4	Jonas Putnam	6
Samuel Parker	4	Nancy Richerson [Richardson]	3
*Samuel Parker	4	Stephen Richardson	8
Isaac W. Pierce	5	Isaac Rogers	4
Joseph Pine	6	Stephen Rowe	6
Martin H. Peck	6	John Rulison	8
*Alanson Pettingill	5	Enoch S. Sanborn	5
*William Perry	4	Lucius N. Scovil	4
Jared Porter	3	William Shuman	7
*William D. Pratt	4	*Otis Shumway	7

Names	Number in Family
*Stephen Shumway	3
*Elias Smith	3
Warren Smith	7
*Gardner Snow	3
George Snow	2
Nathan Staker	6
*Stephen Starks	6
Arnold Stevens	6
*Henry Stevens	3
George Stringham	6
James Strop [or Stray]	6
John Sweat	10
John Tanner	10
*Charles Thompson	2

Names	Number in Family
Ira Thornton	7
Oliver Thornton	6
John Thorp	7
Cornelius Vanleuven	3
*Frederick Vanleuven	6
John Vanleuven, Jr.	9
Alba Whittle	6
*B. S. Wilber	2
*Levi B. Wilder	6
*Jeremiah Willey	4
William Willson	3
*Abraham Wood	4
Alexander Wright	1
Asa Wright	10

Names	Number in Family	Names	Number in Family
Aaron. M York		*Joseph Young*	
Aaron M. York	4	•Joseph Young	

(The following individuals also signed the constitution but their names were crossed off and in some instances an explanation was written after their names that they had withdrawn:)

Names	Number in Family
•Solomon Angell	?
•Harrison Burgess	?
Hezekiah Fisk	4
•Dana Jacobs	4
•Daniel S. Miles	3
•Daniel Wood	6
John Young, Sr.	1

Notes

Chapter 1. The Birth of Mormonism in Ohio

[1]Doctrine and Covenants [D&C] 32:1-3. See also D&C 28:8; 30:5.

[2]Amos Sutton Hayden, *Early History of the Disciples in the Western Reserve, Ohio*, p. 210; Parley P. Pratt, *Mormonism Unveiled*, p. 41. For an excellent account of the introduction of Mormonism in Ohio, see Richard Lloyd Anderson, "Impact of the First Preaching in Ohio," *BYU Studies* 11 (Summer 1971): 474:96. See also Josiah Jones, "History of the Mormonites," *Evangelist* 9 (June 1, 1841): 132-34.

[3]Joseph Smith, *History of the Church* (HC) 1:122-24. In a letter dated July 1868, Sidney Rigdon insisted that when Oliver Cowdery introduced the gospel to him in Mentor, he was devoted to the study of the Bible, which was "the only book of revelation he had until his acquaintance" with the Book of Mormon. Post Collection, microfilm copy, Archives of The Church of Jesus Christ of Latter-day Saints, Salt Lake City, Utah (hereafter cited as Church Archives) and Harold B. Lee Library, Special Collections, Brigham Young University, Provo, Utah (hereafter cited as BYU).

[4]HC 1:124.

[5]Ibid.

[6]*Painesville Telegraph*, February 15, 1831, p. 1. A similar description of Sidney Rigdon's problem concerning the authority claimed by the missionaries was recorded by Parley P. Pratt in *Mormonism Unveiled*, p. 41.

[7]*Saints' Herald* 29 (1882): 192.

[8]Parley P. Pratt, *Autobiography of Parley Parker Pratt*, p. 48.

[9]"Mary Elizabeth Rollins Lightner," *Utah Genealogical Historical Magazine* 17 (July 1926): 193-94.

[10]Journal of John Murdock, pp. 8-9.

[11]Ibid., p. 9; autobiography of John Murdock, pp. 5-6.

[12]Journal of John Murdock, pp. 8-9; autobiography of John Murdock, p. 8.

[13]HC 1:125.

[14]*Painesville Telegraph*, February 15, 1831, p. 1.

[15]Pratt, *Autobiography*, p. 47.

[16]*Painesville Telegraph*, February 15, 1831, p. 1; Pratt, *Mormonism Unveiled*, pp. 40-41.

[17]*Painesville Telegraph*, February 15, 1831, p. 1; Pratt, *Mormonism Unveiled*, p. 41; Jones, "History," pp. 133-34. Although "M.S.C.," Parley P. Pratt, and Josiah Jones dated the baptism of Sidney Rigdon as November 15, two other contemporary accounts record the date as November 14; however, the latter two accounts were recorded long after the ones I have cited in this work. See *Saints' Herald* 29 (1882): 192; Frederick G. Mather, "The Early Days of Mormonism," *Lippincott's Magazine* 26 (August 1880): 206-7.

[18]Edward and Lydia Partridge, "Writings," pp. 6-7; Andrew Jenson, *Latter-day Saint Biogrpahical Encyclopedia* 1:51, 223; Jones, "History," p. 133.

[19]"Philo Dibble's Narrative" in *Early Scenes in Church History*, pp. 74-76.

[20]Orson Hyde, "History of Orson Hyde," *Deseret News*, May 5, 1858.

[21]An account of Oliver Cowdery's introduction of the gospel to the Shaker community at North Union was reproduced in Richard Lloyd Anderson's article "Impact of the

First Preaching in Ohio," *BYU Studies* 11 (Summer 1971): 489. This extract was taken from the journal of Ashbel Kitchell, copied by Henry C. Blinn, and is in the collection of the Shaker Museum, Old Chatham, New York: "Late in the fall a member of that society came to our house to visit the Believers. His name was Oliver Cowdery. He stated that he had been one who assisted in the translation of the golden Bible, and had seen an angel, and also had been commissioned by him to go out and bear testimony that God would destroy this generation. By his request we gave liberty for him to bear his testimony in our meeting. But finding he had nothing for us, we treated him kindly and labored to find out their manner of spirit. He appeared meek and mild."

[22]The estimate of 130 members joining the Church during the first three weeks of November 1830 is based on the report of John Whitmer, "The Book of John Whitmer," p. 1; an article appearing in the *Evening and Morning Star* 1 (April 1833), when Oliver Cowdery was co-editor; and journal of Lyman Wight, cit. in Joseph Smith, *History of the Church of Jesus Christ of Latter Day Saints*, ed. Heman C. Smith 1:153 (hereafter cited as Heman C. Smith, ed., *History of the Church*). Parley P. Pratt recorded a similar estimate of "127 souls" in his *Autobiography*, p. 48.

[23]Pratt, *Autobiography*, pp. 31-32. Hayden, *Early History of the Disciples*, pp. 193-94, 237-38; Grand River Baptist Association Records, 1817-1842, pp. 83, 86; Alexander Campbell, ed., *The Christian Baptist*, pp. 451-52; *Millennial Harbinger* 1 (Aug. 2, 1830): 370-73.

[24]"History of Joseph Smith," *Times and Seasons* 4 (May 1, 1843): 177-78. *Minutes of the Beaver Baptist Association*, 1820, p. 4; S. Williams, *Mormonism Exposed*, p. 2. A biographical sketch of Sidney Rigdon was published in the *Times and Seasons* "from authentic sources" at a time when he was available for consulation and assistance, and has been reprinted in *HC* 1:120-21. See also F. Mark McKiernan, *The Voice of One Crying in the Wilderness*, pp. 13-19.

[25]"History of Joseph Smith," *Times and Seasons* 4 (May 15, 1843): 193-94; Robert Richardson, *Memoirs of Alexander Campbell* 2:44-45; Williams, *Mormonism Exposed*, p. 2. Alexander Campbell's faith in the popular creeds of Christendom had been shaken while he was studying theology in Scotland, and upon arriving in America in 1809, he united with his father, Thomas Campbell, in rejecting all denominations and endorsing the New Testament as the only guide for religious truth. Three years later this former Presbyterian preacher was baptized by a Baptist elder; he then led the independent congregation of about thirty who supported him and his father into the Baptist fold, uniting the Brush Run society with the Redstone Baptist Association in 1815. When Alexander Campbell joined that alliance, he claimed that he did not present a creed to that body, only a written declaration of faith that he did not consider binding as a term of communion. As he continued to proclaim his views, he met opposition from the association. Consequently, in 1823 he became pastor of a Baptist society in Wellsburg composed mainly of members dismissed from the society at Brush Run; the following year he united with Baptists who had formed the Mahoning Association in 1820. Campbell, *The Christian Baptist*, pp. 92-93; *Minutes of the Redstone Baptist Association*, 1815, pp. 4-5.

[26]"History of Joseph Smith," *Times and Seasons* 4 (June 1, 1843): 209; Grand River Baptist Association Records, pp. 60, 66-67, 74-75; Hayden, *Early History of the Disciples*, p. 191.

²⁷Record of the Mahoning Baptist Association, pp. 76-78, 80-82.
²⁸Hayden, *Early History of the Disciples*, p. 71; Walter Scott, *The Gospel Restored*, p. vi. Scott claimed that he taught the concept of baptism for the remission of sins to Alexander Campbell and Sidney Rigdon and that Rigdon converted the Mormon missionaries to that belief. Although it appears that this doctrine was not emphasized in the preaching of most reformers before 1827, Campbell and Rigdon understood it before that date. This doctrine was also clearly enunciated in the Book of Mormon and in the instructions of John the Baptist to the Prophet Joseph Smith, and was thereby endorsed by Latter-day Saints before the Latter-day Saint missionaries arrived in Ohio. For the views of Scott on this subject, see Walter Scott to Br. Emmons, October 22, 1851, Disciples Historical Society, Nashville, Tennessee.
²⁹Hayden, *Early History of the Disciples*, pp. 193-94.
³⁰Campbell, *The Christian Baptist*, p. 452.
³¹Grand River Baptist Association Records, pp. 83, 86, 99.
³²Mary A. Smith, "A History of the Mahoning Baptist Association," p. 93. The first church of the Campbell movement in the Mahoning Association area to reject its creed was the society in Mantua and Hiram, which was organized January 27, 1827. The following November, the Baptists in New Lisbon abandoned their articles of religion, and in 1828 a similar action was taken by the members of the Braceville church. Ibid, pp. 93-94.
³³Campbell, *The Christian Baptist*, p. 664; *Millennial Harbinger* 1 (January 4, 1830): 1. Campbell also proclaimed in 1830 that "the American Revolution is but the precursor of a revolution of infinitely more importance to mankind. . . . A more glorious work is reserved for this generation— . . . the emancipation of the human mind from the shackles of superstition." *Millennial Harbinger* 1 (July 5, 1830): 307.
³⁴Hayden, *Early History of the Disciples*, pp. 183-86.
³⁵Journal of Lyman Wight, cit. in Heman C. Smith, ed. *History of the Church* 1:51-52; Williams, *Mormonism Exposed*, p. 2; Hayden, *Early History of the Disciples*, p. 209.
³⁶Campbell, *The Christian Baptist*, pp. 454-55.
³⁷Ibid., pp. 89-91, 95.
³⁸Edward Partridge, Papers, May 26, 1839.
³⁹Jenson, *Biographical Encyclopedia* 1:223.
⁴⁰Pratt, *Autobiography*, pp. 27-32.
⁴¹Ibid., pp. 31-32.
⁴²Ibid., p. 32.
⁴³Ibid., pp. 35-37; Pratt, *Mormonism Unveiled*, p. 41.
⁴⁴Pratt, *Autobiography*, pp. 37-42; Pratt, *Mormonism Unveiled*, p. 41.
⁴⁵Pratt, *Autobiography*, pp. 42-45.
⁴⁶HC 1:118-22. Prior to their departure, the four missionaries endorsed a covenant of cooperation dated "Manchester, October 17, 1830." In this covenant Oliver Cowdery promised that he would walk humbly before God, obeying the commandment that he should go forth "to proclaim glad tidings of great joy" to the Lamanites "by presenting unto them the fulness of the gospel." The three other elders covenanted that they would assist him faithfully in this work and would obey his "words and advice." Copies of this covenant along with some of the early revelations recorded by Joseph Smith were published by Ezra Booth, one of the early members who left the Church, in *Ohio Star*, December 8, 1831.

Chapter 2. Ohio in the 1830s

[1]U.S. Bureau of the Census, *Historical Statistics of the United States, Colonial Times to 1957*, pp. 7, 16.

[2]Francis P. Weisenburger, *The Passing of the Frontier*, pp. 3-4.

[3]B. Drake and E. D. Mansfield, *Cincinnati in 1826*, p. 11.

[4]*Historical Statistics*, p. 13.

[5]Weisenburger, *Passing of the Frontier*, pp. 47-54.

[6]John Struthers Stewart, *History of Northeastern Ohio* 1:68-78, 82, 97; Warren Jenkins, *Ohio Gazetteer*, p. 536.

[7]Weisenburger, *Passing of the Frontier*, pp. 233-35, 269-70. Early in 1835 Latter-day Saints in Kirtland began publishing a newspaper, *Northern Times*, that supported candidates of the Democratic party. *Painesville Telegraph*, February 20, 1835, p. 3; *Northern Times*, August 7, 1835, and October 9, 1835.

[8]Milton V. Backman, Jr., *American Religions and the Rise of Mormonism*, pp. 277, 283, 308-9.

[9]*Cleveland Herald*, September 8, 1831.

[10]Alexis de Tocqueville, *Democracy in America*, p. 95.

[11]C. S. Griffin, *The Ferment of Reform, 1830–1860*, p. 1.

[12]Merle Curti, *The Growth of American Thought*, pp. 365-66.

[13]*Painesville Telegraph*, June 29, 1830, p. 2; October 11, 1831, p. 3; April 26, 1831, p. 1.

[14]*Loraine Gazette* (Elyria, Ohio), March 5, 1830, p. 3. Before 1831 many Methodist, Presbyterian, and Baptist congregations agreed to support the temperance crusade, thereby becoming energetic temperance societies. Lewis Curtis, ed., *The General Conferences of the Methodist Episcopal Church from 1792 to 1896*, pp. 76, 82, 105; Records of the Presbytery of Geneva, Book C, p. 109; Minutes of the Presbytery of Grand River, 1829-1836, p. 79; *Ohio Baptist Convention: Records of Annual Meetings*, p. 16.

[15]*Cleveland Herald*, January 21, 1830, p. 3; March 18, 1830, p. 3; April 8, 1830, p. 3.

[16]"Extracts from a Brief History of the Congregational Church of Kirtland, Ohio," copied by Marion A. Crary, p. 2; Grand River Baptist Association Records, 1817-1842, pp. 94, 106; *Geauga Gazzette*, July 20, 1832, p. 1; Christopher G. Crary, *Pioneer and Personal Reminiscences*, p. 25.

[17]"Intemperance—Insanity," *Journal of Health* 1 (1829): 13-14; "On the Use and Abuse of Ardent Spirits," ibid., 1 (1830): 157-59; ibid., 1 (1829): 96; ibid., 1 (1830): 153-55, 219-20, 297-99, 330-31; "Wines," ibid., 1 (1830): 136-38. See also Sylvester Graham, *Lectures on the Science of Human Life*, pp. i-iv.

[18]*Millennial Harbinger* 1 (June 7, 1830): 281-83; *Catholic Telegraph* (Cincinnati), January 17, 1834, p. 112; June 20, 1834, p. 235; *Chardon Spectator and Geauga Gazette*, October 5, 1833, p. 1; *Western Courier* (Ravenna, Ohio), October 24, 1833, p. 2.

[19]Griffin, *Ferment of Reform*, pp. 44-45.

[20]George Rogers Taylor, *The Transportation Revolution, 1815-1860*, pp. 22-24; Harlan Hatcher, *The Buckeye Country*, pp. 132-40.

[21]Taylor, *Transportation Revolution*, pp. 58, 65.

[22]Brigham Young, "History of Brigham Young," *Deseret News*, February 10, 1858, p. 384. See also Elden Jay Watson, comp., *Manuscript History of Brigham Young, 1801-1844*, p. 18.

[23]Taylor, *Transportation Revolution*, pp. 58-60, 138-42.
[24]Ibid., pp. 32, 52, 79.
[25]Harry N. Scheiber, *Ohio Canal Era*, pp. 28, 48, 50, 235-36.
[26]*Latter-day Saints' Messenger and Advocate* 2 (September 1836): 374.

Chapter 3. The Gathering

[1]U.S. Bureau of Census, Fourth Census: 1820, Microcopy no. 33, Roll no. 91, Ohio, pg. 105A; U.S. Bureau of Census, Fifth Census: 1830, Microcopy no. 19, Roll no. 131, pp. 267-73.
[2]Since there is no complete Church membership record for the 1830s, the author with the assistance of various researchers, including Thomas Gregory and Rick Brown, prepared a list of members from various sources, including *History of the Church*; Kirtland Council Minute Book, Church Archives; *Messenger and Advocate*; a record of the First Quorum of Elders Belonging to the Church of Christ in Kirtland, Geauga County, Ohio, 1836-1870, Archives, Reorganized Church of Jesus Christ of Latter Day Saints, Independence, Missouri; Far West, Kirtland, and Nauvoo Teachers Quorum Minutes, 1834-1845, Church Archives; Far West Record, Certificate Record Book, 1836-1838, Church Archives; and a Church membership file (located in the Church Genealogical Society and based on information taken from patriarchal blessing books, records kept by Seventies, and other records). Throughout this work this list has been employed to determine Church members and membership during the 1830s. A comparison of the names appearing in the Kirtland census of 1830 with known members of the Church indicates that eight men listed in that census joined the Church. These eight heads of families were John M. Burk, Reynolds Cahoon, Algernon S. Gilbert, Selah J. Griffin, Isaac Morley, Newel K. Whitney, Lyman Wight, and Frederick G. Williams. Calvin Beebe of Parkland owned land in Kirtland in 1830, and Mary Rollins was living with her uncle, A. S. Gilbert. Since several individuals living there had the same name, it is difficult to determine whether or not the name on one record refers to the same person as the same name on another record. Genealogical dates (births, deaths, marriages, etc.) and other information relating to members of the Kirtland Branch and participants in the march of Zion's Camp have been published in Milton V. Backman, Jr., Susan Easton, and Keith Perkins, comps., *A Profile of Latter-day Saints of Kirtland, Ohio, and Members of Zion's Camp: 1830-1839.*
[3]*History of Geauga and Lake Counties, Ohio*, p. 246.
[4]Ibid.
[5]Lucy Diantha Allen, "Recollections of Her Ancestry Taken in 1901," pp. 2-3; Vera Morley Ipson, "History and Travels of the Life of Isaac Morley, Sr." (taken from histories written by his daughters Cordelia and Lucy), p. 1.
[6]Allen, "Recollections," pp. 2-3; Ipson, "Life of Isaac Morley," pp. 1-2.
[7]Kirtland Township Record Book 1:1.
[8]Ibid.; Anne B. Prusha, "A History of Kirtland, Ohio," p. 47.
[9]Ibid., pp. 58-62; Elizabeth G. Hitchcock, "Grandison Newell, A Born Trader," pp. 1-3.

[10]*History of Geauga and Lake Counties,* p. 247.

[11]Ibid., p. 246.

[12]"Records of the Presbyterian Church of Kirtland," copied from the original by Lucy M. Morley; "Extracts from 'A Brief History of the Congregational Church of Kirtland, Ohio,'" p. 2; Mary B. Sim, "Old South Congregational Church," *Historical Society Quarterly, Lake County, Ohio* 2 (Summer 1960): 2.

[13]Christopher G. Crary, *Kirtland: Personal and Pioneer Reminiscences,* p. 20; John Marshall Barker, *History of Ohio Methodism,* p. 109.

[14]Grand River Baptist Association Records, 1817-1842, p. 81.

[15]Extracts from the journal of Lydia Partridge, p. 5; "Philo Dibble's Narrative," in *Early Scenes in Church History,* p. 77. See also John Whitmer, "The Book of John Whitmer," p. 2; John Corrill, *A Brief History of the Church of Christ of Latter Day Saints,* p. 17.

[16]Larry C. Porter, "A Study of the Origins of The Church of Jesus Christ of Latter-day Saints in the States of New York and Pennsylvania, 1816-1831," pp. 269-73, 285; Lucy Mack Smith, *History of Joseph Smith,* pp. 191-92. While the more popular edition published by Bookcraft has been cited, the references included in this work have been compared with the original publication, and any major changes in the editions are mentioned in the footnotes. The original publication of Lucy's biography was titled *Biographical Sketches of Joseph Smith the Prophet, and His Progenitors for Many Generations* (Liverpool, England: published for Orson Pratt by S. W. Richards, 1853).

[17]Lucy Mack Smith, *History of Joseph Smith,* p. 192; Jenson, *Biographical Encyclopedia* 1:219.

[18]D&C 35:4-9.

[19]D&C 36:1-6.

[20]*Painesville Telegraph,* January 18, 1831, p. 3.

[21]John Whitmer, History, p. 10.

[22]Autobiography of John Murdock, pp. 8-9.

[23]Journal History of the Church, December 31, 1830.

[24]D&C 37; 38:31-32.

[25]3 Nephi 20:22; 21:23; 1 Nephi 13:37.

[26]D&C 28:9.

[27]Porter, "A Study of the Origins of the Church," pp. 199-204, 294, 305.

[28]John Whitmer, "The Book of John Whitmer," p. 6.

[29]The names of the New York Saints who are known to have participated in this migration are recorded in Porter, "A Study of the Origins of the Church," pp. 299-302, 314-16.

[30]Ibid., pp. 290-94; HC 1:145-46; "Joseph Knight's Incidents of History from 1827-1844," probably compiled from loose sheets in Joseph Knight's possession, August 16, 1862, by Thomas Bullock, p. 2, Church Archives.

[31]Orson F. Whitney, *Through Memory's Hall,* p. 13; Jenson, *Biographical Encyclopedia* 1:223-24.

[32]Edward W. Tullidge, *The Women of Mormondom,* pp. 41-43; Jenson, *Biographical Encyclopedia* 1:223.

[33]HC 1:145-46.

[34]Porter, "A Study of the Origins of the Church," pp. 290-94.

[35]Jacob Morris Papers, #1656, Olin Research Library, Cornell University, Ithaca, New York, cited in Porter, "A Study of the Origins of the Church," pp. 303-4.

[36]Frederic G. Mather, "The Early Days of Mormonism," *Lippincott's Magazine* 26 (1880): 204.

[37]Journal History, May 16, pp. 1-4; "Joseph Knight's Incidents of History from 1827-1844," p. 2.

[38]Lucy Smith, *History of Joseph Smith*, pp. 195-99.

[39]Ibid., pp. 203-4. Reference to this miracle, which was related by early Latter-day Saints, appeared in "Mormonism," *Niles' Weekly Register* 40 (July 16, 1831): 352.

[40]*History of Geauga and Lake Counties, Ohio*, p. 248.

[41]*Painesville Telegraph*, May 17, 1831, p. 3.

[42]Journal History, February 22, 1831; Joseph Smith to Martin Harris, February 22, 1831, Joseph Smith Collection, Church Archives.

[43]*Wayne Sentinel* (Palmyra, New York), May 27, 1831.

[44]Pratt, *Autobiography*, p. 61; *Mormonism Unveiled*, p. 41. Pratt's estimates are probably excessive for the first half of 1831. See Samuel George Ellsworth, "A History of Mormon Missions in the United States and Canada, 1830-1860," p. 90.

[45]Based on a study by Mark Grandstaff, approximately 78 percent of the Latter-day Saints who settled in Kirtland were born in New England or New York. Prior to their conversions, they were not transients, but were stable residents of their communities. The median years in which pre-Mormon emigrants to Ohio lived in a community prior to their move to the Western Reserve was 11.7. Their migration pattern was generally one long move from New England to Ohio or from New England to New York and then to Ohio, where they located in a previously settled area rather than in the frontier. See Table 1. Backman, Easton, and Perkins, *A Profile of Latter-day Saints of Kirtland, Ohio*, pp. 85-87.

Chapter 4. The Critics Respond

[1]HC 1:158.

[2]E. D. Howe, *Autobiography and Recollections of a Pioneer Printer*, pp. 1, 4, 21, 46; *History of Geauga and Lake Counties, Ohio*, pp. 29, 223-24. After Howe retired, his younger brother, Asahel Howe, became publisher with M. G. Lewis acting as editor.

[3]See Milton V. Backman, Jr., "Contemporary Accounts of the Latter-day Saints and Their Leaders Appearing in Early Ohio Newspapers."

[4]*Painesville Telegraph*, January 5, 1830, p. 2.

[5]Ibid., December 27, 1831, p. 3.

[6]*Painesville Telegraph*, March 22, 1831, p. 2; March 29, 1831, p. 2; August 9, 1832, p. 1; *Ohio Repository* (Canton), August 30, 1833, p. 2; September 1, 1836, p. 2.

[7]*Painesville Telegraph*, March 8, 1831, p. 3; March 22, 1831, p. 2; May 9, 1834, p. 3; November 20, 1835, p. 3.

[8]Ibid., March 22, 1831, p. 2; March 29, 1831, p. 2.

[9]Ibid., March 29, 1831, p. 2.

[10]Ibid., September 13, 1831, p. 1.

[11]Ibid., March 1, 1831, p. 3; Francis W. Kirkham, *A New Witness for Christ in America* 2:89-96.

[12] Joseph Smith, "To the Editor," *Times and Seasons* 4 (May 15, 1843): 194.

[13] *Cleveland Herald*, November 25, 1830, p. 3; *Ashtabula Journal*, December 4, 1830, p. 2; *Western Reserve Chronicle* (Warren, Ohio), December 9, 1830, p. 1.

[14] *Painesville Telegraph*, March 15, 1831, p. 1.

[15] Ibid., September 22, 1829, p. 3; *American Friend and Marietta Gazette*, January 15, 1831, p. 4.

[16] *Ohio Star*, December 9, 1830, p. 2.

[17] *Painesville Telegraph*, March 8, 1831, p. 3.

[18] *HC* 1:158.

[19] *Painesville Telegraph*, April 5, 1831, p. 3.

[20] Ibid., January 18, 1831, p. 3.

[21] Ibid., September 13, 1831, p. 1.

[22] Ibid., March 13, 1832, p. 3.

[23] *HC* 1:158.

[24] *Ohio Star*, December 8, 1831, p. 1; December 29, 1831, p. 3; *Painesville Telegraph*, January 17, 1832, p. 1. D&C 78, received in March 1832, was the first revelation in which fictitious names were inserted in the printed account. When the reason for this concealment was no longer necessary, the real names of those addressed in the revelation were added in parentheses. The 1981 edition of the Doctrine and Covenants discontinued use of the code names, noting that "since there exists no vital need today to continue the code names, the real names only are now used herein, as given in the original manuscripts." See heading to section 78.

[25] Joseph Smith, "To the Elders of the Church of Latter Day Saints," *Messenger and Advocate* 1 (September 1835): 180.

[26] *Painesville Telegraph*, November 16, 1830, p. 3; *Ohio Star*, December 9, 1830, p. 2; Milton V. Backman, Jr., *Christian Churches of America: Origins and Beliefs*, pp. 143-45, 163-66.

[27] John Whitmer, "The Book of John Whitmer," p. 22.

[28] Joseph Smith, "Try the Spirits," *Times and Seasons* 3 (April 1, 1842): 747.

[29] Autobiography of Levi Hancock, p. 41.

[30] George A. Smith in *Journal of Discourses* 11:3-4 (hereafter cited as *JD*).

[31] John Whitmer, "The Book of John Whitmer," pp. 18-19.

[32] D&C 43:1-7. This concept had also been enunciated in an earlier revelation. See D&C 28:1-7.

[33] Joseph Smith, "Try the Spirits"; Pratt, *Autobiography*, p. 61; John Corrill, *A Brief History of the Church*, p. 16; *Painesville Telegraph*, February 15, 1831, p. 1.

[34] Pratt, *Autobiography*, p. 61.

[35] Ibid., pp. 61-62.

[36] D&C 50:23-24, 31.

[37] Autobiography of Jared Carter, pp. 4-5.

[38] *HC* 2:33-34; Joseph Smith, "Try the Spirits." For additional information on the abnormal spiritual exercises and apostasy of early converts, see Max H. Parkin, "The Nature and Cause of Internal and External Conflict of the Mormons in Ohio Between 1830 and 1838," chapters 3, 4.

[39] See D&C 93:36.

Chapter 5. The Law of Consecration

[1]D&C 38:24, 36. This revelation was initially published in the Book of Commandments for the Government of the Church of Christ 40 (Zion [Independence], Missouri, 1833): 21-22. There are some differences in the wording in these published
editions. Believing in the principle of continual revelation, Latter-day Saints hold
that authorized leaders have the authority to edit (in the form of additions or explanations) the revelations. Joseph Smith, who recorded the original revelations,
supervised the editing and publication of these writings when they were printed in
the 1835 edition of the Doctrine and Covenants.

[2]John Whitmer, "The Book of John Whitmer," p. 11.

[3]HC 1:146-47.

[4]Leonard J. Arrington, "Early Mormon Communitarianism: The Law of Consecration
and Stewardship," Western Humanities Review 7 (Autumn 1953): 346-50.

[5]For additional information on the Shakers, see Edward Andrews, The People Called
Shakers, and for general information on utopian societies of early America, see Arthur Eugene Bestor, Jr., Backwoods Utopias.

[6]D&C 41:9-11.

[7]D&C 42:30-35. The basic ideas included in this revelation were initially published by
Latter-day Saints in the July 1832 issue of the Evening and the Morning Star under the
title "Extracts from the Laws for the Government of the Church of Christ." This information was later included in the Book of Commandments, chapter 44, and in a
more expanded version in a reprint in the Evening and Morning Star issued at Kirtland. It was originally printed in the Doctrine and Covenants (1835 edition) as section 13.

[8]D&C 51:2-3.

[9]John Whitmer, "The Book of John Whitmer," pp. 29-30; HC 1:180; "Newel Knight's
Journal," Scraps of Biography, pp. 69-70; autobiography of Jared Carter, p. 3. Copley's given name is spelled Leman and Lemon in various records.

[10]D&C 54.

[11]The names of these emigrants are included in Porter, "A Study of the Origins of the
Church," pp. 299-303.

[12]D&C 52:2-3, 7-12, 22-32. These missionaries were told to travel in pairs or small
groups, to take different routes, and to preach and baptize while traveling west.

[13]D&C 53:1-5; 55:1-6.

[14]HC 1:188-89. See also "History of Orson Pratt," Deseret News, June 2, 1858, and published in Elden J. Watson, comp., The Orson Pratt Journals, p. 11. Pratt wrote that
while traveling to Missouri, he and his brother Parley held about fifty meetings and
baptized eleven converts. Meanwhile, Joseph Smith discussed gospel principles in
Cincinnati with Walter Scott, one of the leaders of the restorationist movement and
an early associate of Sidney Rigdon.

[15]HC 1:189.

[16]HC 1:189-202; D&C 57, 58, 59, 60.

[17]HC 58:35-38.

[18]HC 1:196-99.

[19]D&C 61:9, 22-23.

[20]HC 1:206.

[21]D&C 63:39; 64:20.

[22]D&C 64:21, 26.

[23]D&C 63:42-46; John Whitmer, "The Book of John Whitmer," p. 37.

[24]Geauga County, Ohio, Deed Records, Book 15, pp. 490-92 (hereafter cited as Geauga Deed Records); Book 17, p. 32, microfilm copy, BYU and Church Genealogical Department; Geauga County, Ohio, Kirtland, Tax Records, 1830-1833, microfilm copy, BYU and Church Genealogical Department.

[25]D&C 70:1-3, 7, 14; Far West Record, p. 31; Kirtland Council Minute Book, p. 108.

[26]D&C 72:7-8; 84:112; 104:40-42. Bishop Whitney's mercantile establishment was called Newel K. Whitney and Company and served as an agency to distribute goods to the needy. A similar storehouse, called Gilbert, Whitney and Company, was located in Missouri. Leonard J. Arrington, Feramorz Y. Fox, and Dean L. May, *Building the City of God*, pp. 31, 435.

[27]D&C 96:1-8; 104:20-50; HC 1:353, 363; Far West Record, p. 32; Kirtland Council Minute Book, pp. 13, 24; Arrington, Fox, and May, *Building the City of God*, pp. 31, 435.

[28]Feramorz Y. Fox, "United Order: Discrimination in the Use of Terms," *Improvement Era* 47 (July 1944): 432. One of the bases from which the United Firm grew was the Gilbert-Whitney store in Kirtland; after A. Sidney Gilbert was called by revelation to settle in Missouri, this business was expanded to two mercantile establishments. D&C 57:6, 9; 63:42-45.

[29]This land was purchased by Frederick G. Williams from Isaac Moore, who was one of the first land speculators to benefit from the arrival of the Saints in Kirtland. Moore had purchased seventy acres for $200 and seventy-five acres for $360, after which he sold most of his land to Latter-day Saints for $2,000. Geauga Deed Records, Book 15, pp. 425-26; Book 16, pp. 22-23. See also Geauga, Kirtland, Tax Records for the 1830s. Frederick G. Williams, "Frederick Granger Williams of the First Presidency of the Church," *BYU Studies* 12 (spring 1972): 247; F. G. Williams, "Statement of Facts Relative to Joseph Smith and Myself," Church Archives.

[30]Geauga Deed Records, Book 17, p. 359; Book 18, pp. 480-81; Geauga, Kirtland, Tax Records, 1834, 1835.

[31]Geauga, Kirtland, Tax Records, 1830-1839.

[32]D&C 104:47-53.

[33]Geauga Deed Records, Book 18, pp. 487-88; D&C 104:20.

[34]Geauga Deed Records, Book 18, p. 479; D&C 104:27-30.

[35]Geauga Deed Records, Book 18, pp. 478-80; D&C 104:24-26, 43-46.

[36]D&C 104:34, 39-41. Property taxes for most of the French farm (approximately one hundred acres in lot 17) were paid from 1834 to 1836 by the Whitney Company and in 1837 by John Johnson.

[37]D&C 58:27-28.

[38]HC 1:365-67. Copies of some of these contracts are located in the Church Archives. See Edward Partridge papers.

[39]Joseph Smith to William W. Phelps, November 27, 1832, cited in HC 1:297-99.

[40]Joseph Smith, Jr., to Edward Partridge, May 2, 1833, Edward Partridge papers, cited in O. F. Whitney, "The Aaronic Priesthood," *Contributor* 6 (October 1884): 6-7.

[41]D&C 51:5. This statement does not appear in the earliest copies of this revelation as found in the Kirtland Revelation Book, Church Archives, and the Book of Commandments. However, the statement was included as verse five in the first edition of the Doctrine and Covenants (1835).

[42]D&C 49:20. For additional information on the law of consecration and stewardship, see Hyrum Andrus, *Doctrines of the Kingdom*, pp. 222-96, and the bibliography in Arrington, Fox, and May, *Building the City of God*.

[43]HC 2:205-6; Geauga, Kirtland, Tax Records, 1830-1839; "About the Mormons," B. C. Fowles papers, Western Reserve Historical Society.

[44]Kirtland Council Minute Book, pp. 214-17.

[45]*Painesville Telegraph*, September 13, 1831, p. 1; *Warren News-letter* and *Trumbull County Republican*, September 13, 1831, p. 1; *Western Reserve Chronicle* (Warren), September 22, 1831, p. 4.

[46]Autobiography of Heber C. Kimball, pp. 8-19, 32-34, Church Archives.

Chapter 6. Revelations and Confrontations

[1]Although the wife of John Johnson is referred to in some contemporary records as Elsa or Elsey, she was also called Alice in a family Bible. A tombstone located in the cemetery next to the Kirtland Temple includes the following inscription: "In Memory of Mary E., daughter of John and Alice Johnson, who died March 30, 1833, in the fifteenth year of her age." Geauga Deed Records, Book 18, pp. 478-79; Book 24, p. 100; Book 25, pp. 15, 409, 440. For additional information on the John Johnson family, see Keith Perkins, "A House Divided: The John Johnson Family," *Ensign* 9 (February 1979): 54-59.

[2]Hayden, *Early History of the Disciples*, p. 250. The account of the healing of Elsa Johnson was included in a funeral sermon delivered by B. A. Hinsdale on August 3, 1870, entitled "Life and Character of Symonds Ryder." See also Luke Johnson, "History of Luke Johnson," *Deseret News*, May 19, 1858, p. 53; "Philo Dibble's Narrative," in *Early Scenes in Church History*, p. 79; and HC 1:215n-16n.

[3]HC 1:215; Hartwell Ryder, "A Short History of the Foundation of the Mormon Church," typescript, Hiram College, p. 3.

[4]Robert J. Matthews, *A Plainer Translation: Joseph Smith's Translation of the Bible*, pp. 8-20.

[5]Ibid., pp. 11-12. See also D&C 45:60-61; 73:3-4; 76:15; and HC 1:238-39, 131-33.

[6]HC 1:245.

[7]Matthews, *A Plainer Translation*, pp. 12-13.

[8]Ibid., pp. 26-28, 39-40, 55-58, 91-95.

[9]Ibid., p. 96.

[10]Ibid., pp. 53-54.

[11]See D&C 45:60-61. D&C 76:15-18, 77, and probably sections 84, 86, 88, 107, and 132 were recorded in connection with this project.

[12]HC 1:98; Matthews, *A Plainer Translation*, pp. 26-27.

[13]D&C 45:60-61.

[14]Matthews, *A Plainer Translation*, p. 31.

[15]HC 1:211.

[16]It is not clear whether Joseph Smith translated the books of the New Testament in the order in which they appear in the King James Version or whether he passed from one section to another. Some revisions were made after he had completed his first revision and was reviewing what he had previously translated. We also do not know if some of the revelations in the Doctrine and Covenants (such as section 74) were received while he was actually translating a particular book or whether he received the revelation while he was pondering over a concept recorded in the New Testament.

[17]HC 1:245.

[18]D&C 76:20-24.

[19]1 Corinthians 7:14; D&C 74:7.

[20]D&C 77.

[21]D&C 76:25-112.

[22]D&C 76:28.

[23]"Recollections of the Prophet Joseph Smith," *Juvenile Instructor* 27 (May 15, 1892): 303-4.

[24]HC 1:295.

[25]HC 1:324, 368-69; Kirtland Council Minute Book, p. 8; Joseph Smith to the Brethren (in Zion), July 2, 1833, Church Archives, cited in HC 1:368-70.

[26]Matthews, *A Plainer Translation*, pp. 15-16, 41-47.

[27]Ibid., pp. 52, 207-18.

[28]Far West Record, pp. 18-19.

[29]HC 1:104.

[30]Richard P. Howard, *Restoration Scriptures*, pp. 197-98.

[31]Pratt, *Autobiography*, p. 62.

[32]Far West Record, pp. 18-19; HC 1:222-24, 270.

[33]D&C 1:17-24, 37.

[34]Far West Record, p. 19.

[35]D&C 67:6-7.

[36]HC 1:226. There are many variations in the spelling of McLellin in contemporary records, such as McLellan, McLelland, and M'Lellin. The 1981 edition of the Doctrine and Covenants spells it McLellin.

[37]HC 1:229.

[38]D&C 69:1-2.

[39]HC 1:229-34; D&C 133.

[40]D&C 133:9, 13, 25-26, 62-64.

[41]D&C 1, 67-70, 133.

[42]Far West Record, pp. 19-20.

[43]D&C 70.

[44]HC 1:226.

[45]Howard, *Restoration Scriptures*, p. 199.

[46]Ibid., p. 200.

[47]HC 1:390, 411; John Taylor, statement, April 15, 1858, Church Archives, cited in Journal History, July 20, 1833, pp. 3-4.

[48]HC 2:165, 243-51; Kirtland Council Minute Book, p. 76. Howard, *Restoration Scriptures*, p. 200; *Evening and Morning Star* (Kirtland reprint), 1 (June 1833): 16.

[49]Charles H. Ryder, "History of Hiram," 1864, typescript, Hiram College, Hiram, Ohio.

[50]Hayden, *Early History of the Disciples*, p. 251. In addition to Ezra Booth and Symonds

Ryder, Joseph Smith noted that Eli Johnson, Edward Johnson, and John Johnson, Jr., apostatized during that early period in the history of the Church. HC 1:260.

[51]D&C 52:23.

[52]D&C 52:37.

[53]Far West Record, p. 4; HC 1:260-61; Hayden, Early History of the Disciples, p. 252. Although Ryder's name was spelled "Simonds Rider" in the Far West Record, his name was spelled "Symonds Rider" in minutes of the church in which he served as pastor. In other records, including a newspaper article he wrote, his name was spelled "Symonds Ryder." Ohio Star, December 29, 1831, p. 3. Hartwell Ryder, "Short History of the Mormon Church," p. 4.

[54]Hayden, Early History of the Disciples, p. 252.

[55]Ohio Star, November 10, 1831, p. 3; November 24, 1831, p. 1. Joseph Smith learned through revelation that one of Booth's problems was that he lost the Spirit of the Lord because he did not keep the commandments of God. D&C 64:15-16.

[56]Ohio Star, November 24, 1831, p. 1.

[57]HC 1:241; D&C 56:4.

[58]Ohio Star, November 10, 1831, p. 3; November 17, 1831, p. 3.

[59]Ibid., November 24, 1831, p. 1.

[60]Ibid.

[61]HC 1:216-17; Hyrum M. Smith and Janne M. Sjodahl, Doctrine and Covenants Commentary, p. 165.

[62]Ohio Star, November 10, 1831, p. 3.

[63]HC 1:241; Parkin, "Conflict at Kirtland," p. 117; Messenger and Advocate 1 (January 1835): 62.

[64]Ohio Star, December 15, 1831, p. 3; December 29, 1831, p. 3.

[65]HC 1:241.

[66]Charles H. Ryder, "History of Hiram," p. 16; George A. Smith in JD 2:5.

[67]Luke Johnson estimated that the mob consisted of about forty or fifty men, while Hartwell Ryder estimated that the band consisted of about sixty men who divided into two groups, one attacking Joseph Smith and the other Sidney Rigdon. Meanwhile, Charles Ryder wrote that the men who tarred and feathered Joseph Smith and Sidney Rigdon lived in Shalersville, Garrettsville, and Hiram. Luke Johnson, "History of Luke Johnson," Millennial Star 26 (1864): 834; Hartwell Ryder, "History of the Mormon Church," p. 4; Charles Ryder, "History of Hiram," p. 16.

[68]Joseph Smith's recording of the mobbing in Hiram appears in Book A-1, pp. 205-9, Church Archives, and was initially printed in "History of Joseph Smith," Times and Seasons 5 (August 1844): 611-12. See also HC 1:265.

[69]HC 1:261.

[70]HC 1:261-62. Luke Johnson identified Warren Waste as the man Joseph Smith kicked as he left the home. Waste, Johnson added, was one of the strongest individuals living in the Western Reserve and boasted that he alone could take the Prophet out of the house. But after struggling with the Prophet and being knocked off the steps, he cried, "Do not let him touch the ground, or he will run over the whole of us." He is reported to have said afterwards that Joseph Smith was "the most powerful man" he had ever held in his life. Luke Johnson, "History," Millennial Star 26 (1864): 835.

[71]HC 1:262. This is not a direct quotation from the Prophet's history. Hartwell Ryder later wrote that while his father, Symonds Ryder, had been accused of being one of the leaders of the mob who tarred and feathered Josehp Smith, he did not believe the

accusation was correct, for he remembered that his father had been sick that night. He believed that his father remained home throughout the night, not leaving until late the next morning. Hartwell Ryder, "History of the Mormon Church," p. 4.

72HC 1:262-63. Luke Johnson reported that after Joseph Smith was taken from his father's home, the mob stretched him on a board and "tantalized him in a most insulting and brutal manner." He further stated that the mob planned to emasculate him, and Dr. Dennison was to perform the operation; but when the doctor saw the Prophet stretched on the plank, he changed his mind and refused to perform the operation. Johnson then substantiated Joseph Smith's account that after the Prophet was beaten and scratched, the mobsters attempted to "pour some vial of some obnoxious drug into his mouth," which broke one of his front teeth. Luke Johnson, "History," p. 835.

73HC 1:263.

74HC 1:264; Luke Johnson, "History," p. 835; autobiography of Lucy Walker Kimball, March 25, 1832.

75HC 1:263-64; Luke Johnson, "History," p. 835.

76HC 1:264; "Katherine Hulet Winget," in Kate B. Carter, comp., *Our Pioneer Heritage* 13:489; autobiography of Lucy Walker Kimball, March 25, 1832. In addition to the references cited above, a few other contemporary accounts refer to this mobbing. See *Geauga Gazette*, April 17, 1832, p. 1: *Ohio Argus and Franklin Gazette* (Lebanon, Ohio), June 8, 1832, p. 1; Amasa Lyman, "History," *Deseret News*, September 8, 1858, p. 2; *Portage County Democrat* (Ravenna, Ohio), February 15, 1860, p. 1. The *Geauga Gazette* stated: "On Saturday night, March 24, a number of persons, some say 25 or 30, disguised with coloured faces, entered the rooms in Hiram, where the two Mormonite leaders, Smith and Rigdon, were sleeping, and took them together with the pillows on which they slept, carried them a short distance and after besmearing their bodies with tar, applied the contents of the pillows to the same."

77HC 1:265.

78HC 1:265-66. Since there was another visitor in the Whitney home when Emma Smith arrived in Kirtland during Joseph's second trip to Missouri, Emma stayed at the homes of Reynolds Cahoon, Joseph Smith, Sr., and Frederick G. Williams. Book A-1, p. 209, Church Archives; "History of Joseph Smith," *Times and Seasons* 5 (September 2, 1844): 624.

Chapter 7. The Call to Preach

1HC 1:467-69.

2*Here Is Lake County, Ohio*, pp. 24-25; Robert Kent Fielding, "The Growth of the Mormon Church in Kirtland, Ohio," p. 57; Alma Saari, "The Fairport Harbor Story," *Historical Society Quarterly* 8 (May 1966): 1-5.

3D&C 4:3-4.

4Journal of John Murdock, pp. 1-2.

5Journal of Levi Ward Hancock, pp. 36-39.

6Autobiography of Jared Carter, pp. 1-8.

7Autobiography of Zera (Zerah) Pulsipher, pp. 5-6.

8Florence A. Hall, "Sketch of Zera Pulsipher," pp. 3-4.

[9]Ibid.; autobiography of Zera Pulsipher, p. 7; "Autobiography of Wilford Woodruff," *Tullidge's Quarterly Magazine* 3 (October 1883): 2.

[10]Watson, *Manuscript History of Brigham Young*, pp. 5-6.

[11]D&C 42:6, 63. See also 44:3; 45:64; 52:10.

[12]D&C 44:1, 3.

[13]D&C 45:64; 44:4.

[14]D&C 88:81.

[15]D&C 49:1.

[16]Richard Lloyd Anderson, "First Preaching in Ohio," *BYU Studies* 11 (Summer 1971): 489.

[17]D&C 52:7-10, 22-32.

[18]D&C 52:35.

[19]D&C 60:5-9.

[20]D&C 66:1, 5-8.

[21]D&C 75:7, 9, 17.

[22]D&C 75:13-15.

[23]D&C 75:30-36.

[24]D&C 79:1.

[25]D&C 80:1-3.

[26]D&C 99:1.

[27]D&C 112:1-4.

[28]D&C 103:21-22, 29-30, 37-40.

[29]Autobiography of Jared Carter, p. 10.

[30]*HC* 2:441.

[31]*HC* 2:514.

[32]*HC* 2:28.

[33]*HC* 2:35. The Kirtland high council decided in August 1835 that it was not advisable at that time for an elder to take his wife on a mission. Kirtland Council Minute Book, p. 97.

[34]D&C 107:23-25.

[35]*HC* 2:209. A description of the missionary activities of the Twelve in 1835 is found in Journal History, September 26, 1835.

[36]*HC* 2:431-32. Journal History, April 1836 to November 1836; December 1836 to April 1837. During the winter of 1837, nine of the apostles served missions in Ohio.

[37]"Extracts from the Journal of Heber C. Kimball," *Millennial Star* 26 (1864): 584-85.

[38]Ibid., pp. 599, 711.

[39]*HC* 1:468. This announcement appeared in the *Evening and Morning Star,* published in Kirtland in December 1833.

[40]*HC* 2:394-95, 406; Kirtland Council Minute Book, pp. 138-39.

[41]William Smith, *William Smith on Mormonism,* pp. 20-21.

[42]*HC* 2:403-4.

[43]*HC* 2:446; Elders Licenses Issued at Kirtland, 1836-1838.

[44]For a description of educational programs sponsored by Latter-day Saints in Kirtland, see chapter 15.

[45]*HC* 1:467-69.

[46]*HC* 2:431.

[47]Journal History, June 2, 1835.

[48]Davis Bitton, "Kirtland as a Center of Missionary Activity, 1830-1838," *BYU Studies* 11 (Summer 1971): 502-3.

[49]Ibid., p. 499. See also diary of Hyrum Smith (1831-35).

[50]Bitton, "Kirtland as Center of Missionary Activity," pp. 500-502. Reminiscences and journal of Lorenzo Barnes (1812-35), pp. 1-7; journal of Lorenzo Barnes, 1835-39.

[51]*HC* 1:188-205, 265-72; 2:63-139, 518-28; 3:1-8.

[52]*HC* 1:295.

[53]*HC* 1:416-23.

[54]*HC* 2:40-45, 168-69.

[55]*HC* 2:253.

[56]*HC* 2:463-66. Watson, *Manuscript History of Brigham Young,* p. 14.

[57]*Messenger and Advocate* 3 (April 1837): 491; *HC* 2:502-3, 518-28.

[58]*HC* 1:188-205, 265-72, 295, 416-23; 2:40-45, 63-139, 168-69, 253, 463-66, 518-28.

[59]O. F. Whitney, "Newel K. Whitney," *Contributor* 5 (January 1885): 127; *HC* 2:40-45, 518; *Messenger and Advocate* 3 (April 1837): 491; autobiography of Nathan Tanner, p. 21.

[60]Ebenezer Robinson, "Items of Personal History of the Editor," p. 12.

[61]*D&C* 111:1, 8.

[62] *HC* 2:464-66.

[63]Diary of Joseph Smith, 1832-34, pp. 5-6; Dean C. Jessee and William G. Hartley, "Joseph Smith's Missionary Journal," *New Era* 4 (February 1974): 35. An account of this missionary experience was included in the Prophet's history; see *HC* 1:416-23.

[64]Diary of Joseph Smith, 1832-34, pp. 6-7.

[65]*D&C* 100:1-12.

[66]In his diary, Joseph Smith referred to Eleazer Freeman Nickerson as Freeman A. Nickerson. Diary of Joseph Smith, 1832-34, pp. 5-6. See also Jessee and Hartley, "Joseph Smith's Missionary Journal," and Freeman Nickerson papers, Church Archives.

[67]Diary of Joseph Smith, 1832-34, pp. 6-13.

[68]Ibid., pp. 14-15; Journal History, October 27, 1833.

[69]Diary of Joseph Smith, 1832-34, pp. 16-17.

[70]Ibid., pp. 17-18.

[71]Journal History, December 20, 1833.

[72]*Messenger and Advocate* 1 (October 1834): 7-8.

[73]"Extracts from the Journal of Heber C. Kimball," *Millennial Star* 26 (1864): 569.

[74]Eliza R. Snow, comp., *Biography and Family Record of Lorenzo Snow,* p. 15.

[75]Memoirs of George A. Smith, p. 29.

[76]"History of John E. Page," *Deseret News,* June 16, 1858, p. 69.

[77]Orson Hyde, "History of Orson Hyde," *Deseret News,* May 5, 1858, p. 45; Howard H. Barron, *Orson Hyde: Missionary, Apostle, Colonizer,* pp. 27-101.

[78]Journal of Erastus Snow, pp. 2-26.

[79]Ibid., pp. 26-45.

[80]Journal of Levi Jackman, p. 3.

[81]Journal of Evan M. Greene, p. 18 (March 28, 1833).

[82]Journal History, February 16, 1835, pp. 2-3.

[83]*Messenger and Advocate* 1 (June 1835): 141; journal of Lorenzo Barnes (1812-1835), p. 7; George A. Smith, "My Journal," *Instructor* 81 (December 1946): 565.

[84]*Messenger and Advocate* 1 (January 1835): 63-64, memoirs of George A. Smith, pp. 30-31.

[85]George A. Smith, "My Journal," p. 564. Protestant meetinghouses were sometimes available to traveling preachers of various faiths, and the facilities in the Kirtland Temple were also made available to others. *Messenger and Advocate* 3 (October 1836): 395-96.

[86]*Messenger and Advocate* 1 (March 1835): 93; 2 (August 1836): 365-67.

[87]Autobiography of Luman Andros Shurtliff, p. 27. Pratt, *Autobiography*, pp. 128-29; John Whitmer, "The Book of John Whitmer," chapter 4.

[88]Pratt, *Autobiography*, pp. 48-51.

[89]Ibid., pp. 128-29; Parkin, "Conflict at Kirtland," pp. 153-54.

[90]HC 2:222.

[91]HC 2:431.

[92]Journal History, September 26, 1837.

Chapter 8. Growth of the Church in Kirtland

[1]This estimate of the Mormon and non-Mormon population in Kirtland is based on an analysis of membership information gathered by the author and tax records of Kirtland for the 1830s. See Table 2, p. 140.

[2]For a description of themes emphasized by early Latter-day Saint missionaries, see Bitton, "Kirtland as a Center of Missionary Activity, 1830-1838," p. 504; Parkin, "Conflict at Kirtland," pp. 134-38; and Barbara McFarlane Higdon, "The Role of Preaching in the Early Latter-day Saint Church, 1830-1846."

[3]HC 1:312-16.

[4]Kirtland Council Minute Book, p. 44.

[5]Journal History, October 1, 1831.

[6]*Messenger and Advocate* 2 (July 1836): 342-46.

[7]Diary of Elias Smith, June 19 to September 19, 1837.

[8]Journal of Orson Pratt, 1833; Watson, *Orson Pratt Journals*, pp. 18-22, 66-69.

[9]Journal of Joseph Fielding, Book 1, pp. 4-7; Pratt, *Autobiography*, pp. 143-50

[10]Journal of Lorenzo Barnes, pp. 7-9. Punctuation, spelling, and capitalization in this quotation have been changed for the sake of clarity.

[11]High Priest Minutes, Spanish Fork, February 5, 1878, Church Archives; autobiography of Jonathan Crosby, p. 3. See also autobiography of Warren Foote, p. 4, and autobiography of William Huntington, p. 2.

[12]Autobiography of Nancy Alexander Tracy, p. 23.

[13]Journal of Wilford Woodruff, December 1833; "Autobiography of Wilford Woodruff," *Tullidge's Quarterly Magazine* 3 (October 1883): 2.

[14]"Autobiography of Wilford Woodruff," p. 2; journal of Wilford Woodruff, December 1833; Cowley, *Wilford Woodruff*, p. 35.

[15]Roberts, *The Life of John Taylor*, pp. 31-41; Pratt, *Autobiography*, pp. 135-51.

[16]Eliza R. Snow, comp., *Biography and Family Record of Lorenzo Snow*, pp. 5-7; autobiography of Eliza R. Snow, p. 8.

[17]Watson, *Manuscript History of Brigham Young*, pp. 1-3.

[18]Autobiography of Eliza R. Snow, p. 6; Eliza R. Snow, *Eliza R. Snow: An Immortal*, pp. 5-6.

[19]Autobiography of Phebe W. Woodruff, p. 1.

[20]Autobiography of Joseph Holbrook, pp. 30-31.

[21]Autobiography of Oliver B. Huntington, pp. 5-6; autobiography of William Huntington, pp. 1-2.

[22]Autobiography of Mary Ann Stearns Winters, daughter of Mary Ann Stearns Pratt, pp. 1-2.

[23]For accounts of the journey to Kirtland, see autobiography of Zadoc Knapp Judd, pp. 4-5; autobiography of Nancy A. Tracy, p. 6; autobiography of Mary Ann Stearns Winters, pp. 2-3; autobiography of Joseph Holbrook, pp. 30-31; autobiography of Warren Foote, p. 10; Journal History, May 1, 1833; and autobiography of Benjamin F. Johnson, p. 9 (hereafter cited as "My Life's Review").

[24]Autobiography of Nathan Tanner, pp. 5-8; autobiography of Elizabeth Beswick Tanner, p. 1.

[25]Autobiography of Nathan Tanner, pp. 10-11.

[26]HC 1:389, 410; 2:180, 253, 281; journal of Oliver B. Huntington, p. 9.

[27]HC 2:468-69.

[28]Journal of Samuel H. Rogers, p. 4; Watson, *Manuscript History of Brigham Young*, pp. 4-6.

[29]Watson, *Manuscript History of Brigham Young*, p. 4.

[30]Journal History, October 29, 1833; autobiography of Wandle Mace, p. 37; Pratt, *Autobiography*, p. 45. For additional contemporary accounts of Joseph Smith see "Joseph Smith, the Prophet," *Young Woman's Journal* 17 (December 1906): 537-48; *Millennial Star* 3 (May 1842): 8; and Hyrum L. Andrus, *Joseph Smith, the Man and the Seer*, pp. 11-17.

[31]Cowley, *Wilford Woodruff*, p. 39.

[32]Autobiography of Joseph Bates Noble, pp. 4-5; Jenson, *Biographical Encyclopedia* 4:691.

[33]Autobiography of Jonathan Crosby, p. 13.

[34]*Juvenile Instructor* 27 (January 1, 1892): 24.

[35]Watson, *Manuscript History of Brigham Young*, p. 4.

[36]Narrative of Nancy Alexander Tracy, p. 8.

[37]Autobiography of Mary Adeline Beman Noble, pp. 17-20; journal of Joseph Bates Noble, pp. 10-13.

[38]In November 1835, the Prophet spent many hours discussing religion with Robert Matthias, a controversial preacher who claimed to be a prophet; Mr. Messenger, a Universalist preacher from New York; Erastus Holmes, an investigator from Newbury, Ohio; Elder Josiah Clark from Kentucky; and Henry Capron, from Manchester, New York. HC 2:304-7, 311-12, 321-22.

[39]"An Account 'About the Mormons,'" B. C. Fowles Papers, Western Reserve Historical Society, Cleveland, Ohio.

[40]Diary of Reynolds Cahoon, p. 8; diary of Levi W. Hancock, p. 47; "Memoirs of President Joseph Smith [III] (1832-1914)," Mary Anderson, ed., *Saints' Herald*, November 6, 1934, p. 1413; Lucy Mack Smith, *History of Joseph Smith*, p. 224.

[41]Geauga Deed Records, Book 20, p. 526; Book 21, p. 467; Book 22, p. 151; Book 23, p. 94; Book 25, p. 168; Book 26, p. 141.

[42]*Messenger and Advocate* 2 (July 1836): 348-49. See also Geauga Deed Records, Book 24, pp. 200, 325, 361-62, 384; and Book 25, pp. 409, 620.

[43]George A. Smith in *JD* 12:150.

[44]Joseph Smith estimated in October 1835 that about 500 or 600 persons communed in

the chapel, and approximately 1,000 members lived in "the vicinity" of Kirtland (possibly meaning the Western Reserve). The estimate of 800 includes children of members and is based primarily upon an identification of families living in Kirtland in 1835. HC 2:296.

[45]The non-Mormon population estimates for the 1830s are based upon the census reports for 1830 and 1840 and the relationship between the census and the personal property tax payers for the 1830s. The author has identified the Mormon and non-Mormon taxpayers for every year during the 1830s, based upon a comparison of those who paid taxes with various records that contain the names of members. For estimates of Church membership in Joseph Smith's history, see HC 1:366; 2:64, 296, 379, 430, 435. Some of these estimates probably do not include unbaptized children. The average Latter-day Saint family in Kirtland was slightly smaller (fewer than six members per household) than the average nonmember family in Ohio (6.3 per household). Latter-day Saints who gathered to Kirtland were also generally young (the average age of a head of a household was thirty) and their families were, therefore, not yet complete. See Mark Grandstaff, "Marriage Patterns of the Mormon Community at Kirtland, Ohio, 1830-1838," BYU Special Collections. The size of non-LDS families declined from 6.3 in 1830 to 6 in 1840.

[46]Jenkins, The Ohio Gazetteer, p. 248.

[47]Ibid., pp. 55, 99, 126, 158, 348, 455, 488; Marvin S. Hill, C. Keith Rooker, and Larry T. Wimmer, The Kirtland Economy Revisited, p. 15.

[48]Northern Times, October 2, 1835, pp. 3-4.

[49]Hill, Rooker, and Wimmer, Kirtland Economy Revisited, p. 13.

Chapter 9. A Temple on a Hill

[1]D&C 88:119.

[2]D&C 38:32. See also D&C 95:8.

[3]Geauga, Kirtland, Tax Records, 1833.

[4]Benjamin Johnson, "My Life's Review," pp. 10-11.

[5]HC 1:349. See also autobiography of Heber C. Kimball, p. 19.

[6]HC 1:335.

[7]HC 1:336; autobiography of Joel Hills Johnson; Benjamin Johnson, "My Life's Review," pp. 10-11; Robert Kent Fielding, "The Growth of the Mormon Church in Kirtland, Ohio," p. 81.

[8]Lucy Mack Smith, History of Joseph Smith, pp. 230-31.

[9]D&C 82:11-12.

[10]D&C 92:1-2; 96:6; Fielding, "Growth of the Mormon Church in Kirtland, Ohio," p. 81.

[11]Benjamin Johnson, "My Life's Review," pp. 10-11.

[12]HC 1:335; Geauga Deed Books, Book 17, p. 32; Book 18, p. 487; Book 19, p. 203; D&C 104:20; Fielding, "Growth of the Mormon Church in Kirtland, Ohio," p. 80.

[13]D&C 95:3, 11-17.

[14]HC 1:342-43, 349-50, 353-54.

[15]HC 1:353; "Lorenzo Dow Young's Narrative" in Fragments of Experience: Sixth Book of the Faith-Promoting Series, p. 42; memoirs of George A. Smith, p. 10.

[16]HC 1:353; Kirtland Council Minute Book, p. 12.

[17]Lucy Mack Smith, *History of Joseph Smith*, p. 230.

[18]Autobiography of Truman O. Angell, p. 4.

[19]"Extract from Journal of Elder Heber C. Kimball," *Times and Seasons* 6 (January 15, 1845): 771.

[20]Autobiography of George W. Johnson, p. 2.

[21]*Ohio Observer* (Hudson), August 11, 1836; *Cincinnati Journal and Western Luminary*, August 25, 1836, p. 4.

[22]Orson Pratt in *JD* 14:273.

[23]Brigham Young in *JD* 1:133-35; *HC* 1:400; Journal History, July 23, 1833. According to George A. Smith, the twenty-four elders who participated in the service in which the cornerstones were laid according to the order of the holy priesthood were Joseph Smith, Jr., Hyrum Smith, Joseph Smith, Sr., Newel K. Whitney, Orson Hyde, Frederick G. Williams, John Smith, Sidney Rigdon, Samuel H. Smith, Reynolds Cahoon, Joseph C. Kingsbury, Joel H. Johnson, Don Carlos Smith, William Smith, Gideon Carter, Solomon Humphrey, Edmund Durfee, Harpin Riggs, Sylvester Smith, Joseph Coe, Jared Carter, Jacob Bump, Levi W. Hancock, and David Elliot.

[24]Heber C. Kimball in *JD* 10:165; *HC* 2:161.

[25]Heber C. Kimball in *JD* 10:165-66. See also "Extracts from H. C. Kimball's Journal," *Times and Seasons* 6 (April 15, 1845): 867.

[26]Autobiography of Artemus Millet, p. 1.

[27]*HC* 1:342; D&C 90:28-30.

[28]Autobiography of Nathan Tanner, pp. 25-27.

[29]*HC* 1:349-50. A copy of this letter is located in the Church Archives. See also Oliver Cowdery to John F. Boynton, May 6, 1834, Church Archives.

[30]*HC* 2:24-25.

[31]*HC* 2:34-35, 239, 252, 375.

[32]Oliver Cowdery to John F. Boynton, May 6, 1834, Church Archives.

[33]Phinehas Howe Young, "History," *Millennial Star* 25:390-91.

[34]*HC* 2:44.

[35]*HC* 2:175.

[36]*HC* 2:234, 281, 287-88.

[37]*HC* 1:347; 2:288, 293; D&C 94:13-14.

[38]*The Orson Pratt Journals*, p. 26; *HC* 1:451, 465.

[39]*HC* 2:2. See also "History of the Church," Book B, Agenda, p. 4, Joseph Smith Collection, Church Archives.

[40]*HC* 1:418; 2:169. See also Oliver Cowdery to Ambrose Palmer, October 30, 1833, microfilm copy, Church Archives; *HC* 1:417-19, 465; 2:142, 169-70, 384-85.

[41]The first issue of the *Evening and Morning Star* printed in Kirtland was dated December 1833. In October 1834, the first issue of the *Latter-day Saints' Messenger and Advocate* appeared. The Latter-day Saint press in Kirtland continued to print material for the Church until December 1837, when this printing establishment was "burned to the ground." *HC* 2:528.

[42]*HC* 2:142, 169.

[43]*HC* 2:64. See also chapter 11 in this work.

[44]*HC* 2:167. See also "History of Orson Pratt," *Deseret News*, June 2, 1858.

[45]Autobiography of William Burgess, Jr., pp. 1-2. See also autobiography of William Draper, p. 1, and "Extracts from H. C. Kimball's Journal," *Times and Seasons* 6 (April 15, 1845): 867.

[46]Mrs. Peter S. Hitchcock, "Joseph Smith and the Kirtland Temple," *Historical Society Quarterly, Lake County, Ohio* 7 (November 1965): 3.

[47]Ibid.; Harry Black, *Kirtland Temple*, p. 10. Black walnut, oak, cherry, and white wood were used in the construction of the temple.

[48]*HC* 2:363; Black, *Kirtland Temple*, p. 13; autobiography of Artemus Millet, p. 6. Although tradition says that women gave their china and glassware to the building project so that it could be crushed and mixed with the stucco, there are no known contemporary accounts relating to this sacrifice. "There is no doubt that dishes and glassware were mixed with the stucco, but whether they were old or discarded dishes or the ladies' best is not known." Linda K. Newell and Valeen T. Avery, "Sweet Counsel and Seas of Tribulation," *BYU Studies* 20 (Winter 1980): 155-56.

[49]*HC* 2:363; Hitchcock, "Kirtland Temple," p. 129. The two contracts that were issued for the plastering of the temple are the only known contracts granted to members of the Church for laboring on this temple.

[50]Hitchcock, "Kirtland Temple," p. 3.

[51]*HC* 2:399; Watson, *Manuscript History of Brigham Young*, p. 12.

[52]*HC* 2:399.

[53]Fields, "History of the Kirtland Temple," pp. 26-27. There was no bell in the tower before 1890.

[54]Robert Winter, in "Architecture on the Frontier: The Mormon Experiment," *Pacific Historical Review* 43 (1974): 52, notes that "the practice of mixing Gothic and classical details, as in the Kirtland temple, was not unknown in eastern architecture," for it was seen in buildings in New England, New York, and Pennsylvania. Therefore, the mixture of various types of architectural forms was not what was unique about the architecture of the Kirtland Temple; rather, the distinctive characteristic of this building was the precise nature of the blending.

[55]D&C 94:4-5; 1 Kings, ch. 6.

[56]Black, *Kirtland Temple*, pp. 13-14; Hitchcock, "Kirtland Temple," p. 3. There are thirty-two Gothic and five colonial windows in the temple.

[57]Autobiography of Heber C. Kimball (enlarged version), pp. 33-34, manuscript, Church Archives; Black, *Kirtland Temple*, pp. 15-16.

[58]Autobiography of Heber C. Kimball (enlarged version), p. 33; "Kirtland," *Messenger and Advocate* 3 (1837): 490. The major cost of the building was for the purchase of glass and special tools for cutting and carving wood.

Chapter 10. The Crisis in Missouri

[1]*HC* 1:374-76; *Evening and Morning Star* 2 (December 1833): 114-15.

[2]*HC* 1:374-76.

[3]*Painesville Telegraph*, August 30, 1833, p. 2; *Ohio State Journal* (Columbus), August 24, 1833, p. 3; *Cleveland Herald*, August 31, 1833, p. 3. For additional information on reasons Latter-day Saints were persecuted in Missouri, see Richard L. Bushman, "Mormon Persecutions in Missouri," *BYU Studies* 3 (Autumn 1960): 11-20; Warren A. Jennings, "The Expulsion of the Mormons from Jackson County, Missouri," *Missouri Historical Review* 64 (October 1969): 42; Warren A. Jennings, "Zion Is Fled: The Expulsion of the Mormons from Jackson County, Missouri," pp. 109, 119-37.

[4]*HC* 1:398. These demands were printed in many American newspapers, including

Painesville Telegraph, August 30, 1833, p. 2, and *Cleveland Herald*, August 31, 1833, p. 3.

[5]*Times and Seasons* 1 (December 1839): 18. *Ohio State Journal* (Columbus), August 24, 1833, p. 3, reported that the Mormon leaders were granted two hours to accept the demands of the Missourians, while a memorial prepared by members of the Church and sent to Governor Daniel Dunklin reported that the Mormon leaders were given only fifteen minutes to consider these demands. *Evening and Morning Star* 2 (December 1833): 114-15.

[6]*HC* 1:390-91; *Times and Seasons* 1 (December 1839): 18; autobiography of Edward Partridge, p. 15; *Painesville Telegraph*, August 16, 1833, p. 3.

[7]*HC* 1:399-400; *Evening and Morning Star* 2 (December 1833): 114-15; *Evening and Morning Star* 2 (January 1834): 122-23; *Times and Seasons* 1 (December 1839): 18-19.

[8]*Painesville Telegraph*, August 16, 1833, p. 3.

[9]*Cleveland Herald*, August 24, 1833, p. 3.

[10]*Ohio Argus* (Lebanon), September 6, 1833, p. 3.

[11]*HC* 1:417.

[12]*HC* 1:446; *Evening and Morning Star* 2 (December 1833): 118-19.

[13]Ibid., p. 118.

[14]Ibid., pp. 118-19.

[15]Ibid., pp. 118-19.

[16]Ibid., p. 120.

[17]Lucy Mack Smith, *History of Joseph Smith*, p. 225.

[18]Oliver Cowdery to Elizabeth Cowdery, December 6, 1833, copy of Cowdery Letters, Huntington Library, San Marino, California; microfilm copy in Church Archives.

[19]Joseph Smith to Edward Partridge, W. W. Phelps, and John Whitmer, December 5, 1833, Church Archives, cited in *HC* 1:448-51.

[20]Ibid.

[21]Joseph Smith to the exiled Saints in Missouri, cited in *HC* 1:453-56.

[22]Ibid.

[23]D&C 101:1-2, 6-8.

[24]D&C 101:16-21. See also Heber C. Kimball in *JD* 9:27 and Brigham Young in *JD* 11:324.

[25]Joseph Smith to W. W. Phelps, January 14, 1833, Church Archives, cited in *HC* 1:316-17, and B. H. Roberts, *A Comprehensive History of the Church* 1:315-16.

[26]*HC* 1:426-28; *Evening and Morning Star* 2 (January 1834): 124-25; *Times and Seasons* 1 (December 1839): 18.

[27]*HC* 1:429-31; Pratt, *Autobiography*, pp. 99-100; "Philo Dibble's Narrative," *Early Scenes in Church History*, pp. 83-85.

[28]*HC* 1:433-35; *Evening and Morning Star* 2 (January 1834): 125-26; *Times and Seasons* 1 (January 1840): 33-35.

[29]*HC* 1:436-38; Pratt, *Autobiography*, pp. 102-3; *Times and Seasons* 1 (January 1840): 35; *Evening and Morning Star* 2 (January 1834): 126.

[30]"Philo Dibble's Narrative," in *Early Scenes in Church History*, p. 85.

[31]Pratt, *Autobiography*, p. 103.

[32]*HC* 1:457-58.

[33]*Evening and Morning Star* 2 (January 1834): 126.

³⁴Oliver Cowdery to Samuel Bent, January 7, 1834, Oliver Cowdery Papers, Church Archives.

³⁵Lyman Cowdery letter dated January 13, 1834, Church Archives.

³⁶HC 2:39; Kirtland Council Minute Book, pp. 41-42; Pratt, *Autobiography*, p. 109.

³⁷Peter Crawley and Richard L. Anderson, "The Political and Social Realities of Zion's Camp," *BYU Studies* 14 (Summer 1974): 4, 10-11.

³⁸D&C 101:51, 55-56.

³⁹HC 2:39-40; Kirtland Council Minute Book, pp. 41-42.

Chapter 11. Zion's Camp Marches West

¹D&C 103:21-23, 29-30, 35-40.

²D&C 103:30-34.

³D&C 103:11-15, 20.

⁴Pratt, *Autobiography*, p. 109; *Orson Pratt Journals*, p. 35.

⁵Autobiography of Joseph Holbrook, p. 30.

⁶HC 2:44; Kirtland Council Minute Book, pp. 42-43.

⁷HC 2:44.

⁸Journal of Wilford Woodruff, 1833-1837, April 1834.

⁹HC 2:48-49. Joseph Smith had returned to Kirtland on March 28, 1834.

¹⁰HC 2:50, 52; Kirtland Council Minute Book, pp. 43-47. The Prophet also recorded in his history that about April 1, he received in letters from eastern Saints the sum of $251.60 "towards the deliverance of Zion." HC 2:61.

¹¹Watson, *Manuscript History of Brigham Young*, p. 8. Charles C. Rich later served as an apostle of the Church (1849-83).

¹²Heman C. Smith, ed., *History of the Church* 1:445-46, 462; Lyman Omer Littlefield, *Reminiscences of Latter-day Saints*, p. 29; Journal of the Branch of the Church of Christ in Pontiac, Michigan, 1834, Church Archives.

¹³"Speech delivered by Heber C. Kimball," *Times and Seasons* 6 (July 15, 1845): 972; HC 2:64.

¹⁴Watson, *Manuscript History of Brigham Young*, pp. 7-8; S. Dilworth Young, "Here Is Brigham," pp. 89-91; Tullidge, *Women of Mormondom*, p. 106.

¹⁵Memoirs of George A. Smith, p. 11. For preparations for the journey west, see also Heber C. Kimball, "Journal," *Times and Seasons* 6 (January 15, 1845): 771.

¹⁶HC 2:61; diary of Moses Martin, p. 1; journal of Wilford Woodruff, May 1, 1834.

¹⁷Memoirs of George A. Smith, pp. 10-11.

¹⁸"Incidents of the History of Zion's Camp," *Millennial Star* 26 (December 10, 1864): 793; Memoirs of George A. Smith, p. 21; journal of Wilford Woodruff, May 1, 1834; diary of Moses Martin, p. 1; Wayne Allan Jacobson, "A Prosopographical Study of the Zion's Camp Marchers," pp. 17-18. On February 14, 1835, following the march of Zion's Camp to Missouri, fifty-five of the participants in this journey attended a meeting held in Kirtland, which is another indication that about fifty of the participants were Kirtland Saints. Kirtland Council Minute Book, pp. 147-48.

¹⁹Autobiography of Heber C. Kimball, p. 7; "Autobiography of Wilford Woodruff," *Tullidge's Quarterly Magazine* 1 (October 1883): 3.

[20]Oliver Cowdery and Sidney Rigdon to the "Churches," May 10, 1834, Oliver Cowdery Letters, Church Archives.

[21]HC 2:64; autobiography of Joseph Holbrook, p. 31; autobiography of Joseph Bates
Noble, p. 6; Kimball, "Journal," p. 771. Nathan Baldwin wrote in his journal that
the soldiers of Zion's Camp carried a small white flag with the word "PEACE" en-
scribed on it in large red letters. Autobiography of Nathan Baldwin, p. 12.

[22]Wilburn D. Talbot, "Zion's Camp," pp. 35, 132-36; Times and Seasons 6 (January 1,
1846): 1074; autobiography of Joseph B. Noble, p. 9; Kimball, "Journal," pp. 771,
840; autobiography of Nathan Baldwin, pp. 9, 15.

[23]Autobiography of Joseph Holbrook, p. 31; "Journal of the Branch of the Church of
Christ in Pontiac, Michigan," on its journey to Zion, pp. 1, 8, Church Archives.

[24]HC 2:64-87. In the initial publication of Joseph Smith's history of Zion's Camp in
Times and Seasons (6 [January 1, 1845]: 1074-78), the number leaving New Portage
was estimated at 150. This number has been corrected in the current edition of this
history to 130, which seems to be a more accurate estimate.

[25]Pratt, Autobiography, pp. 114-15.

[26]This estimate is based on the assumption that about 130 men left New Portage.

[27]HC 2:87; journal of Levi Ward Hancock, p. 81; memoirs of George A. Smith, p. 23.
In addition to the 204 men of Zion's Camp listed in the History of the Church (2:183-
85), three other men who participated in this march were Jesse Smith, Lewis Zobriskie, and Gad Yale. Thomas Bullock, an early LDS historian, also identified Horace
Evans and Thomas Turner as participants. Meanwhile, David W. Patten and William D. Pratt had been sent from Kirtland in advance of the army, carrying dispatch-
ers to the Saints in Missouri. See appendix A. For additional information on the
march of Hyrum Smith's division, see Roger Dale Lannius, "Zion's Camp and the
Redemption of Jackson County, Missouri," pp. 104-5, 114-16.

[28]HC 2:87-88. Kimball, "Journal," p. 772.

[29]HC 2:64. See also Kimball, "Journal," p. 771. The description of the march of Zion's
Camp published in Joseph Smith's History of the Church was taken primarily from the
journal of Heber C. Kimball. The historians who compiled that portion of this history, in referring to Joseph Smith, used the first rather than the third person. See
Dean C. Jessee, "The Reliability of Joseph Smith's History," Journal of Mormon History 3 (1976): 34-39; Howard C. Searle, "Authorship of the History of Joseph Smith:
A Review Essay," BYU Studies 21 (Winter 1981): 101-22.

[30]HC 2:73; Pratt, Autobiography, pp. 114-15; journal of Wilford Woodruff, May 1834;
autobiography of Joseph B. Noble, pp. 6-7; Kimball, "Journal," p. 772; journal of
Reuben McBride, p. 3.

[31]Pratt, Autobiography, pp. 114-15.

[32]HC 2:79-80; Times and Seasons 6 (January 1, 1846): 1076; journal of Wilford Woodruff, 1834; journal of Levi Ward Hancock, p. 79; autobiography of Heber C. Kimball, p. 11; Kimball, "Journal," p. 788; memoirs of George A. Smith, p. 20; diary of
Moses Martin, pp. 7-8; journal of Reuben McBride, pp. 3-4.

[33]HC 2:70; diary of Moses Martin, p. 5.

[34]HC 2:69-70.

[35]Memoirs of George A. Smith, p. 25.

[36]Ibid., p. 12.

[37]Ibid., p. 22; diary of Moses Martin, p. 4; journal of Levi Ward Hancock, p. 80.

[38]Memoirs of George A. Smith, p. 20; Kimball, "Journal," p. 788; autobiography of Joseph B. Noble, p. 8; autobiography of Harrison Burgess, pp. 2-3.

[39]HC 2:88-89.

[40]Daniel Dunklin to W. W. Phelps and others, February 4, 1834, cited in HC 1:476-78. See also Daniel Dunklin to W. W. Phelps and others, January 22, 1836, cited in HC 2:178-79.

[41]Pratt, Autobiography, p. 115; HC 2:94.

[42]HC 2:86.

[43]HC 2:94-95.

[44]HC 2:103-4.

[45]Zion's Camp journal of Charles C. Rich, p. 5.

[46]Journal of Wilford Woodruff, 1834, cited in HC 2:104n; autobiography of Nathan Baldwin, p. 12; autobiography of Joseph Holbrook, pp. 33-34; journal of Levi Ward Hancock, p. 81.

[47]HC 2:96-97; The Advocate (Newark, Ohio), July 19, 1834, p. 4.

[48]HC 2:113-14.

[49]D&C 105:2-6, 9.

[50]Autobiography of Nathan Tanner, p. 13; autobiography of William F. Cahoon, p. 43; Kimball, "Journal," p. 804. According to an article published in the Deseret News Weekly, October 19, 1864 (reprinted in Millennial Star 26 [December 10, 1864]: 792-94), two members of Zion's Camp left the Church because of their desire to fight in Jackson County. Very few members of this army immediately apostatized. An examination of the lives of 169 survivors of Zion's Camp (no information was located on 22 individuals, and 12 died of cholera) revealed that 132 died in the faith and 30 apostatized after being active in the Church for several years following their discharge; the dates when 7 others apostatized are unknown. Talbot, "Zion's Camp," pp. 113-14.

[51]HC 2:114-20; Kimball, "Journal," pp. 804, 838-40; journal of Levi Ward Hancock, p. 82; autobiography of Harrison Burgess, p. 3. The men who died of cholera were John S. Carter, Eber Wilcox, Seth Hitchcock, Erastus Rudd, Alfred Fisk, Edward Ives, Noah Johnson, Jesse B. Lawson, Robert McCord, Elial Strong, Jesse Smith, and Warren Ingalls. Evening and Morning Star (Kirtland edition) 2 (July 1834): 351-52; HC 2:120.

[52]HC 2:120: Watson, Manuscript History of Brigham Young, p. 9.

[53]HC 2:122-23; autobiography of Joseph B. Noble, p. 9; journal of Wilford Woodruff, July 1834.

[54]HC 2:135, 139; memoirs of George A. Smith, p. 27.

[55]Memoirs of George A. Smith, p. 29; Painesville Telegraph, July 25, 1834, p. 3.

[56]Chardon Spectator and Geauga Gazette, July 12, 1834, p. 3; Ohio Respository (Canton), July 18, 1834, p. 2; Ohio Atlas and Elyria Advertiser (Elyria), July 17, 1834, p. 2; memoirs of George A. Smith, p. 27.

[57]Painesville Telegraph, July 18, 1834, p. 3.

[58]Painesville Telegraph, August 8, 1834, p. 2; HC 2:144.

[59]Daniel Dunklin to Colonel J. Thornton, June 6, 1834, cited in HC 2:84-87.

[60]HC 2:142-44, 150-60; Kirtland Council Minute Book, pp. 58-72; Messenger and Advocate 1 (October 1834): 10-11.

[61]Talbot, "Zion's Camp," pp. 121-22. See also Orson Pratt in JD 15:360.

[62]Joseph Young, *History of the Organization of the Seventies*, pp. 1-2, cited in HC 2:181n.

[63]Joseph Young, *History of the Seventies*, p. 14, cited in HC 2:182n.

[64]Ibid. See also autobiography of Harrison Burgess, pp. 2-3, and Kimball, "Journal," p. 840.

[65]HC 2:187, 203-4. Of the original apostles, only Thomas B. Marsh, William E. McLellin, and John F. Boynton did not serve in Zion's Camp.

[66]Klaus J. Hansen, *Quest for Empire*, pp. 48-49.

[67]Brigham Young in JD 2:10. See also JD 20:20, 76.

[68]Autobiography of Marshall M. Hubbard.

[69]Autobiography of Joseph B. Noble, p. 9.

[70]Wilford Woodruff in JD 13:158.

Chapter 12. An Attempt to "Unvail" Mormonism

[1]*Painesville Telegraph*, February 7, 1834, p. 3. Most of the ten members of the Kirtland committee who hired Hurlbut to gather derogatory information about the Prophet were large property holders in Kirtland, owning from 45 to 247 acres in 1833 and 1834. See Geauga, Kirtland, Tax Records, 1833. 1834. Solomon Spaulding's name is spelled differently in contemporary records. Sometimes it is spelled Spaulding and other times Spalding. I have employed in this work the spelling most commonly used in later histories and the one employed by his widow, Mrs. Matilda Davison. See Matilda Davison, "The Mormon Bible," *The Family Magazine* 7 (1840): 38-39.

[2]HC 1:352, 354-55; Kirtland Council Minute Book, pp. 21-22; Benjamin F. Johnson, "My Life's Review," p. 19. Sidney Rigdon wrote that Hurlbut was guilty of using obscene language in the presence of a young lady. Sidney Rigdon to editors of the Boston Journal, May 27, 1839, cited in Samuel M. Smucker, ed., *The Religious, Social, and Political History of the Mormons*, pp. 45-47.

[3]HC 2:46-47; Ohio, Geauga County, Court of Common Pleas Records, Book P, pp. 431-32.

[4]HC 1:475; E. D. Howe, *Mormonism Unvailed*, pp. 232-62; Richard Lloyd Anderson, "Joseph Smith's New York Reputation Reappraised," *BYU Studies* 10 (Spring 1970): 286-90.

[5]HC 1:1, 6-7.

[6]Alma 39:5.

[7]Milton V. Backman, Jr., *Joseph Smith's First Vision*, p. 117; Orsamus Turner, *History of the Pioneer Settlement of Phelps and Gorham's Purchase, and Morris' Reserve*, p. 214.

[8]William H. Kelley, "The Hill Cumorah, and the Book of Mormon . . . from late interviews," *Saints' Herald* (Plano, Illinois), June 1, 1881, p. 162.

[9]Charles H. Whittier and Stephen W. Stathis, "The Enigma of Solomon Spalding," *Dialogue* 10 (Autumn 1977): 70-72; Davison, "The Mormon Bible," p. 429. See also Benjamin Johnson, "My Life's Review," pp. 19-20.

[10]Whittier and Stathis, "The Enigma of Solomon Spalding," pp. 71-72.

[11]Solomon Spaulding, manuscript, Oberlin College Archives, Oberlin, Ohio. One of a number of publications of this manuscript is The *"Manuscript Story," of Reverend Sol-*

omon Spalding; or "manuscript found" (Lamoni, Iowa: Reorganized Church of Jesus Christ of Latter Day Saints, 1908).

[12] Whittier and Stathis, "The Enigma of Solomon Spalding," p. 72.

[13] Howe, *Mormonism Unvailed*, pp. 278-81.

[14] Ibid.

[15] Lester E. Bush, Jr., "The Spalding Theory: Then and Now," *Dialogue* 10 (Autumn 1977): 42-44.

[16] Howe, *Mormonism Unvailed*, p. 289.

[17] *Public Discussion of the Issues between the Reorganized Church . . . and the Church of Christ (Disciples)*, p. 82.

[18] Bush, "The Spalding Theory," p. 54; James H. Fairchild, *Manuscript of Solomon Spaulding and the Book of Mormon*, p. 197.

[19] Bush, "The Spalding Theory," p. 42; Howe, *Mormonism Unvailed*, pp. 287-88.

[20] HC 2:269-70; *Messenger and Advocate* 2 (1835): 228; *Elders' Journal* 1 (August 1838): 59-60.

[21] Howe, *Mormonism Unvailed*, pp. 288-90.

[22] Ibid., pp. 102-4, 107.

[23] *Painesville Telegraph*, November 28, 1834, p. 3; *Ohio Repository* (Canton), September 1, 1836, p. 2; *Aurora*, September 24, 1836, p. 4; Bush, "The Spalding Theory," pp. 49-53.

[24] Bush, "The Spalding Theory," pp. 49-53.

[25] Orson Hyde to George J. Adams, June 7, 1841, cited in John E. Page, *The Spaulding Story*, p. 10.

[26] Sidney Rigdon to editors of the Boston Journal, May 27, 1839, cited in Smucker, *History of the Mormons*, pp. 45-47.

[27] Benjamin Winchester, *The Origin of the Spaulding Story*, p. 13.

[28] Fairchild, *Manuscript of Solomon Spaulding*, pp. 193-96. The Spaulding manuscript, which was located in Hawaii, is currently being preserved in the Oberlin College Library, Oberlin, Ohio.

[29] Joseph F. Smith, "The Manuscript Found," *The Improvement Era* 3 (February, March, April 1900): 241-49; 351-57; 377-83.

[30] Bush, "The Spalding Theory," pp. 56-63; Dean C. Jessee, "'Spalding theory' reexamined," *Church News*, August 20, 1977, pp. 4-6.

Chapter 13. Unfolding the Doctrines of the Kingdom

[1] Two distinct teachings of the Book of Mormon relate to the doctrines of the Fall and the Atonement. This scripture tells us how man benefits from the Fall and informs us that as a consequence of the Atonement, all men will be resurrected.

[2] Earl E. Olson, "The Chronology of the Ohio Revelations," *BYU Studies* 11 (Summer 1971): 329-33.

[3] Robert J. Matthews, "The 'New Translation' of the Bible, 1830-1833: Doctrinal Development During the Kirtland Era," *BYU Studies* 11 (Summer 1971): 420.

[4] HC 2:477.

[5]HC 5:402.

[6]Kirtland Council Minute Book, pp. 43-44. Warren Foote wrote that some members left the Church because they could not accept the revelation relating to the three degrees of glory. Journal of Warren Foote, p. 5.

[7]Richard P. Howard, *Restoration Scriptures*, p. 199.

[8]Ibid., pp. 196-97. The Kirtland Revelation Book is preserved in the Church Archives.

[9]HC 2:165; Kirtland Council Minute Book, p. 76.

[10]Melvin J. Petersen, "A Study of the Nature of and the Significance of the Changes in the Revelations as found in a Comparison of the Book of Commandments and Subsequent Editions of the Doctrine and Covenants," pp. 145-49.

[11]Ibid., pp. 152-53.

[12]Howard, *Restoration Scriptures*, p. 201.

[13]*Evening and Morning Star*, Kirtland reprint 1 (January 1835): 16. Italics were not included in the initial publication of this editorial.

[14]D&C 8:2; 9:7-9.

[15]Richard Lloyd Anderson, "By the Gift and Power of God," *Ensign* 7 (September 1977): 83.

[16]D&C 1:24. See also 2 Nephi 31:3; Ether 12:39.

[17]Brigham Young in *JD* 2:314.

[18]Orson Pratt, "Priesthood," *Millennial Star* 19 (April 25, 1857): 260.

[19]HC 2:243-46; Kirtland Council Minute Book, pp. 98-106.

[20]Two sections bore the number LXVI. The last section was numbered XCIX and was dated November 1834, which is section 106 in the current edition of the Doctrine and Covenants. The first section in the appendix is also counted in the 101 revelations; it is now section 133.

[21]HC 2:246n; Kirtland Council Minute Book, p. 106.

[22]James R. Clark, *Story of the Pearl of Great Price*, p. 28.

[23]A printed copy of chapter 24 of Matthew is found in the BYU Library. See Richard Lloyd Anderson, "Joseph Smith's Insights into the Olivet Prophecy," pp. 57-58.

[24]Portions of what is today section 88 of the Doctrine and Covenants were printed in February 1833 in the *Evening and Morning Star*.

[25]For many years, the most frequently cited account of the discovery and movement of the mummies from Egypt to America was an account by Oliver Cowdery that was published in the *Messenger and Advocate* in December 1835. This report, based on what Oliver learned from Michael Chandler, contains a number of factual errors. The most accurate account available today on this aspect of history is Jay Todd's *The Saga of the Book of Abraham* (Salt Lake City: Deseret Book Co., 1969). Since this work was published, additional research by Dr. H. Donl Peterson of Brigham Young University, Dan Jorgensen, former president of the Northern Italian Mission, and others has brought forth additional knowledge concerning Lebolo and Chandler. Many details, however, remain unresolved, especially concerning the transporting of the mummies after they left Egypt and before they arrived in America. A copy of the death notice in Catholic parish records of Castillamonte, Italy, that identifies Lebolo's death date and place is found in Dan Jorgensen, "New Facts on the Life and History of Giovanni Pietra Antonio Lebolo," typescript and photocopies, Church Archives.

[26]Todd, *Saga of the Book of Abraham*, pp. 123-34.

[27]Joseph Coe to Joseph Smith, January 1, 1844, Joseph Smith Collection, Church Ar-

chives. Todd, *Saga of the Book of Abraham*, pp. 160-62; *Painesville Telegraph*, March 27, 1835, p. 3; Jay M. Todd, "The Historical Background of the Book of Abraham," *Pearl of Great Price Symposium*, November 22, 1975, p. 29. See also *Times and Seasons* 3 (May 2, 1842): 774-75.

28Orson Pratt in *JD* 20:65.
29HC 2:235.
30HC 2:236.
31*Ohio Repository* (Canton), March 22, 1838, p. 1, which is a reprint from the *Republican* (Painesville), February 5, 1838.
32Orson Pratt in *JD* 7:176.
33HC 2:238.
34HC 2:286.
35HC 2:289.
36HC 1:318, 320, 334.
37HC 2:520-21.
38Todd, *Saga of the Book of Abraham*, pp. 180-86, 194-211.
39D&C 42:40-42, 54, 74-75, 79, 85-87.
40D&C 59:9-10.
41D&C 42:6, 63; 44:3; 45:64; 52:10.
42D&C 88:78-79; 93:53.
43D&C 42:30-31; 52:40; 56:16; 104:15-16.
44Matthews, *Joseph Smith's Translation of the Bible*, pp. 260-61, 316-17; Matthews, "Doctrinal Development During the Kirtland Era," pp. 409-10.
45*Evening and Morning Star* 1 (October 1832); D&C 68:25-26.
462 Nephi 31:13; Mosiah 18:14; Alma 39:17-19; Jacob 4:4-5; Mosiah 13:33-35; Helaman 8:14-18.
47*Evening and Morning Star* 1 (April 1833); Moses 6:52.
48*Evening and Morning Star* 1 (April 1833); Moses 5:6-7.
49Genesis 14:18-20; Alma 13:18; *Evening and Morning Star* 1 (April 1833). See also Matthews, *Joseph Smith's Translation of the Bible*, pp. 382-84.
50Pratt, *Autobiography*, pp. 297-98.
51Moses 3:5.
52D&C 29:36; Moses 4:1-4.
53D&C 27:11; Oliver Cowdery to John Gilbert, January 1, 1834, Oliver Cowdery Letters, Huntington Library, San Marino, California. A photocopy is in the Church Archives. See also Joseph Fielding Smith, comp., *Teachings of the Prophet Joseph Smith*, p. 157.
54D&C 93:29. See also D&C (1835) 82:5.
55Book of Abraham 3:22-23; *Times and Seasons* 3 (March 15, 1842): 720.
56Ether 13:3-11.
571 Nephi 22:26; D&C 42:35-36.
58Alma 11:43-44; 40:23; Mormon 7:6; 9:13; 10:34.
59Alma 40:11-14.
60D&C 84:2-4; Moses 7:62-63.
61D&C 29:17; 101:25; 133:22-24.
62D&C 87:6. This revelation was recorded in the Kirtland Revelation Book, pp. 32-33. It was preceded by the revelation that is now section 86 of the Doctrine and Covenants and followed by today's section 88. The revelation was circulated in manu-

script form after its recording on Christmas day in 1832 and was initially printed in 1851 in the Pearl of Great Price. See Orson Pratt in JD 18:224; Hyrum M. Smith and Janne M. Sjodahl, *Doctrine and Covenants Commentary*, pp. 538-39.

63HC 1:301.

64William W. Freehling, *Prelude to Civil War*, pp. ix-x, 139-43, 255-59.

65Ibid., pp. 265-95.

66Ibid., pp. 25, 48, 203, 265, 271.

67HC 5:324.

68D&C 87:1-4.

69D&C 87:8. See also 45:32.

70Matthew 13:24-30; D&C 101:64-67.

71D&C 133:19-35; 110-11. Section 133 is known as the Appendix of the Doctrine and Covenants and was recorded on November 3, 1831.

72D&C 77:6-7, 12.

73D&C 133:56; 63:49, 54; 29:11-12.

74D&C 29:12.

75D&C 87:6; 65:5; 38:22; 45:59.

76D&C 63:50-51; 101:29-31.

77Daniel 2:35, 45; 7:27; D&C 65:2; 84:19-22.

78D&C 101:32-34.

79D&C 88:17-20, 110-114; 29:23; 43:31.

80D&C 76:51-70; 88:28.

81D&C 76:71-79; 88:30.

82D&C 76:81-88, 101-105; 19:4-12.

83D&C 76:32-39. See also 29:27-30. For additional information on Joseph Smith's contribution to an understanding of the doctrine of last things, see Bruce R. McConkie, *Mormon Doctrine*; Russell Swensen, "The Influence of the New Testament upon Latter-day Saints Eschatology from 1830-1846"; and Louis G. Reinwand, "An Interpretive Study of Mormon Millennialism During the Nineteenth Century with Emphasis on Millennial Developments in Utah."

84HC 2:380-81; Joseph Smith, Diary (1835-36), pp. 136-37.

85*Messenger and Advocate* 3 (March 1837): 470-71.

86HC 1:334-35; 2:382, 387, 432.

87Joseph Smith, Diary (1835-36), pp. 23-24, cited in Milton V. Backman, Jr., *Joseph Smith's First Vision*, pp. 158-59.

88Backman, *Joseph Smith's First Vision*, pp. 155-57, 160-65. The account of the First Vision that appears in the Pearl of Great Price was initially written by the Prophet in 1838, shortly after Joseph moved from Ohio to Far West, Missouri. HC 3:25.

89D&C 76:22-23; Minutes of the Salt Lake School of the Prophets, October 3, 1883, p. 59, Church Archives; High Priests Records of Spanish Fork, September 1880, September 1881, August 13, 1883, June 3, 1886, June 2, 1887, Church Archives; John Whitmer, "The Book of John Whitmer," ch. 7.

90W. W. Phelps wrote that before he joined the Church, he believed the Father and the Son were "two distinct characters." *Messenger and Advocate* 1 (May 1835): 115. In a sermon delivered on June 16, 1844, Joseph Smith instructed Latter-day Saints that whenever he preached on the subject of Deity, he spoke on the "plurality of Gods." "It had been preached by the Elders for fifteen years," he added. "I have always declared God to be a distinct personage, Jesus Christ a separate and distinct personage

and a Spirit: and these three constitute three distinct personages and three Gods."
HC 6:474.
[91]*Lectures on Faith* 5:2.
[92]D&C 93:33.
[93]D&C 131:7; 130:22.
[94]Truman Coe, "Mormonism," *Ohio Observer* (Hudson), August 11, 1836, pp. 1-2, and
  reprinted in the *Cincinnati Journal and Western Luminary,* August 25, 1836, p. 4.
  Several Latter-day Saints wrote in the 1830s that they rejected the traditional belief
  that God was an immaterial being, without body and parts. See Vinson Knight to his
  mother, June 24, 1835, typescript, BYU; Parley P. Pratt, *Mormonism Unveiled,* p.
  42, reprinted in Parley P. Pratt, *Writings of Parley Parker Pratt,* pp. 232-33.
[95]Matthews, *Joseph Smith's Translation of the Bible,* pp. 309-10.
[96]HC 6:477-78; D&C 76:58-59. See also Van Hale, "The Doctrinal Impact of the King
  Follett Discourse," *BYU Studies* 18 (Winter 1978): 213-14, and Andrew F. Ehat and
  Lyndon W. Cook, comps., *The Words of Joseph Smith,* pp. 378-83.
[97]HC 6:478-79.
[98]D&C 84:38.
[99]D&C 88:107; Hale, "The Doctrinal Impact of the King Follett Discourse," p. 214.
[100]E. R. Snow, *Biography and Family Record of Lorenzo Snow,* p. 10.
[101]LaRoy Sunderland, *Mormonism Exposed and Refuted,* p. 35.
[102]Pratt, *Mormonism Unveiled,* p. 27.
[103]Brigham Young in *JD* 12:158.
[104]D&C 89.
[105]Roy W. Doxey, *The Word of Wisdom Today,* p. 2.
[106]D&C 98:12.

Chapter 14. Church Policies, Programs, and Administration

[1]HC 4:541.
[2]D&C 20:2-3, 38-64; 21:1.
[3]James R. Moss, "The Historical Development of the Church Court System," p. 75.
[4]D&C 42:3; autobiography of Luman Andros Shurtliff, p. 19; LeRoi C. Snow, "How
  Lorenzo Snow Found God," *Improvement Era* 40 (February 1937): 82-84; George A.
  Smith in *JD* 11:7; "Elder Daniel D. McArthur," *Juvenile Instructor* 27 (February 15,
  1892): 128-29.
[5]D&C 41:9-11; 42:30-36.
[6]John Whitmer, "The Book of John Whitmer," p. 28; John Corrill, *A Brief History of
  the Church of Christ of Latter Day Saints,* p. 18; Jenson, *Biographical Encyclopedia*
  1:219-21; 235-36.
[7]D&C 72:8-19.
[8]Diary of Reynolds Cahoon, 1832; HC 2:228.
[9]D&C 58:18.
[10]D&C 84:112.
[11]Kirtland Revelation Book, pp. 84-86. See also D&C 107:68-72, 87-88. This revelation, which was copied in the Kirtland Revelation Book, was later included in the

Revelation on the Priesthood, which is now section 107 of the Doctrine and Covenants, beginning with verse 59 and continuing to verse 100 with the exception of verses 69, 70, 73, 76, 77, 88, 90, and 93-98.

[12]*Far West Record,* p. 3; John Whitmer, "The Book of John Whitmer," pp. 27-28 (chapter VII); HC 1:176n.

[13]D&C 68:19.

[14]D&C 84:111.

[15]D&C 107:1-19.

[16]HC 1:243n. Joseph Fielding Smith taught that the President of the High Priesthood presides over all the priesthood of the Church, and since he holds the keys of that priesthood, he has the authority to regulate it. Jospeh Fielding Smith, *Church History and Modern Revelation* 3:80.

[17]"Duty of Bishops, March 1832," Newel K. Whitney Collection, BYU.

[18]Kirtland Revelation Book, pp. 10-11; D&C, introduction to section 81.

[19]*Far West Record,* p. 32; D. Michael Quinn, "The Evolution of the Presiding Quorums of the LDS Church," *Journal of Mormon History* 1 (1974): 23-24. Frederick G. Williams was serving as a counselor to the Prophet in January 1832. Kirtland Council Minute Book, p. 6.

[20]D&C 81:2. Initially this revelation was addressed to Jesse Gause. Kirtland Revelation Book, pp. 17-18. According to Joseph Fielding Smith, members of the First Presidency have a right to officiate in all the offices of the Church and "hold the keys of all the spiritual blessings of the Church." He further taught that the President of the Church is the presiding officer who presides over the membership of the Church. *Church News,* September 9, 1933, p. 4; Joseph Fielding Smith, *Church History and Modern Revelation* 3:80.

[21]D&C 90:16.

[22]D&C 107:22.

[23]D&C 107:9, 80.

[24]D&C 68:20-22. This information was inserted in section 68 after the First Presidency had been organized.

[25]D&C 107:22; Quinn, "Evolution of the Presiding Quorums," p. 25. See also D&C 124:95 and Glen Mouritsen, "The Office of Associate President of The Church of Jesus Christ of Latter-day Saints," pp. 41-54.

[26]HC 4:190; Quinn, "Evolution of the Presiding Quorums," p. 26; Book of Patriarchal Blessings, September 1835, Church Archives.

[27]HC 3:381.

[28]HC 3:381; D&C 86:8-10; 107:40; 124:91-92; Andrew F. Ehat and Lyndon W. Cook, *The Words of Joseph Smith,* p. 6; Earnest M. Skinner, "Joseph Smith, Sr.: First Patriarch to the Church," pp. 86-89.

[29]D&C 107:40, 41, 57; Skinner, "Joseph Smith, Sr.," pp. 75, 96-103.

[30]Quinn, "Evolution of the Presiding Quorums," p. 26; Earnest M. Skinner, "Joseph Smith, Sr., First Patriarch to the Church," chapter 6.

[31]Edward Stevenson, "Incidents of My Early Days in the Church," *Juvenile Instructor* 29 (September 1, 1894): 551-52.

[32]HC 2:446-47, 467; Journal History, May 10, 1836; Journal of John Smith, 1836. Following the death of Joseph Smith, Sr., in 1840, Hyrum Smith was ordained Patriarch to the Church (on January 24, 1841), followed by William B. Smith (or-

dained on May 24, 1845); after William B. Smith's excommunication, John Smith, brother of Joseph Smith, Sr., was ordained on January 1, 1849.

[33]Isaiah 54:2. See also Isaiah 33:20.

[34]3 Nephi 22:2; Moroni 10:31; Sidney B. Sperry, *Doctrine and Covenants Compendium*, pp. 201-2.

[35]D&C 82:13.

[36]D&C 94:1.

[37]Kirtland Council Minute Book [KCMB], pp. 29-31; HC 2:25. There were at least fifteen members of this first high council: the Presidency of the Church and the twelve high councilors.

[38]KCMB, pp. 29, 32; HC 2:28-31; D&C 102. The twelve high priests who were called to serve on the first high council of the Church were Joseph Smith, Sr., John Smith, Joseph Coe, John Johnson, Martin Harris, John S. Carter, Jared Carter, Oliver Cowdery, Samuel H. Smith, Orson Hyde, Sylvester Smith, and Luke Johnson.

[39]KCMB, pp. 32-35; D&C 102; HC 2:28-29.

[40]HC 2:124; *Far West Record*, pp. 46-47.

[41]KCMB, p. 38.

[42]KCMB, p. 206.

[43]KCMB, pp. 48, 214-17, 245, 248.

[44]KCMB, p. 211.

[45]KCMB, pp. 108-10.

[46]KCMB, p. 207.

[47]KCMB, p. 239.

[48]KCMB, pp. 251-52, 254.

[49]KCMB, pp. 120, 135, 261-64.

[50]KCMB, pp. 239, 261-64.

[51]KCMB, pp. 24-25, 107, 136, 139.

[52]KCMB, p. 108.

[53]KCMB, p. 107.

[54]KCMB, p. 252.

[55]D&C 27:12. See also D&C 20:2-3; 21:1. This title of apostle did not have the same connotation as it does today.

[56]D&C 18:9, 37.

[57]HC 2:187, 195.

[58]KCMB, p. 147; HC 2:181-82.

[59]KCMB, p. 149; HC 2:186-89; "Extracts from Heber C. Kimball's Journal," *Times and Seasons* 6 (April 15, 1845): 868; autobiography of Joseph B. Noble, p. 10.

[60]KCMB, pp. 151-54; HC 2:189-93.

[61]KCMB, pp. 157-58; HC 2:193-94; Wilburn D. Talbot, "The Duties and Responsibilities of the Apostles," pp. 16-17.

[62]KCMB, pp. 158-64; HC 2:189-98; D&C 18:27. See also KCMB, pp. 86-88.

[63]KCMB, pp. 187-88; HC 2:220, 382. The ranking of apostles according to their temporal ages pertained only to the initial organization of the Twelve. Prior to 1844, a combined criterion of chronological age and date of ordination was used for determining the relative positions of the members of the Quorum of the Twelve Apostles. Only when two apostles were set apart on the same day did age determine their seniority. Reed C. Durham, Jr. and Steven H. Heath, *Succession in the Church*, p. 46.

64HC 2:372-74. Under the date of January 16, 1836, Joseph Smith recorded the following information in his diary: "I next proceeded to explain the subject of the duty of the twelve, and their authority, which is next to the present presidency, and that the arrangement of the assembly in this place, on the 15th instant, in placing the high councils of Kirtland next [to] the presidency was because the business to be transacted was business that related to that body in particular which was to fill the several quorums in Kirtland; not because they were first in office, and that the arrangement was [the] most judicious that could be made on the occasion; also the 12 are not subject to any other than the first presidency, viz., myself, S. Rigdon and F. G. Williams." Diary of Joseph Smith, 1835-36, pp. 122-23, cited in HC 2:373-74.

65KCMB, p. 198; HC 2:209-10; D&C 107:1-58; Heber C. Kimball Papers, A Revelation Given at Kirtland (Book 94B), pp. 22-23.

66HC 2:209, 222-26; Talbot, "Duties and Responsibilities of the Apostles," pp. 23-24.

67HC 2:430-32.

68Quinn, "Evolution of the Presiding Quorums," p. 28. During the Nauvoo period, the functions and jurisdiction of the apostles were expanded. The apostles began to regulate affairs within the stakes, for example, served as members of the city countil, were placed in charge of Church publications, and were given the responsibility of preparing for a westward migration. Ibid., pp. 29-30.

69Joseph Young, History of the Organization of the Seventies, p. 2; HC 2:181n.

70HC 2:201-2.

71Messenger and Advocate 2 (January 1836): 253; KCMB, pp. 99, 175-76, 187.

72D&C 107:25-27, 34, 93, 97-99.

73KCMB, pp. 98-99; HC 2:243-44, 388; Quinn, "Evolution of the Presiding Quorums," p. 32n.

74HC 2:393. Minutes of the Seventies, Book A, pp. 6-9, Church Archives.

75Minutes of the Seventies, p. 9; Journal of Wilford Woodruff, December 20, 1836; Dean C. Jessee, "The Kirtland Diary of Wilford Woodruff," BYU Studies 12 (Summer 1972): 375.

76Minutes of the Seventies, p. 18; Joseph Young, History of the Seventies, pp. 4-5. The five high priests who were released as presidents of the First Quorum of Seventy were Hazen Aldrich, Leonard Rich, Zebedee Coltrin, Lyman Sherman, and Sylvester Smith (leaving Joseph Young and Levi Hancock in the council); and the five elders who filled the vacancies in the presidency were James Foster, Josiah Butterfield, John Gaylord, Daniel S. Miles, and Salmon Gee.

77D&C 107:85-88. This revelation also stated that the president of the elders quroum was to preside over ninety-six elders. D&C 107:89.

78Robert L. Marrott, "History and Functions of the Aaronic Priesthood," pp. 25-26.

79HC 2:243, 246; KCMB, pp. 99, 105.

80HC 2:411.

81Journal of Edward Partridge, January 26, March 29, 1836; HC 2:430; George A. Smith in JD 2:214-15; Journal of Wilford Woodruff, April 3-4, 1837; Jessee, "Kirtland Diary of Wilford Woodruff," pp. 387-88.

82Marrott, "History of the Aaronic Priesthood," pp. 19-20. For approximately one hundred years, the word conference had a dual meaning in the Church. It meant a local geographical area outside the organized stakes and also a meeting of the Saints. There was also no distinction in the early history of the Church between local and general conferences. Jay R. Lowe, "A Study of the General Conferences of the Church," pp. 14-15.

[83]Marrott, "History of the Aaronic Priesthood," pp. 34-35; HC 4:393; Messenger and Advocate 3 (January 1837): 446.

[84]Marrott, "History of the Aaronic Priesthood," pp. 32-34; Pratt, Autobiography, p. 42; Times and Seasons 1 (March 1840): 77-78; Elders' Journal 1 (November 1837): 22; Far West Record, p. 152.

[85]Messenger and Advocate 2 (June 1836): 332.

[86]Marrott, "History of the Aaronic Priesthood," p. 36.

[87]D&C 107:78-82; 102:27.

[88]D&C 134:1, 4-5, 7-11; Richard O. Cowan, Doctrine and Covenants: Our Modern Scripture, pp. 204-5.

[89]3 Nephi 27:3-9. Many religious communities in the early republic used the title "Church of Christ." Local Congregational churches, for example, were called the Church of Christ of Middleboro or the Church of Christ of Plymouth. Some of the leaders of the restoration movement of the early nineteenth century also used this title, while the Presbyterians of Geneva, New York, referred to their church as the "Church of Jesus Christ." "Records of the Church of Christ, In the Joining borders of Bridgewater and Middleborough"; Records of the Church of Christ in Geneva, State of New York.

[90]HC 2:62-63; Evening and Morning Star 2 (May 1834): 158-60; KCMB, p. 49.

[91]KCMB, pp. 84, 134, 144, 180, 200; HC 1:483; 2:126, 146, 239, 246; John Smith to Elias Smith, October 19, 1834, copy in Special Collections, University of Utah.

[92]D&C 115:4. When an extract of this revelation identifying the name of the Church was printed in the Elders' Journal, the title appeared as follows: "The Church of Jesus Christ of Latter Day Saints." Elders' Journal 2 (August 1838): 52.

[93]Autobiography of Elizabeth Beswick Tanner, p. 1.

[94]Journal History, May 26, 1835.

[95]Joel H. Johnson, Voice from the Mountains, p. 12.

[96]"The Word of Wisdom," Times and Seasons 3 (June 1, 1842): 800; Brigham Young in JD 13:277.

[97]Minutes of the Salt Lake School of the Prophets, October 11, 1883, Church Archives; Constitution of the Kirtland Camp, Church Archives (see Appendix D).

[98]KCMB, pp. 39-40; HC 2:34-35; Messenger and Advocate 3 (November 1836): 412. The position advocated by Orson Pratt in this controversy is the policy of the Church today.

[99]Messenger and Advocate 3 (November 1836): 412.

[100]Messenger and Advocate 3 (May 1837): 510-11.

[101]HC 2:223-25.

[102]Autobiography of Mary Ann Stearns Winters, p. 3.

[103]Messenger and Advocate 3 (May 1837): 511. Minutes of the Seventies, p. 21, 32.

[104]HC 2:482.

[105]Record of the First Quorum of Elders, October 19, 1837, Research Library and Archives, Reorganized Church of Jesus Christ of Latter Day Saints.

[106]HC 2:522-24; Far West Record, p. 87.

[107]Journal of Wilford Woodruff, December 4, 1836; Jessee, "Kirtland Diary of Wilford Woodruff," p. 373.

[108]*Far West Record,* pp. 139-41; Paul H. Peterson, "An Historical Analysis of the Word of Wisdom," p. 26.

[109]*HC* 2:252.

[110]*HC* 2:218.

[111]*HC* 2:442.

[112]*HC* 3:18-19; *Far West Record,* p. 92; *Des Moines Daily News,* October 16, 1886, cited in Peterson, "Historical Analysis of the Word of Wisdom," p. 20.

[113]Joseph F. Smith, *Eighty-Fourth Semiannual Conference Report,* October 13, 1913, p. 14.

[114]*D&C* 43:16; 66:11; 87:8; 89:18-21; 95:8; 98:1-2, 18, 24; 101:65.

Chapter 15. Life among the Early Saints

[1]"History of the Life of Joseph Smith, Jr.," pp. 1-2, Kirtland Letter Book, Joseph Smith Collection, Church Archives.

[2]Brigham Young in *JD* 13:176.

[3]Orlen Curtis Peterson, "A History of the Schools and Educational Programs of the Church of Jesus Christ of Latter-day Saints in Ohio and Missouri, 1831-1832," p. 3; *Messenger and Advocate* 1 (February 1835): 80.

[4]*D&C* 55:4.

[5]*D&C* 93:36.

[6]*D&C* 93:40, 24.

[7]*D&C* 131:6; Peterson, "History of the Schools in Ohio and Missouri," p. 5.

[8]*Elders' Journal* 1 (August 1838): 53.

[9]Robert E. Chaddock, *Before 1850,* pp. 140, 144-46; W. W. Boyd, "Secondary Education in Ohio Previous to the Year 1840," *Ohio Archaeological and Historical Publications* 25 (1916): 119.

[10]*History of Geauga and Lake Counties, Ohio,* p. 246; Journal of Levi Hancock, pp. 47-48; Benjamin F. Johnson, "My Life's Review," p. 15; Crary, *Reminiscences,* pp. 45-46; Kirtland Township Record Book, March 30, 1834; February 13, 1836.

[11]*D&C* 88:117-41; *HC* 1:316-17. A copy of this letter from Joseph Smith to William W. Phelps is in the Church Archives.

[12]*D&C* 88:118, 79.

[13]*D&C* 88:118.

[14]*D&C* 90:15.

[15]*D&C* 88:70-74, 85.

[16]*HC* 1:322-24; Journal History, February 18, 1833; Minutes, School of the Prophets, October 3, 1883; October 11, 1883, Church Archives.

[17]*D&C* 88:127-41; Minutes, School of the Prophets, 1870-74; October 3, 1883; October 8, 1883.

[18]*HC* 1:323-24.

[19]Minutes, School of the Prophets, November 12, 1870.

[20]Minutes, School of the Prophets, June 3, 1871.

[21]*HC* 1:334.

[22]*HC* 1:316. A copy of this letter is in the Church Archives.

[23]KCMB, p. 17; *HC* 1:334-35; *Times and Seasons* 5 (December 15, 1844): 738; Joseph Smith, History, Book A-1, p. 281, Church Archives.

[24]Minutes, School of the Prophets, October 3, 1883.

[25]Journal of John Murdock, 1833.

[26]Minutes, School of the Prophets, October 3, 1883; October 11, 1883; Brigham Young in *JD* 12:158; journal of Levi Hancock, p. 74; *HC* 1:323.

[27]*HC* 2:169-70, 175-76, 200, 287, 301.

[28]*HC* 2:176, 218, 315, 430-33, 476.

[29]*HC* 2:218; autobiography of William Draper, p. 2.

[30]*HC* 2:169-70. Henry Howe, *Historical Collections of Ohio* (1848), p. 282.

[31]*HC* 2:218.

[32]*HC* 2:376.

[33]*HC* 2:436.

[34]*HC* 2:175-76; Oliver Cowdery to William Frye, December 22, 1835, copy in Church Archives; Peterson, "History of Schools in Ohio and Missouri," p. 35; H. S. Salisbury, "History of Education in the Church of Jesus Christ of Latter Day Saints," *Journal of History* 15 (1922): 264-65.

[35]*HC* 2:176n; *Messenger and Advocate* 1 (May 1835): 122-26.

[36]*HC* 2:200; Johnson, "My Life's Review," p. 16; Journal History, November 14, 1835.

[37]*HC* 2:287, 309, 318, 430-32.

[38]Journal of Lorenzo Barnes, pp. 41-43, 54.

[39]*HC* 2:376.

[40]*HC* 2:299-300, 318-19; Burton E. Levinson, "The Western Reserve: Its Hebrew Influence," pp. 73, 129-30.

[41]*HC* 2:355-56; LeRoi C. Snow, "Who Was Professor Joshua Seixas?," *Improvement Era* 39 (1936): 67-71. See also Louis Zucker, "Joseph Smith as a Student of Hebrew," *Dialogue* 3 (Summer 1968): 41-55.

[42]*HC* 2:356.

[43]*HC* 2:382, 384.

[44]Snow, "Professor Seixas," pp. 69-70.

[45]*HC* 2:385-86, 390-91; H. S. Salisbury, "History of Education in the Church of Jesus Christ of Latter Day Saints," *Journal of History* 15 (1922): 266; journal of Lorenzo Barnes, p. 42 (February 9, 1836); Hyrum Smith to Elias Smith, February 27, 1836, Church Archives.

[46]*HC* 2:396-97.

[47]Autobiography of Caroline Barnes Crosby, 1836.

[48]William W. Phelps papers; *Orson Pratt Journals*, p. 74; *HC* 2:396.

[49]*Messenger and Advocate* 1 (February 1835): 80; Heber C. Kimball, "Journals," 6 (April 15, 1845): 867; *HC* 2:200.

[50]"Our Village," *Messenger and Advocate* 3 (January 1837): 444; autobiography of George A. Smith, pp. 87-88; *HC* 2:474-75.

[51]Johnson, "My Life's Review," p. 16; autobiography of Eliza R. Snow, p. 7.

[52]*HC* 2:317-18, 334, 340.

[53]*HC* 2:356, 407, 409, 412, 474; autobiography of Caroline Barnes Crosby, 1836.

[54]*Orson Pratt Journals*, p. 74.

[55]Journal of Lorenzo Barnes, December 9, 1835.

[56]Autobiography of Eliza R. Snow, p. 7.

[57]D&C 59:9-12.

[58]Autobiography of Zadoc Knapp Judd, p. 5.

[59]High Priest Minutes, Spanish Fork, February 5, 1878, Church Archives; Joseph Smith

to Vienna Jacques, September 4, 1833, Joseph Smith Collection, Church Archives; journal of Levi Ward Hancock, pp. 47-48; memoirs of George A. Smith, pp. 10-11; Lucy Mack Smith, *History of Joseph Smith*, p. 226.

60Autobiography of Nancy Alexander Tracy, 1835; Lucius A. Goldsmith, "Rigdon the First Mormon Elder," Manuscript, Western Reserve Historical Society; autobiography of Truman O. Angell, p. 2.

61Sketch Book of Oliver Cowdery, January 24 and 31, February 7 and 28, and March 6, 1836; journal of Lorenzo Barnes, p. 2; *HC* 2:312, 319.

62*HC* 2:291-92, 299, 304, 312, 322, 330, 345, 363, 399, 408, 480.

63*HC* 2:376.

64*HC* 2:290, 396; autobiography of William Burgess, Jr., p. 1.

65*HC* 2:347. See also *HC* 2:301, 316, 344.

66*HC* 2:346-47.

67*HC* 3:362. See also journal of Samuel H. Rogers, pp. 5-7, and autobiography of Luman Andros Shurtliff, p. 27.

68"History of Brigham Young," *Deseret News*, February 10, 1858, p. 385, reprinted in *Millennial Star* 15 (1863): 439. For additional accounts of this meeting, see Levi Ward Hancock statement, November 1832, Church Archives; and autobiography of Heber C. Kimball, p. 6, manuscript, Church Archives. Elder Kimball wrote that this was the first occasion when Joseph Smith heard someone speaking in tongues. Prior to this meeting, however, this gift had been manifest among members in Columbia, Pennsylvania, and Mendon, New York. This gift was later manifest among the Saints in Missouri in June 1983. John Whitmer, "The Book of John Whitmer," p. 39.

69Benjamin F. Johnson, "My Life's Review," p. 21.

70E. R. Snow, comp., *Biography and Family Record of Lorenzo Snow*, p. 12; Tullidge, *The Women of Mormondom*, pp. 99-101; autobiography of Mary Ann Stearns Winters, p. 3.

71"Our Village," *Messenger and Advocate* 3 (January 1837): 444.

72Ibid.; *HC* 2:399.

73*A Collection of Sacred Hymns for the Church of the Latter Day Saints: Selected by Emma Smith*, p. iii.

74D&C 25:11-12.

75Ibid.; *HC* 1:270, 390; *Evening and Morning Star* 1 (June 1832). Hymns were also printed on the last page of each issue of the *Star* throughout 1832 and from February through July 1833, the latter being the last issue of this monthly publication. Ten of the thirty-three hymns printed in the initial *Evening and Morning Star* are included in the hymnal currently used in the Church. Six of these hymns were written by Church members. William W. Phelps wrote "Redeemer of Israel," "Earth with Her Ten Thousand Flowers," "We're Not Ashamed to Own Our Lord," "Now Let Us Rejoice," and "Awake, O Ye People, the Savior Is Coming." The other hymn written by a Latter-day Saint was Philo Dibble's "The Happy Day Has Rolled On." The four hymns in our present hymnal that were printed in Missouri and were written by non-Latter-day Saints are John Newton's "Glorious Things of Thee Are Spoken," Isaac Watts's "He Died! The Great Redeemer Died" and "Joy to the World," and Robert Robinson's "Guide Us, O Thou Great Jehovah." Newell B. Weight, "The Birth of Mormon Hymnody," *Dialogue* 10 (Spring 1975-76): 41.

76*HC* 2:273. "Gently Raise the Sacred Strain" was one of the hymns by William W.

Phelps that was printed in the June 1835 issue of the *Messenger and Advocate*. The following month the first hymns that included tunes were printed. These hymns were also written by Phelps: "Awake, for the Morning Is Come" (set to "Chinese Chant") and "O God, the Eternal Father" (set to "From Greenland's Icy Mountains"). Weight, "Birth of Mormon Hymnody," p. 42.

[77] For additional information on this hymnal and early Latter-day Saint hymns, see J. Spencer Cornwall, *Stories of Our Mormon Hymns*; N. B. Weight, "An Historical Study of the Origin and Character of Indigenous Hymn Tunes of the Latter-day Saints"; William Leroy Wilkes, Jr., "Borrowed Music in Mormon Hymnals"; Lowell M. Durham, "The Role and History of Music in the Mormon Church"; Lowell M. Durham, "On Mormon Music and Musicians," *Dialogue* 3 (summer 1968): 19-40; William E. Purdy, "Music in Mormon Culture 1830-1876"; and Ruth Alene Symons, "The Song of the Righteous: An Historical and Literary Analysis of the Latter-day Saint Hymnal, 1835-1871."

[78] HC 2:320. See also HC 2:369, 376-78, 398, 408.

[79] HC 2:400, 402, 405, 503; autobiography of Zadoc Knapp Judd, p. 5; autobiography of Mary Ann Stearns Winters, p. 2.

[80] Robert Riegel, *Young America 1830-1840* (Norman: University of Oklahoma Press, 1949), pp. 345, 351-59; KCMB, pp. 251-53, 256-58.

[81] HC 2:345.

[82] Autobiography of Mary Ann Stearns Winters, p. 6. Mary Ann was about six or seven when this incident occurred.

Chapter 16. A Pentecostal Season

[1] HC 2:287, 309, 380-82; William W. Phelps to Sally Phelps, November 14, 1835; Journal History, November 14, 1835; autobiography of Milo Andrus, p. 5; autobiography of Levi Jackman, pp. 8-17.

[2] Orson Pratt in *JD* 18:132.

[3] HC 2:309, 432; diary of Joseph Smith, 1835-36, pp. 34-35, 189, holograph, Joseph Smith Collection, Church Archives.

[4] Oliver Cowdery, Sketch Book, January 16, 1836, Church Archives, reproduced in Leonard J. Arrington, "Oliver Cowdery's Kirtland-Ohio 'Sketch Book,'" *BYU Studies* 12 (Summer 1972): 410-26. See also diary of George Burkett, p. 6.

[5] Cowdery, Sketch Book, January 21, 1836. Cowdery mentioned that John Corrill also attended this meeting. HC 2:379; Joseph Smith diary (1835-36), p. 135. When the Prophet used the term *presidency*, he referred to various individuals who held positions of presidency, including his two counselors in the First Presidency, Sidney Rigdon and Frederick G. Williams, and three other counselors, Oliver Cowdery, Hyrum Smith, and Joseph Smith, Sr. Three other men in Kirtland at that time were also called by the title of president: David Whitmer, president of the high council and the Church in Missouri, and his two counselors, William W. Phelps and John Whitmer. HC 2:124, 126, 176, 219, 239, 283, 364, 366.

[6] Journal of Edward Partridge, January 21, 1836; autobiography of Heber C. Kimball, p. 33.

[7] HC 2:356, 379; diary of Joseph Smith, 1835-36, pp. 135-36.

8HC 2:379-81; diary of Joseph Smith, 1835-36, pp. 135-38.

9HC 2:379-81; diary of Joseph Smith, 1835-36, pp. 135-36; journal of Edward Partridge, January 21, 1836.

10HC 2:380; diary of Joseph Smith, 1835-36, p. 136; journal of Edward Partridge, January 21, 1836.

11HC 2:380-81; D&C 137; diary of Joseph Smith, pp. 137-38.

12HC 2:28, 124, 356-57, 366-67; KCMB, pp. 200-203; journal of Edward Partridge, January 7, 1836.

13HC 2:382; diary of Joseph Smith, 1835-36, p. 139; journal of Edward Partridge, January 21, 1836.

14HC 2:382; diary of Joseph Smith, 1835-36, p. 139.

15Journal of Edward Partridge, January 21, 1836; Cowdery, Sketch Book, January 21, 1836.

16HC 2:382; diary of Joseph Smith, 1835-36, p. 139; journal of Edward Partridge, January 21, 1836.

17HC 2:382-83; diary of Joseph Smith, 1835-36, pp. 140-41; journal of Edward Partridge, January 22, 1836.

18A Record of the First Quorum of Elders Belonging to the Church of Christ in Kirtland, Geauga County, Ohio, 1836-1870, January 25, 28, 1836; Cowdery, Sketch Book, January 25, 1836.

19HC 2:386-87; diary of Joseph Smith, 1835-36, pp. 143-44.

20High Priests Minute Book of Spanish Fork, Utah, April 29, 1866, to December 1, 1898, Church Archives.

21Autobiography of Harrison Burgess, pp. 3-4. See also diary of Stephen Post, January 1836.

22HC 2:387; diary of Joseph Smith, 1835-36, p. 144.

23Autobiography of Heber C. Kimball, p. 35.

24HC 2:391-92; diary of Joseph Smith, 1835-36, pp. 151-52.

25Cowdery, Sketch Book, March 26, 1836.

26HC 2:410. Joseph Smith's account of the dedicatory service as printed in his History of the Church is based on a record he wrote in his diary. See diary of Joseph Smith, 1835-36, pp. 173-85.

27HC 2:411.

28HC 2:410-11, 433; journal of Edward Partridge, March 31, 1836.

29HC 2:412-13.

30HC 2:413-15. An account of the dedicatory service written by Oliver Cowdery was printed in the March 1836 edition of the Messenger and Advocate. Cowdery, Sketch Book, March 27, 1836; Messenger and Advocate 2 (March 1836): 274-81.

31Snow, Eliza R. Snow: An Immortal, p. 59.

32HC 2:416.

33HC 2:417-18; Messenger and Advocate 2 (March 1836): 276-77.

34HC 2:419.

35HC 2:420-26; Messenger and Advocate 2 (March 1836): 277-80. This prayer was initially included in the 1876 edition of the Doctrine and Covenants as section 109 (the same section in the current edition of this work) and included the following introductory statement: "The following Prayer was given by revelation to Joseph Smith, the Seer, and was repeated in the Kirtland Temple at the time of its dedication, March 27th, 1836." See also Orson Pratt in JD 18:132.

³⁶HC 2:426. This hymn was included in Emma's hymnal, published in 1835.

³⁷HC 2:427-28; *Messenger and Advocate* 2 (March 1836): 281; diary of Joseph Smith, 1835-36, pp. 184-85; diary of Stephen Post, March 27, 1836.

³⁸Autobiography of Truman O. Angell, p. 5; Heber C. Kimball in *JD* 9:376; George A. Smith in *JD* 2:10; journal of Edward Partridge, March 27, 1836.

³⁹Autobiography of Heber C. Kimball (enlarged version), p. 66; Heber C. Kimball in *JD* 9:376.

⁴⁰HC 2:427-28; diary of Joseph Smith, 1835-36, p. 185.

⁴¹HC 2:428; *Messenger and Advocate* 2 (March 1836): 281.

⁴²George A. Smith in *JD* 2:215 and 11:10; Cowdery, Sketch Book, March 27, 1836; diary of Stephen Post, March 27, 1836.

⁴³Orson Hyde Elliott, *Reminiscences, in the Life of Orson Hyde Elliott*, p. 44; George A. Smith in *JD* 2:215; autobiography of Aroet L. Hale, p. 4.

⁴⁴Benjamin Brown, *Testimonies for the Truth*; autobiography of A. L. Hale, pp. 4-5; George A. Smith in *JD* 2:215; Cowdery, Sketch Book, March 27, 1836.

⁴⁵Autobiography of William Hyde, p. 7.

⁴⁶Benjamin Brown, *Testimonies for the Truth*, pp. 10-11.

⁴⁷Snow, *Writings*, pp. 58, 62.

⁴⁸Autobiography of Nancy Alexander Tracy, p. 9.

⁴⁹HC 2:308-9.

⁵⁰HC 2:429-30; diary of Joseph Smith, 1835-36, pp. 186-87; journal of Edward Partridge, March 27, 1836.

⁵¹HC 2:430-33; diary of Joseph Smith, 1835-36, pp. 187-90; journal of Edward Partridge, March 30, 1836. George Burkett recorded in his diary (p. 6) that he attended a pentecostal feast in the temple on April 16, 1836, during which he participated in the ordinance of washing of feet. Summarizing his experiences in the Kirtland Temple, he wrote, "Great are the blessings that the Saints enjoy in this place."

⁵²HC 2:434-36; diary of Joseph Smith, 1835-36, pp. 191-93. This is the last entry in Joseph Smith's Kirtland diary of 1835-36.

⁵³HC 4:211; 6:184, 251-52.

⁵⁴Autobiography of Heber C. Kimball (enlarged version), pp. 36-37.

⁵⁵Autobiography of William Draper, p. 2; autobiography of A. L. Hale, April 4-6, 1836. Aroet Hale quotes from the journal of his father, Jonathan H. Hale.

⁵⁶Ebenezer Robinson, "Items of Personal History," *The Return* 1:88-91.

⁵⁷Autobiography of Ira Ames, 1836; autobiography of Luke Johnson, *Millennial Star* 26 (1864): 834-36; *Millennial Star* 27 (1865): 5-7; autobiography of Chapman Duncan, p. 3.

⁵⁸"Minutes of a Conference," *Millennial Star* 26 (January 1864): 51.

⁵⁹Autobiography of Nathan Tanner, 1836.

⁶⁰Autobiography of George A. Smith, p. 82.

⁶¹Pratt, *Autobiography*, p. 130. See also autobiography of Milo Andrus, p. 5.

⁶²Watson, *Manuscript History of Brigham Young*, p. 12; autobiography of Joel Hills Johnson, p. 2.

⁶³Newel Knight, *Scraps of Biography*, p. 94.

⁶⁴E. R. Snow, *Biography and Family Record of Lorenzo Snow*, p. 11. See also B. F. Johnson, "Show Us a Sign," in *Early Scenes in Church History*, p., 11.

⁶⁵Autobiography of Nancy Alexander Tracy, pp. 9-10.

⁶⁶Snow, *Biography and Family Record of Lorenzo Snow*, pp. 12-13; autobiography of Eliza

R. Snow, p. 7; Tullidge, *Women of Mormondom*, pp. 65, 99, 100; Mary Fielding to Mercy R. Thompson, July 8, 1837, typescript, Church Archives.

[67]Tullidge, *Women of Mormondom*, p. 207.

[68]Ibid., pp. 207-8.

[69]Ibid., pp. 208-9.

[70]Journal of Wilford Woodruff, April 2-4, 1837. Portions of this record have been reproduced in Dean C. Jessee, "The Kirtland Diary of Wilford Woodruff," *BYU Studies* 12 (Summer 1972): 365-99.

[71]Jessee, "Kirtland Diary of Wilford Woodruff," pp. 389-91.

[72]Ibid., pp. 391-92.

[73]Ibid., pp. 392-93.

[74]Ibid., p. 396.

[75]Ibid., p. 397.

[76]Daniel Tyler, "Incidents of Experience," *Scraps of Biography*, pp. 32-33.

[77]Benjamin Winchester, "Primitive Mormonism," *Salt Lake Tribune*, September 22, 1889, p. 2. After leaving the Church, Benjamin Winchester claimed that at the time of the dedication of the Kirtland Temple, a number of Latter-day Saints became intoxicated and the dedicatory service "ended in a drunken frolic." Such an accusation conflicts with many other contemporary accounts and is inconsistent with the Latter-day Saint attitude toward intemperance. If such behavior had been manifest, individuals would have undoubtedly recorded the information in their diaries or letters in 1836, but the negative reports emerged long after the events had transpired and among vindictive critics who had become enemies of the Church.

[78]Autobiography of Nancy Alexander Tracy, p. 9.

Chapter 17. Conflict in Kirtland

[1]Watson, *Manuscript History of Brigham Young*, pp. 15-16.

[2]E. R. Snow, comp., *Biography and Family Record of Lorenzo Snow*, pp. 20-21. See also journal of Oliver B. Huntington, pp. 28-29; HC 2:529; 3:1.

[3]A copy of the plan prepared by Joseph Smith for the City of Kirtland is in the Church Archives.

[4]Jessee, "Kirtland Diary of Wilford Woodruff," p. 391. Punctuation has been added for clarity.

[5]Ibid., p. 371.

[6]*Messenger and Advocate* 3 (January 1837): 444.

[7]Geauga, Kirtland, Tax Records, 1836. These estimates of the amount of property the average LDS and non-LDS family owned were determined by estimating the Mormon and the non-Mormon population of Kirtland and then evaluating property holdings of individuals in Kirtland based on property tax records of the mid-1830s. The non-Mormon population was determined by using a formula based on residents (tax payers who paid a personal property tax during the 1830s) who paid land taxes and on personal property tax records in Kirtland. See Hill, Rooker, and Wimmer, *Kirtland Economy Revisited*, pp. 5-14. The estimate of land purchased in the 1830s was sometimes not taxed until one or two years after the purchase had been consummated.

[8]*HC* 2:479-80.

[9]Between the spring of 1836 and early 1838, the taxable land held by members of the Church increased from about 1200 to almost 3,000 acres. Geauga, Kirtland, Tax Records, 1836, 1837, 1838.

[10]Hill, Rooker, and Wimmer, *Kirtland Economy Revisited*, pp. 17, 21-22.

[11]Crary, *Pioneer and Personal Reminiscences*, p. 34; *Messenger and Advocate* 3 (June 1837): 521. See also autobiography of Heber C. Kimball, p. 40. Kirtland was not the only community in Geauga County that was experiencing inflationary conditions in the mid-1830s. In January 1836, contemporary reports estimated that the population of Painesville Township had increased "fifty per cent during the last year"; that the price of city lots in Painesville had increased in a few months from $10 to an estimated $50 to $75 per foot; and that one piece of property increased in value in a few weeks from $10,000 to more than $20,000. *Painesville Telegraph*, January 29, 1836, p. 3. According to Mark Grandstaff, there was not only a relationship in the growth of the LDS population in Kirtland and rising land prices but the increase in the land prices caused some non-Mormons in Kirtland to emigrate. Mark Grandstaff, "The Kirtland Community: 1815-1840," BYU Special Collections, pp. 15-18.

[12]In April 1837, Joseph Smith wrote that the unliquidated debt on the temple was about $13,000. *HC* 2:480.

[13]Hill, Rooker, and Wimmer, *Kirtland Economy Revisited*, pp. 25-29, 40.

[14]Ibid., pp. 41-42.

[15]Ibid., p. 43; Scott H. Partridge, "The Failure of the Kirtland Safety Society," BYU *Studies* 12 (Summer 1972): 443-45; C. C. Huntington, "A History of Banking and Currency in Ohio Before the Civil War," *Ohio Archaeological and Historical Publications* 24 (1915): 348, 355, 375.

[16]Hill, Rooker, and Wimmer, *Kirtland Economy Revisited*, p. 43.

[17]*HC* 2:467-68; Hill, Rooker, and Wimmer, *Kirtland Economy Revisited*, pp. 67, 81-82.

[18]*HC* 2:468.

[19]Ibid.; Huntington, "History of Banking and Currency in Ohio," pp. 372-73, 377. The Bank of Manhattan was organized at Toledo, Ohio, on March 25, 1836.

[20]*HC* 2:470-72; *Messenger and Advocate* 3 (January 1837): 441-43; 3 (July 1837): 535.

[21]Huntington, "History of Banking and Currency in Ohio," pp. 265, 417, 446.

[22]*Messenger and Advocate* 3 (January 1837): 443; D. Paul Sampson and Larry T. Wimmer, "The Kirtland Safety Society: The Stock Ledger Book and the Bank Failure," BYU *Studies* 12 (Summer 1972): 427-36; Hill, Rooker, and Wimmer, *Kirtland Economy Revisited*, pp. 59-61.

[23]Hill, Rooker, and Wimmer, *Kirtland Economy Revisited*, pp. 54-58, 70.

[24]Ibid., p. 44; Cleveland Daily Gazette, January 25, 1837; *Western Reserve Chronicle*, February 7, 1837, p. 3.

[25]J. W. Swan, comp., *Statutes of the State of Ohio*, pp. 136-39; Hill, Rooker, and Wimmer, *Kirtland Economy Revisited*, p. 44.

[26]*HC* 2:487-88, 507-8; Kirtland Safety Society Ledger Book, p. 273.

[27]*Elders' Journal* 1 (August 1838): 58; George A. Smith in *JD* 11:11; autobiography of Nathan Tanner, pp. 23-24; autobiography of Truman O. Angell, p. 4.

[28]Geauga County, Court of Common Pleas Record Book U, pp. 359-64.

[29]Hill, Rooker, and Wimmer, *Kirtland Economy Revisited*, p. 44.

[30]Ibid., p. 66.

[31]Ibid., p. 46; HC 2:487-88; *Conneaut Gazette*, January 27, 1837, p. 2; *Western Reserve Chronicle*, February 7, 1837, p. 3; *Painesville Republican*, January 19, 1837, p. 2; *Messenger and Advocate* 3 (July 1837): 535-36; George A. Smith in *JD* 11:11; autobiography of Heber C. Kimball, p. 40; autobiography of Jonathan Crosby, pp. 14-15.

[32]*Messenger and Advocate* 3 (July 1837): 535-41; *Painesville Republican*, January 19, 1837, p. 2; Geauga County, Court of Common Pleas, Record Book U, pp. 359-64.

[33]HC 2:488; autobiography of Heber C. Kimball, p. 40; Hill, Rooker, and Wimmer, *Kirtland Economy Revisited*, p. 51.

[34]Autobiography of William Draper, p. 2; autobiography of Nathan Tanner, p. 24; autobiography of Oliver B. Huntington, p. 10; Benjamin F. Johnson, "My Life's Review," pp. 15-16.

[35]Hill, Rooker, and Wimmer, *Kirtland Economy Revisited*, p. 65.

[36]Ibid., pp. 25-29, 69.

[37]Ibid., pp. 29-40, 68-69. Once the Saints began selling large sections of land in Kirtland as they prepared to migrate west, the value of the land decreased sharply. When the Prophet was forced to flee from Kirtland in January 1838, an angry mob in pursuit, he left behind many disgruntled creditors. He recognized his obligation to pay his debts, and after he moved west, he called Oliver Granger to travel to Ohio to locate individuals who had loaned him money and to pay them. As late as 1843, with the help of other members of the Church, he was still trying to pay debts incurred while he lived in Kirtland. *HC* 3:164-65. See also "Recommendatory Letters," October 19, October 26, October 27, 1838, Joseph Smith Collection, Church Archives; Journal History, May 4, 1838.

[38]Huntington, "History of Banking and Currency in Ohio," pp. 385-90; Hill, Rooker, and Wimmer, *Kirtland Economy Revisited*, pp. 51-53. The Bank of Canton closed its doors on April 13, 1838.

[39]Brigham Young in *JD* 1:215.

[40]HC 2:502.

[41]*Painesville Telegraph*, June 30, 1837, p. 3; journal of Joseph Fielding, p. 12.

[42]HC 2:502; Journal History, July 27, 1837; Watson, *Manuscript History of Brigham Young*, pp. 20-21.

[43]Mary Fielding to Mercy R. Thompson, 1837, typescript, Mary Fielding Papers, Church Archives.

[44]Hill, Rooker, and Wimmer, *Kirtland Economy Revisited*, p. 29.

[45]Snow, *Biography and Family Record of Lorenzo Snow*, p. 20.

[46]Jessee, "Kirtland Diary of Wilford Woodruff," p. 382.

[47]Autobiography of Heber C. Kimball, p. 40, cited in *Woman's Exponent* 9 (May 1, 1881): 178.

[48]*Messenger and Advocate* 3 (May 1837): 505-10.

[49]2:487; Watson, *Manuscript History of Brigham Young*, p. 15; autobiography of Aroet L. Hale, pp. 4-5; Ebenezer Robinson, "Items of Personal History," *The Return*; p. 19; autobiography of Heber C. Kimball, p. 39. For additional information on LDS speculation in land sales in the 1830s, see Parkin, "Conflict at Kirtland," pp. 284-86.

[50]Autobiography of Ira Ames, 1837.

[51]Pratt, *Autobiography*, p. 168.

[52]Jessee, "Kirtland Diary of Wilford Woodruff," p. 385.

[53]HC 2:487-88.

[54]*Painesville Republican*, February 9, 1837, p. 2; Kirtland Council Minute Book, p. 236; HC 2:487-88.

[55]KCMB, p. 236; HC 2:510.

[56]HC 2:493; Parkin, "Conflict at Kirtland," p. 312.

[57]"Life Incidents," *Woman's Exponent* 9 (May 15, 1881): 186.

[58]*Elders' Journal* 1 (August 1838): 50. See also Parkin, "Conflict at Kirtland," pp. 287-89.

[59]George A. Smith in JD 7:115. See also *Elders' Journal* 1 (August 1838): 57.

[60]Benjamin F. Johnson, "Letter to George A. Gibbs," p. 8. See also Oliver Cowdery to Warren Cowdery, January 21, 1838, Huntington Library, San Marino, California, microfilm copies at Church Archives and BYU; Danel W. Bachman, "A Study of the Mormon Practice of Plural Marriage Before the Death of Joseph Smith," pp. 82-83; and John Whitmer, "The Book of John Whitmer," p. 86.

[61]Johnson, "Letter to George A. Gibbs," pp. 8-10.

[62]George Q. Cannon, "History of the Church," *Juvenile Instructor* 16 (September 15, 1881): 206. See also Joseph F. Smith in JD 20:29.

[63]Johnson, "Letters to George A. Gibbs," p. 8.

[64]HC 2:509-11; KCMB, pp. 234-37; Watson, *Manuscript History of Brigham Young*, p. 23; Journal History, September 3-4, 1837.

[65]HC 2:512; KCMB, p. 240; *Elders' Journal* 1 (July 1838): 36.

[66]HC 2:528; *Elders' Journal* 1 (July 1838): 36-38; George A. Smith in JD 7:115; Snow, *Biography and Family Record of Lorenzo Snow*, pp. 20-21; autobiography of Caroline Barnes Crosby, 1837; Thomas Marsh to Wilford Woodruff, April 30, 1838, Wilford Woodruff papers, Church Archives.

[67]Quinn, "Organizational Development and Social Origins of the Mormon Hierarchy, 1832-1932," pp. 248-91. This estimate of the number who left the Church in 1837 and 1838 is based on reports of persons who united with apostate groups and records that reveal excommunications of members during that period. Approximately 87 percent of the Kirtland Saints have been identified on Missouri, Nauvoo, Iowa, or Utah records, and almost one hundred persons remained in Kirtland.

[68]After arriving in Far West, Missouri, in March 1838, Joseph Smith learned that members had held a court and had released the Far West Presidency, consisting of David Whitmer, William W. Phelps, and John Whitmer, from their positions and excommunicated the latter two leaders. One month later, David Whitmer and Oliver Cowdery were excommunicated. According to Parkin, Whitmer's and Cowdery's problems were caused in part by a union with dissidents in Kirtland; and although the men were not excommunicated until after they had moved to Missouri, the roots of their difficulties stem back to problems that had occurred while they were living in Kirtland. Parkin, "Conflict at Kirtland," p. 318n; journal of Joseph Fielding, p. 13. A biographical profile of the General Authorities, including the dates of their callings and excommunications or disfellowshipment when applicable, is in Quinn, "Organizational Development annd Social Origins of the Mormon Hierarchy 1832-1932," pp. 248-91. See also Benjamin Johnson, "My Life's Review," pp. 23-24, and Ebenezer Robinson, "Items of Personal History," p. 29.

[69]Among the leaders cited in the text who returned and died in full fellowship in the Church were Oliver Cowdery, Frederick G. Williams, Martin Harris, Luke S. Johnson, John Gould, and Salmon Gee. John Gaylord also returned but later joined the Reorganized Church of Jesus Christ of Latter Day Saints.

⁷⁰Autobiography of Oliver B. Huntington, p. 15.

⁷¹Watson, *Manuscript History of Brigham Young*, pp. 23-24.

⁷²Ibid., pp. 23-24; Parley P. Pratt in *JD* 1:85.

⁷³Memoirs of George A. Smith, pp. 10, 28-29, 47; Lucy Mack Smith, *History of Joseph Smith*, p. 231. See also chapter 18.

⁷⁴Heber C. Kimball in *JD* 9:374; *HC* 2:2; Benjamin F. Johnson, "My Life's Review," p. 19; memoirs of George A. Smith, p. 10; journal of Levi Ward Hancock, p. 77; Oliver Cowdery to W. W. Phelps, January 21, 1834, photocopy, Church Archives.

⁷⁵Joseph Smith to Edward Partridge, W. W. Phelps, and John Whitmer, December 5, 1833, Joseph Smith Collection, Church Archives, and cited in *HC* 1:448-51. See also *HC* 3:1.

⁷⁶Backman, *American Religions*, pp. 168-69. For additional information on intolerance in colonial America and the birth of religious liberty in this country, see chapter 4 in that work.

⁷⁷Alexis de Tocqueville, *Democracy in America*, p. 202.

⁷⁸Robert Boyd, *Personal Memoirs: Together with a Discussion Upon the Hardships and Sufferings of Itinerant Life* (Cincinnati, 1868), pp. 184-85, cited in William Warren Sweet, *Religion in the Development of American Culture*, p. 136.

⁷⁹Robert Price, "The Ohio Anti-slavery Convention of 1836," *Ohio State Archaeological and Historical Quarterly* 45 (1936): 185; Gilbert H. Barnes and Dwight L. Dumond, eds., *Letters of Theodore Dwight Weld, Angelina Grimke Weld and Sarah Grimke, 1822-1844* 1:236-38, 261-61; Benjamin F. Thomas, *Theodore Weld*, p. 174.

⁸⁰Thomas, *Theodore Weld*, p. 107; Henry Howe, *Historical Collections of Ohio* 2:80-81.

⁸¹Russel B. Nye, "Marius Robinson, A Forgotten Abolitionist Leader," *Ohio State Archaeological and Historical Quarterly* 55 (1946): 147.

⁸²An excellent account of a non-Mormon view of Latter-day Saint beliefs in the mid-1830s was written by Truman Coe and published in the *Cincinnati Journal and Western Luminary*, August 25, 1836, p. 3. For additional information, see the author's collection of articles on Mormonism in Ohio newspapers during the 1830s, Church Historical Library and Brigham Young University.

⁸³Oliver Cowdery to John A. Bryan, October 15, 1835; *Northern Times*, October 9, 1835; August 7, 1835. In 1836, 396 people in Kirtland Township voted for Van Buren (Democratic candidate) and only 116 for Harrison (Whig), while in Geauga County 1,487 voted for Van Buren and 3,274 for Harrison. After the Mormons emigrated, the political pattern in Kirtland shifted, with only 103 voting for Van Buren in 1840 and 191 for Harrison (with Harrison also winning in Lake County, the country where Kirtland was located in 1840). *Painesville Telegraph*, November 24, 1836, and November 19, 1840.

⁸⁴Max H. Parkin, "Mormon Political Involvement in Ohio," *BYU Studies* 9 (Summer 1969): 487; *Messenger and Advocate* 3 (July 1837): 537-38.

⁸⁵*Painesville Telegraph*, February 20, 1835, p. 3. *Northern Times* continued to be circulated almost weekly for at least one year. Parkin, "Conflict at Kirtland," pp. 187-88.

⁸⁶Kirtland Township Record Book 1:137, 151; Parkin, "Mormon Political Involvement in Ohio," p. 492.

⁸⁷*Painesville Telegraph*, April 17, 1835, p. 3.

⁸⁸Parkin, "Conflict at Kirtland," pp. 174-77; *Messenger and Advocate* 3 (April 1837): 496. See also Danel W. Bachman, "New Light on an Old Hypothesis: the Ohio Ori-

gins of the Revelation on Eternal Marriage," *Journal of Mormon History* 5 (1978): 29-31.

[89]"An Account 'About the Mormons,'" B. C. Fowles Papers, Western Reserve Historical Society; *Messenger and Advocate* 2 (July 1836): 349; 3 (January 1837): 443; *HC* 2:468-69.

[90]Journal History, December 18, 1835.

[91]Autobiography of Jonathan Crosby, pp. 15-16.

[92]*Messenger and Advocate* 2 (July 1836): 349.

[93]*Messenger and Advocate* 3 (January 1837): 443. See also *HC* 2:468-69.

[94]Swan, *Statutes of the State of Ohio*, pp. 634-36; Kirtland Township Record Book, October 1833; memoirs of George A. Smith, p. 28.

[95]*Painesville Telegraph*, January 31, 1834, p. 3.

[96]Memoirs of George A. Smith, pp. 28-29.

Chapter 18. The Exodus from Kirtland

[1]Watson, *Manuscript History of Brigham Young*, pp. 23-24; S. Dilworth Young, *"Here Is Brigham,"* pp. 178-79.

[2]*HC* 3:1; Hepzibah (Hepsy) Richards to Willard Richards, January 22, 1838, typescript, Richards Family Papers, Church Archives. Hepzibah wrote that Joseph and Sidney left Kirtland on Saturday night, January 14. According to Zera Pulsipher, Joseph was placed in a box that was nailed on an ox-cart and was driven out of town "to save his life." Autobiography of Zera Pulsipher, pp. 7-8.

[3]Lucy Mack Smith, *History of Joseph Smith*, p. 247.

[4]Snow, *Biography and Family Record of Lorenzo Snow*, p. 22. See also autobiography of Caroline Barnes Crosby, 1838; autobiography of Daniel Wood, pp. 6-7; journal of John Lyman Smith, p. 1. John Lyman Smith wrote that the people persecuted Joseph Smith and his followers "so much that they were compelled" to flee from Ohio. See also autobiography of Julian Moses, p. 16.

[5]*HC* 3:1.

[6]Luke S. Johnson, "History of Luke Johnson," *Millennial Star* 27 (January 7, 1865): 5-6.

[7]*HC* 3:2-3.

[8]*HC* 3:2; Watson, *Manuscript History of Brigham Young*, pp. 24-25.

[9]*HC* 3:3, 8-9. Because of his wife's illness, Sidney Rigdon remained temporarily at Dublin and followed the Prophet's group to Far West, arriving there on April 4. F. Mark McKiernan, *The Voice of One Crying in the Wilderness*, p. 82.

[10]Luke S. Johnson, "History of Luke Johnson," pp. 5-6; Snow, *Biography and Family Record of Lorenzo Snow*, pp. 22-23.

[11]Snow, *Biography and Family Record of Lorenzo Snow*, pp. 23-24; Lucy Mack Smith, *History of Joseph Smith*, pp. 248-49; autobiography of Oliver B. Huntington, p. 15.

[12]Lucy Mack Smith, *History of Joseph Smith*, pp. 249, 252-53; *HC* 3:43.

[13]Hepzibah Richards to Willard Richards, January 18, 1838; Manuscript History of the Great Lakes Mission–Ohio, January 18, 1838, Church Archives.

[14]Hepzibah Richards to Willard Richards, January 22, 1838; Hepzibah Richards to friends, January 28, 1838.

[15]Hepzibah Richards to friends, February 19, 1838.

[16]Hepzibah Richards to friends, March 23, 1838.

[17]Autobiography of Zadoc Knapp Judd, p. 7.

[18]Nathan B. Cheney, life sketch, p. 2; Sadie Foss Elliott, "Life Sketch of Nathan Calhoun Cheney and Eliza Ann Beebe Cheney."

[19]Autobiography of Daniel Wood, pp. 6-7.

[20]Autobiography of Luman Andros Shurtliff, p. 30.

[21]Hepzibah Richards to friends, March 23, 1838.

[22]Autobiography of Luman Andros Shurtliff, pp. 30-31; Hepzibah to friends, March 23, 1838.

[23]Manuscript History of the Great Lakes Mission—Ohio, January 17, 1838, Church Archives; autobiography of Caroline Barnes Crosby, 1838.

[24]Benjamin F. Johnson wrote that one of the Kirtland Saints, Lyman R. Sherman, set fire to the printing office to thwart the plans of Joseph's enemies. Benjamin F. Johnson, "My Life's Review," p. 24. Other Latter-day Saints, however, accused their enemies of destroying the building. Journal of Jonathan H. Hale, Book 2, p. 10; *Elders' Journal* (July 1838): 34.

[25]Hepzibah Richards to Willard Richards, January 18, 1838.

[26]*Painesville Telegraph*, May 31, 1838, pp. 2-3. Zera Pulsipher wrote that although mobbers claimed that the seventies set fire to the Methodist church, "we knew we were innocent" of this charge. He added that there was no doubt in his mind that their enemies were thus trying to destroy them. Autobiography of Zera Pulsipher, pp. 9-10.

[27]Crary, *Pioneer and Personal Reminiscences*, p. 35.

[28]Journal of William Huntington, pp. 3-4. Huntington reported that he arrived in Far West after traveling more than eight weeks, but that his tools were never delivered.

[29]Autobiography of Nathan Tanner, pp. 25-27; autobiography of Elizabeth Beswick Tanner, p. 2; Leonard J. Arrington, "The John Tanner Family," *Ensign* 9 (March 1979): 46-47.

[30]Autobiography of Luman Andros Shurtliff, pp. 31-32.

[31]Some of the best accounts of the journey of the Saints to Missouri in 1838 are found in the following works: autobiography of Anson Call, pp. 3-5; journal of John Smith, April 5, 1838, to June 16, 1838; Lucy Mack Smith, *History of Joseph Smith*, pp. 251-53; Snow, *Biography and Family Record of Lorenzo Snow*, pp. 24-25; HC 3:1-3, 8, 43, 100-148; diary of Samuel D. Tyler, pp. 1-56; and autobiography of Luman Andros Shurtliff, pp. 31-32.

[32]HC 3:87-98; Gordon Orville Hill, "A History of Kirtland Camp," pp. 10-16; autobiography of Zera Pulsipher, p. 8.

[33]HC 3:87-89.

[34]HC 3:89-91.

[35]Autobiography of Zera Pulsipher, p. 8.

[36]Autobiography of John Pulsipher, p. 2. See also autobiography of George W. Johnson, p. 2, and autobiography of Luman Andros Shurtliff, p. 31.

[37]HC 3:94-95.

[38]HC 3:90-91.

[39]Hepzibah Richards to friends, March 23, 1838; Hill, "A History of Kirtland Camp," p. 16.

[40]The names of the persons and the number of persons in their respective families who subscribed to the constitution of Kirtland Camp are in HC 3:91-93. Only about 33

percent of those who signed the constitution paid taxes in Kirtland during the 1830s, indicating that many of these members were among the poorest Saints. See also the journal of George Johnson, p. 2; autobiography of John Pulsipher, p. 2.

[41]Parkin, "Conflict at Kirtland," p. 330; autobiography of Zera Pulsipher, p. 9.

[42]Hill, "A History of Kirtland Camp," p. 22; HC 3:98-100; autobiography of John Pulsipher, p. 4; journal of Jonathan H. Hale, p. 11. Estimates of the number in this company who left Kirtland on July 6 or shortly thereafter vary slightly but not significantly. The two best accounts of the journey of Kirtland Camp are the diary of Samuel D. Tyler and the record kept by the camp historian, Elias Smith, which has been published in volume 3 of Joseph Smith, History of the Church.

[43]Autobiography of John Pulsipher, p. 4.

[44]Autobiography of Charles Pulsipher, p. 69.

[45]HC 3:100.

[46]Autobiography of Jeremiah Willey, p. 13. The spelling in this quotation has been corrected. See also autobiography of Caroline Barnes Crosby, 1838.

[47]Journal of William F. Cahoon, cited in Stella Cahoon Shurtleff and Brent Farrington Cahoon, Reynolds Cahoon and His Stalwart Sons, p. 28.

[48]HC 3:103-5; diary of Samuel Tyler, pp. 1, 10; Hill, "History of Kirtland Camp," pp. 26, 88.

[49]HC 3:100-116. The men who probably participated in both the march of Zion's Camp and the journey of Kirtland Camp were Nathan Baldwin, George Brooks, John Carter, John Folger, Sherman Gilbert, Michael Griffith, Joseph B. Noble, John Parker, William B. Pratt, and Joseph Young.

[50]HC 3:89-90; Jenson, Biographical Encyclopedia 1:187, 192-94, 719-21.

[51]HC 3:102-3; diary of Samuel Tyler, pp. 19, 27; autobiography of Aroet L. Hale, 1838, p. 9; autobiography of John Pulsipher, p. 4.

[52]HC 3:114.

[53]Diary of Samuel Tyler, pp. 6-7; HC 3:101, 107-8, 112, 116-17, 123, 125-26, 129, 131.

[54]HC 3:113; diary of Samuel Tyler, p. 13; Early Scenes in Church History, pp. 73-74; autobiography of Aroet L. Hale, pp. 11-12.

[55]Diary of Samuel Tyler, pp. 14, 21-23. See also pages 26 and 28 for references of healing among participants of Kirtland Camp.

[56]Autobiography of Jeremiah Willey, pp. 13-14. For references to those who died while journeying with Kirtland Camp, see Hill, "History of Kirtland Camp," pp. 33, 75, 76, 81, 89, 93, 94, 96-100, 107, 111.

[57]HC 3:106.

[58]HC 3:108-9; diary of Samuel Tyler, pp. 7-8; autobiography of Aroet L. Hale, 1838, p. 11; journal of Jonathan H. Hale, book 2, p. 15.

[59]Diary of Samuel Tyler, p. 16. For additional references to the non-Mormon response to Kirtland Camp, see Clermont Courier (Batavia, Ohio), June 15, 1868, p. 2; Ohio Repository (Canton), July 18, 1838; Herald and Gazette (Cleveland), July 25, 1838, p. 2; and Western Citizen and Urbana Gazette, July 31, 1838, p. 3.

[60]Diary of Samuel Tyler, pp. 11, 19, 23, 43.

[61]Ibid., pp. 18-19. See also HC 3:119-32.

[62]Diary of Samuel Tyler, p. 19.

[63]Autobiography of Zera Pulsipher, pp. 10-11; HC 3:131-32.

[64]HC 3:132-41; diary of Samuel Tyler, pp. 30-45.

[65]HC 3:103, 137-46; diary of Samuel Tyler, p. 40.

66*HC* 3:137-38; diary of Samuel Tyler, p. 39.

67*HC* 3:139-40; autobiography of Joel Hills Johnson, p. 19.

68Diary of Samuel Tyler, p. 42.

69Hill, "History of Kirtland Camp," pp. 113-14.

70Diary of Samuel Tyler, p. 46.

71Ibid., pp. 48-49; *HC* 3:143.

72Diary of Samuel Tyler, p. 50; *HC* 3:144-45.

73Diary of Samuel Tyler, p. 55; *HC* 3:147.

74Diary of Samuel Tyler, p. 56.

75*HC* 3:175.

76*HC* 3:323-25. Amanda Smith, wife of Warren Smith, whose description of the massacre at Haun's Mill was published in Joseph Smith's *History*, left Kirtland Camp with her family on September 18, 1838. Hill, "History of Kirtland Camp," pp. 113-14.

77Autobiography of Oliver B. Huntington, p. 12.

78George Q. Cannon in *JD* 23:362.

Chapter 19. The Aftermath

1D&C 117:1. See also Gordon Orville Hill, "History of Kirtland Camp," pp. 25-26, and Davis Bitton, "The Waning of Mormon Kirtland," *BYU Studies* 12 (Summer 1972): 455.

2Jenson, *Biographical Encyclopedia* 1:226, 283.

3Watson, *Manuscript History of Brigham Young*, pp. 57-58. See also journal of Theodore Turley, November 1839.

4Journal History, April 27, 1840.

5*HC* 4:204-5, 225-26; *Times and Seasons* 2 (July 1, 1841): 458-60.

6*Times and Seasons* 2 (July 1, 1841): 458-60. According to the minutes of this conference, the following branches comprised Kirtland Stake: Kirtland, Brownhelm, Charleston, Nelson, Madison, Harrisonville, Brooklyn, Grafton, Gustavus, and Andover. Some of the leaders of this stake, such as Zebedee Coltrin and Almon W. Babbitt, returned to Kirtland after migrating to Missouri and Illinois; others, such as Hiram Kellogg and Salmon Gee, continued to live in Kirtland after most of the Saints had left in 1838. Jenson, *Biographical Encyclopedia* 1:190, 192-93, 284-85.

7Journal History, October 19, 1841.

8Journal History, October 28, 1842; October 29, 1842; October 31, 1842.

9D&C 124:83.

10*HC* 4:443-44; *Times and Seasons* 3 (November 15, 1841): 589. See also Artel Ricks, "Hyrum's Prophecy," *Improvement Era* 59 (May 1956): 305ff.

11*Times and Seasons* 4 (August 1, 1842): 282-84.

12Brigham Young to the "Brethren" (Kirtland Saints), January 21, 1845, photocopy, Church Archives. In October 1845, Brigham Young received a letter from Reuben McBride informing him that "apostates were doing everything they could to injure the Saints," that they had broken into the Lord's House and "taken possession of it," and that they were "trying to take possession of the Church farm." *HC* 7:484.

13*Times and Seasons* 6 (April 15, 1845): 871-72.

14*Deseret News*, December 13, 1851. The letter was dated August 7, 1851. Elder Bay also wrote that there were "quite a number of scattered Saints in Ohio, and most of them are willing to gather." In 1846, Henry Howe, a non-Mormon writer, visited Kirtland and wrote that after the Mormons left, "most of the dwellings went to decay, and it now has somewhat the appearance of a depopulated and broken down place." Howe, *Historical Collections of Ohio (1847)*, p. 282. See also Bitton, "The Waning of Mormon Kirtland," pp. 459-63.

[15] HC 7:484; Fields, "History of the Kirtland Temple," p. 93; *History of Geauga and Lake Counties*, pp. 39-40; Howe, *Historical Collections of Ohio*, p. 282. In 1847 apostates held several conferences in the temple. See *The Ensign of Liberty of the Church of Christ* 1 (1847): 1, 14.

[16] Ricks, "Hyrum's Prophecy," p. 340; Richard W. Young, "In the Wake of the Church," *Contributor* 4 (December 1882): 106-8.

[17] According to Paul E. Reimann, the Reorganized Church of Jesus Christ of Latter Day Saints secured title to the property through adverse possession. See Paul E. Reimann, *The Reorganized Church and the Civil Courts*, and Clarence L. Fields, "History of the Kirtland Temple," pp. 89-101.

[18] Ricks, "Hyrum's Prophecy," p. 340.

[19] Richard W. Young, "In the Wake of the Church," p. 108.

[20] Autobiography of Jesse Wentworth Crosby, pp. 5-6.

Bibliography

Reference and Bibliographical Guides

A Catalogue of Theses and Dissertations Concerning The Church of Jesus Christ of Latter-day Saints, Mormonism and Utah. Provo: Brigham Young University Printing Services, 1971.

Andrus, Hyrum L., and Richard E. Bennett, eds. *Mormon Manuscripts to 1846: A Guide to the Holdings of the Harold B. Lee Library.* Provo: Harold B. Lee Library, Brigham Young University, 1977.

Backman, Milton V., Jr., comp. "Contemporary Accounts of the Latter-day Saints and Their Leaders Appearing in Early Ohio Newspapers." 3 vols. Photocopy, Brigham Young University, and Church Historical Library.

Backman, Milton V., Jr., Susan Easton, and Keith Perkins, comps. *A Profile of Latter-day Saints of Kirtland, Ohio, and Members of Zion's Camp, 1830–1839.* Provo: Religious Studies Center, Brigham Young University, 1983.

Bitton, Davis. *Guide to Mormon Diaries and Autobiographies.* Provo: Brigham Young University Press, 1977.

Gutgesell, Stephen. *Guide to Ohio Newspapers, 1793–1973: Union Bibliography of Ohio Newspapers Available in Ohio Libraries.* Columbus: Ohio Historical Society, 1976.

Flake, Chad J. *A Mormon Bibliography: 1830–1930.* Salt Lake City: University of Utah Press, 1978.

Jenson, Andrew. *Latter-day Saint Biographical Encyclopedia.* 4 vols. Salt Lake City: Andrew Jenson History Co., 1901.

Johnson, Jeffery O. *Register of the Joseph Smith Collection in the Church Archives.* Salt Lake City: Historical Department of The Church of Jesus Christ of Latter-day Saints, 1973.

Larson, David R., ed. *Guide to Manuscripts, Collections, and Institutional Records in Ohio.* Society of Ohio Archivists, 1974.

Primary Sources

Minute Books and Other Church Records

Book of Patriarchal Blessings. Vol. 1, Church Archives.

Elders Licenses Issued at Kirtland, 1836–1838. Microfilm, Brigham Young University.

Extracts from a Brief History of the Congregational Church of Kirtland, Ohio. Lake County Historical Society, Mentor, Ohio.

Far West Record: Minutes of The Church of Jesus Christ of Latter-day Saints, 1830–1844. Edited by Donald Q. Cannon and Lyndon W. Cook. Salt Lake City: Deseret Book, 1983.

Grand River Baptist Association Records. Western Reserve Historical Society, Cleveland, Ohio.

High Priest Minutes, Spanish Fork, 1866–1898. Church Archives.

Journal History of the Church. Church Archives.

Journal of the Branch of the Church of Christ in Pontiac, Michigan, 1834. Church Archives.

Kirtland Council Minute Book, 1832-1837. Church Archives.

Kirtland Revelation Book. Church Archives.

Manuscript History of the Great Lakes Mission–Ohio. Church Archives. (Contains selections from the Journal History of the Church.)

Minutes of the Beaver Baptist Association, 1820. Warren, Ohio, 1820.

Minutes of the Presbytery of Grand River, 1829–1836. Western Reserve Historical Society, Cleveland, Ohio.

Minutes of the Redstone Baptist Association, 1815. Pittsburgh, 1815.

Minutes of the Salt Lake School of the Prophets, 1883. Church Archives.

Minutes of the Seventies, Book A (1835–1838). Church Archives.

Ohio Baptist Convention: Records of Annual Meetings. Norwalk, Ohio, 1890.

Teachers Quorum Minute Book, December 25, 1834–February 12, 1845. Church Archives.

Record of the First Quorum of Elders Belonging to the Church of Christ in Kirtland, Geauga Co., Ohio, 1836–1870. Library–Archives, Reorganized Church of Jesus Christ of Latter Day Saints, Independence, Missouri.

Record of the Mahoning Baptist Association. Hiram College, Hiram, Ohio.

Records of the Church of Christ in Geneva, State of New York. Geneva, New York: First Presbyterian Church.

Records of the Church of Christ, in the Joining Borders of Bridgewater and Middleborough, 1747–1754. Middleboro, Massachusetts: North Congregational Church.

Records of the Presbyterian Church of Kirtland. Western Reserve Historical Society.

Records of the Presbytery of Geneva, Book C. Microfilm copy located in the Harold B. Lee Library, Brigham Young University.

Whitmer, John. "The Book of John Whitmer: Kept by Commandment." Library–Archives, Reorganized Church of Jesus Christ of Latter Day Saints, Independence, Missouri.

Government Documents

Kirtland Township Record Book, vols. 1-2. Microfilm, Church Genealogical Department.

Geauga County, Ohio, Book of Deeds, books 15-25. Microfilm, Church Genealogical Department.

Geauga County, Ohio, Court of Common Pleas, record book U. Microfilm, Church Genealogical Department and Brigham Young University.

Geauga County, Ohio, Land Records. Microfilm, Church Genealogical Department and Brigham Young University.

Geauga County, Probate Records. Microfilm, Church Genealogical Department and Brigham Young University.

Geauga County, Ohio, Tax Records, 1830–1839. Microfilm, Church Genealogical Department and Brigham Young University.

Swan, J. W., comp. Statutes of the State of Ohio. Columbus, Ohio, 1841.

U.S. Bureau of Census, Fourth census: 1820.

U.S. Bureau of Census, Fifth census: 1830.

U.S. Bureau of the Census. Historical Statistics of the United States, Colonial Times to 1957. Washington, D.C.: U.S. Government Printing Office, 1969.

Diaries, Journals, Autobiographies, and Other Unpublished Contemporary Writings

Allen, Lucy Diantha. "Recollections of Her Ancestry Taken in 1901." Brigham Young University.

Ames, Ira. Autobiography. Microfilm of holograph, Church Archives.

Andrus, Milo. Autobiography. Typescript, Church Archives.

Angell, Truman O. Autobiography. Microfilm of holograph. Church Archives and typescript, Brigham Young University.

Baldwin, Nathan. Autobiography. Photocopy of typescript, Church Archives.

Barnes, Caroline. Autobiography. Microfilm of holograph, Church Archives.

Barnes, Lorenzo. Journal. Holograph, Church Archives.

Brown, Lorenzo, Journals. Holograph and typescripts, Church Archives.

Burgess, Harrison. Autobiography. Photocopy of holograph, Church Archives.

Burgess, William Jr. Autobiography. Typescript, Brigham Young University.

Burkett, George. Diary. Typescript, Church Archives.

Cahoon, Reynolds. Diary, 1832. Holograph, Church Archives.

Cahoon, William F. Autobiography. Microfilm of holograph, Church Archives.

Carter, Jared. Autobiography. Typescript. Church Archives.

Carter, Jared. Journal. Holograph, Church Archives.

Cheney, Nathan B. "A Sketch of the Life and Labors of Elder Nathan B. Cheney," Brigham Young University.

Cowdery, Oliver. Papers. Church Archives.

Cowdery, Oliver. Papers. Huntington Library, San Marino, California.

Crosby, Caroline Barnes. Autobiography. Microfilm of holograph, Church Archives.

Crosby, Jesse Wentworth. Autobiography. Typescript of holograph, Brigham Young University.

Crosby, Jonathan. Autobiography. Holograph, Church Archives.

Draper, William. Autobiography. Typescript, Brigham Young University and Church Archives.

Duncan, Chapman. Autobiography. Typescript, Brigham Young University.

Fielding, Joseph. Journal. Holograph, Church Archives.

Fielding, Mary. Papers, Church Archives.

Foote, Warren. Journal. 3 vols. Holograph, Church Archives.

Gilbert and Whitney Store Day Book, 1836–1837. Library–Archives, Reorganized Church of Jesus Christ of Latter Day Saints, Independence, Missouri.

Greene, Evan M. Journal. Holograph, Church Archives.

Hale, Aroet L. Autobiography. Holograph, Church Archives.

Hale, Jonathan H. Journal. Holograph, Church Archives.

Hancock, Levi Ward. Journal. Holograph, Church Archives, and typescript, Brigham Young University.

Hancock, Mosiah. Journal. Holograph, Church Archives, and typescript, Brigham Young University.

Holbrook, Joseph. Autobiography. Typescript, Church Archives.

Hubbard, Marshall M. Autobiography. Church Archives.

Huntington, Oliver Boardman. Diaries. Typescript, Utah State Historical Society, Salt Lake City, Utah.

Huntington, William. Journal. 2 vols. Holograph, Brigham Young University.

Hyde, William. Autobiography. Typescript, Church Archives.

Jackman, Levi. Autobiography. Typescript, Brigham Young University.

Johnson, Benjamin F. "Letter to George A. Gibbs." Typescript, Church Archives and Brigham Young University.

Johnson, Benjamin F. "My Life's Review." Typescript, Church Archives.

Johnson, George W. Autobiography. Typescript, Brigham Young University.

Johnson, Joel Hills. Autobiography. Typescript, Church Archives.

Judd, Zadoc Knapp. Autobiography. Typescript, Brigham Young University.

Kimball, Heber C. Journals and Papers. Church Archives.

Kimball, Lucy Walker. Autobiography. Microfilm of holograph, Church Archives.

Kirtland Safety Society Ledger Book. Chicago Historical Society; microfilm copy, Brigham Young University.

Knight, Joseph. "Incidents of History from 1827–1844." Church Archives.

Lightner, Mary Elizabeth Rollins. Journal. Photocopy of typescript, Brigham Young University.

Mace, Wandle. Autobiography. Journal typescript, Brigham Young University.

Martin, Moses. Diary. Holograph, Church Archives.

McArthur, Daniel D. Autobiography. Photocopy of holograph, Brigham Young University.

McBride, Reuben. Journal. Microfilm of holograph, Church Archives.

Millet, Artemus. Autobiography. Holograph, Church Archives.

Morris, Jacob. Papers. Olin Research Library, Cornell University, Ithaca, New York.

Murdock, John. Journal. Holograph, Church Archives, and typescript, Brigham Young University.

Nickerson, Freeman. Papers. Church Archives.

Noble, Joseph B. Journal. Holograph, Church Archives and typescript, Brigham Young University.

Noble, Mary Adeline Beman. Autobiography. Typescript, Brigham Young University.

Partridge, Edward. Autobiography. Typescript of holograph, Church Archives.

Partridge, Edward. Papers. Church Archives.

Partridge, Edward and Lydia. "Writings." Compiled by Edward Partridge. Typescript, Church Archives.

Patten, David W. Journal. Holograph, Church Archives.

Phelps, William W. Papers. Church Archives.

Pratt, Orson. Journal. Holograph, Church Archives.

Post, Stephen. Diary. Holograph, Church Archives.

Pulsipher, Charles. Autobiography. Typescript, Brigham Young University.

Pulsipher, John. Autobiography. Typescript, Brigham Young University.

Pulsipher, Zera. Autobiography. Typescript, Brigham Young University.

Rich, Charles C. Zion's Camp Journal. Church Archives.

Richards, Willard. Papers. Church Archives.

Rigdon, Sidney. Letters. Post Collection, microfilm copy, Church Archives.

Rogers, Samuel H. Journal. Typescript of holograph, Brigham Young University.

Scott, Walter. Letters. Disciples Historical Society, Nashville, Tennessee.

Shurtliff, Luman Andros. Autobiography. Typescript of holograph, Brigham Young University.

Smith, Elias. Diary. Holograph, Church Archives.

Smith, George A. Memoirs. Typescript, Brigham Young University.

Smith, Hyrum. Collection. Church Archives.

Smith, John Lyman. Journal. Holograph, Church Archives.

Smith, Joseph, Jr. Collection. Church Archives.

Snow, Eliza R. Autobiography. Holograph, Bancroft Library, University of California, and microfilm of holograph, Church Archives.

Snow, Erastus. Journal. Typescript, Brigham Young University.

Snow, Lorenzo. Journal. Holograph, Church Archives.

Spaulding, Solomon. Manuscript. Oberlin College Archives, Oberlin, Ohio.

Tanner, Elizabeth Beswick. Autobiography. Photocopy of typescript, Brigham Young University.

Tanner, Nathan. Autobiography. Photocopy of holograph, Brigham Young University.

Tracy, Nancy Alexander. Autobiography. Bancroft Library, University of California, and typescript, Church Archives.

Turley, Theodore. Journal, 1829-40. Holograph, Brigham Young University.

Tyler, Samuel D. Diary. Typescript of holograph, Church Archives.

Whitney, Newel K. Collection. Brigham Young University.

Willey, Jeremiah. Autobiography. Holograph, Church Archives.

Williams, Frederick G. Papers. Church Archives.

Winters, Mary Ann Stearns. Autobiography. Typescript, Church Archives.

Wood, Daniel. Autobiography. Holograph, Church Archives.

Woodruff, Phebe W. Autobiography. Bancroft Library, University of California, and microfilm copy, Church Archives.

Woodruff, Wilford. Journals and papers. Church Archives.

Published Sources

Writings of Contemporaries

Arrington, Leonard J. "Oliver Cowdery's Kirtland, Ohio, 'Sketch Book.'" *BYU Studies* 12 (Summer 1972): 410-26.

Book of Commandments, for the government of the Church of Christ. Organized according to law, on the 6th of April, 1830. Independence, Missouri: W. W. Phelps and Co., 1833.

Book of Mormon. 2d ed. Kirtland: O. Cowdery and Co., 1837.

Barnes, Gilbert H., and Dwight L. Dumond, eds. *Letters of Theodore Dwight Weld, Angelina Grimke Weld and Sarah Grimke, 1822-1844.* 2 vols. New York: Da Capo Press, 1970.

Brown, Benjamin. *Testimonies for the Truth.* Liverpool, England, 1853.

Campbell, Alexander. *Delusions.* Boston, 1832.

Carter, Kate, B., comp. *Our Pioneer Heritage.* Salt Lake City: Daughters of the Utah Pioneers.

Cheney, Nathan B. "A Sketch of the Life and Labors of Elder Nathan B. Cheney." Photocopy of typescripts, Brigham Young University.

Chesney, James M. *An Antidote to Mormonism: A Warning Voice to the Church and Nation.* New York, 1838.

Collection of Sacred Hymns for the Church of the Latter Day Saints: Selected by Emma Smith. Kirtland: F. G. Williams and Co., 1835.

Corrill, John. *A Brief History of the Church of Christ of Latter Day Saints.* St. Louis, 1839.

Cowdery, Oliver. *Supplement to J. Seixas' Manual Hebrew Grammar for the Kirtland, Ohio, Theological Institution.* New York, 1836.

Crary, Christopher G. *Pioneer and Personal Reminiscences.* Marshalltown, Iowa, 1893.

De Tocqueville, Alexis. *Democracy in America.* Edited by Richard D. Heffner. New York: New American Library, 1956.

Doctrine and Covenants of the Church of the Latter Day Saints. Kirtland: F. G. Williams and Co., 1835.

Doctrine and Covenants of The Church of Jesus Christ of Latter-day Saints. Salt Lake City: The Church of Jesus Christ of Latter-day Saints, 1981.

Early Scenes in Church History: Eighth Book of the Faith-Promoting Series. Salt Lake City, 1882.

Ehat, Andrew F., and Lyndon W. Cook, comp. *The Words of Joseph Smith.* Provo, Utah: Religious Studies Center, Brigham Young University, 1980.

Elliott, Orson Hyde. *Reminiscences, in the Life of Orson Hyde Elliott.* San Francisco, 1899.

Fragments of Experience: Sixth Book of the Faith-Promoting Series. Salt Lake City, 1862.

Graham, Sylvester. *The Aesculapian Tablets of the Nineteenth Century.* Providence, 1834.

———. *Lectures on the Science of Human Life.* Boston, 1839.

"History of John E. Page." *Deseret News*, June 16, 1858.

Howe, E. D. *Autobiography and Recollections of a Pioneer Printer.* Painesville, 1878.

———. *Mormonism Unvailed.* Painesville, 1834.

Howe, Henry. *Historical Collections of Ohio.* Cincinnati, 1847.

———. *Historical Collections of Ohio.* 2 vols. Cincinnati, 1891.

Hyde, Orson. "History of Orson Hyde," *Deseret News*, May 5, 1838.

Jenkins, Warren. *The Ohio Gazeteer.* Columbus, 1837.

Jessee, Dean C. "The Kirtland Diary of Wilford Woodruff." *BYU Studies* 12 (Summer 1972): 365-99.

Johnson, Joel H. *Voice from the Mountains.* Salt Lake City, 1881.

Jones, Josiah. "History of the Mormonites." *The Evangelist* 9 (June 1, 1841): 132-34.

Journal of Discourses. 26 vols. London: Latter-day Saints Book Depot, 1854–1886.

Kelley, William H. "The Hill Cumorah, and the Book of Mormon . . . from late interviews." *The Saints Herald* (Plano, Illinois), June 1, 1881.

Kimball, Heber C. "Journal." *Times and Seasons* 6 (1845).

Kirkham, Francis W. *A New Witness for Christ in America.* 2 vols. Independence, Missouri, 1942.

Littlefield, Lyman Omer. *Reminiscences of Latter-day Saints.* Logan, Utah, 1888.

Lundwall, Nels B., comp. *A Compilation Containing the Lectures on Faith.* Salt Lake City: N.B. Lundwall, n.d.

"Mary Elizabeth Rollins Lightner." *Utah Genealogical Historical Magazine* 17 (1926): 193-205, 250-60.

Messages of the First Presidency of the Church . . . 1833–1964. 6 vols. Edited by James R. Clark. Salt Lake City: Bookcraft, 1965-75.

Page, John E. *The Spaulding Story Concerning the Origin of the Book of Mormon.* Pittsburgh, 1843.

Pratt, Orson. *The Orson Pratt Journals*. Compiled by Elden J. Watson. Salt Lake City: Elden Jay Watson, 1975.

Pratt, Parley P. *Autobiography of Parley Parker Pratt*. Edited by Parley P. Pratt, Jr. Salt Lake City: Deseret Book, 1964.

———. *Mormonism Unveiled: Zion's Watchman Unmasked*. New York, 1838.

———. *Writings of Parley Parker Pratt*. Edited by Parker Pratt Robinson. Salt Lake City: Deseret News Press, 1952.

Public Discussion of the Issues between the Reorganized Church of Jesus Christ of Latter Day Saints and the Church of Christ (Disciples) Held in Kirtland, Ohio, Beginning February 12th, and Closing March 8th, 1844. Lamoni, Iowa, 1913.

Richardson, Robert. *Memoirs of Alexander Campbell*. Cincinnati, 1872.

Robinson, Ebenezer. "Items of Personal History." *The Return*. Photocopy, Brigham Young University Library.

Scott, Walter. *The Gospel Restored*. Cincinnati, 1836.

Scraps of Biography. Salt Lake City: Juvenile Instructor, 1883.

Smith, George A. "My Journal." *Instructor* 81-84 (1946–1949).

Smith, Joseph. *History of the Church of Jesus Christ of Latter-day Saints*. 7 vols. Edited by B. H. Roberts. Salt Lake City: The Church of Jesus Christ of Latter-day Saints, 1932-51.

———. *History of the Church of Jesus Christ of Latter Day Saints*. 4 vols. Edited by Heman C. Smith. Independence, Missouri: Reorganized Church of Jesus Christ of Latter Day Saints, 1920–1922.

Smith, Joseph Fielding, comp. *Teachings of the Prophet Joseph Smith*. Salt Lake City: Deseret Book, 1961.

Smith, Lucy Mack. *History of Joseph Smith*. Edited by Preston Nibley. Salt Lake City: Bookcraft, 1954.

Smith, William. *William Smith on Mormonism*. Lamoni, Iowa, 1883.

Snow, Eliza R. *Eliza R. Snow: An Immortal: Selected Writings of Eliza R. Snow*. Compiled by Nicholas G. Morgan. Salt Lake City: Nicholas G. Morgan Sr. Foundation, 1957.

Snow, Eliza R., comp. *Biography and Family Record of Lorenzo Snow*. Salt Lake City: Deseret News, 1884.

Stevenson, Edward. "Incidents of My Early Days in the Church." *Juvenile Instructor* 29 (September 1, 1894): 551-52.

Sunderland, LaRoy. *Mormonism Exposed and Refuted*. New York, 1838.

Towle, Nancy. *Vicissitudes: Illustrated, in the Experience of Nancy Towle in Europe and America*. Charleston, 1832.

Tullidge, Edward W. *The Women of Mormondom*. New York, 1877.

Watson, Elden Jay, ed. *Manuscript History of Brigham Young, 1801–1844*. Salt Lake City: Smith Secretarial Service, 1968.

Williams, S. *Mormonism Exposed*. Photocopy, Brigham Young University.

Winchester, Benjamin. *The Origin of the Spaulding Story*. Philadelphia, 1840.

Woodruff, Wilford. "Autobiography of Wilford Woodruff." *Tullidge's Quarterly Magazine* 3 (October 1883): 1-25.

Periodicals

Christian Baptist. Edited by Alexander Campbell. 7 vols. in 1. Cincinnati, 1835.

Contributor (Salt Lake City). 1879–1896.

Evening and Morning Star (Independence, Missouri, and Kirtland, Ohio), 1832–1833, 1834–1836.
Elders' Journal of the Church of Latter Day Saints (Kirtland, Ohio, and Far West, Missouri). 1837–1838.
Ensign (Salt Lake City). 1971–present.
Historical Record (Salt Lake City). 1882–1890.
Improvement Era (Salt Lake City). 1897–1970.
Journal of Health (Phildelphia). 1829–1830.
Latter Day Saints' Messenger and Advocate (Kirtland, Ohio). 1834–1837.
Millennial Harbinger (Bethany, Virginia). 1830– 1870.
Millennial Star (Liverpool, England). 1840–present.
New Era (Salt Lake City). 1971–present.
Northern Times (Kirtland, Ohio). 1835–1836.
Times and Seasons (Nauvoo, Illinois). 1839–1846.
Young Women's Journal (Salt Lake City). 1889– 1929.
Woman's Exponent (Salt Lake City). 1872–1914.

Secondary Works

Ahlstrom, Sydney E. *A Religious History of the American People*. New Haven: Yale University Press, 1972.
Anderson, Richard Lloyd. "By the Gift and Power of God." *Ensign* 7 (1977): 78-85.
———. "The Impact of the First Preaching in Ohio." *BYU Studies* 11 (Summer 1971): 474-96.
———. "Joseph Smith and the Millenarian Time Table." *BYU Studies* 3 (Spring-Summer 1961): 55-66.
———. "Joseph Smith's Insights into the Olivet Prophecy: Joseph Smith 1 and Matthew 24. *Pearl of Great Price Symposium*. Brigham Young University, November 22, 1975 (rev. ed., Provo: Brigham Young University, 1977), pp. 57-58.
———. "Joseph Smith's New York Reputation Reappraised." *BYU Studies* 10 (Spring 1970): 283-314.
Andre, Laurel B. Blank. "The Nineteenth-Century Temple Architecture of the Latter-day Saints." Ph.D. diss., University of Michigan, 1973.
Andrews, Edward. *The People Called Shakers: A Search for the Perfect Society*. New York: Oxford University Press, 1953.
Andrus, Hyrum L. *Doctrines of the Kingdom*. 3 vols. Salt Lake City: Bookcraft, 1973.
———. *Joseph Smith, the Man and the Seer*. Salt Lake City: Deseret Book, 1960.
Andrus, Hyrum L., and Helen Mae Andrus. *They Knew the Prophet*. Salt Lake City: Bookcraft, 1974.
Arrington, Leonard J. *Charles C. Rich, Mormon General and Western Frontiersman*. Provo: Brigham Young University Press, 1974.
———. "Early Mormon Communitarianism: The Law of Consecration and Stewardship." *Western Humanities Review* 7 (Autumn 1953): 341-69.
———. *Great Basin Kingdom: An Economic History of the Latter-day Saints, 1830–1900*. Cambridge, Massachusetts: Harvard University Press, 1958.
Arrington, Leonard J., Feramorz Y. Fox, and Dean L. May. *Building the City of God: Community and Cooperation Among the Mormons*. Salt Lake City: Deseret Book, 1976.

Bacheler, Origen. *Mormonism Exposed, Internally and Externally.* New York, 1838.

Bachman, Danel W. "New Light on an Old Hypothesi: The Ohio Origins of the Revelation on Eternal Marriage." *Journal of Mormon History* 5 (1978): 19-32.

———. "A Study of the Mormon Practice of Plural Marriage before the Death of Joseph Smith." M.A. thesis, Purdue University, 1975.

Backman, Milton V., Jr. *American Religions and the Rise of Mormonism.* 2d ed. Salt Lake City: Deseret Book, 1970.

———. *Christian Churches of America: Origins and Beliefs.* Rev. ed. New York: Charles Scribner's Sons, 1983.

———. "Kirtland: The Crucial Years," *Ensign* 8 (January 1979): 24-28.

———. *Joseph Smith's First Vision. The First Vision in Its Historical Context.* 2d ed. rev. Salt Lake City: Bookcraft, 1980.

———. "Truman Coe's 1836 Description of Moronism." *BYU Studies* 17 (Spring 1977): 347-55.

———. "The Quest for a Restoration: The Birth of Mormonism in Ohio." *BYU Studies* 12 (Summer 1972): 346-64.

Barker, John Marshall. *History of Ohio Methodism.* Cincinnati, 1898.

Barrett, Ivan J. *Joseph Smith and the Restoration. A History of the LDS Church to 1846.* Provo: Young House, Brigham Young University Press, 1973.

Barron, Howard H. *Orson Hyde: Missionary, Apostle, Colonizer.* Bountiful, Utah: Horizon, 1977.

Baumgarten, James N. "The Role and Function of the Seventies in L.D.S. Church History." M.A. thesis, Brigham Young University, 1960.

Berrett, Lamar C. "History of the Southern States Mission, 1831–1861." M.S. thesis, Brigham Young University, 1960.

Bestor, Arthur Eugene, Jr. *Backwoods Utopias: The Sectarian and Owenite Phases of Communitarian Socialism in America, 1663–1829.* Philadelphia: University of Pennsylvania Press, 1950.

Bicentennial Edition: The Historical Society Quarterly Lake County, Ohio. Painesville, Ohio: Painesville Publishing Co., 1976.

Bitton, Davis. "Kirtland as a Center of Missionary Activity, 1830–1838." *BYU Studies* 11 (Summer 1971): 497-516.

———. "The Waning of Mormon Kirtland." *BYU Studies* 12 (Summer 1972): 455-64.

Black, Harry. *Kirtland Temple.* Independence, Missouri, n.d.

Bowen, Walter Dean. "The Versatile W. W. Phelps: Mormon Writer, Educator, and Pioneer." M.S. thesis, Brigham Young University, 1958.

Boyd, W. W. "Secondary Education in Ohio Previous to the Year 1840." *Ohio Archaeological and Historical Publications* 25 (1916): 118-34.

Brown, Richard Maxwell. *Strain of Violence.* New York: Oxford University Press, 1975.

Bryan, James D. "Multi-colored Maps from False Color Separations: Kirtland Examples (1800–1900)." M.S. thesis, Brigham Young University, 1980.

Bush, Lester E., Jr. "The Spaulding Theory: Then and Now." *Dialogue* 10 (Autumn 1977), 40-69.

Bushman, Richard L. "Mormon Persecutions in Missouri, 1833." *BYU Studies* 3 (Autumn 1960): 11-20.

Cannon, George Q. *Life of Joseph Smith the Prophet.* Salt Lake City: Deseret Book, 1958.

Chaddock, Robert E. *Before 1850.* New York: Columbia University, 1908.

Clark, James R. *The Story of the Pearl of Great Price.* Salt Lake City: Bookcraft, 1955.

Clark, John A. *Gleanings by the Way*. Philadelphia, 1842.

Cook, Lyndon W. *The Revelations of the Prophet Joseph Smith*. Provo: Seventy's Mission Bookstore, 1981.

Corbett, Pearson H. *Hyrum Smith, Patriarch*. Salt Lake City: Deseret Book, 1963.

Cornwall, J. Spencer. *Stories of Our Mormon Hymns*. Salt Lake City: Deseret Book, 1961.

Cowan, Richard O. *Doctrine and Covenants: Our Modern Scripture*. Provo: Brigham Young University Press, 1978.

Cowley, Matthias F. *Wilford Woodruff: History of His Life and Labors as Recorded in His Daily Journals*. Salt Lake City: Bookcraft, 1964.

Crawley, Peter, and Richard L. Anderson. "The Political and Social Realities of Zion's Camp." *BYU Studies* 14 (Summer 1974): 406-20.

Curti, Merle E. *The Growth of American Thought*. New York: Harper and Brothers, 1951.

Curtis, Lewis, ed. *The General Conference of the Methodist Episcopal Church*. Cincinnati, 1900.

Davison, Matilda. "The Mormon Bible." *Family Magazine* 7 (1840): 38-39.

Doxey, Roy W. *The Word of Wisdom Today*. Salt Lake City: Deseret Book, 1975.

Drake, E., and E. D. Mansfield. *Cincinnati in 1826*. Cincinnati, 1827.

Durham, Lowell M. "On Mormon Music and Musicians." *Dialogue* 3 (Summer 1968): 19-40.

————. "The Role and History of Music in the Mormon Church." M.A. thesis, University of Iowa, 1942.

Durham, Reed, Jr., and Steven H. Heath. *Succession in the Church*. Salt Lake City: Bookcraft, 1970.

Dyer, Alvin R. *The Refiner's Fire: The Significance of Events Transpiring in Missouri*. 3rd ed. rev. Salt Lake City: Deseret Book, 1972.

Elliott, Sadie Foss. "Life Sketch of Nathan Calhoun Cheney and Eliza Ann Beebe Cheney as told by their Daughters Helen Mar Cheney Miller and Eliza Jane Cheney Rawson." Typescript, Brigham Young University.

Ellsworth, Samuel George. "A History of Mormon Missions in the United States and Canada, 1830–1860." Ph.D. diss., University of California, Berkeley, 1951.

Esplin, Ronald K. "The Emergence of Brigham Young and the Twelve to Mormon Leadership, 1830–1841." Ph.D. diss., Brigham Young University, 1981.

Fairchild, James H. *Manuscript of Solomon Spaulding and the Book of Mormon*. Cleveland, 1886.

Fielding, Robert Kent. "The Growth of the Mormon Church in Kirtland, Ohio." Ph.D. diss., Indiana University, 1957.

Fields, Clarence L. "History of the Kirtland Temple." M.S. thesis, Brigham Young University, 1963.

Filler, Louis. *The Crusade Against Slavery, 1830–1860*. 2d ed. New York: Harper and Row, 1971.

Flake, Lawrence R. *Mighty Men of Zion*. Salt Lake City: Karl D. Butler, 1974.

Fogarty, R. S., ed. *American Utopianism*. Itasca, Illinois: F. E. Peacock, c. 1972.

Fox, Feramorz. "United Order: Discrimination in the Use of Terms." *Improvement Era* 47 (1944): 432, 459-62.

Freehling, William W. *Prelude to Civil War: The Nullification Controversy in South Carolina, 1816–1836*. New York: Harper and Row, 1968.

Gentry, Leland Homer. "A History of the Latter-day Saints in Northern Missouri from 1836 to 1839." Ph.D. diss., Brigham Young University, 1965.

———. "What of the Lectures on Faith?" *BYU Studies* 19 (Fall 1978): 5-19.

Goldsmith, Lucus A. "Rigdon the First Mormon Elder." Western Reserve Historical Society.

Grandstaff, Mark R. "Marriage Patterns of the Mormon Community at Kirtland, Ohio: 1830–1838." Special Collections, Harold B. Lee Library, Brigham Young University.

Griffin, C. S. *The Ferment of Reform, 1830–1860.* New York: Thomas Y. Crowell Co., 1967.

Gunn, Stanley R. *Oliver Cowdery, Second Elder and Scribe.* Salt Lake City: Bookcraft, 1962.

Hale, Van. "The Doctrinal Impact of the King Follett Discourse." *BYU Studies* 18 (Winter 1978): 209-25.

Hall, Florence, "Sketch of Zera Pulsipher." Typescript, Brigham Young University.

Hansen, Klaus J. *Quest for Empire.* East Lansing: Michigan State University Press, 1967.

Hatcher, Harlan. *The Buckeye Country.* New York: H. K. Kinsey and Co., 1940.

Hayden, Amos Sutton. *Early History of the Disciples in the Western Reserve, Ohio.* Cincinnati, 1876.

Here Is Lake County, Ohio. Cleveland: Howard Allen, 1964.

Higdon, Barbara Joan McFarlane. "The Role of Preaching in the Early Latter Day Saint Church, 1830–1846." Ph.D. diss., University of Missouri, 1961.

Hill, Gordon Orville. "A History of Kirtland Camp: Its Initial Purpose and Notable Accomplishments." M.A. thesis, Brigham Young University, 1975.

Hill, Marvin S. "Cultural Crisis in the Mormon Kingdom: A Reconsideration of the Causes of Kirtland Dissent." *Church History* 49 (September 1980): 286-97.

Hill, Marvin S., C. Keith Rooker, and Larry T. Wimmer. *The Kirtland Economy Revisited* (Provo: Brigham Young University Press, 1977).

History of Geauga and Lake Counties, Ohio. Philadelphia, 1878.

Hitchcock, Elizabeth G. "Grandison Newell, A Born Trader." *Historical Society Quarterly, Lake County, Ohio* 10 (May 1968): 1-4.

Hitchcock, Mrs. Peter S. "Joseph Smith and the Kirtland Temple." *Historical Society Quarterly, Lake County, Ohio* 7 (November 1965): 1-4.

Howard, Richard P. *Restoration Scriptures: A Study of Their Textual Development.* Independence, Missouri: Herald Publishing House, 1969.

Huntington, C. C. "A History of Banking and Currency in Ohio Before the Civil War." *Ohio Archaeological and Historical Publications* 24 (1915): 235-539.

Ipson, Vera Morley. "History and Travels of the Life of Isaac Morley, Sr." Brigham Young University.

Irving, Gordon. "Numerical Strength and Geographical Distribution of the LDS Missionary Force, 1830–1974." *Task Papers in LDS History*, no. 1. Salt Lake City: Historical Department of The Church of Jesus Christ of Latter-day Saints, 1975.

Jacobson, Wayne Allan. "A Prosopographical Study of the Zion's Camp Marchers." History 780 Research Paper, University of Utah, 1976. Photocopy, Church Historical Library.

Jennings, Warren A. "The Army of Israel Marches into Missouri." *Missouri Historical Review* 62 (Winter 1968): 107-35.

———. "The Expulsion of the Mormons from Jackson County, Missouri.*Missouri Historical Review* 64 (October 1969): 41-63.

———. "Factors in the Destruction of the Mormon Press in Missouri, 1833." *Utah Historical Quarterly* 35 (Winter 1967): 56-76.

———. "Zion Is Fled: The Expulsion of the Mormons from Jackson County, Missouri." Ph.D. diss., University of Florida, 1962.

Jessee, Dean C. "The Reliability of Joseph Smith's History." *Journal of Mormon History* 3 (1976): 34-39.

Jessee, Dean C., and William G. Hartley. "Joseph Smith's Missionary Journal." *New Era* 4 (1974): 34-36.

Jorgensen, Dan. "New Facts on the Life and History of Giovanni Pietro Antonio Lebolo." Typescript of photocopies, Church Archives.

Keller, Karl., ed., "I Never Knew a Time When I Did Not Know Joseph Smith: A Son's Record of the Life and Testimony of Sidney Rigdon." *Dialogue* 1 (Winter 1966): 15-42.

Kemp, Thomas Jay. *The Office of the Patriarch to the Church in The Church of Jesus Christ of Latter-day Saints.* Stanford, Connecticut: Thomas J. Kemp, 1972.

Kidney, Walter C. *Historic Building in Ohio.* Pittsburgh, Pennsylvania: Ober Park Associates, 1972.

Launius, Roger Dale. "Zion's Camp and the Redemption of Jackson County, Missouri." M.A. thesis, Graceland College, 1978.

Layton, Robert L. "A Perspective on Time and Place." *BYU Studies* 11 (Summer 1971): 423-38.

Levinson, Burton E. "The Western Reserve: Its Hebrew Influence." Typescript, American Jewish Archives, Cincinnati, Ohio. (A photocopy of this typescript is in the Brigham Young University Library.)

Lowe, Jay R. "A Study of the General Conferences of The Church of Jesus Christ of Latter-day Saints, 1830–1901." Ph.D. diss., Brigham Young University, 1972.

Lundwall, Nels B., comp. *Compilation Containing the Lectures on Faith.* Salt Lake City: N. B. Lundwall, n.d.

Lyon, T. Edgar. "Independence, Missouri, and the Mormons, 1827–1833." *BYU Studies* 13 (Autumn 1972): 10-19.

Marrott, Robert L. "History and Functions of the Aaronic Priesthood and the Offices of Priest, Teacher, and Deacon in The Church of Jesus Christ of Latter-day Saints, 1829 to 1844." M.A. thesis, Brigham Young University, 1976.

Mather, Frederick G. "The Early Days of Mormonism." *Lippincott's Magazine of Popular Literature and Science* 26 (1880): 198-211.

Matthews, Robert J. "The 'New Translation' of the Bible, 1830-1833: Doctrinal Development during the Kirtland Era." *BYU Studies* 11 (Summer 1971): 400-422.

———. *"A Plainer Translation": Joseph Smith's Translation of the Bible; a History and Commentary.* Provo: Brigham Young University Press, 1975.

M'Chesney, James. *An Antidote to Mormonism.* Revised by G. J. Bennet. New York, 1838.

McConkie, Bruce R. *Mormon Doctrine.* 2d ed. Salt Lake City: Bookcraft. 1966.

McGavin, E. Cecil. *The Family of Joseph Smith.* Salt Lake City: Bookcraft, 1963.

McGrane, Reginald Charles. *The Panic of 1837.* Chicago: University of Chicago Press, 1924.

McKiernan, F. Mark. "The Conversion of Sidney Rigdon to Mormonism," *Dialogue* 5 (Summer 1970): 71-78.

———. *The Voice of One Crying in the Wilderness: Sidney Rigdon, Religious Reformer 1793–1876.* Lawrence, Kansas: Coronado Press, 1971.

Moss, James R. "The Historical Development of the Church System." *The First Annual Church Educational System Religious Educators Symposium.* Provo: Brigham Young University, 1977.

Mott, F. L. *American Journalism: A History, 1690-1960.* 3rd ed. New York: Macmillan, 1962.

Mouritsen, Robert Glen. "The Office of Associate President of The Church of Jesus Christ of Latter-day Saints." M.A. thesis, Brigham Young University, 1972.

Newell, Linda K., and Valeen T. Avery. "Sweet Counsel and Seas of Tribulation: The Religious Life of the Women in Kirtland." *BYU Studies* 20 (1980): 151-62.

Nibley, Hugh. "The Meaning of the Kirtland Egyptian Papers." *BYU Studies* 11: (Summer 1971): 350-99.

Nye, Russel B. "Marius Robinson, A Forgotten Abolitionist Leader." *The Ohio State Archaeological and Historical Quarterly* 55 (1946): 138-54.

Olson, Earl E. "The Chronology of the Ohio Revelations." *BYU Studies* 11 (Summer 1971): 329-49.

Pancoast, Eva L. "Mormons at Kirtland." M.S. thesis, Western Reserve University, 1929.

Parkin, Max H. "A History of the Latter-day Saints in Clay County, Missouri, from 1833 to 1837." Ph.D. diss., Brigham Young University, 1976.

———. "Kirtland: A Stronghold for the Kingdom." Edited by Mark McKiernan, Alma R. Blair, and Paul Edwards. *The Restoration Movement: Essays in Mormon History.* Lawrence, Kansas: Coronado Press, 1973.

———. "Mormon Political Involvement in Ohio." *BYU Studies* 9 (Summer 1969): 484-502.

———. "The Nature and Cause of Internal and External Conflict of the Mormons in Ohio Between 1830 and 1838." M.A. thesis, Brigham Young University, 1966.

Partridge, Scott H. "The Failure of the Kirtland Safety Society." *BYU Studies* 12 (Summer 1972): 437-54.

Pearl of Great Price Symposium, Brigham Young University, November 22, 1975. Rev. ed. Provo: Brigham Young University, 1977.

Perkins, Keith. "A House Divided: The John Johnson Family." *Ensign* 9 (February 1979): 54-59.

Petersen, Lauritz G. "The Kirtland Temple." *BYU Studies* 12 (Summer 1972): 400-409.

Petersen, Melvin J. "A Study of the Nature of and the Significance of the Changes in the Revelations as Found in a Comparison of the Book of Commandments and Subsequent Editions of the Doctrine and Covenants." M.S. thesis, Brigham Young University, 1955.

Peterson, Paul H. "An Historical Analysis of the Word of Wisdom." M.A. thesis, Brigham Young University, 1972.

Peterson, Orlen Curtis. "A History of the Schools and Educational Programs of The Church of Jesus Christ of Latter-day Saints in Ohio and Missouri, 1831–1839." M.A. thesis, Brigham Young University, 1972.

Phelps, Gary L. "Home Teaching—Attempts by the Latter-day Saints to Establish an

Effective Program during the Nineteenth Century." M.S. thesis, Brigham Young University, 1975.

Porter, Larry C. "A Study of the Origins of The Church of Jesus Christ of Latter-day Saints in the States of New York and Pennsylvania 1816–1831." Ph.D. diss., Brigham Young University, 1971.

Poulsen, Larry N. "The Life and Contributions of Newel Kimball Whitney." M.A. thesis, Brigham Young University, 1966.

Price, Robert. "The Ohio Anti-slavery Convention of 1836." *Ohio State Archaeological and Historical Quarterly and Historical Quarterly* 45 (1936): 173-88.

Prusha, Anne B. "A History of Kirtland, Ohio." M.A. thesis, Kent State University, 1971.

––––––. *A History of Kirtland, Ohio.* Mentor, Ohio: Lakeland Community College Press, 1982.

Purdy, William E. "Music in Mormon Culture 1830–1876." Ph.D. diss., Northwestern University, 1960.

Quinn, D. Michael. "Organizational Development and Social Origins of the Mormon Hierarchy, 1832–1932: A Prosopographical Study." M.S. thesis, University of Utah, 1973.

––––––. "The Evolution of the Presiding Quorums of the LDS Church." *Journal of Mormon History* 1 (1974): 21-38.

Reimann, Paul E. *The Reorganized Church and the Civil Courts.* Salt Lake City: Utah Printing Co., 1961.

Reinwand, Louis G. "An Interpretive Study of Mormon Millennialism during the Nineteenth Century with Emphasis on Millennial Developments in Utah." M.A. thesis, Brigham Young University, 1971.

Reynolds, George. *The Myth of the "Manuscript Found"; or, The Absurdities of the Spaulding Story.* Salt Lake City, 1883.

Riegel, Robert E. *Young America 1830–1840.* Norman: University of Oklahoma Press, 1949.

Roberts, B. H. *A Comprehensive History of The Church of Jesus Christ of Latter-day Saints, Century 1.* 6 vols. Salt Lake City: The Church of Jesus Christ of Latter-day Saints, 1930.

––––––. *The Missouri Persecutions.* Salt Lake City: Bookcraft, 1965.

––––––. *The Life of John Taylor.* Salt Lake City: Bookcraft, 1963.

Ryder, Charles. "History of Hiram." 1864. Typescript, Hiram College, Hiram, Ohio.

Ryder, Hartwell. "A Short History of the Foundation of the Mormon Church." Typescript, Hiram College, Hiram, Ohio.

Saari, Alma. "The Fairport Harbor Story." *Historical Quarterly, Lake County, Ohio* 8 (May 1966): 1-5.

Salisbury, H. S. "History of Education in the Church of Jesus Christ of Latter Day Saints." *Journal of History* 15 (1922): 257-81.

Sampson, D. Paul, and Larry T. Wimmer. "The Kirtland Safety Society: The Stock Ledger Book and the Bank Failure." *BYU Studies* 12 (Summer 1972): 427-36.

Searle, Howard C. "Authorship of the History of Joseph Smith: A Review Essay." *BYU Studies* 21 (1981): 101-22.

Scheiber, Harry N. *Ohio Canal Era: A Case Study of Government and the Economy, 1820–1861.* Athens: Ohio University Press, 1969.

Shurtleff, Stella Cahoon, and Brent Farrington Cahoon. *Reynolds Cahoon and His Stalwart Sons.* Salt Lake City: Paragon Press, 1960.

Sim, Mary B. "Old South Congregational Church." *Historical Society Quarterly, Lake County, Ohio* 2 (Summer 1969): 1-4.

Skinner, Earnest M. "Joseph Smith, Sr., First Patriarch to the Church." M.S. thesis, Brigham Young University, 1958.

Smith, Hyrum M., and Janne M. Sjodahl. *The Doctrine and Covenants Commentary.* Rev. ed. Salt Lake City: Deseret Book, 1950.

Smith, Joseph Fielding. *Church History and Modern Revelation.* 4 vols. Salt Lake City: Deseret Book, 1946–1949.

———. *Essentials in Church History.* 26th ed. Salt Lake City: Deseret Book, 1973.

Smith, Mary A. "A History of the Mahoning Baptist Association." Master's thesis, West Virginia University, 1943.

Smith, Thomas H. *An Ohio Reader: 1750 to the Civil War.* Grand Rapids, Michigan: William B. Eerdmans, 1975.

Smucker, Samuel M., ed. *The Religious, Social, and Political History of the Mormons, or Latter-day Saints.* New York, 1857.

Snow, LeRoi C. "How Lorenzo Snow Found God." *Improvement Era* 40 (1937): 82-84.

———. "Who Was Professor Joshua Seixas?" *Improvement Era* 39 (1939): 67-71.

Sperry, Sidney B. *Doctrine and Covenants Compendium.* Salt Lake City: Bookcraft, 1960.

Stephens, Calvin Robert. "The Life and Contributions of Zebedee Coltrin." M.A. thesis, Brigham Young University, 1974.

Stewart, John Struthers. *History of Northeastern Ohio.* 3 vols. Indianapolis, Indiana: Historical Publishing Company, 1935.

Sunderland, LaRoy. *Mormonism Exposed and Refuted.* New York, 1838.

Sweet, William Warren. *Religion in the Development of the American Culture.* New York: Charles Scribner's Sons, 1952.

Swensen, Russell. "The Influence of the New Testament upon Latter-day Saint Eschatology from 1830–1846." M.A. thesis, University of Chicago, 1931.

Symons, Ruth Alene. "The Song of the Righteous: An Historical and Literary Analysis of the Latter-day Saint Hymnal, 1835–1871." M.A. thesis, Brigham Young University, 1971.

Tagg, Melvin S. "A History of the Church . . . in Canada, 1830–1963." Ph.D. diss., Brigham Young University, 1963.

Talbot, Wilburn D. "The Duties and Responsibilities of the Apostles of The Church of Jesus Christ of Latter-day Saints, 1835–1945." Ph.D. diss., Brigham Young University, 1978.

———. "Zion's Camp." M.S. thesis, Brigham Young University, 1973.

Taylor, George Rogers. *The Transportation Revolution, 1815–1860.* New York: Harper and Row, 1968.

Temin, Peter. *The Jacksonian Economy.* New York: W. W. Norton, 1969.

Thomas, Benjamin F. *Theodore Weld: Crusader for Freedom.* New Brunswick: Rutger University Press, 1950.

Thornton, Willis. "Gentile and Saint at Kirtland." *Ohio State Archaeological and Historical Quarterly* 63 (January 1954): 8-33.

Todd, Jay M. "The Historical Background of the Book of Abraham," *Pearl of Great Price*

Symposium. Rev. ed. Provo: Brigham Young University, 1977.

————. *The Saga of the Book of Abraham.* Salt Lake City: Deseret Book Co., 1969.

Turner, Orasmus. *History of the Pioneer Settlement of the Phelps and Gorhams's Purchase, and Morris' Reserve.* Rochester, 1852.

Tyler, Alice Felt. *Freedom's Ferment.* New York: Harper and Row, c. 1944.

Van Deusen, Glyndon G. *The Jacksonian Era: 1828–1848.* New York: Harper and Brothers, 1959.

Walters, Ronald G. *American Reformers, 1815–1860.* New York: Hill and Wang, 1978.

Weight, Newell B. "An Historical Study of the Origin and Character of Indigenous Hymn Tunes of the Latter-day Saints." M.A. thesis, University of Southern California, 1961.

————. "The Birth of Mormon Hymnody." *Dialogue* 10 (Spring 1975–1976): 40-48.

Weisberger, Bernard A. *The American Newspaperman.* Chicago: University of Chicago Press, 1961.

————. *They Gathered at the River: The Story of the Great Revivalists and Their Impact upon Religion in America.* Boston: Little, Brown, 1958.

Weisenburger, Francis P. *The Passing of the Frontier.* Vol. 3 of *The History of the State of Ohio.* Ed. Carl Wittke. Columbus: Ohio State Archaeological and Historical Society, 1941.

West, William S. *A Few Interesting Facts Respecting the Rise, Progress and Pretensions of the Mormons.* Warren, Ohio, 1837.

————. "An Historical Study of the Origin and Character of Indigenous Hymn Tunes of the Latter-day Saints." M.A. thesis, University of Southern California, 1961.

Whitney, Orson F. *Life of Heber C. Kimball.* 2d ed. Salt Lake City: Stevens and Wallis, 1945.

————. *Through Memory's Hall.* Independence, Missouri: Zion's Printing and Publishing Co., 1930.

Whittier, Charles H., and Stephen W. Stathis. "The Enigma of Solomon Spaulding." *Dialogue* 10 (Autumn 1977): 70-73.

Wilkes, William Leroy, Jr. "Borrowed Music in Mormon Hymnals." Ph.D. diss., University of Southern California, 1957.

Williams, Frederick G. "Frederick Granger Williams of the First Presidency of the Church." *BYU Studies* 12 (Spring 1972): 243-61.

Winter, Robert. "Architecture on the Frontier: The Mormon Experiment." *Pacific Historical Review* 43 (1974): 50-60.

Woodford, Robert. "The Historical Background of the Doctrine and Covenants." Ph.D. diss., Brigham Young University, 1974.

Young, Joseph. *History of the Organization of the Seventies.* Salt Lake City, 1878.

Young, S. Dilworth. *"Here Is Brigham."* Salt Lake City: Bookcraft, 1964.

Zucker, Louis C. "Joseph Smith as a Student of Hebrew." *Dialogue* 3 (Summer 1968): 41-55.

Index

Aaronic Priesthood, 237; bishop presides over, 240; quorums of, 254-55

Abolitionists, 26, 28, 332-33

Abraham: writings of, 218-21; paid tithes, 223; was righteous spirit, 224

Accountability, age of, 221-22

Adam, 222, 224

Adam-ondi-Ahman, 366

Affidavits against Joseph Smith, 202-3

Aldrich, Hazen, 328, 426n.76

Alexander, Nancy, 128, 136

Allen, Charles, 164

American Revivalist and Rochester Observer, 126

American Temperance Union, 27

Ames, Ira, 254, 304, 324

Amherst, Ohio, 62, 106, 241

Angel, Solomon, 132, 176

Angell, Truman O., 147-48, 299

Angels: accompanying Zion's Camp, 186; resting upon Kirtland Temple, 305

Anointings, 286-87, 303; spiritual manifestations following, 287-93, 303-4

Apostasy, 93-97; after frustrations of Zion's Camp, 192; among General Authorities, 308-9; spirit of, in Kirtland, 310-11; following prosperity, 323; due to immorality, 326-27; extent of, in Kirtland, 327-28

Apostles, Quorum of Twelve, 108, 199; testify to truth of revelations, 216-17; calling and ordaining of, 248-50; missionary assignments of, 251-52; apostates among, 308; ranking of, 425n.63; Joseph

Smith defines duty of, 426n.64; duties of, expanded in Nauvoo, 426n.68

Architecture of Kirtland Temple, 147-49, 157-61

Army of Saints. *See* Zion's Camp

Arson, 349-50

Ashley, Major N., 106

Ashtabula Journal, 54

Astronomy, ancients' understanding of, 220

Atonement, 419n.1

Authority: to baptize, 6; lack of, was recognized by many, 16-17; assumed by Protestants, 57; certificates of, issued to missionaries, 110-11; to perform marriages, 337

Avon, New York, 137, 176

Babbitt, Almon W., 369, 442n.6

Babbitt, Erastus, 254

Babcock, Amos, 369

Bailey, Lydia, 117, 282

Bainbridge, Ohio, 12

Baker, Samuel, 181, 188

Baldwin, Nathan, 191, 416n.21, 441n.49

Banks, 314-15

Baptism: by authority, 4, 6; of many in Kirtland, 8; for remission of sins, 13, 395n.28; at age eight, 221; was practiced by ancients, 222

Baptists: Sidney Rigdon's ministry among, 12-13; views of, regarding baptism, 13; farm preachers of, 25; growing population of, in Kirtland, 39

Barber, Andrew, 168-69, 171

Barnes, Lorenzo, 113, 127-28, 272

461

Wealth, inordinate desires for, 323-24

Weld, Theodore, 332

Western Reserve, 23, 43

Western Reserve Chronicle, 54

Western Reserve Teachers' Seminary, 372

Weston, Samuel, 170

Whig party, 24, 335

Whitmer, David, 96, 245, 248; excommunication of, 261; performs anointing, 289; support for, to replace Joseph Smith, 310; is accused of transgression, 327; president of high council in Missouri, 431n. 5; excommunicated, 437n. 68

Whitmer, Jacob, 171

Whitmer, John: presides over Kirtland branch, 41-42; teaches incorrect principle, 59; carries revelations to Missouri, 91; on ordinations of high priests, 240; in Missouri high council, 245; called by title of "president," 431n. 5; excommunicated, 437n. 68

Whitmer, Peter, 1, 19, 67, 115, 288

Whitney, Elizabeth Ann, 45, 305

Whitney, Newel K.: joins Church, 8; prays for Holy Ghost, 16; store owned by, 37, 70, 137-38; Joseph Smith meets, and calls by name, 45; called "Ahashdah" in some revelations, 58; was to remain in Kirtland, 69; is called on fund-raising mission, 70; is called as bishop in Kirtland, 71, 239-40; stewardship of, 74; purchases land in Kirtland, 146; house of, meeting held at, 278; anointing of, 287; is summoned to Missouri, 368; listed in 1830 Kirtland census, 397n. 2; business of,

402n. 26; lays cornerstone of temple, 412n. 23

Whitney, William, 171

Wight, Lyman: first meeting of, with missionaries, 4-5; joins Church, 8; endorsed communitarian system, 15; reports on Missouri trials, 173-74; recruits for Zion's Camp, 177, 179; second officer of Zion's Camp, 185; discharges Zion's Camp members, 194; vision of, of Savior, 240; high councilor, 288; visit of, to Kirtland, 370; listed in 1830 Kirtland census, 397n. 2

Wilbur, Benjamin, 358, 360

Willey, Bathsheba, 360

Willey, Jeremiah, 357

Williams, Frederick G.: joins Church, 8; travels through Ohio with missionaries, 9-10; travels to Missouri, 67, 102; was to remain in Kirtland, 69; land purchased by, 71-73, 138; stewardship of, 73; asks for contributions to Church, 79; newspaper published by, 141; supervises brick making, 144; sees Kirtland Temple in vision, 147-49; age of, in Zion's Camp, 181; paymaster of Zion's Camp, 182; helps prepare revelations for publication, 214; exhibits mummies around Kirtland, 220; counselor in First Presidency, 241, 431n. 5; washes Joseph Smith's feet, 266; apostasy of, 328; listed in 1830 Kirtland census, 397n. 2; lays cornerstone of temple, 412n. 23; returns to Church, 437n. 69

Willoughby, Ohio, 23

Wilson, Calves, 106

Winchester, Benjamin, 181, 209, 434n. 77